# Fostering 21st Century Digital Literacy and Technical Competency

Antonio Cartelli

*University of Cassino and Southern Lazio, Italy*

Information Science
REFERENCE

| Managing Director: | Lindsay Johnston |
| Editorial Director: | Joel Gamon |
| Book Production Manager: | Jennifer Yoder |
| Publishing Systems Analyst: | Adrienne Freeland |
| Assistant Acquisitions Editor: | Kayla Wolfe |
| Typesetter: | Christy Fic |
| Cover Design: | Jason Mull |

Published in the United States of America by
Information Science Reference (an imprint of IGI Global)
701 E. Chocolate Avenue
Hershey PA 17033
Tel: 717-533-8845
Fax: 717-533-8661
E-mail: cust@igi-global.com
Web site: http://www.igi-global.com

Library of Congress Cataloging-in-Publication Data

Fostering 21st century digital literacy and technical competency / Antonio Cartelli, editor.
    p. cm.
 Includes bibliographical references and index.
 Summary: "This book offers the latest in research on the technological advances on computer proficiency in the educational system and society, bringing together theories and experiences in order to create a common framework"--Provided by publisher.
   ISBN 978-1-4666-2943-1 (hardcover) -- ISBN 978-1-4666-2944-8 (ebook) -- ISBN 978-1-4666-2945-5 (print & perpetual access)  1.  Computer literacy--Study and teaching.  2.  Technological literacy--Study and teaching.  I. Cartelli, Antonio, 1954- II. Title: Fostering twenty-first century digital literacy and technical competency.
   QA76.9.C64 F67
   004--dc23
                                        2012037384


British Cataloguing in Publication Data
A Cataloguing in Publication record for this book is available from the British Library.

The views expressed in this book are those of the authors, but not necessarily of the publisher.

# Table of Contents

**Section 3**
**Digital Technologies, Blended Learning, and Reflecting Competences**

## Section 4
## Digital Technologies and Competences for Education and Communication

## Section 5
## Digital Technologies and Literacy

# Detailed Table of Contents

## Section 1
## Digital Literacy and Culture

This article highlights the importance of the concepts of media literacy, and digital and informational literacy to understand the multimodal meaning of multiliteracies and their interfaces. An analogy with Babel is used to understand the different ways in which this concept articulates the linguistic, visual, audio, spatial, and gestural dimensions in digital culture. In this framework, the question of convergence is highlighted in learning experiences undertaken in formal and informal contexts. To qualify the meaning of this learning for the subject, the article mentions the concept of personal literacy to locate the importance of subjectivity in the interactions that the multiliteracies offer. Finally, in an exercise of representation of the components of the multiliteracies, the article presents a diagram that highlights the importance of mediation and the forms of appropriation that express concepts and experiences in search of a transformative pedagogical practice, as an opportunity to understand the multiliteracies as a condition of dialog, expression and participation in the culture.

Longitudinal research projects into social practices are both subject to and capture changes in society, meaning that research is conducted in a fluid context and that new research questions appear during the project's life cycle. In the present study emerging new performances and uses of ICT are examined and the relation between network society competences, learners' informal learning strategies and ICT in formalized school settings over time is studied. The authors find that aspects of ICT like multimodality, intuitive interaction design and instant feedback invites an informal bricoleur approach. When integrated into certain designs for teaching and learning, this allows for Formalized Informal Learning and support is found for network society competences building.

For a number of years, there has been a concerted effort by the United Arab Emirates to take a prominent role in introducing e-business initiatives throughout the Gulf region, and this effort has translated into widespread access of internet technology for its own citizens. The country, in setting out to become a hub for foreign and domestic companies, realized that to achieve these goals it must provide appropriate e-business frameworks and infrastructures, which it has successfully done. Although, while not the only means of acquiring digital literacy, regular exposure to the internet does contribute to gaining these necessary 21st century skills. It might be expected that with such widespread access to the internet the population would contribute to becoming digitally competent. Using an ethnographic case study methodology, this paper investigates issues contributing to what might be a new form of digital divide; cultural issues which limit the acquisition of such digital skills.

## Section 2
## Digital Literacy Evaluation and Development in Students, Teachers, and Adults

The topic of the individual learning conditions creation can be analysed from the technological as well as pedagogical side. In both cases there is the same fundamental point: how to create valuable and as much as possible natural learning environment? The experience in the application of technologies for personalisation, analysed in scientific literature, reveals newer possibilities for the individual activities support. This encourages taking a different route in analysing individual learning – to interdisciplinary combine the content of close concepts. The paper deals with basic concepts of interdisciplinary content analysis – informatics and information technology impact to an individual learning in primary school.

In this paper the behaviors and tendencies in the use of digital technologies by university students are analyzed. After a short discussion of former studies and the presentation of the model for digital literacy structure and assessment in students attending compulsory school, the investigation carried out by the authors is described and the results obtained from the analysis of the university students' answers is reported. The survey was submitted to 331 students in the Faculty of Humanities at the University of Cassino, Italy, and the students' answers show a contradictory reality: on one side, digital technologies are mainly used to communicate in social networks or to play music and movies, on another side it is evident the students' interest for the most recent aspects of the application of digital technology and for the improvement in the quality of their use.

## Chapter 6

*Valentina Dagienė, Vilnius University, Lithuania*

Starting from the key competencies for a knowledge society, this paper examines the information and communication technology (ICT) competency needed by teachers for effective teaching in the 21st-century. The paper analyzes the existing pre-service education programmes for teachers' ICT competency in Lithuanian universities and colleges, self-evaluation of future teachers of their technological and pedagogical ICT competency, and comparison of these results with the course requirements for the teachers' educational ICT literacy, based on the existing Lithuanian requirements for teachers' pedagogical ICT literacy programmes. The paper is based on the data of the research study "Teachers' Training on ICT Application in Education" developed by the Institute of Mathematics and Informatics in 2009. Conclusions and recommendations of the study have been proposed to implement deeper content-based modules for pedagogical ICT competency and skills in all-level pre-service teacher education as well as in-service training courses.

## Chapter 7

*Antonella Nuzzaci, University of Valle d'Aosta, Italy*

This article describes the new requirements of the European Higher Education Area (EHEA) - international and cross-cultural, Information and Communication Technologies (ICTs) that are important in all fields of university studies and take on a central role for learning and teaching. The literature review showed that, despite the considerable attention focused on the technological know-how of university teaching, few studies have examined the characteristics of these actors. The purpose is to focus more on teachers, clearly defining the technological skills necessary to develop the new European System of Higher Education in order to facilitate the development of skills, general learning, disciplinary, and professional digital education. This paper analyzes why this adaptation is necessary, the difficulties encountered, the objectives, and the response of teachers to these changes. On the other hand, university education acts on three fronts: the integration and use of new educational technologies in universities, the European convergence and application of ICT, the innovation and education needed to bridge the gap between universities, and teachers facing reality, both socially and professionally. This study contributes to the debate on the interactions between academic literacy, technological skills, and employment prospects for university teachers.

## Chapter 8

*Jeffrey Hsu, Fairleigh Dickinson University, USA*
*Zhongxian Wang, Montclair State University, USA*
*Karin Hamilton, Fairleigh Dickinson University, USA*

The needs of adult learners are different from those of traditional undergraduate students, and programs must be designed to meet this need. In particular, digital and technology literacy needs, including general computing skills, computerized communications, online and distance learning, and Web 2.0 tools make navigating coursework an additional challenge. In this paper, the authors examine the technology and digital literacy needs and backgrounds of adult learner students and discuss research on the interaction between technology and adult learner education. Using the features of intensive weekend classroom sessions, on-line distance learning, and specialized teaching methods, an improved learning environment tailored to unique needs and career goals can be offered to business undergraduate adults. An important component is the development of technology and digital literacy skills to "fill the gaps" of students who may have extensive business or working experience, but are less than proficient in the use of technology. More depth and analysis is given to the following areas: digital and technology skills and knowledge improvement, pedagogical features, the use of intensive weekend and evening sessions, and the role of distance learning to supplement the classroom sessions.

## Section 3
## Digital Technologies, Blended Learning, and Reflecting Competences

### Chapter 9

*M. Esther del Moral Pérez, University of Oviedo, Spain*
*Lourdes Villalustre Martínez, University of Oviedo, Spain*

The M.A.T.R.I.X (Modalities of Telematic Learning and Inter-university Results that can be Extrapolated to Blended Learning)1 project identified and described the diverse teaching methods and practices applied in a representative sample of virtual and blended learning degree courses taught at different Spanish Universities using the G92 Shared Virtual Campus. The purpose was to extrapolate the experiences considered as "good practice" in the new blended learning contexts and methodologies proposed by the EHEA, using as indicators the quality of the learning design as assessed by experts, the satisfaction level of the students taking the courses, their effective contribution to attaining specific and generic competence in different subjects.

### Chapter 10

*Dimitrios Roussinos, University of Peloponnese, Greece*
*Athanassios Jimoyiannis, University of Peloponnese, Greece*

Wikis are currently gaining in popularity in schools and higher education institutions and they are widely promoted as collaborative tools supporting students' active learning. This paper reports on the investigation of university students' beliefs and perceptions of a wiki authoring activity, designed to support blended and collaborative learning. The study was administered in the context of an authentic coursework project activity in a first semester university course on Information and Communication Technologies (ICT), attended by 47 first year students. Research findings indicated that the students in the sample were generally positive about the collaborative experience offered through the wiki and the consequent learning outcomes. Students' perceptions of the functionality and usability of the wiki environment were also positive. They considered the wiki as an effective and easy to use technology. In overall, they evaluated positively the wiki assignment, as well as the technical and learning support they received on-line, through the wiki pages, and by their instructors during the class sessions.

**Chapter 11**

*Antonella Nuzzaci, Université de la Vallée d'Aoste, Italy*

This study examines the effects of an activity of reflection on a group of students enrolled in the Master for Intercultural Education and European dimension of distance education, who participated in the construction of the model for a "reflection participant" and a self-evaluation tool to be used for training teachers. The activity is part of the research carried out within the Leonardo da Vinci "REFLECT" - "reflective practice for training the trainers" - Reflective Practice and VET (Vocational Education and Training), aimed at the creation of a specific methodology for the implementation of reflective practices in VET contexts, so that new processes of updating and re-professionalization required by the challenges of today's society can be started. It envisaged the creation of a testing laboratory, organized within the Faculty of Education at the University of Valle d'Aosta, which brings together teaching and research functions, contemplating an experiment involving the direct training of educators and teachers and demonstrating how to make a significant change in the actors who take part in the process. The study results show that it is possible to develop, enhance and strengthen skills through reflective mode online. The study indicates in post-treatment that the impact of such differences is based on the contextual features of the training.

**Section 4**
**Digital Technologies and Competences for Education and Communication**

**Chapter 12**

*Carlo Giovannella, University of Rome Tor Vergata, Italy*
*Claudia Di Lorenzo, University of Rome Tor Vergata, Italy*
*Simona Scarsella, University of Rome Tor Vergata, Italy*
*Corrado Amedeo Presti, University of Rome Tor Vergata, Italy*

This paper reports and discusses the result of a survey focused on the perceptions and expectations on TEE applications, conducted among 500 Italian educators (university, high/middle/elementary schools and professionals) involved in on-line or blended learning practices. The expectations are quite basic ones, although may depend on the educational level: support to content sharing and production, communication, assessment and team working are at the top of rank; much less relevant appear to be items like: support to socialization, process design and personalization. Very similar results have been obtained also from a survey among schools' teachers, novices for TEE, attending a Master in "e-learning: methods, techniques and applications". The survey was conducted after the conclusion of the first part of the master carried on according to a very traditional distance learning process: content download, self-evaluation tests, tutor assistance upon request. However, after the participation to the second part of the Master, organized as a collaborative, design inspired P3BL (problem, project and process based learning) experience, their opinions on TEE changed in a considerable manner. This indicates how necessary a dissemination action on a large scale among educators with regard to both TEE potentialities and design literacy would be.

One of the challenges facing university and college professors is the use of effective and efficient communication with their students. One solution could be the use of social networking sites to engage students and the U.S. 2010 Digital Year in Review (2011), social networking continues to grow as one of the web's top activities with 9 out of every 10 U.S. Internet users accessing break down communication barriers, according to a social networking site every month. The study includes an in-depth review of the uses, benefits and risks of social networking sites as well as how they might be utilized in a college or university setting. The researcher in this study surveyed university business students at a private, four-year, Hispanic-serving institution in Texas about their use of social networking sites and how professors might integrate these sites into the curriculum.

Learning a foreign language takes time and effort. In the last few years, too much emphasis has been placed on oral communication skills and English teachers make their students speak English without paying enough attention to grammatical accuracy. As a result, while students' ability in terms of fluency has improved, they often cannot communicate appropriately in English due to a lack of grammatical knowledge. The aim of the study was to explore the potential of Precision Teaching software developed for the improvement of English grammar rules. Two groups were compared, one having used the software and the other following a traditional textbook-based approach. The students who used the software showed significantly higher learning scores than students who did not. In addition, after using the software students show increased scores in some cognitive abilities that are related to foreign language learning.

**Section 5**
**Digital Technologies and Literacy**

This study explores the use of the Internet by medical practitioners in private hospitals in Warri Delta State, Nigeria. Descriptive survey design was adopted and questionnaire was the instrument used to collect data. The total population and sample for the study were 137 medical practitioners from 30 private hospitals in Warri. Findings revealed that most medical practitioners used the Internet on a regular basis; a majority of the medical practitioners started using the Internet between 1 – 5 years ago; most of the medical practitioners spend 2 – 5 hours using the Internet per visit; a majority of medical practitioners used the Internet without assistance. Medline, journals and PubMed were the Internet resources used by most of the medical practitioners. Internet use enables the respondents to improve patient care, keep up-to-date; high cost of Internet access and lack of access to the Internet were some of the problems facing most of medical practitioners. The study recommends that hospital management should provide their medical practitioners with Internet facilities to enable them access to the most recent and accurate information for effective service delivery. The findings will help health care authorities especially in developing countries to improve on Internet access facilities to medical practitioners.

This paper examines literacy as it affects Space Technology in Nigeria. The place of digital technology enables a proper understanding of literacy in Nigeria. The paper is divided into four parts. The first section redefines literacy in order to understand the possibilities of meanings based on the perceptions of James (1984), Onukaogu (2008), Arua (2009) and Ajayi (2009) that conceptualize the complex nature of literacy and its indispensability. The second part visualizes the role played by literacy in educating technological advancement in Nigeria, bearing in mind that in 1999, the Federal Government of Nigeria approved the Nigerian Space Policy and the implementation of the space program. The third section underscores the socio-economic relevance of literacy in enhancing global space technology for Nigeria while the fourth section relates Ajayi's (2009) projection in a meta-critical manner, so that Nigeria can become a world power. The theoretical framework for this paper is the "Transformational Theory". The theory opines that "learning occurs as a result of transformation of participation in culturally valued activities" such as space technology. The paper emphasizes practical findings to stimulate excellence and literacy relevance in science and technology.

# Chapter 17

Today, satellite communication networks are being integrated into the infrastructure of modern Terrestrial communication networks and becoming popular for the delivery of educational content and data, as well as education-centric services, including information, tele-conferencing, entertainment, or "edutainment" services. With fresh demand for new services and applications, it is becoming essential that wireless network architecture seamlessly interoperate with new and existing technologies, protocols and standards. This paper presents recent work on the use of hybrid wireless network infrastructures for delivering tele-education and e-learning applications to remote communities by combining a variety of satellite, terrestrial and wireless technologies, and provides the results from live scenarios carried out employing various methods of interoperability testing. The analysis of the results examines a number of different issues such as delay, jitter, packet loss, latency, throughput measurement, and bandwidth. By combining satellite and terrestrial (wireless) technologies, full coverage and high capacity can be achieved for true broadband services for delivering educational content. The interoperability among such diverse networks imposes a number of challenges regarding service provision and management.

# Preface

The massive and exponential spreading of digital equipment during last two decades has greatly influenced human way of living. As never before it has been possible to get, to manage and to share any kind of information by means of little, handy and relatively cheap instruments, like mobile phones and smartphones. Furthermore, the digital structure of information, made of thousands and millions of bits, independent each other, and the Internet with its social networks, led people to easily develop the features of "personal authoring for information and its wide spreading"; as a consequence anyone has been persuaded that information could be acquired, stored, modified, and suddenly made available as new information.

The evidence for the above statements can be easily found in recent events like the Muslim spring, or Arab spring; notwithstanding the difficulties still evident in the societies of Northern Africa and Middle East in fact, the wishes and aspirations of those people may never become a collective desire and lead to the request of profound social changes, whether digital instruments, digital communication and the Internet were not available.

The target of a global communication, which looked easy and possible without bulky and expensive equipments and with less or no skills and competences, induced many people to think that a new season for the participation in democratic life was now available and new digital literacy, developed in a personal and intuitive way, was finally possible.

The same result is implicitly included in Prensky (2001) definitions, and especially in the separation he proposes between "digital natives" and "digital immigrants." The formers, born in a context populated of a multitude of digital equipments, develop an intuitive and personal interaction with the new instruments, and are able to use them without being forced to think about their structure and functioning.

The main conclusion from what has been reported until now is that some kind of information, especially that made of sounds, images and movies, can be today easily managed by people, who capture them from the environment they are immersed in, and make them available to others with the simple transmission on social networks.

These behaviours and the undertaken actions, on another hand, do not exclude many and profound consequences for mankind; at least, they solicit questions on the connection between new and traditional features, skills and competences in human subjects, like the following ones:

- What skills and competences are needed in today society, to be better citizens and to easily adapt to its continuous changes?
- How much "new competences," and digital competences among them, are connected to more traditional ones?

- What literacy are needed in formal and informal education to help people better learn and develop the competences needed in the knowledge society?
- What role must play school, at all levels of education, to help people hit the targets suggested above while changing its connection with knowledge and education?

No complete and final answer has been given until now to any of the former questions, probably for the cross-disciplinary features of the underlying problems.

Some attempts have been made to propose possible solutions, first from computing scholars and soon after from researchers and scientists in other different fields.

Computing scientists have long questioned on the topics to be included in education to let students be more clever and able in solving different kind of problems; they also made great efforts to analyze human-computer interaction and the influence of computing on human thinking, and they are still working on these fields to make computers better and better. As regards the relation between computer and education they are today mainly focused on computer education and computing curricula, while many other institutions and organizations are debating on more general topics like the computing core topics to be included in school curricula and the digital competences to be developed in the youth and for lifelong learning.

Historically speaking, the first step in the proposal of instruments and methods for the development of suitable computing knowledge, and consequently for the improvement of personal knowledge, has been the definition of new literacy, i.e. computing, IT and ICT literacy. The main idea supporting those definitions suggested that people could develop new learning strategies and use the new digital instruments while learning the basic elements of information technology.

On this side, many associations of Computer Professionals, like AICA in Italy and CEPIS in Europe, developed since 1997 special curricula: ECDL syllabus (European Computer Driving Licence) and EUCIP syllabus (European Certification of Informatics Professionals), to let people get the certification concerning the basic knowledge and skills for personal computing or for network management.

Different hypotheses and suitable proposals were developed by other institutions all over the world on this side.

The Committee on Information Technology of the Computer Science and Telecommunications Board in the US National Research Council (1999), published the report "Being fluent with Information Technology," by which educational institutions were explicitly invited to propose special training activities to the students, on the abilities specifically needed for the information society.

The Association of College and Research Libraries (ACRL 2000) proposed a definition for the information literacy: "the group of skills needed for individual development in modern-day societies" and described the features of these skills.

The UNESCO (2002), on another hand, defined media education as the education allowing people to develop the understanding of the means of communication in the society they live, and settled the skills needed to use these means in relation to others. UNESCO, first among the organizations proposing instruments and methods for a new literacy, considered these skills an essential part of the civic training.

For the ETS (2002), the ICT literacy has the following meaning: "digital technology, communications tools, and/or networks, to access, manage, integrate, evaluate and create information in order to function in a knowledge society."

The basic differences between the above proposals have been grouped in the following two categories by M. Tornero (2004):

- **Scope:** The ACRL proposal refers to information management in general, regardless of the means through which it may be accessed; UNESCO refers to the means of communication in a broader sense; ETS confines itself to digital means;
- **Framework of applicability:** UNESCO makes its proposal within a framework of democratic society, and therefore within a collective context; the ACRL and the ETS make their proposals within the framework of individual competence, which is cognitive and technological.

More recently a great attention has been devoted to the impact that new technologies have on mankind, when passing from the discussion on how people use digital resources and processes, to the analysis of what they must know and be able to do with technologies.

The shift in the focus attention, from a discipline centered paradigm to a human centered paradigm, implies the growing of the interest of scientific community for the development of individual competences, which are seen as active involvement of subjects in their interaction with reality, and people knowledge and skills are considered much more important than the knowledge of instruments and processes (Le Boterf, 1990).

On this side a great effort has been made by European Institutions to define the basic skills and competences for lifelong learning, which are considered essential to be the citizens in the European "knowledge society." The result of this effort has been a recommendation for all countries belonging to the European Community, by which the set of key competences has been settled; digital competences, the fourth among them, are considered especially important because of their cross cultural features with respect to language (reading/writing) and calculus competences (Council of European Parliament 2005).

The definition reported in the recommendation of the European parliament states that digital competence involves the confident and critical use of Information Society Technology (IST) for work, leisure and communication. It is underpinned by basic skills in ICT: the use of computers to retrieve, assess, store, produce, present and exchange information, and to communicate and participate in collaborative networks via the Internet.

In other words digital competence requires a sound understanding and knowledge of the nature, role and opportunities of IST in everyday contexts: in personal and social life as well as at work. The skills needed include: the ability to search, collect and process information and use it in a critical and systematic way, assessing relevance and distinguishing real from virtual while recognising the links. Individuals should have skills to use tools to produce, present and understand complex information and the ability to access, search and use internet-based services; they should also be able to use IST to support critical thinking, creativity and innovation.

It must be noted that the opinions and statements by computing scientists and public institutions reported until now, mark the evolution of "thinking about IT/ICT" when passing from "teaching IT/ICT structure and functioning" to "teaching in a proficient way how to use IT/ICT." The possible last step on the way of the connection between human knowledge and IT/ICT is the "teaching-learning in a world populated of IT/ICT," where it is clear that the use of digital technologies influences human way of learning and building new knowledge. On this side new meanings are emerging for digital literacy and digital competence, and we'll report in what follows the proposals of the scientific community at least from two different perspectives: by the organization sciences and by the human and social sciences.

As regards the first viewpoint, digital literacy and competence are strictly connected with the application of the ideas, instruments and methods of knowledge management, both in corporate and organizations and in the subjects belonging to them.

The deep changes in knowledge construction phenomena evidenced in the knowledge management practices induced to think that suitable instruments and methods could be used to help students in the creation of an ecology of information and in the successful use of technology for the building of new knowledge. This strategy has been called Personal Knowledge Management (PKM).

The term PKM was first introduced in 1999 in two North American Universities (Sorrentino, 2008): UCLA (University of California at Los Angeles) and Millikin University (in Decatur). The two places assigned different meanings and perspectives to PKM also if they essentially agreed on some key features for it.

At UCLA, in the Anderson School of Management, professors aimed at the creation of a program for their MBA students, it had to help students to face the information explosion that the Internet was producing. The main aim of the PKM program was to teach students some basic Knowledge Management principles and their application, like using computer-based tools; students would then acquire a mindset and a methodology enabling them to process information and transform it into knowledge. The training for PKM concentrated around five tasks:

- Searching/finding
- Categorizing/classifying
- Naming things/making distinctions
- Evaluating/assessing
- Integrating/relating

At Millikin University PKM was better viewed as based on a set of problem solving skills that have both a logical or conceptual as well as physical or hands-on component. The program, as defined at Millikin University, consisted of seven "information" skills:

- Retrieving information
- Evaluating information
- Organizing information
- Collaborating around information
- Analyzing information
- Presenting information
- Securing information

These skills were, and still are, thought capable of the improving of individual's performances and of intrapersonal/interpersonal relationships.

It has to be noted that special tools are integral part of PKM because of the need of the technological support for enacting this discipline. Furthermore, several changes intervened in recent years to amplify the above set of skills. For instance, sharper skills are today required to exploit the new generation of "super-search engines," to manage the new media, to access qualified information (less ranked by authorities, and more by crowds) etc.

Among the most used tools for PKM there are: new aggregators, feeds, blog engines, metadata creation tools, multimedia management tools, mind mappers, concept mappers, tools for voice and video conferencing, personal schedulers, web assistants etc.

The pioneers of PKM stated that the development of skills for creating and maintaining "personal" knowledge is not a casual activity. Skills can be taught in an academic environment, they can be instigated and facilitated in an enterprise environment but, in all cases, an act of self-responsibility on the part of the individual is fundamental and necessary. As a result PKM requires a continuous investment in time and resources by people who decide to adopt them.

On the side of human and social sciences two main positions must be reported, both involving the constructivist psycho-pedagogical paradigm.

First, the interactivist followers applied the ideas of Piaget and Ausubel, and suggested that digital equipments can be used to solicit the highest way of thinking in children and more generally in people, that is to construct mental models for the understanding of the world. S. Papert (1991), probably the best known among them, invented the term "constructionism" for the description of the human way of knowing and interpreting phenomena and created special instruments to give concreteness to the above idea; the graphics programming Logo language, the better known product by Papert, has been used in many experiences all over the world to teach pupils the basic ideas of computer programming and the algorithmic way of problem solving. Otherwise stated, digital literacy and the development of digital competences are the natural requisite for new ways of learning and interpreting phenomena.

On another hand the socio-constructivist followers, started from the local and situated learning experiences involving the use of digital equipments, to state how important these equipments could be to induce collaborative learning and to create communities of learning, by stimulating communication among subjects and peer-to-peer learning among the members of the community.

In this last case the author's experience with students in a Faculty of Humanities attending the course of Latin Paleography, can be useful to understand the different perspectives by which phenomena can be explored and discussed (Cartelli, 2005). The different viewpoints emerging from the studies carried out can be synthesized in the following statements:

1.  The communities of students involved in the use of information systems for teaching and research had all the features of CoLs or FCL as described by Brown and Campione (1996). Some new features never observed before were also detected in the students' skills: working in a group (in traditional paleography courses it is a very rare experience), easier facing of complex tasks (thanks to the help each student could have from their colleagues), and raising of the individuals' peculiarities within the community (for the orientation to specializing in doing something when people work together on a common commitment). The ICT also had a great role in the paleography teaching experiences because they helped students in experimenting a meta-cognitive environment and cognitive apprenticeship strategies, involved them in the discussion and evaluation of the procedures they took part in, and let them experiment meaningful learning.

2.  The same communities of students had many features of the communities of practice (CoPs). With respect to the corresponding communities in organizations and corporations, which are autonomously created and have no hierarchies, the presence of a hierarchical structure has to be noted (professors and their collaborators organize the work, suggest what to do, support everyday activity, etc.). Further differences between groups of students and CoPs are: (a) community skills are mostly induced/transmitted by professors and not freely shared among individuals, (b) community memory is not made of the repositories of expertise but it is made of the data in the databases (i.e., it is mostly represented by the scientific knowledge available from sites browsing and database querying).

Nevertheless, the groups of students can be considered CoPs because (a) there is a common task shared among all community members, (b) there is a reciprocal commitment regulating interactions and sharing of experiences among the subjects in the community, (c) there is a shared repertoire of knowledge, instruments and methods by means of which common knowledge is preserved and transmitted (Wenger, 1998).

3.  At last, the groups of students involved in the teaching of paleography, based on the use of special information systems, had the features of virtual communities. This conclusion emerged from the collaboration of many national and foreign scholars, who worked on the systems via the Internet, and usually did not know the students involved in the project. Nonetheless their contribution were very important for students and for the construction of the community memory. As soon as the students became familiar with the digital instruments and the information systems they were able in participating in community discussions and work on the documents to be analyzed.

It has to be noted that the different contexts of application for the considerations reported until now, mostly coming from the fields of high and adult education, had their counterpart on schools experiences, at all levels of education and all over the world. In Italy they inspired many experiments funded by the Ministry of Education, on the introduction of IWB (Interactive Whiteboards) in the classes and on the construction of new learning experiences (some names for the corresponding education projects were innovate-school, innovate-teaching, classes 2.0 etc.).

Furthermore, as usually happens, the experiences carried out in the schools are still limited to the role of experiments and do not influence everyday teaching in a more structured and articulated planning and practice of teachers' work; nonetheless teachers perceive the need of changing the strategies to be adopted at school to let it be less distant from the students' life experiences.

The complex situation today present at school has been well synthesized by L. Galliani (2004), who has proposed an integrated model for the use e-learning strategies at school; in his model web based learning (WBL) and computer mediated communication (CMC), both have an important role and determine the development of knowledge, skills and competences in the students. The contexts they produce and the experiences they can induce lead to a wide panorama of possible educational environments where information processes, knowledge processes and learning processes have different complexity depending on the involvement of technology use (see Figure 1).

The problems and the experiences reported until now and the attempt to answer the questions formulated formerly, resulted in the writing of this book, where the issues discussed and the proposals of the different authors induced to create five different sections.

The first section is devoted to the analysis of the links and connections between digital literacy and culture. The second section discusses the evaluation and development of digital literacy in students, teachers, professors and more generally in adults; the proposal of technological environments for the development of digital competences in students, the digital experiences from teachers in their training courses and the difficulties in the use of digital equipments in university students are only some topics among the ones discussed in this section. The third section looks at the connection between digital technologies, blended learning and reflecting competences. The fourth section focuses on digital technologies and digital competences for education in the attempt of discussing the finding of new fields of application for them and the fifth and last section reports of different experiences on digital technologies and literacy.

In what follows the different section are analyzed with a special attention to the explanation of the contribution by the different authors.

*Figure 1. Structure of the technological educational environments teachers can use at school*

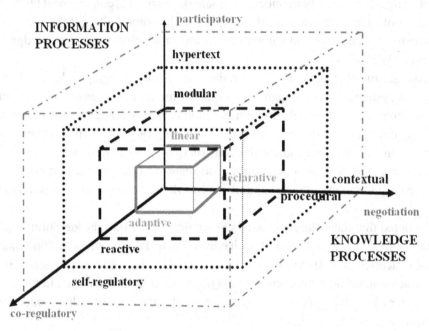

LEARNING PROCESSES

Section 1 begins with *Beyond Babel: Multiliteracies in Digital Culture* by Monica Fantin. The paper highlights the importance of the concepts of media literacy, and digital and informational literacy, to understand the multimodal meaning of multiliteracies and their interfaces. An analogy with Babel is used to help understand the different ways that this concept articulates the linguistic, visual, audio, spatial, and gestural dimensions in digital culture. In this context learning experiences in formal and informal environments are discussed. The concept of personal literacy is also presented in order to state the importance of subjectivity in the interactions that the multiliteracies offer. At last a diagram that highlights the importance of mediation and the forms of appropriation that express concepts and experiences in search of a transformative pedagogical practice is reported to understand the multiliteracies as a condition of dialog, expression and participation in the culture.

Chapter 2, by Karin Tweddell Levinsen, Birgitte Holm Sørensen, titled *Formalized Informal learning – ICT and Learning for the 21st Century,* reports research in a fluid context, the everyday school experience. In their study emerging new performances and uses of ICT are observed and provide the opportunity to study the relation between network society competences, learners' informal learning strategies and ICT in formalized school settings over time. Longitudinal research-projects into social practices are both subjects to and capture changes in society. The study has found that aspects of ICT such as multimodality, intuitive interaction design and instant feedback invites an informal bricoleur approach. When integrated into certain designs for teaching and learning this allows for what the authors call *Formalized Informal Learning* and find support for network society competences building.

Chapter 3, by Tony Jewels & Rozz Albon, *Reconciling Culture and Digital Literacy in the United Arab Emirates,* starts by analyzing the effort the United Arab Emirates made to take a prominent role in introducing e-business initiatives throughout the Gulf region; this effort was translated into widespread access of the Internet technology for their citizens, under the hypotheses that:

- Appropriate e-business frameworks and infrastructures needed such instruments and suitable competences for people,
- Regular exposure to the Internet does contribute to gaining these necessary 21$^{st}$ century skills, although, it is not the only means of acquiring digital literacy.

It might be expected that with such widespread access to the Internet the population would become digitally competent, but an ethnographic case study methodology carried out by the authors shows that a new form of digital divide limiting the acquisition of such digital skills can be detected.

Section 2 starts with *Transformation of Individual Learning through Informatics and Information Technology Activities in Primary School* by Valentina Dagiene and Vaiva Grabauskiene. The authors analyze the support to individual learning both from the technological and pedagogical sides. Their starting point is the creation of natural learning environments, which are naturally inter-disciplinary. They propose the use of digital technologies for the personalization of learning, to interdisciplinary combine the content of close concepts. The paper deals with basic concepts of interdisciplinary content analysis – informatics and information technology impact to an individual learning in primary school.

Chapter 5 was written by Antonio Cartelli and Angela Di Nuzzo, and titled *Digital Literacy and Competence in Students Attending a Faculty of Humanities*. The paper aims at discussing and verifying the contradictions reported in former studies, on the behaviors of students at different stages of schooling when using digital equipments. First of all the behaviors and the tendencies in the use of digital technologies by university students are discussed. Soon after the model for digital literacy structure and assessment is reported. At last an investigation on university students is described and the results emerging from the analysis of their answers is discussed. The survey has been submitted to 331 students in a Faculty of Humanities, and the students' answers have confirmed the presence of a contradictory reality: digital technologies are mainly used to communicate in social networks or to play music and movies, not to manage information concerning the topics to be studied, but it is evident the students' interest for the most recent aspects of the application of digital technology and for the improvement in the quality of their use.

Chapter 6, *Transformation of Individual Learning through Informatics and Information Technology Activities in Primary School,* by Valentina Dagiene, deals with the information and communication technology (ICT) competency needed by teachers for effective teaching in the 21st century. It first aims at the analysis of the existing pre-service education programmes for teachers' ICT competency in Lithuanian universities and colleges, soon after it reports strategies for self-evaluation of future teachers technological and pedagogical ICT competency, and at last compares the results with the course requirements for the teachers' educational ICT literacy, based on the existing Lithuanian requirements for teachers' pedagogical ICT literacy programmes. The paper is based on the data of the research study "Teachers' Training on ICT Application in Education" developed by the Institute of Mathematics and Informatics in 2009. Conclusions and recommendations for the study are proposed to implement deeper content-based modules for pedagogical ICT competency and skills in all-level pre-service teacher education as well as in-service training courses.

In chapter 7, Antonella Nuzzaci writes on *Technological Literacy in the Profile of Skills of University Professor in the New European Higher Education System*. The paper first describes the requirements of the European Higher Education Area (EHEA) - international and cross-cultural, Information and Communication Technologies (ICTs), that appear increasingly important in all fields of university studies. From the analysis of the literature review it emerges that, despite the considerable attention focused on the technological know-how of university teaching, few studies examine these elements. Educational research in the field of ICT is in fact mainly devoted to the design of digital systems.

The paper aims at focusing on professors, by defining the technological skills necessary to develop the new European System of Higher Education, in order to facilitate the development of skills, general learning, disciplinary, and professional digital education. To hit this target the paper highlights the three perspectives guiding university education: the integration and use of new educational technologies in universities, the European convergence and application of ICT, the innovation and education needed to bridge the gap between universities and teachers facing reality, both socially and professionally. Main purpose of the study is to contribute to the debate on the interactions between academic literacy, technological skills and employment perspectives for university teachers.

Jeffrey Hsu, Zhongxian Wang, and Karin Hamilton, authors of *Developing and Managing Digital/ Technology Literacy and Effective Learning Skills in Adult Learners,* start by observing how different the needs of adult learners are from those of traditional undergraduate students, and consequently hypothesizes a suitable design for adult education programs to meet this needs. In particular, as emerges from scientific literature, digital and technology literacy needs, including general computing skills, computerized communications, online and distance learning, and web 2.0 tools make navigating coursework an additional challenge aside from the content itself.

The authors' main hypothesis for adult education experiences is based on the use of intensive weekend classroom sessions, on-line distance learning, and specialized teaching methods; an improved learning environment tailored to unique needs and career goals can be offered to business undergraduate adult students (those who are older, have substantial business experience and knowledge). An important component of the authors' work is the development of technology and digital literacy skills, to "fill the gaps" of students who may have extensive business or working experience, but are less than proficient in the use of technology. Relevant theories and frameworks from education and psychology are used to support the techniques and methods discussed. A model of adult learner technology integration is created based on both a review of theory/relevant research and experiences gained with an adult business undergraduate program. Examples relating to specific kinds of courses and situations are also included.

Section 3 begins with authors Esther del Moral Pérez and Lourdes Villalustre Martínez, and their contribution, *Good Teaching Practice and Good Quality Indicators for Virtual and Blended Learning: Project MATRIX.* The M.A.T.R.I.X (Modalities of Telematic Learning and Inter-university Results that can be Extrapolated to Blended Learning) project identified and described the diverse teaching methods and practices applied in a representative sample of virtual and blended learning degree courses taught at different Spanish Universities using the G9 Shared Virtual Campus. The author purpose is to extrapolate the experiences considered as "good practice" in the new blended learning contexts and methodologies proposed by the EHEA, using as indicators the quality of the learning design as assessed by experts, the satisfaction level of the students taking the courses, their effective contribution to attaining specific and generic competence in different subjects etc.

Chapter 10 was written by Dimitrios Roussinos and Athanassios Jimoyiannis. *Blended collaborative learning through a wiki-based project: A case study on students' perceptions* reports on the investigation the authors made on university students' beliefs and perceptions of a wiki authoring activity, designed to support blended and collaborative learning. The research started from the popularity that wikis are gaining in schools and higher education institutions and from the literature promoting them as collaborative tools supporting students' active learning. The study has been administered in the context of an authentic coursework project activity in a first semester university course on Information and Communication

Technologies (ICT), attended by 47 first year students. The authors found that the students in the sample were generally positive about the collaborative experience offered through the wiki and the consequent learning outcomes. Students' perceptions of the functionality and usability of the wiki environment were also positive, because they considered the wiki as an effective and easy to use technology.

Antonella Nuzzaci, author of chapter 11, *Developing a Reflective Competence for a Master Level Program on E-learning: the Leonardo Project REFLECT*, reports of the effects of an activity of reflection on a group of students enrolled in the Master for Intercultural Education and European dimension of distance education, who participated in the construction of the model for a "reflection participant" and a self-evaluation tool to be used for training teachers. The teaching activity was part of the research carried out within the Leonardo da Vinci project "REFLECT" - "reflective practice for training the trainers" - Reflective Practice and VET (Vocational Education and Training), aimed at the creation of a specific methodology for the implementation of reflective practices in VET contexts and, more generally, for the acquisition of learning, so that new processes of updating and re-professionalization required by the challenges of today's society could be started. During the experience a testing laboratory was created, it was inside the Faculty of Education at the University of Valle d'Aosta, and aimed at bringing together teaching and research functions within the higher education system; the target was hit with an experiment involving the direct training of educators and teachers, which showed how deep were the changes induced in the actors involved in the process. The main result of the study is concerned with the development, enhancement and strengthening of skills through online reflective mode, with the use of tools which determine specific reflexive patterns especially centered on the contexts.

Section 4 begins with a work by Carlo Giovannella, Claudia Di Lorenzo, Simona Scarsella, and Corrado Amedeo Presti. Their paper, *Educators' expectations on Technology Enhanced Education (TEE): should and could they be modified?* reports and discusses the result of a survey focused on the perceptions and expectations on TEE applications, conducted among 500 Italian educators (university, high/middle/elementary schools and professionals) involved in on-line or blended learning practices. The authors show that whether the expectations may depend on the educational level, they are quite basic: support to content sharing (78%) and production (65,5%), communication (59%), assessment (59%) and team working (59%) are at the top of rank; much less relevant appear to be items like: support to socialization, process design and personalization. The authors report also that very similar results have been obtained from a survey on schools' teachers, novices for TEE, attending a Master in "e-learning: methods, techniques and applications." The survey was conducted after the conclusion of the first part of the master made according to a very traditional old-fashion distance learning process: content download, self-evaluation tests, tutor assistance upon request. However, after the participation to the second part of the Master, organized as a collaborative, design inspired, P$^3$BL (problem, project and process based learning) experience, the students' opinions on TEE changed in a fairly considerable manner, and more complex and broad-spectrum expectations on technologies emerged.

*Benefits and Risks of Social Networking Sites: Should they Also Be Used to Harness Communication in a College or University Setting?* by Angelina I. T. Kiser is chapter 13. The paper starts from the analysis of the challenges university and college professors are facing in the use of effective and efficient communication with their students. From literature revue the use of social networking sites to engage students and the U.S. 2010 Digital Year in Review (2011) appear as possible solutions to the problem, mostly because the social networking continues to grow as one of the web's top activities with 9 out of every 10 U.S. Internet users accessing break down communication barriers. The study includes an in-depth review of the uses, benefits and risks of social networking sites as well as how they might be utilized in a college or university setting. The researcher in this study surveyed university business students at a private, four-year, Hispanic-serving institution in Texas about their use of social networking sites and how professors might integrate these sites into the curriculum.

Francesca Cuzzocrea, Anna Maria Murdaca, and Patrizia Oliva author chapter 14: *Using Precision Teaching Method to Improve Foreign Language and Cognitive Skills in University Students.* The paper first analyzes the difficulties in learning a foreign language by high school students. It emerges that in the last few years too much emphasis has been placed on oral communication skills so that English teachers made their students speak English without paying enough attention to grammatical accuracy. As a result, the authors suggest that while students' ability in terms of fluency has improved, they often cannot communicate appropriately in English due to a lack of grammatical knowledge. The study explores the potential of Precision Teaching software developed for the improvement of English grammar rules. Two groups were compared, one having used the software and the other following a traditional textbook-based approach. The students who used the software showed significantly higher learning scores than students who did not. In addition, after using the software students show increased scores in some cognitive abilities that are related to foreign language learning.

The final section, Section 5 begins with *Use of the Internet by Medical Practitioners in Private Hospitals in Warri, Delta State, Nigeria,* by Esharenana E. Adomi and Ericson Egbaivwie. This study was intended to explore the use of the Internet by medical practitioners in private hospitals in Warri Delta State, Nigeria. Descriptive survey design was adopted and a questionnaire was the instrument used to collect data. The sample population under analysis for the study were one hundred and thirty-seven (137) medical practitioners from thirty (30) private hospitals in Warri. The findings revealed that most medical practitioners used the Internet on a regular basis; a majority of the medical practitioners started using the Internet between 1 – 5 years ago; most of the medical practitioners spend 2 – 5 hours using the Internet per visit; a majority of medical practitioners used the Internet without assistance. Medline, journals and PubMed were the Internet resources used by most of the medical practitioners. Main results of the investigation are: a) the Internet use enable the respondents to improve patient care, keep them up-to-date; b) the high cost of the Internet access and the lack of access to the Internet by most patients were some of the problems most part of medical practitioners had to face.

The study recommends that hospital management should provide their medical practitioners with Internet facilities to enable them have access to the most recent and accurate information for effective service delivery.

Christopher Babatunde Ogunyemi, author of *Literacy and Space Technology in Nigeria,* examines literacy as it affects Space Technology in Nigeria. It explains how literacy is applied to space development and its digital importance. The paper is divided into four parts. The first section redefines literacy in order to understand the possibilities of meanings based on the perceptions of James (1984), Onukaogu (2008), Arua (2009) and Ajayi (2009) that conceptualize the complex nature of literacy and its need. The second part visualizes the role played by literacy in educating technological advancement in Nigeria, bearing in mind that in 1999, the Federal Government of Nigeria approved the Nigerian Space Policy and the implementation of the space program. As outlined in the policy, the program started with the establishment of a National Space Research and Development Agency (NASRDA), under the Federal Ministry of Science and Technology. The third section underscores the socio-economic relevance of literacy in enhancing global space technology for Nigeria while the fourth section relates Ajayi's projection in a meta-critical manner, to see how literacy rethinks the state of the mind in enhancing excellent technology, so that Nigeria can become a world power. The theoretical framework for this paper is the

"Transformational Theory," by which "learning occurs as a result of transformation of participation in culturally valued activities," such as space technology. Friere (1972), Rogoff (1994), Stolle (2007) and Ikpeze (2009) define this theoretical framework by stimulating knowledge, reading and interpretation of concept to human society. The paper emphasizes practical findings to stimulate excellence and literacy relevance in science and technology.

Munir Abbasi and Lampros K. Stergioulas wrote chapter 17, *Hybrid Wireless Networks for E-learning and Digital Literacy – Testing and Evaluation*. The paper starts by considering how satellite communication networks are today increasingly integrated into the infrastructure of modern Terrestrial communication networks and are becoming popular for the delivery of educational content and data, as well as education-centric services, including information, tele-conferencing, entertainment or 'edutainment' services. With fresh demand for new services and applications, it is becoming essential that wireless network architecture should seamlessly interoperate with new and existing technologies, protocols and standards. The paper reports of recent work on the use of hybrid wireless network infrastructures for delivering tele-education and e-learning applications to remote communities, by combining a variety of satellite, terrestrial and wireless technologies, and provides the results from live scenarios carried out employing various methods of interoperability testing. The analysis of the results examines a number of different issues such as delay, jitter, packet loss, latency, throughput measurement and bandwidth. By combining satellite and terrestrial (wireless) technologies, full coverage and high capacity can be achieved for truc broadband services for delivering educational content. The interoperability among such diverse networks imposes a number of challenges regarding service provision and management. The end-to-end quality of service management implies that features such as service scalability between different networks have to be available. On the other hand, wireless QoS provides a promising diversified platform for a wide range of seamless applications.

*Antonio Cartelli*
*University of Cassino and Southern Lazio, Italy*

## REFERENCES

ACRL. (2000). *Information literacy competency standards for higher education*. Chicago, IL: Association of College & Research Libraries.

Brown, A. L., & Campione, J. (1996). Psychological theory and the design of innovative learning environments: On procedure, principles and systems. In Schaube, L., & Glaser, R. (Eds.), *Innovation in learning* (pp. 289–375). Mahwah, NJ: Lawrence Erlbaum.

Cartelli, A. (2005). ICT, COLS, COPS and virtual communities. In Dasgupta, S. (Ed.), *Encyclopedia of virtual communities and technologies* (pp. 248–252). Hershey, PA: Idea-Group Inc. doi:10.4018/978-1-59140-563-4.ch047

Committee on Information Technology Literacy. (1999). *Being fluent with information technology*. Washington, DC: National Academy Press.

Council of European Parliament. (2005) *Recommendation of the European Parliament and of the Council on key competences for lifelong learning.* Retrieved from http://ec.europa.eu/education/policies/2010/doc/keyrec_en.pdf

Educational Testing Service. (2002). *Digital transformation. A framework for ICT literacy. A report from the ICT Literacy Panel.* Princeton, NJ: Author.

Galliani, L. (2004). *La scuola in rete.* Bari, Italy: Laterza.

Le Boterf, G. (1990). *De la compétence: Essai sur un attracteur étrange.* Paris, France: Les Ed. de l'Organisation.

Papert, S., & Harel, I. (1991). *Constructionism.* New York, NY: Ablex Publishing Corporation.

Prensky, M. (2001). Digital natives, digital immigrants. *Horizon, 9*(5). doi:10.1108/10748120110424816

Sorrentino, F. (2008). From knowledge to personal knowledge management. In Cartelli, A., & Palma, M. (Eds.), *Encyclopedia of information communication technology* (pp. 510–517). Hershey, PA: Information Science Reference. doi:10.4018/978-1-59904-845-1.ch067

Tornero, J. M. P. (2004). *Promoting digital literacy: Final report (EAC/76/03).Understanding digital literacy.* Barcelona, Spain: UAB. Retrieved December 4th, 2007, from http://ec.europa.eu/education/archive/elearning/doc/studies/dig_lit_en.pdf

UNESCO. (2002). *Recommendations addressed to the UNESCO.* Youth Media Education Conference, Seville, 15-16 February 2002.

Wenger, E. (1998). *Communities of practice. Learning, meaning and identity.* New York, NY: Cambridge University Press.

# Section 1
# Digital Literacy and Culture

# Chapter 1
# Beyond Babel:
## Multiliteracies in Digital Culture

**Monica Fantin**
*Universidade Federal de Santa Catarina (UFSC), Brazil*

## ABSTRACT

*This article highlights the importance of the concepts of media literacy, and digital and informational literacy to understand the multimodal meaning of multiliteracies and their interfaces. An analogy with Babel is used to understand the different ways in which this concept articulates the linguistic, visual, audio, spatial, and gestural dimensions in digital culture. In this framework, the question of convergence is highlighted in learning experiences undertaken in formal and informal contexts. To qualify the meaning of this learning for the subject, the article mentions the concept of personal literacy to locate the importance of subjectivity in the interactions that the multiliteracies offer. Finally, in an exercise of representation of the components of the multiliteracies, the article presents a diagram that highlights the importance of mediation and the forms of appropriation that express concepts and experiences in search of a transformative pedagogical practice, as an opportunity to understand the multiliteracies as a condition of dialog, expression and participation in the culture.*

## INTRODUCTION

Upon discussing the concepts of media literacy, digital literacy and information literacy and their specificities in the fields of education and communication (Fantin, 2010), we see that if all media require literacy and if all language needs to be appropriated, we can think of a broad concept of literacy. This concept should be updated according to the demands of social practice and different socio-cultural contexts, and should dialectically consider the micro and macro dimensions of these processes in their specificities and generalities. This leads us to think at the frontiers of the

DOI: 10.4018/978-1-4666-2943-1.ch001

concepts, practices and uses of the multiliteracies based on their multiple faces – written, oral, visual, artistic, spatial, gestural and tactile modes of representation – which reveal their multimodal character and the interfaces articulated in various dimensions of languages.

Given the Babelic condition of human language and its potential for appropriation, this plural condition does not only signify the difference *between* languages, but a "multiplicity of languages *within* language, in any language, Therefore, any language is multiple, since *one* singular language is also an invention(...)" according to Larrosa (2004)

Without considering the merit of the discussion between tongue and language, this Babelized condition of language can also signify encounters, because beyond the confusion and catastrophe that the myth of Babel represents, the plurality of language, more than an excess, can imply different forms of dialog and mediation. Babel appears to run through any human phenomenon of communication and of construction of meanings and given the multiplicity of cultural practices, it is more than ever necessary to deal with its different forms of translation, interpretation and appropriation.

## Babelized Languages and Learning

Different forms of written, audiovisual, digital language, and so forth, have their codes and specificities and the process for these learning styles is complex, involving basic dimensions and abilities that concern common issues. Based on the specificities of the languages and the media and of that which is common to the different learning processes, we can discuss how the concepts of literacy are intertwined in the multiliteracies.

If the concept of literacy is discussed today as multimedia literacy, as Buckingham says, digital literacy "can be seen as one of the multiple literacies that are required by the contemporary media" (Buckingham, 2005). Thus, instead of the simple

inclusion of digital literacy in curriculums, Buckingham defends a broader reconceptualization of what is understood by literacy and by autoliteracy.

In this respect, Rivoltella (2008) also affirms that, more important than including media education in a new school discipline, a transversal approach and attention is needed in the curriculum, so that students can learn about digital culture in an environment in which teachers adopt media and communication as a teaching style. As a style of teaching, digital media involves convergences and this leads us to consider the perspective of multiliteracies.

For the New London Group the notion of multiliteracies:

*is an attempt to comprehend and target the multiple text forms that have resulted from the new technologies and new media forms, through a pedagogy that allows students to comprehend and deal with the ' increasing complexity and interrelationship as different modes of meaning' (Iyer & Luke, 2010)*

For those who defend multiliteracies, the emphasis on the plurality of literacies does not refer only to the various media or modes of communication, but also to the social nature of literacy and its various forms of use in cultures and societies. It is by understanding reading and writing as social activities that some researchers prefer to refer to 'literacy practices' instead of simply literacy, according to Buckingham (2005).

In this conceptual expansion, Hobbs (2006) once again presents the idea of media literacy based on the concept of multimedia literacy and on the areas of the emerging syntheses. Situating the terms along with visual literacy, media literacy, critical literacy, informational literacy and technology literacy, the author expands the concept of literacy in its forms of expression and visual, electronic and digital communication, including the respective objects of study and analysis. Reviewing key disciplinary and conceptual traditions of some of the new literacies, the author examines the consensuses and disagreements so that:

*A model that synthesizes this literature is created in order to support the work of scholars interested in investigating how teachers translate the "big ideas" of multiliteracies into classroom practice and to support the development of measures to assess students' learning (Hobbs, 2006)*

From this perspective, the author elaborates three key-ideas for multiliteracies that concern AA (authors and audiences), MM (messages and meanings) and RR (representations and reality), individualizing them in a framework that situates each literacy. This helps identify its applicability and offers a view of the different emphases and aspects of its similarities and differences.

In this reconceptualization and synthesis of the different perspectives:

*All of the proponents reflect an appreciation that visual, electronic, and digital media are reshaping the knowledge, skills and competencies required for full participation in contemporary society, and all view these abilities as fundamentally tied to the intellectual and social practices known as literacy (New London Group, 1996; Hobbs, 2006).*

This understanding of multiliteracies recognizes that "the acquisition and development of these competencies require changes in the learning environment" (Buckingham Hobbs, 2006) and this includes significant changes in teaching and the functioning of education: projects, experiences, access to tools and material resources, forms of mediation, classroom organization, and related issues.

More recently, educational work with ICT based on the concepts of digital literacy and information literacy allows making advances in the concepts of multimodal and multimedia literacy, as originally proposed by the New London Group

in the sense of a critical pedagogy and critical and multiliteracies, and place at the center of the concept the "transformative pedagogy aimed at affective leanings across social and cultural differences, and across different learning styles" (Iyer & Luke, 2010). For these authors, multiliteracies and multimodal literacies understand that the integration of linguistic, social and cultural diversity promotes a project that results in student agency and transformative pedagogy.

*Multiliteracies aim to target literacy practices currently favored in schools as well as literacy practices children acquire at home, and in other informal settings. In this sense, multiliteracy approaches are mindful and inclusive of the diverse and complex cultural perspectives of learners and theirs diverse learning styles (Iyer & Luke, 2010).*

For this reason, it is essential to think of media literacy, digital literacy and information literacy as multiliteracies, or that is, as a repertoire of related capacities, some more generic and others more specific, related to the medias, as Bazagette (2005) emphasizes. From this perspective, the teaching and learning of multiliteracies is associated to art, science, narrative and the ludic, as fundamental languages in which the subject expresses and communicates his or her feelings, ideas and experiences in the most varied forms: oral, written, artistic, corporal, electronic, digital.

This means that the teacher needs to learn to use various types of media and learn different forms of teaching. This demands teacher training that deals with expression and creation not only based on scientific knowledge but also as a possibility of belonging and digital inclusion.

From this perspective, multiliteracies can be understood as a condition for citizenship, because digital inclusion must include social, cultural, technological and intellectual dimensions in order to favor belonging and assure the effective participation of people in the culture, as Fantin and Girardello (2008) affirm. In school contexts, an articulation between different languages and contents involves a collaborative work of experimentation, creation, and discovery. It also involves dialog, negotiation, polyphony, openness, flexibility, criticism, and collaboration.

*In this process, the languages of different fields of knowledge can be understood based on different perspectives: as a form of expression of the subject of the culture, as a means of communication, as a form of interaction and human development, and also as a social-cultural object of knowledge (Fantin & Girardello, 2008)*

That is, to think of the concept of multiliteracies implies thinking not only of the theoretical bases that give foundation to and legitimate this concept but also of public policies and investments in teacher education to work with this new perspective. This is not reduced to specialized courses, because it involves thinking of the potential place for media-education in initial and continued teacher education within educational institutions at their various levels of education. This teacher education should work with approximation to and distancing from the various literacies, not only to assure the movement between conceptual and institutional continuities and ruptures, but also to reconsider what is considered to be "new." At a time in which large and rapid changes are occurring at stunning speed, the validity of classical and contemporary knowledge need to be considered in a new dimension. And although new media require new competencies, we cannot always remain at the mercy of the novelties, understood as something good or bad in and of themselves.

Equally important to the resignification and updating of certain practices is the search for concepts that can express this movement, and in this search we can find broader and hybrid terms that represent the complexity of these questions, which preserve and maintain important elements, while also transforming them. Thus, educational thinking and action, understood as cultural prac-

tices, can not only be in better harmony with the current challenges, but act in the construction of a route:

*That recognizes and respects the new forms of culture and the new modes of acting which they generate, but which does not sacrifice, and does not change the compulsive and frenetic innovation, the incessant search for meaning and quality of life. It is the search for a space for a type of "third path" of a cultural nature that allows crossing horizons to a new intelligence of the world and of life, which is capable of intervening in the local, but with a global understanding and vision (Pinto, 2005).*

In this search for paths and meanings, the author refers to an "ecology of communication" (idem), which understands communicative practices not only as information and transmission, but as relation, dialog and connection. This idea can be expanded to educational practices, relating them to a concept of multiliteracies that redimensions the role of the subject, and its ties and relations with the other, with the social surroundings and with the cultural scenario.

To help understand this plurality of relations of the subject and her subjectivity in the context of multiliteracies, we can aggregate the concept of personal literacy, understood as a "process of expressing desires and complex motive states in an articulate manner" (Fiumara, Cole, & Moyle, 2010). Considering that the educational context involves questions of power and that the use of social technologies requires increasingly cooperative practices, the analytical capacity, logic and critical evaluation demanded by the other literacies are necessary abilities but also involve other spaces, times and subjectivities.

In the context of an experience guided by the concept of multiliteracies, Cole and Moyle (2010) affirm that personal literacy refers to the work of each individual in a group, and her projects and the articulation between the personal and cultural identities in the activity that "involves activation of her modes of creativity including imagination, memory and synthetic thought about who they would like to become."

At this time, I mention personal literacy only to call attention to this important concept to be considered in the larger framework of the interfaces that compose multiliteracies. Alongside the linguistic, visual, audio, spatial gestural and digital dimensions, this idea can advance the understanding of the concept, qualifying the understanding of the integrated learning that occur in the social and cultural context of multiliteracies.

## CONCLUSION

Considering the Babelic condition of multiliteracies, we see that their interfaces involve media literacy, digital literacy, information literacy as well as personal literacy, mediated by the idea of convergence. With this we seek to offer conceptual and cultural instruments to understand what

multiliteracies and their concepts, practices and uses signify.

As a provisional synthesis to represent this complex process involving multiliteracies, instigated by Cartelli, I have made a diagram to represent the factors mentioned in the article and their possible articulations. In Figure 1, I also include other elements related to the condition of being fluent in multiliteracies, which concern different mediations and opportunities to appropriate this multimodal experience and the idea of convergence.

For each one of the components that represent the idea of multiliteracies, the realms of the different literacy are part of one another and dialog with each other. The lines, which sustain and form the design, can be understood as threads that cross the dimension and highlight the specificity of each frontier, woven by the idea of mediation, appropriation and convergence. We can also include indicators that qualify the texture of the mediation and its educational, technological and cultural emphases, as well as the possibilities for

*Figure 1. Components of the multiliteracies*

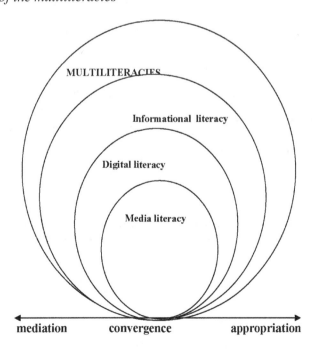

instrumental, critical, ethical-aesthetic, and creative and shared appropriation. This would allow recognition of different opportunities to achieve fluency in multiliteracies as well as recognition of the significance of learning as a search for dialog, expression and participation in the culture.

# REFERENCES

Bazalgette, C. (2005). Incontro com Cary Bazalgette nel suo ufficio. *Boletim da Academia Nacional de Medicina, 3.*

Buckingham, D. (2005). *Media education: Literacy, learning and contemporary culture.* Cambridge, UK: Polity Press.

Cole, D., & Moyle, V. (2010). Cam-capture literacy and its incorporation into multiliteracies. In Pullen, D. L., & Cole, D. (Eds.), *Multiliteracies and technology enhanced education: social practice and the global classroom* (pp. 116–129). Hershey, PA: IGI Global.

Fantin, M. (2006). *Mídia-educação: Conceitos, experiências e diálogos Brasil Itália.* Florianópolis, Brazil: Cidade Futura.

Fantin, M. (2008) Os cenários culturais e as multiliteracies na escola. *Revista Comunicação e Sociedade, 13.*

Fantin, M. (2010). Perspectives on media literacy, digital literacy and information literacy. *International Journal of Digital Literacy and Digital Competence, 1*(4), 10–15. doi:10.4018/jdldc.2010100102

Fantin, M., & Giradello, G. (2008). Digital literacy and cultural mediations to the digital divide. In Rivoltella, P. C. (Ed.), *Digital literacy: Tools and methodologies for information society* (pp. 310–340). Hershey, PA: IGI Global.

Hobbs, R. (2006). *Multiple vision of multimedia literacy: Emerging areas of synthesis.* Retrieved December, 17, 2007, from http://reneehobbs.org/renee's%20web%20site/publications/Hobbs%20final%20PDF%20Literacy%20and%20Technology%20Vol%202.pdf

Larrosa, J. (2004). *Linguagem e educação depois de Babel.* Belo Horizonte, Brazil: Autêntica.

Pinto, M. (2005). A busca da comunicação na sociedade multi-ecrãs: Perspectiva ecológica. *Comunicar, 25,* 259–264.

Rivoltella, P. C. (2005). *Media education: Fondamenti didattici e prospettive di ricerca.* Brescia, Italy: La Scuola.

Rivoltella, P. C. (2008). From Media Education to Digital Literacy: A Paradigm Change? In Rivoltella, P. C. (Ed.), *Digital literacy: Tools and methodologies for information society* (pp. 217–229). Hershey, PA: IGI Global.

Yier, R., & Luke, C. (2010). Multimodal, multiliteracies: Texts and literacies for the 21st century. In Pullen, D. L., & Cole, D. (Eds.), *Multiliteracies and technology enhanced education: Social practice and the global classroom* (pp. 18–34). Hershey, PA: IGI Global.

# Chapter 2
# Formalized Informal Learning:
## ICT and Learning for the 21st Century

**Karin Tweddell Levinsen**
*Aarhus University, Denmark*

**Birgitte Holm Sørensen**
*Aarhus University, Denmark*

## ABSTRACT

*Longitudinal research projects into social practices are both subject to and capture changes in society, meaning that research is conducted in a fluid context and that new research questions appear during the project's life cycle. In the present study emerging new performances and uses of ICT are examined and the relation between network society competences, learners' informal learning strategies and ICT in formalized school settings over time is studied. The authors find that aspects of ICT like multimodality, intuitive interaction design and instant feedback invites an informal bricoleur approach. When integrated into certain designs for teaching and learning, this allows for Formalized Informal Learning and support is found for network society competences building.*

## 1. INTRODUCTION – RESEARCH IN A FLUID ENVIRONMENT

This paper presents findings from a large-scale longitudinal, qualitative study – Project ICT and Learning (PIL) – that engaged the participation of eight primary schools in Denmark, and was conducted between 2006 and 2008. The research design was based on action research, involving teachers and other relevant stakeholders, as well as participant observations in the classroom documented by thick descriptions, formal and informal interviews and focus group interviews. The aim of the study was to explore and identify relations between designs for teaching and learning and the students' learning of school subjects within defined learning goals and curricula along with various implementations of ICT in the pedagogical everyday practice (Levinsen & Sørensen, 2008).

DOI: 10.4018/978-1-4666-2943-1.ch002

However, another research strand – the topic of this paper – emerged during the project's life cycle as a consequence of ongoing changes in society and technology. Thus, the first part of the paper is dedicated to the presentation of the gradual formulation and grounding of the research design for this new strand.

During the study, interactive whiteboards gradually came into use as a significant implementation of ICT while the students initiated the use of Web 2.0 resources in the school by simply using them. Occasional use of mobile phones initiated by the students was also observed. Gradually, the relation between the students' informal and the teachers' traditional approach to ICT emerged as an important theme, as it was observed how the students performed certain ICT-related activities at a higher level than the teachers and that the traditional teacher-student relation became challenged in both positive and negative ways; e.g. it was observed that in relation to the students' formal learning involving the use of Web 2.0, some school classes produced genuine trivia in terms of simple copy-paste solutions in fulfilling formal tasks, while other classes expanded beyond the defined learning goals of their grade levels. These phenomena were to a higher degree observed in relation to the introduction of Web 2.0 in the classroom than in relation to the traditional use of ICT in terms of applications and learning objects. These further raised questions such as: Does ICT or instances of ICT play a role in the observed changes in the classroom when Web 2.0 and occasionally mobile phones are used? If the answer is yes, then what kind of role is it? What can we learn from that? Do the students' informal strategies encompass qualities that may be useful for a school's general adjustment to the challenges of society's ever-increasing e-permeation?

As a consequence of these emerging phenomena, a new research strand emerged and the project had to formulate additional research questions and identify new empirical fields of attention for data collection, along with analytical categories.

In order to achieve this, it became necessary to frame an understanding of the character of society's transition from industry to network society, and grasp core concepts such as key competences and ICT-related competences or ICT literacy. In the beginning, it was perceived that this would entail an uncomplicated adjustment to the project; however, it soon turned out to be a bit more complex. Therefore, the next section of the paper is dedicated to a discussion about the transition from industry to network society and related core concepts that helped ground the research questions for PIL's new research strand and the subsequent modifications of the project's research design.

## 2. FROM INDUSTRY TO NETWORK SOCIETY

In his book, The Hypercomplex Society (1998), Qvortrup states that our society moves towards increasing hypercomplexity and that the industrial mode of production gradually has come to be replaced by the hypercomplex society's mode of production in which companies produce and process knowledge and offer network services as commodities. At the same time, the production units have come to be ad hoc – open and transparent project organisations that are made possible by the global digital network. According to Qvortrup the individual and organisational challenge is to deal with and reduce the hypercomplexity in adequate ways. The relations between globalisation, networked and ad hoc organisational forms and digitalisation are explored further by Manuel Castells in his acclaimed sociological study, The Information Age (2000). According to Castells, the industrial era of wireline networks saw the role of ICT as a tool in relation to production whereas ICT tools were allocated and delineated to definable locations. In the network society this view of ICT makes no sense because ICT has become ubiquitous and is just as integrated in such domains as politics, the military, economic power, society and citizenship, and interpersonal relations, as it is in activities of production (Castells, 2000).

With mobile and wireless technologies, multimodal digital media and Web 2.0 social software, ICT literally dissolves or penetrates physical structures and offers virtual environments that we can either choose to participate in or have forced upon us. In the same process, human interaction with ICT has expanded from being a mere interaction with tools to what has become an interaction as agency; users being actors, participants, producers and peers. Consequently, digitalisation has become a partly invisible but a constituting dimension in the world, and ICT must be understood as something that is interwoven in the social structure and culture. Table 1 outlines the most profound differences between the industrial and the network society's modes of production.

The increasing e-permeation of all aspects of everyday life has radically changed the role and place of ICT in society from affecting limited parts of our lives, to profoundly impacting the way we live and how we perceive the world and our mutual relations. Additionally, the transformation has impacted fundamental epistemological and ontological questions. In the industrial era, the basic conditions were perceived and treated as ontologically stable and predictable while universal and true knowledge was considered

possible to achieve. In contrast, the basic ontological condition in the world of the network society is fluidity – that is, instability and unpredictability – while knowledge is equally subject to constant (re)construction and (re)negotiation. Accordingly, science and technology studies (STS) have increasingly developed towards constructivist and social constructivist positions (Latour & Wolgar, 1986; Law, 1999).

The fluid nature of the network society causes its mode of production to be highly dependent on the individual's ability to navigate in a fluid context. In contrast to Qvortrup who focuses on a system's (individuals and organisations) reaction towards a hypercomplex environment and how the system may reduce the hypercomplexity, Castells focuses on individuals' and organisations' ability to be proactive and think ahead when dealing with and performing in a complex and fluid environment (Castells, 2000). According to the emerging demands of the global economy, Castells divides individuals as employees of the global economy into two dominant types: self-programmable and generic labour. Self-programmable labour aligns with the demands of the network society and is equipped with the competences for lifelong learning and the ability to retrain and adapt to new conditions and challenges. As such, the self-programmable individual reduces hypercom-

*Table 1. Differences between the industry and network society modes of production*

|  | The industrial mode of production | Network society's mode of production |
|---|---|---|
| World view | Predictable and stable | Uncertain and fluid |
| Commodity | Products | Services |
| Organisation | Linear and hierarchical | Flexible network |
| Core organisation | Companies | Ad hoc project organisations |
| Competition factors | Skills and values | Knowledge |
| Means of control | Rules to follow | Probability and choice |
| Strategy of action | Re-action | Pro-action and interaction |
| Role of ICT | Tool | Tool, personal identity, social structure and culture |
| Role of ICT user | User of tools | User, actor, participant, producer, peer … |
| Competencies | Generic (and self-programming) | Self-programming |

plexity through future-oriented performance of self-management and self-initiated learning. In contrast, generic labour aligns with the demands of the industrial society, needs instruction, and is both interchangeable and disposable. Thus, the generic individual reduces hypercomplexity through reactions oriented primarily towards the present and does not perform self-management or self-initiated learning. As the two types of labour are linked to employers' needs and visions about available employees and do not denote actual people, Castells argues that for a society to remain competitive in the global economy, the educational systems should devote particular efforts to the education of individuals who possess self-programmable rather than generic competences.

In the search of an approach to the emerging performances that were being observed in the PIL-study, the concept of self-programming was deemed a useful theoretical tool, as it became apparent that there were some successful mixtures of students and teachers, curriculum and Web 2.0, which also seemed to bear similarities to self-programming.

## 3. UNDERSTANDING KEY COMPETENCES

### Key Competences in the Network Society

Castells' theory has had a major impact on the international definitions of key competences for the network society that are used as guidelines for governmental decisions about education (OECD, 2001; European Commission, 2003; Rychen & Salganik, 2003; G8, 2006); e.g. the European Commission's Directorate-General for Education and Culture states:

*… the fact that the world is e-permeated means that those who can understand and comfortably use e-facilities are significantly advantaged, in terms*

*of educational success, employment prospects and other aspects of life (Martin, 2005)*

The currently agreed upon list of key competences was developed in the period 1998-2003 when the OECD carried-out the project Definition and Selection of Competences (DeSeCo, 2002). In Denmark, the key competences are included in the Danish government's educational strategy; this is the result of its own project – The National Account of Competences – which was realised in 2005 and which was based on DeSeCo. The DeSeCo key competences are listed below (see Table 2) and divided by the author into general competences that are relevant for any agent in most social formations, and the competences that relate to the self-programmable individual, which are specifically relevant in the network society.

The DeSeCo self-programmable competences constitute a step towards the concretisation of PIL's new research strand. However, they do not specifically relate to ICT. One place to look for a relation between key competences and ICT rests in the body of studies regarding New Learners or Power Users. The terms refer to the members of the generation born into a world where ubiquitous ICT was already present, for whom the Internet, wireless and mobile solutions have become everyday phenomena. It is generally accepted that New Learners exhibit competences that cannot be reduced to basic device-operating skills and a number of studies show that students' use of the

*Table 2. DeSeCo key competences sorted in general and self-programmable competences*

| General key competences | Self-programmable competences |
|---|---|
| Literacy<br>Social competence<br>Communication competence<br>Democratic competence<br>Environmental competence<br>Cultural competence<br>Competence in health and body | Learning (to learn) competence<br>Self-management competence<br>Creativity and innovation competence |

media is far more sophisticated and differentiated outside schools than in schools (Drotner, 2001; Livingstone & Bowill, 2001; Sørensen, Jessen, & Olesen, 2002; Media Council for Children and Young People, 2003; Stald, 2009). They exhibit high-level informal IT-related competences, often surpassing their teachers with respect to both operational skills, as well as communication and networking competences.

## The Challenge of Building Key Competences

Studies by Sørensen et al. (2004) and Malyn-Smith (2004) found that the informal play-related approach to acquiring key competences of the network society and ICT is a challenge to the educational system and schools' adaptation to the network society. It was found that the educational system perceives formal practice and informal learning strategies as contradictory. There have been indications of there being difficulties in accepting that for the first time in history, the system is forced to learn more from its surroundings and from its students rather than the other way around in order to adapt to the present and future e-permeated society.

In correspondence to the observations in the PIL-study, the studies of children's and young people's informal learning strategies towards ICT indicate that ICT may actually play a major role in schools' adaptation to the network society and in the development and building of network society key competences. Thus, in order to collect empirical data that may help to answer the challenges and questions, it became essential to formulate areas of awareness to guide the researchers' attention towards relevant observations. DeSeCo points this awareness towards three competences: creativity and innovation, learning (to learn) and self-management. The performance of the New Learners (Dede, 2005) points towards observable actions related to ICT such as:

- Fluency in multiple media as well as in simulation-based virtual settings;
- Communal learning involving diverse, tacit, situated experience, with knowledge distributed across a community and a context as well as within an individual;
- A balance among experiential learning, guided mentoring, and collective reflection;
- Expressiveness through non-linear, associational webs of representations;
- Co-design of learning experiences personalised to individual needs and preferences;

DeSeCo's definitions and standards are limited in telling us about the desired destination and outcome of digital and key competence-building, while studies of the New Learners' performance and agency are limited because they present a rather abstract and descriptive list of attributes related to self-programmable behaviour. Castells argued that society should devote particular efforts to the education of self-programmable individuals. But neither the definitions of key competences nor studies of the New Learners cue us towards what it takes to educate people to become self-programmable individuals. The basic challenge for the educational system is thereby twofold: 1) The actual making of digitally literate, key competent, self-programmable social actors; and 2) How to develop adequate designs for teaching and learning that allow informal learning strategies to unfold in a formalised context. Questions that seem obvious are never asked, for instance:

- What do self-programmable individuals do when they self-program?
- How do adults learn to become self-programmable, if they are not – e.g. teachers?
- How do we ensure that new generations grow up to be self-programmable rather than generic?
- What are the designs for teaching and learning that scaffold the building of the self-programmable individuals' competences?

In conclusion, we lack research and knowledge about what it means to teach and to learn to become a self-initiated lifelong learner or a self-programmable individual. We lack research that aims at describing the phenomenology of acquiring digital literacy and self-programming as a competence. We also lack research related to the role technology has in these processes. Ultimately, we need to be able to identify and design relevant learning objectives and scaffolding. In this perspective, the emerging performance and use of ICT observed during the PIL-study provided the possibility for researchers to enter into this important research area and provide new knowledge. The first formulation of the research questions for the new strand in the PIL-study became:

*Do instances of key competence-building occur?*

*If so, which key competences are documented?*

*Does ICT play a role in the building of key competences?*

*If so, what role does ICT play in competence-building and how is it enacted?*

## 4. FUTURE-ORIENTED COMPETENCE

The empirical challenge of PIL is to observe in a fluid field where also key concepts such as ICT-related competences and key competences are "essentially contested concepts" (Connolly, 1993); that is, they are both ill-defined and subject to an ongoing negotiation of meaning. It is a challenge to observe competence-building as a process rather than the supposed or best practice outcomes of a competence-building process. The following section discusses the concepts of competence and competence-building and their possible phenomenological appearances in relation to the research questions of PIL's new research strand in

order to encircle the phenomena for observation. As an outcome of this discussion, a new concept – Future-Oriented Competence – is suggested, which encompasses the current understanding of network society competences and offers a framework for the observation of learning activities?

## Digital Literacy

In the early era of everyday use of ICT, computer literacy was understood as the functional and basic skills required when undertaking particular operations. Additionally, users were subdivided according to Dreyfus & Dreyfus' Model of Skill Acquisition (1988): novices, competent users and experts. As search engines spread, search strategies and data management skills were added and later, the repertoire was supplemented with: ability to reflect upon, differentiate between and select among search results (Breivik, 2005; Katz, 2007). As digital media became increasingly complex, the user's cognitive ability to interpret representational forms and modes of interaction became important, and the term multimodal competence was introduced (Tyner, 1998; Jewitt & Kress, 2003; Erstad, 2005).

As users of digital resources are no longer recipients but actors who consume, participate, produce, publish, collaborate and share information, the educational focus has changed from the transfer of best practices to an accommodation of general education or buildung for the network society. Buckingham (2003) claims that as part of their digital building, it is imperative that users-as-actors are able to meta-reflect on their interaction with other actors and on multimodal means of expression, while also understanding how agency and the virtual environment are intertwined, that they dialectically constitute and are constituted by one another. Martin (2006) expands on digital buildung – which he names digital literacy – to further encompass the lifelong ability to act in the fluid digital infrastructure of the 21st century and contends that digital literacy is fundamental for all citizens. Drawing on Bateson (1991), Martin argues that e-permeation demands that meta-reflection on one's personal digital development and learning must be part of digital literacy along with the ability to act and transfer knowledge to new contexts and deal with the yet unknown. Martin defines three stages or levels of engagement in the lifelong construction of digital literacy:

- **Digital competence:** The basic skills required for learning and undertaking particular operations through learning by doing;
- **Corpus of digital uses:** Basic insight and agency that allow for critical reflection, transfer of knowledge and best practices between digital solutions in the digitalised environment;
- **Digital transformation:** Ability to meta-reflect and change the basic premise for agency in the digitalised environment and enable creativity as an integrated part of the agency.

Martin's standpoint implies that the original ICT skills and competences are still relevant, but that their acquisition cannot be seen as a measurable threshold that one can pass. Acquisition must be seen as an ongoing and lifelong learning process. The competences are not successive, rather, they are interwoven and they flow together into the buildung process that Martin (2006) names digital transformation. People who master digital transformation as a self-initiated learning process align with Castells' self-programmable individual and the self-programmable key competences as defined by OECD (see Table 1). With Martin's definition, we get another step closer to unfolding what it means to be or become self-programmable and the kind of agency that self-programming implies. Accordingly, we also get a step closer to operationalising what the researcher may guide his or her awareness towards when collecting data regarding the new research strand.

- In relation to data collection, this means that the observer must be sensitive towards situations where the actors display: computer literacy, the ability search for and process data, multimodal constructive and interpretive competences, and Martin's corpus of digital uses based on the transfer of knowledge and digital transformation.

## Learning, Proactivity and Learning Competences

According to Wenger (1998) learning processes that are similar to acquiring digital transformation competences constitute a continuous negotiation and re-negotiation of meaning when coping with "...the interaction of the planned and the emergent". Thus, according to Wenger, learning is a dialectical process that oscillates between reflection and action; and following this, the self-programmable learner is expected to be able to evaluate his or her own learning process.

- In relation to data collection, this means that the observer must be sensitive towards situations where the actors encounter something unexpected or unknown and observe their agency and strategies over time in relation to acquiring an understanding of the new and to overcome obstacles.

To navigate between the planned and the emergent is, in the world of projects in fluid environments, called process management (Christensen & Kreiner, 1991). According to Acroff (1976) and Christiansen et al. (1999) there are four types of strategies to apply when confronted with something unexpected. Acroff (1976) operates by distinguishing between what is a planning and a situated perspective, and by differentiating between what is a passive and an active behaviour. Passive behaviour matches inactive or reactive strategies of action, while an active behaviour is future-oriented and matches proactive and interactive strategies of action (see Table 3). In the large body of business research literature where these concepts are developed, active behaviours as a whole are named proactivity.

Wenger's concept of dealing with the planned or expected corresponds to Acroff's (1976) planning perspective. Moreover, Wenger's concept of dealing with the emergent or unexpected corresponds to Acroff's situated perspective. According to Wenger and Acroff, the self-programmable individual or the learner who masters digital transformation also masters the management of his or her learning process. These individuals are expected to make use of active behaviours or proactivity and perform learning process management (LPM); that is, to oscillate between the planning and the situated perspectives in order to perform process management.

- In relation to data collection, this means that the observer must be sensitive towards situations where the actors oscillate between the positions: being oriented towards the future and planning a head (reflection), and performing interventions in the present (action).

The self-programmable individual's performance or agency occurs over time and therefore the time dimension is important for observations. The proactive oscillation between action and reflection

*Table 3. Acroff's matrix of perspectives and behaviour*

|  | **Passive behaviour** | **Active behaviour** |
|---|---|---|
| **Planning perspective** | Inactive strategy Avoid changes until they are inevitable | Proactive strategy Looks ahead in order to spot trends and be prepared to meet challenges |
| **Situated perspective** | Reactive strategy Tries to meet changes in ways that preserves the known situation | Interactive strategy Performs interventions in order to meet challenges |

may appear similar to Donald Schön's Reflective Practitioner (2001), however, proactivity denotes a strategy that is always a conscious choice while reflection-in-action denotes an experience-based competence that has been built over years of practice. When competences have become tacit (Polanyi, 1968) they may no longer be subject to conscious reflection. Thus, the reflective practitioner may both denote the virtuous expert and the unreflective practitioner characterised by routines. The so-called New Learners may be considered as reflective practitioners in both meanings of the concept. This may explain the observation mentioned above regarding the student-produced trivia; produced by students who are viewed by their teachers as New Learners. Based on this discussion, learners are subdivided into the following groups that correspond with Martin's three levels of digital literacy:

- **Weak learner:** A learner who displays basic difficulties regarding the oscillation pattern;
- **Routine-based learner:** Prefers action to reflection and the situated perspective to the planning perspective;
- **Self-programmable learner:** Oscillates rather effortlessly between reflection and action, as well as between the planning and situated perspectives.
  - In relation to data collection, this means that the observer must be sensitive towards the differentiation of learners and signs of learners' progression over time between levels.

## Informal Strategies – Bricoleur Approach and Play Culture

As discussed earlier, the so-called New Learners and their informal learning strategies when dealing with ICT may function as inspiration for the observer. The New Learners' informal learning strategies are similar to the bricoleur-style's

(Oblinger, 2003; Malyn-Smith, 2004; Sørensen et al., 2004; Dede, 2005; Oblinger & Oblinger, 2005; Levinsen, 2006; Ryberg, 2007; Sørensen, Audon, & Levinsen, 2010). According to Turkle and Papert (1990) a bricoleur approaches challenges by connecting practice and concrete thinking in a process of arrangement and re-arrangement of materiality while constantly negotiating and re-negotiating meaning using either inner dialogue or shared negotiation. This process produces patterns of behaviour that are similar to the play patterns identified in studies of children's play culture – Construction Play and Role Play (Sørensen, 1999; Jessen, 2001; Trageton, 2004) – and generates learning processes that may be described as assimilation and accommodation (Wakefield, 2003).

However, recent studies document that no matter how competent the New Learners may appear to be in relation to new technologies, they do not possess the knowledge and the competences that are necessary to turn ICT into school-relevant perspectives and uses (Levinsen & Sørensen, 2008; Gynther, 2010; Sørensen, Audon, & Levinsen, 2010). Therefore the process of learning and knowledge-sharing between teachers and students and the subsequent implementation of ICT in everyday school practice are closely related and interdependent.

- In relation to data collection, this means that the observer must be sensitive towards play and bricoleur approaches that unfold in formal learning contexts as well as where teachers challenge students to reflect on their informal learning using formalised perspectives.

## Self-Directed Skills of Inquiry

The literature offers a large body of descriptions of the characteristics of informal learning strategies but only few texts address the unfolding of informal learning strategies in formalised primary school contexts. Literature on the formal use of informal strategies refers primarily to adult learners; in his paper on adults' self-directed learning, Malcolm Knowles (1975) offers a description of what self-directed learning may look like and what a teacher may facilitate when supporting self-directed learning. Knowles' theory addresses adults learning and he developed what he called the Andragogical Model that contrasts pedagogy, as he was convinced that adults learn differently than children. Knowles formulated assumptions about the adult self-directed learner (Knowles, Holten, & Swanson, 2005) and argued that maturing means to become self-directed rather that dependent, and that one becomes able to draw on experience and becomes self-motivating rather than instructed. He also put forward that adults need to know why something is relevant, as a subject to learning.

Knowles' arguments for the difference between andragogy and pedagogy have been subject to debate (Davenport, 1993; Jarvis, 1977; Tennant, 1996) and research has documented that children demonstrate the same need as adults in understanding why something is important in the learning, and that children are able to be self-directed and self-motivated (Gynther, 2010; Sørensen, Audon, & Levinsen, 2010). However, as Knowles' description of the self-directed learner bears similarities to the bricoleur approach identified among young New Learners, it is argued that Knowles' theory may work as a useful tool in operationalising what the observer may look for. The learner, who masters what Knowles coins Self-Directed Skills of Inquiry (1975), is able to identify, inquire and explore an unknown subject or topic and to reflect on and reduce the complexity of the gained information and transform it into knowledge that drives the learning process further. Knowles' distinction bears similarity to Vygotsky's (1978) pedagogic distinction between the cognitive processes of externalisation and internalisation. As the present research addresses agency, neither Knowles' andragogic nor Vygotsky's pedagogic concepts are considered adequate.

In the following, the explorative activity is termed expansion, while the reflective and complexity-reducing activity is termed delimitation. As discussed above, only self-programmable learners may, in contrast to the routine-based and weak learners, be expected to perform self-directed learning and oscillate between expansion and delimitation.

- In relation to data collection, this means that the observer must be sensitive to the distinction between expansion and delimitation. Further, the observer must be sensitive to situations where oscillation between the two may occur or be absent.

## Future-Oriented Competence

The DeSeCo key competences and New Learners' behaviour do not encompass the above-discussed qualities of the self-programmable individuals' performed agency in a field of tension between the expected and the emergent in an e-permeated and fluid environment. Accordingly, both the DeSeCo key competences and New Learners' behaviour are considered too narrow-scoped in this study. In

order to integrate the previously discussed aspects of the network society competences and to cope with the "essentially contested" nature of concepts in the fluid conditions of the network society, the term Future-Oriented Competence is suggested as a temporal stabilization (Latour, 1988, 1992) and umbrella-concept that encompasses the aspects discussed above (see Figure 1): ICT-related competences, proactivity, future orientation and self-directed learning.

Stabilising Future-Oriented Competence encompasses the complexity of interrelatedness and interdependence as illustrated in the model above (see Figure 1), in six dimensions. The four dimensions in the centre are formed by the direction of the self-directed inquiry-dimension towards either expansion or delimitation, while the bricoleur practice-dimension moves between arrangement and negotiation.

## 5. THE CASE AND RESEARCH METHODOLOGY

The previous section defined six dimensions of the Future-Oriented Competence that relate to

*Figure 1. Model displaying the complexity of interrelation and interdependence between the dimensions of Future-Oriented Competence, when practiced in a field of tension between bricoleur activity and self-initiated inquiry*

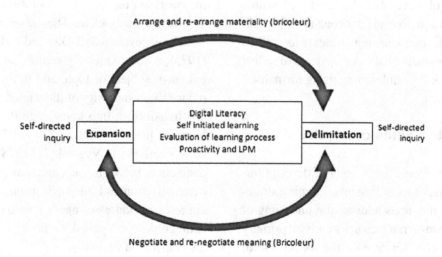

areas of attention that may guide the observer's awareness towards relevant situations during learning activities. Based on the dimensions, the research questions for the new research strand in the PIL-study became:

*Do instances of Future-Oriented Competence-building occur?*

*If so, which dimensions of Future-Oriented Competence are documented?*

*Does ICT play a role in the building of Future-Oriented Competence?*

*If so, what role does ICT play in competence-building and how is it enacted?*

The next step in the development of a methodology was to formulate assumptions of how these situations may phenomenologically appear in practice. These assumptions are the precondition for collecting both the expected and the unexpected during observations. Table 4 shows the relation

*Table 4. The relation between the six dimensions of Future-Oriented Competence and the corresponding*

| Dimensions | Corresponding observable phenomena |
| --- | --- |
| • Digital literacy (Martin's three levels) | ⇒ Do the actors search for and process data?<br>⇒ Do the actors understand and use multimodality in a constructive and interpretive way?<br>⇒ Do the actors display one or more of Martin's three stages of digital literacy? |
| • Learning competences and progression<br>• Weak, routine-based and self-programming learners<br>• Signs of progression over time between levels | ⇒ (How) do the actors formulate requests for help or comments from the teacher?<br>⇒ What kind of support do the actors ask for?<br>⇒ What is the amount and nature of teacher attention the actors need in order to proceed?<br>⇒ Do the actors change strategies and complexity of approach over time? |
| • Informal strategies (bricoleur's style/play) vs. formal strategies (teacher-defined approaches) | ⇒ Do the actors use play patterns as Construction Play and Role Play when exploring something new?<br>⇒ Do the actors arrange/re-arrange materiality (digital objects) while negotiating/re-negotiating meaning?<br>⇒ Do actors combine formal and informal approaches? |
| • Evaluation of one's learning process<br>• Activity of oscillating between the planned and the emergent | ⇒ Do the actors display awareness of discrepancies or alignment between the planned/expected and the emergent?<br>⇒ If so, do the actors express wonder, curiosity or frustration through words and/or body language?<br>⇒ Do the actors formulate and experiment with various strategies in terms of "What to do now"? "Do we need to know more"? "Are we on the right track"?<br>⇒ (How) do the actors negotiate meaning? |
| • Proactivity and learning process management (LPM)<br>• Activity of oscillating between a future-oriented planning perspective and performing interventions in the situated perspective | ⇒ Self-programmers are expected to formulate questions and to develop new strategies in terms of "What if ..." scenarios<br>⇒ Self-programmers are expected to negotiate meaning based on gained knowledge and experience<br>⇒ Generics are expected to look for answers and to repeat a preferred strategy<br>⇒ Generics are expected to ask "What now?" |
| • Self-directed skills of inquiry<br>• Activity of oscillating between expansion and delimitation | ⇒ What do the actors look for and ask for when exploring?<br>⇒ (How) do the actors negotiate meaning?<br>⇒ What do the actors prioritise when reducing complexity?<br>⇒ Do the actors reconsider their assumptions?<br>⇒ Do the actors acquire knowledge about the topic or do they produce trivia? |

between relevant situations and the expected corresponding phenomena that may be interpreted as reifications of Future-Oriented Competence:

After presenting the methodological framework of the new research strand, the case and PIL's research practice are briefly presented. The project was carried out from 2005 to 2007 in a suburb municipality of the Danish capital where primary schools demonstrated adjustments to meet the demands of the 21st century. The schools had been rebuilt to open-plan architecture in order to encourage flexible use of space and the schools had adopted flexible timetables that allow interdisciplinary activities over longer periods of time and across grades. When digital infrastructure, hardware and software were developed and implemented, the intention was to make digital resources accessible to the learners whenever needed throughout the day. These schools were therefore engaged in the process of becoming schools of the network society (Sørensen, Audon, & Levinsen, 2010).

The research was based on the participation of six primary schools in the municipality with 12 classes, ranging from grades 1 to 8. As PIL was a combined development- and research-project, the overall approach was action research. The teachers had formulated model-projects on how they wanted to experiment with combinations of designs for teaching and learning with ICT and accordingly, researchers and the teachers shared knowledge and discussed the actual practice in order to refine the model-projects into genuine educational practice. Data collection was based on anthropological methods such as participatory observation and informal interviews, semi-structured interviews and focus group interviews. Because of the main focus on ICT's learning potential in relation to specific school subjects, the classes were followed in Danish, foreign language teaching, maths and science. Depending on the teacher's model-project design, the observations followed subject-specific classes as well as interdisciplinary activities. The research visits were from one to four hours' dura-

tion, and each class was visited from one to four times, with a total of 38 visits. The use of digital resources ranged from teacher-controlled activities in computer rooms, through learner-centred project work, to the learners' self-initiated and ad hoc use of available ICT resources (Levinsen & Sørensen, 2008). Collected research data included thick descriptions (Geertz, 1973) and recordings of sound, video and stills. The learners' work and teachers' activity-plans were collected; this material has been analysed using methodology as described by Halkier (2008).

## 6. FINDINGS

The empirics were analysed using the six dimensions (see Table 4) as a tool for analysis. The analysis produced a series of indicators for the occurrence and emergence of Future-Oriented Competence in relation to ICT during the observed learning activities. As the six dimensions appear interdependent and interrelated, the following examples were selected because each example accentuates one dimension.

### Digital Literacy (Martin's Three Levels)

When students work with different digital means of expression, they relate to ICT as complex information architecture and technology. They learn to install software and get to know about file types, formats, data transport and the size of data (bytes, megabytes) as well as the technical conditions for accessing the school's intranet from home. But apart from expanding their computer literacy (Martin's level 1) they also progress through Martin's levels 2 and 3.

In the second grade, two boys used MS Word to write a horror story in Danish, and they used CD-Ord, an application originally designed for dyslexics (Levinsen, 2010), as it integrates sound with visualisations of words and lets young writers draw on their ability to listen and see when constructing words and spelling. During the process, the boys expanded their computer literacy as they searched for and downloaded horror-sounds for the story and finally they managed to change the path from the desktop to the memory stick, when they want to share the story. To begin with, they spoke sentences aloud and wrote afterwards, and only discussed single words on the screen. They gradually became able to cope with larger pieces of text and began discussing phrases as they pointed to the text on the screen. They gained experience in their use of keyboard, mouse and interface, and began using the spell-check in an integrated flow when writing, using the right-click functions and word suggestions from CD-Ord. They even managed to move larger pieces of text in order to improve the narrative quality. Throughout the process of writing and editing the text, they gradually built up a repertoire of digital uses for constructing and editing a text.

In language learning where the design for teaching and learning rests on storytelling and ICT, imagination is a necessary process driver. Independent of whether the teacher or the students defined the theme, we observed that students in all age groups formulated visions, pursued ideas and discussed the narrative structure of their storytelling. They produced sketches, storyboards, short lists and staging, and used a variety of digital tools together with digital cameras, mobile devices and internet resources to produce content. As the projects evolved, we observed that the students' digital competences expanded and most students consolidated a corpus of digital uses that allowed them to experiment with the storytelling, using bricoleur strategies. We even saw students progress to digital transformation and managed to redefine the premises for their stories, "kill their darlings" and start all over again with a new design, as well as students who redefined tools e.g. PowerPoint and PhotoStory, from being mere presentation tools to then become bricoleur's style sketching tools and storyboard tools.

Search strategies are central in digital literacy and depend on methodology, skills and imagination. A conscious and successful search depends on the ability to imagine the object of search and to ask questions in ways that exploit the potential of the search engines (Dervin, 1992; Dervin & Frenette, 2003). In a fifth-grade storyline project, two girls worked on a story in English about a mother who died in a car accident. They started a Google Image search for "dead people". At this point, they had no idea how to search or what they were actually looking for, and they used a trial-and-error strategy. Images from the tsunami in 2004 showed-up. "Uh, that's scary. Let's use our names instead," said Sara. Then the images became bimbo-like. "I sure don't wanna be like that!" and Sara searched for "Heidi". Then an image of a girl appeared: "… she looks like someone who lost her mother". They began realising that the Internet does not follow the same logic as their minds: on the Internet, Sara equals bimbo while Heidi equals the healthy girl from Switzerland. During the process, the girls progressed from unreflected trial-and-error to a reflected learning-by-doing strategy. Using Martin's terms, they progressed from simple digital competence to a corpus of digital uses for search engines. In their subsequent search for the father, they began negotiating what they were looking for before starting. "Let's find a father, he is a young man", said Heidi, and Sara wrote: "young man". This change in search strategy represents a change in the basic understanding of what it means to search and accordingly, the two girls moved closer to exploiting the search engine in accordance to Martin's digital transformation.

## Learning Competences and Progression

Weak learners and routine-based learners tend to approach lifelong learning in a generic manner, while self-programmable learners are by definition lifelong learners. Lifelong learning depends on the ability to motivate oneself for learning, but it is also a matter of establishing a habitus (Bourdieu, 1990) for encountering obstacles or challenges with an inner drive even when it seems tedious. The network society's challenge is that it takes time to develop and establish a habitus. The following examples display how working with digital storytelling in role-play setups support the development of a self-programmable habitus while students move from weak to routine-based or even self-programmable learning competence.

In a cross-disciplinary role-play in English and maths, students of the fourth grade had become journalists who were responsible for their own research. They were assigned to an English-speaking location by the teacher, and provided coordinates in Google Earth. Students were to collect and select material about the locality. At the end of the day, students were to deliver oral reports and written English news-features to the editor of the newspaper (the teacher). The assignment also simulated travel to the locations, since students were to e.g. book hotels and flights and keep a fictitious travel budget. Frequently, we saw students expanding on the requirements of the role-play as they invented side-stories that required further research. They also generated more features for the newspaper, e.g. the story of why the statue of a lion appears on many pictures from Singapore, and the story of what the term "trouble" means to Northern Ireland. In the same project, two boys who are weak learners were assigned to explore London. They seemed bored and started to talk about computer games instead. When the teacher asked them how they would proceed, they insisted that the task was boring because they were only interested in beer and soccer. This was meant as a provocation, but the teacher chose to ignore their attempt to avoid doing school work. "Then, why don't you look for different pubs, beers and prices? And you could find the soccer clubs and famous players who play in London", the teacher suggested. The boys accepted the suggestion and they managed to write a feature in English about beer and soccer in London. During this process,

the boys gradually displayed more sophisticated search strategies and they began negotiating meanings in relation to the feature. The teacher was experienced with student-centred pedagogy and gradually the boys changed their attitude from demanding instructions: "What should we do now?" to seeking advice and negotiating their own suggestions. In this example, the boys moved from weak learners towards routine-based learners. We also saw students who became so engaged with this way of working with digital tools and storytelling that they began to produce their own projects when they had finished the formal task. They planned and conducted productions about games (boys) or pets (girls) and they combined and challenged a multitude of tools and possibilities.

In these cases, the school's formal learning approach allowed space for the children's informal learning strategies, and the teachers actively created arenas where lifelong learning habitus could be develop.

## Informal Strategies (Bricoleur/Play)

Fourth-graders collected data about the weather over the period of a month to be used in building their own database in order to store data, compare data, and calculate changes over time. So as to become familiar with the database tool, two groups of students were asked by the teacher to collect data from two other groups: height, weight, shoe number and age, while names and addresses were put into the database's text fields. Most of the students followed instructions, while two girls insisted on finding the right pink colour for the background and changed the format of the shoe number input-field from numbers to numerals because they wanted to write "size 36 and size 37". During this process, they used a bricoleur approach and repeatedly arranged and re-arranged the appearance of their database while they discussed which attributes would be the most appropriate for their purpose. When they came to the part of the exercise where they were supposed to compare results from the whole class, their informal approach turned-out to be fruitful. Suddenly, one of the girls exclaimed: "Oh, that's why – when we use word-numbers we cannot calculate and compare! That's why we have to use real numbers. But then we ought to have place for more than one shoe number". In this example, the girls demonstrated that they had grasped the conceptual difference between numerals and numbers and they indirectly used the concept of intervals. Following this, the girls continued developing and expanding their weather database using a bricoleur approach, and they produced rather sophisticated analyses compared to the learning objectives for the fourth grade.

## Evaluation of One's Learning Process (Reflection/Action)

Seventh-graders were working with evolutionary theory that takes them from the time of the Big Bang to today. They had studied books and other theoretical sources and were assigned to produce a PhotoStory of their findings. They could use the Internet for further information but had to take digital photos. The teacher set a rule that a maximum of 12 photos could be used in the narrative and that only three could be derived from the Internet.

One group was waiting for a digital camera but used the waiting time to discuss narrative strategies and how to take the photos – motives and visual design. They wrote notes on paper and started searching for images of the Big Bang. One of the girls started using PowerPoint. "Why do you use PowerPoint" a boy asked, and the girl answered: "To get an overview of our narrative". Actually she was making a storyboard in PowerPoint and she typed on the first page: "Earth – sun system (as an orange)" and "cell lifecycle" on the second page. The storyboard inspired them to discuss whether Darwin's theory was important and whether Darwin is important. The girl suggested that they use an image of Darwin, because she

found that the storyboard revealed a hole in the narrative. When they tried it out in the storyboard, they realised that the hole was not just about the order of the narrative, but that the hole was that they had not really understood what exactly the theory was about. After reflecting on this new challenge, they searched for additional information on the Internet and decided to act by redesigning the narrative framework and the list of images before they went out to take pictures.

## Proactivity and Learning Process Management (Future Perspective/ Situated Perspective)

Eighth-graders were working on a cross-disciplinary theme that combines Nature and Science with Lego Mindstorms robots. The Mindstorms-part is about constructing and programming robots for the Robolab-competition. Students were divided into groups of four to six students. The groups were supplied with a construction set of bricks, wheels, cogwheels, axles and shafts, a programming brick that controls the robot, a remote control and three engines that drive the movements of the robot. The groups were provided with a task description, exercises, a robot manual and three laptops. In the physics room there was a copy of the track that the robot must be able to complete.

The robot programming software was installed on the laptops and after programming, the students had to upload their programming onto the programming brick and test the robot. In order to construct a functioning robot, the students had to plan and process-manage both research and testing. The groups agreed on a division of work among members. Some members experimented with the physical construction of the final robot whereas others experimented with programming and used "get-started-robots", while continuously negotiating how to proceed in the exploration and construction of a working robot. The construction-students found that if the robot was too delicate it became frail and fell apart when moving, and they additionally discovered that if it was too solid it became too heavy and could not move at all. They discussed ways to change the resistance and test how much weight the engines could work with, the difference between caterpillars and wheels, and they experimented with the construction in order make the robot more stable but lighter. The programming-students tested their "get started-robot" on the track and photo-documented the movements. They explored various solutions for programming movements and used the manual to reflect on and plan new experiments. After ten minutes, a group of girls had managed to construct a robot that was able to run and turn on the track. They began using the remote control, but remote controls are not allowed in the Robolab-competition. The teacher explained that the remote control could work in another way if fastened to the robot. The remote control could then be programmed to make the robot change direction when colliding with something. Soon the programming-girls had found more information in the manual and began testing the remote control together with light-sensors.

When working with the robots, the students demonstrated a high level of complexity in their collaboration. They alternated between the future perspective of proactivity – "what if…" scenarios – and the situated perspective of testing the hypothesis in practice. They reflected on the results at the same time as they negotiated and evaluated the progression as part of managing the learning process.

## Self-Directed Skills of Inquiry Competence (Expansion/ Delimitation)

### Expansion

Groups of two or three students in the first-grade measured a table with their thumbs, the classroom floor with their feet and the hall with a tape measure. They wrote their measurements into a group–post, in the class' database (MINIKORT®), which the teacher had prepared in advance. When all groups had finished their task, the teacher used the interactive whiteboard to display the database and showed various views to the class. The class was then asked to compare the sets of thumb-measurements and think about whether there was something to wonder about. Soon the students raised their hands and said that the groups had produced different results.

When the teacher asked if they could figure out why, they answered that thumbs had different sizes. When the teacher displayed the set of foot-measures, reactions were quick and students started to discuss one measurement that particularly stuck out. Then a boy said: "Oh, it's because I forgot to take my boots off – my boots are big so I counted less feet". In this way, the students used everyday language to formulate complex concepts such as accuracy and they concluded that feet and thumbs were inaccurate because they come in different sizes, while a tape measure is always the same. Because the tape measure ought to be precise, they concluded that the difference in measurements of the hall must have been due to sloppiness. In this case, the teacher facilitated and supported the students' process towards self-directed skills of inquiry.

In a fourth-grade class, students worked with surface measurement and drew their room and furniture on the interactive whiteboard. They visited IKEA's homepage, with its 3-D tool for arranging rooms with furniture. They did not know about volume as a geometric concept, as volume is not part of fourth-grade curriculum. However, they soon realised that some furniture filled the space in ways that could not be expressed only by surface measurements. They began discussing if it could be possible for a person to move about in the room when furnished in certain ways, and whether it would be possible to calculate – rather than actually putting real furniture into the real room – in order to answer those types of questions. Ultimately, the teacher had shown them how to calculate volume and in this way, the students managed to challenge and overpass the curriculum of their grade level. In this case, the students demonstrated that they mastered self-directed skills of inquiry and they expanded their understanding of abstract concepts by transforming "filling the space" into calculation of volume.

## Delimitation

When using search engines, the big challenge is to distinguish between "finding something about X" and "finding something relevant and reliable about X". Critical source criticism and the ability to knowledgably select information are basic requirements in the network society.

A fifth-grade class was investigating Leonardo da Vinci and perspective in Renaissance painting. They Googled the Mona Lisa and the first image that showed up was Mr. Bean as Mona Lisa, followed by some apparently reliable links to reproductions, as well as some other manipulations where Mona Lisa is represented as smoking a cigarette, or has a moustache, or looks like Homer Simpson. These findings were used by the teacher on the interactive whiteboard to initiate a class discussion about findings which are reliable and valid Mona Lisa references, and which are not. However, the findings were also useful for a discussion regarding types of findings that are relevant for specific purposes. In some cases, Mr. Bean or Homer Simpson as Mona Lisa may be the relevant finding, and during the discussion, the class began constructing more robust, reflective and critical attitudes towards searching and selecting from the Internet.

The process of editing, remediating and producing a digital, multimodal presentation of a subject depends on the ability to critically select relevant material from sources. But it also depends on the ability to construct a communicative product which appears meaningful from the perspective of an audience. This is why the production of digital media products is categorised as delimitating, even though a media product may have the potential to function as a lever for expansion regarding the audience. We have observed that the production of all kinds of digital products meant for presentations implies activities such as remediation, inscription and decoding of representational signs and ordering of the media message and narrative. The majority of observed groups working with production discussed and experimented with content, narration, montage, means of expression and aesthetic design. They asked themselves questions such as whether they had gotten the content right, if they had missed information or had maybe not fully understood the subject. They reflected on how to remediate and integrate content derived from the sources in ways that may communicate to an audience. During these processes the students built up multimodal competences and the ability to delimitate and reduce complexity.

## 7. DISCUSSION

The data analysis confirms that various ways of including ICT, digital media and e-learning into designs for teaching and learning may support the students' development and consolidation of Future-Oriented Competence. However, the relation is found not to be deterministic.

The positive effect is observed in relation to cases where the design for teaching and learning involves students' group work in problem-oriented narrative settings such as storyline and role-plays. However, it is not found in cases with traditional teacher-centred approaches involving ICT (Levinsen & Sørensen, 2008). The effect is also found when the objective of the students' task reaches beyond the expansive exploration of a topic and also aims at the delimitative reduction of complexity in terms of: 1) remediation of material for a digital presentation; 2) production of empirical data in science that has to be documented and presented; and 3) when using process-oriented e-portfolios. Constructivist and social constructivist research have convincingly documented learning potential of these approaches and therefore it becomes relevant to ask:

## DOES IT REALLY MAKE A DIFFERENCE THAT ICT IS INVOLVED?

The answer is: Yes. Compared to using the above-mentioned approaches without ICT, we observed that even young students are able to work focused and independent for longer periods of time and that the teachers' interventions change from instructive guidance to constructive coaching. Moreover, we have made several observations where teachers had to remind students of the breaks, though they preferred to continue working. We also – as mentioned above – observed that students challenged and went beyond the official learning goals in language teaching, math and science. So the next logical question is:

## WHAT IS IT ABOUT ICT THAT MAKES A DIFFERENCE?

The ICT applications that support and inspire the acquisition of Future-Oriented Competence all share some important features. They are not necessarily designed for learning purposes and the interactivity is open-ended rather than pre-defined. They offer intuitive user interfaces and a WYSIWIG (What You See Is What You Get) mix of exploration tools and construction tools that are enhanced by easy access to internet resources and the transport of data between applications using copy-paste functionality. These applications allow for user-driven interaction and the manipulation of complex elements such as those offered by the WYSIWIG-principle. They also offer transparent relations between construction, editing, trial-runs, instant feedback, re-construction and re-editing. In short, what these applications invite is the continuing arrangement and re-arrangement of materiality in terms of digital representations, while the user or users negotiate and re-negotiate meaning in terms of inner or shared dialogues. In other words, these applications encourage users of ICT to draw on bricoleur strategies which the students already master in their informal, leisure-time explorations of ICT. Thus, when these applications are implemented in the above-mentioned designs for teaching and learning, students are allowed to expand their formal student role with informal strategies and to exploit and develop these informal strategies while at the same time, work on the formal school assignment.

In conclusion, this is what we call *Formalized Informal Learning*. Variations of ICT that allow for bricoleur strategies to be coupled with designs for teaching and learning that invite self-directed inquiry, are genuinely supporting the building of Future-Oriented Competence. However, as research has also documented (Gynther, 2010; Sørensen, Audon, & Levinsen, 2010), students' learning of the subject-matter and Future-Oriented Competence do not automatically result from this combination of pedagogy and ICT. There is a fair risk of producing digital trivia and therefore, having teachers as coaches and supervisors is equally important.

## REFERENCES

Bateson, G. (1991). A sacred unity. In Donaldson, R. (Ed.), *Further steps to an ecology of mind*. San Francisco, CA: HarperCollins.

Bourdieu, P. (1990). *The logic of practice*. Cambridge, UK: Policy Press.

Breivik, P. S. (2005). 21st century learning and information literacy. *Change, 37*(2), 20–27. doi:10.3200/CHNG.37.2.21-27

Buckingham, D. (2003). *Media education: Literacy, learning and contemporary culture*. Cambridge, UK: Polity Press.

Castells, M. (2000). Materials for an exploratory theory of the network society. *The British Journal of Sociology*, *51*(1), 5–24. doi:10.1080/000713100358408

Christensen, S., & Kreiner, K. (1991). *Projektledelse i løst koblede systemer – ledelse og læring i en ufuldkommen verden*. Copenhagen, Denmark: Jurist- og Økonomforbundets Forlag.

Davenport, J. (1993). Is there any way out of the andragogy mess? In Thorpe, M., Edwards, R., & Hanson, A. (Eds.), *Culture and Processes of Adult Learning*. London, UK: Routledge.

Dede, C. (2005). Planning for neo-millennial learning styles. *EDUCAUSE Quarterly*, *1*, 7–12.

Dervin, B. (1992). From the mind's eye of the user: The sense-making qualitative-quantitative methodology. In Glazier, J. D., & Powell, R. R. (Eds.), *Qualitative research in information management* (pp. 61–84). Englewood, CO: Libraries Unlimited.

Dervin, B., & Frenette, M. (2003). Sense-making methodology: Communicating communicatively with campaign audiences. In Dervin, B., Foreman-Wernet, L., & Lauterbach, E. (Eds.), *Sense-making methodology reader: Selected writings of Brenda Dervin* (pp. 233–250). Cresskill, NJ: Hampton Press.

Dreyfus, H. L., & Dreyfus, S. (1988). *Mind over machine: The power of human intuition and expertise in the era of the computer*. New York, NY: Simon and Schuster.

Drotner, K. (2001). *Medier for fremtiden: Børn, unge og det nye medielandskab*. Copenhagen, Denmark: Høst.

Erstad, O. (2005). *Digital kompetanse i skolen – en innføring*. Oslo, Norway: Universitetsforlaget.

European Information Society. (2003). *eLearning: Better eLearning for Europe*. Brussels, Belgium: Directorate-General for Education and Culture, Office for Official Publications of the European Communities. Retrieved from http://ec.europa.eu/information_society/eeurope/2005/all_about/elearning/index_en.htm

Geertz, C. (1973). Thick description: Toward an interpretive theory of culture. In Geertz, C. (Ed.), *The interpretation of cultures: Selected essays* (pp. 3–30). New York, NY: Basic Books.

Gynther, K. (2010). *Didaktik 2.0*. Aarhus, Denmark: Akademisk Forlag.

Halkier, B. (2008). *Fokusgrupper* (2nd ed.). Copenhagen, Denmark: Samfundslitteratur.

Jarvis, P. (1987). Malcolm Knowles. In Jarvis, P. (Ed.), *Twentieth century thinkers in adult education* (pp. 169–187). London, UK: Croom Helm.

Jewitt, C., & Kress, G. (2003). *Multimodal literacy*. New York, NY: Peter Lang.

Katz, I. R. (2007). *Beyond technical competence: Literacy in information and communication technology*. Retrieved from http://www.ets.org/Media/Tests/ICT_Literacy/pdf/ICT_Beyond_Technical_Competence.pdf

Knowles, M. S. (1975). *Self-directed learning: A guide for learners and teachers*. Englewood Cliffs, NJ: Prentice Hall.

Knowles, M. S., Holten, E. F. III, & Swanson, R. A. (2005). *The adult learner* (6th ed.). Amsterdam, The Netherlands: Elsevier.

Latour, B. (1988). *The pasteurization of France*. Cambridge, MA: Harvard University Press.

Latour, B. (1992). Where are the missing masses? The sociology of a few mundane artifacts. In Bijker, W. E., & Law, J. (Eds.), *Shaping technology/building society: Studies in sociotechnical change* (pp. 225–258). Cambridge, MA: MIT Press.

Latour, B., & Wolgar, S. (1986). *Laboratory life – the Construction of Scientific Facts.* Princeton, NJ: Princeton University Press.

Law, J. (1999). After ANT: Complexity, naming and topology. In Law, J., & Hassard, J. (Eds.), *Actor network theory and after* (pp. 1–14). Oxford, UK: Blackwell Publishers.

Levinsen, K. (2006). Watch out – the power users are coming. *International Electronic Journal of E-learning, 5*(1), 79–86.

Levinsen, K. (2010). Effective use of ICT for inclusive learning of young children with reading and writing difficulties. In Mukerji, S., & Tripathi, P. (Eds.), *Cases on interactive technology environments and transnational collaboration* (pp. 56–73). Hershey, PA: IGI Global.

Levinsen, K., & Sørensen, B. H. (2008). *It, faglig læring og pædagogisk videnledelse.* Copenhagen, Denmark: The Danish University School of Education. Retrieved from http://junior-pc-koerekort. dk/Rapport_PIL_2008.pdf

Livingstone, S., & Bowill, M. (2001). *Children and their changing media environment: A European comparative study.* Mahwah, NJ: Erlbaum.

Malyn-Smith, J. (2004). Power users of technology - Who are they? Where are they going? Why does it matter? *UN Chronicle Online Edition, 2,* 58. Retrieved from http://www.un.org/Pubs/ chronicle/2004/issue2/0204p58.asp

Martin, A. (2005). DigEuLit – A European framework for digital literacy: A progress report. *International Journal of eLiteracy, 2,* 130-136.

Martin, A. (2006). A European framework for digital literacy. *Digital Kompetanse, 2,* 151–161.

Media Council for Children and Young People. (2003). *SAFT.* Retrieved from http://www.medieraadet.dk/html/saft

Oblinger, D. (2003). Boomers, gen-exers and millennials: Understanding the new students. In *Proceedings of the EDUCAUSE Annual Conference, 38,* 36–43.

Oblinger, D., & Oblinger, J. (2005). Educating the net generation. In *Proceedings of the EDUCAUSE Annual Conference.* Retrieved from http://www. educause.edu/educatingthenetgen/

Polanyi, M. (1968). Logic and psychology. *Journal of the American Psychoanalytic Association, 23,* 27–43.

Ryberg, T. (2007). Patchworking as a metaphor for learning: Understanding youth, learning and technology. *E-Learning Lab Publication, 10.*

Rychen, D., & Salganik, L. (2003). *Key Competencies for a Successful Life and Well-Functioning Society.* Cambridge, MA: Hogrefe & Huber.

Sørensen, B. H. (1999). *Projektarbejde fra begyndertrinnet – medier og formidling.* Copenhagen, Denmark: Lærerhøjskole.

Sørensen, B. H., Audon, L., & Levinsen, K. (2010). *Skole 2.0.* Aarhus, Denmark: KLIM.

Sørensen, B. H., Hubert, B., Risgaard, J., & Kirkeby, G. (2004). *Virtuel Skole* (Tech. Rep. No. 153). Copenhagen, Denmark: Danmarks Pædagogiske Universitetsskole.

Sørensen, B. H., Jessen, C., & Olesen, B. R. (2002). *Børn på nettet- kommunikation og læring.* Copenhagen, Denmark: Gads Forlag.

Sørensen, B. H., Olesen, B. R., & Audon, L. (2001). *Det hele kører parallelt - de nye medier i børns hverdagsliv.* Copenhagen, Denmark: Gads Forlag.

Stald, G. (2009). *Globale medier – lokal unge. Institut for Medier, erkendelse, formidling.* Copenhagen, Denmark: Københavns Universitet. Retrieved from http://mef.ku.dk/

Tennant, M. (1996). *Psychology and adult learning*. London, UK: Routledge.

Trageton, A. (2004). *At skrive sig til læsning*. Copenhagen, Denmark: Gyldendal.

Turkle, S., & Papert, S. (1990). Epistemological pluralism: Styles and voices within the computer culture. *Signs, 16*(1), 128–157. doi:10.1086/494648

Tyner, K. (1998). *Literacy in a digital world*. Mahwah, NJ: Erlbaum.

Vygotsky, L. S. (1978). *Mind in society*. Cambridge, MA: Harvard University Press.

Wakefield, J. F. (2003). The development of creative thinking and critical reflection: Lessons from everyday problem finding. In Runco, M. A. (Ed.), *Critical creative processes* (pp. 253–274). New York, NY: Hampton Press.

*This work was previously published in the International Journal of Digital Literacy and Digital Competence, Volume 2, Issue 1, edited by Antonio Cartelli, pp. 7-26, copyright 2011 by IGI Publishing (an imprint of IGI Global).*

# Chapter 3
# Reconciling Culture and Digital Literacy in the United Arab Emirates

**Tony Jewels**
*Zayed University, UAE*

**Rozz Albon**
*Sharjah Higher Colleges of Technology, UAE*

## ABSTRACT

*For a number of years, there has been a concerted effort by the United Arab Emirates to take a prominent role in introducing e-business initiatives throughout the Gulf region, and this effort has translated into widespread access of internet technology for its own citizens. The country, in setting out to become a hub for foreign and domestic companies, realized that to achieve these goals it must provide appropriate e-business frameworks and infrastructures, which it has successfully done. Although, while not the only means of acquiring digital literacy, regular exposure to the internet does contribute to gaining these necessary 21st century skills. It might be expected that with such widespread access to the internet the population would contribute to becoming digitally competent. Using an ethnographic case study methodology, this paper investigates issues contributing to what might be a new form of digital divide; cultural issues which limit the acquisition of such digital skills.*

## INTRODUCTION

As we pass into the second decade of the third millennium the internet has proven to be one the most exceptional innovations to date, with the World Wide Web affecting cultural, social and economic sectors, in both the way we spend our daily lives and in the way we do business. It has brought a wealth of information to our fingertips while heavily improving our educational system in an organized, efficient and effective manner, as well as enhancing our interpersonal relationships. The strategic potential of the medium was recog-

DOI: 10.4018/978-1-4666-2943-1.ch003

nized well over a decade ago by the Organisation for Economic Co-operation and Development (OECD) who stated:

*Our generation stands on the very cusp of the greatest technological revolution that mankind has ever faced. Some compare this age of electronic communication with the arrival of the Guttenberg press, or with the industrial revolution. Yet this revolution when it has run its course may have a greater impact on the planet than anything that has preceded it (OECD, 1997).*

Referring to the internet, Prensky (2001) makes the case that people seeking wisdom will need the use of digital technologies to provide them with unprecedented access to data, information, and knowledge from across the globe. Yet how one uses, filters, and eventually applies these resources will play an important role in the wisdom of their decisions and judgments (Skiba, 2010).

Though within the UAE widespread e-government services are available, there has been no systematic or widespread education of the general population on the use and benefits of internet usage in the country. Even though access to internet facilities is at a level comparative to both the

US and UK (see Figure 1 & Table 1) and is the highest in the Arab world (see Figure 2) many of its citizens have thus failed to understand how to use the medium effectively (Jewels et al., 2009).

Based on autoethnographic observations and anecdotal evidence, UAE internet usage patterns appear to be clearly different from usage patterns of similarly advanced nations. Though the operational benefits of using the internet are generally understood by its citizens, there are many families who are still concerned enough about the medium's more sinister ramifications to effectively curtail its use in the home. In order to effectively navigate the multidimensional and fast-paced digital environment, the term digital literacy has supplanted the traditional meaning of the term literacy (Jones-Kavalier & Flannigan, 2006). UAE children, the so-called 'digital natives' that Prensky (2001) refers to, may in this situation be limited from acquiring all the skills that will ultimately contribute to them being digitally literate in a global environment.

Understanding why this type of paradox exists may be useful in providing alternative means of attaining digital literacy in culturally sensitive situations. The anecdotal evidence indicates there are many parents in the United Arab Emirates

*Figure 1. Internet Access of selected countries (Source: http://www.google.com/publicdata?ds=wb-wdi&met=it_net_user_p2&idim=country:ARE&dl=en&hl=en&q=uae+internet+usage)*

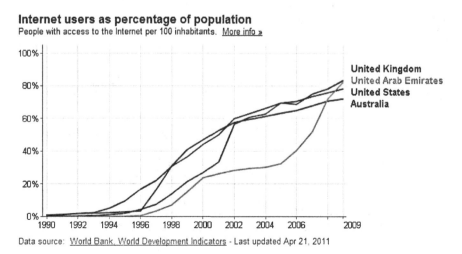

*Table 1. Internet Usage Statistics as provided by International Telecommunications Union (ITU) (Internet World Stats, 2011)*

| Year | Users | Population | % of population |
|------|-------|-----------|-----------------|
| 2010 | 3,777,900 | 4,975,593 | 75.9% |

(UAE) today who are skeptical about the access to undesirable information via the Internet. They see themselves in a quandary: whether or not allowing their children to use the internet is the right thing to do; whether shutting the internet out of their lives might be the safest way to protect their children. It may be said that digital literacy and its partner digital competence in the Internet age are as important as traditional literacy was in the past. The ability to read and write, while still necessary for full engagement in a digital world may be, on its own, no longer sufficient.

## LITERATURE REVIEW

The term digital literacy does not only deal with the ability to communicate but *"to create, to manipu-*

*late, to design, to self-actualize"* (Jones-Kavalier & Flannigan, 2006). Becta (2010) describes the term more simply as "the combination of skills, knowledge and understanding that young people need to learn in order to participate fully and safely in an increasingly digital world". Digital competence on the other hand has been defined by Cartelli (2005) as consisting of being able to explore and face new technological situations in flexible ways. He adds that digital competency allows us to analyze, select and critically evaluate data and information, to exploit technological potentials in order to represent and to solve problems, and to build shared and collaborative knowledge, while fostering awareness of one's own personal responsibilities and the respect of reciprocal rights/obligations. A relatively new term 'digital wisdom' is described by Prensky (2009) as a twofold concept, referring both to wisdom arising *from* the use of digital technology to access cognitive power beyond our innate capacity and to wisdom *in* the prudent use of technology to enhance our capabilities.

Prensky (2001) uses the term 'digital natives' to describe the current generation of children who

*Figure 2. Internet access of selected Middle East countries (Source: http://www.google.com/publicdata?ds=wb-wdi&met=it_net_user_p2&idim=country:ARE&dl=en&hl=en&q=uae+internet+usage)*

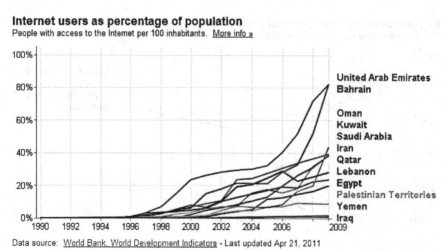

have never experienced a world without ICT. Prensky proffers a list to describe the difference in processing information and the acquired attitudes as result of using and engaging in ICT, This list identifies behaviours and outcomes beyond just reading and writing. Facer, (2003) elaborated Prensky's (2001) description of more digital literate users and both are summarized in Table 2.

Four prominent issues emerged from Jewels et al.'s (2009) investigation of e-business adoption in the UAE:

- **Cultural Issues:** The conservative nature of the local Islamic society and traditional values of UAE inhabitants combine to curb the pace of acceptance of ideas embraced without hesitation by other societies.
- **Lack of Understanding/Education:** There appears to be low confidence levels in the UAE population when conducting e-business.
- **Mistrust in the electronic medium:** In collectivist societies such as the UAE, details of a single incident of internet fraud

will promptly and systematically be widely distributed, and this single incident may soon become regarded as the norm. On the other hand, sharing of consistently successful usage seldom occurs.

- **Language and Regional Factors:** The official language of the UAE is Arabic and this is the primary language of communication by the local population. Many popular global sites do not have an Arabic version.

It is generally agreed, according to Bonnici and de vey Mestdagh (2005) that 'illegal' and 'harmful' are distinct categories of content, and that at an international level there is little agreement as to what content can be 'universally' considered illegal (p. 134). The UAE appears however to be particularly concerned about harmful effects of the internet. A report conducted by the General Command of Abu Dhabi Police (2008), entitled 'Internet and networks, and their effects on society and security,' examined both negative and positive effects of mobile technology and its im-

*Table 2. Comparisons between generations of Internet users*

| Prensky's comparison | Facer's description of digital literate individuals |
|---|---|
| Twitch speed v conventional speed | The ability to process information very quickly, determining what is and is not of relevance to them; the ability to process information in parallel at the same time, from a range of different sources |
| Parallel processing v linear processing | The ability to process information in parallel at the same time from a range of different sources and familiarity with exploring information in a non-linear fashion i.e. by 'jumping' through a range of different information resources |
| Graphics first v text first | The tendency to access information in the first instance through imagery and then using text to clarify, expand and explore |
| Random access v step by step | The ability to create links rather than following a 'story' |
| Connected v stand alone | A familiarity with networked, non-geographically bounded networks of communication |
| Active v passive | Having a model of doing in order to learn rather than learning in order to do |
| Play v work | A relaxed approach to 'play', viewing this as a valid activity and conceptualising the computer as primarily a 'play tool' |
| Pay-off v patience | Expecting rewards for activities |
| Fantasy v reality | A relaxed acceptance of fantasy as a valid space of experience |
| Technology as friend v technology as foe | A view of technology as a friend, familiar through having grown up with it |

pacts on all segments of society (this report was originally published in Arabic and subsequently translated into English). According to this report, the negative impacts of the dissemination of ideas and the promotion of negative beliefs may not be consistent with the beliefs of the community and could lead to Internet addiction and isolation through excessive use.

The Internet may have innumerable benefits, but it is not without some potential costs or negative influence particularly when it concerns children, as noted by Bremer (2005). The 'harmful internet content' principle is developed further by Bonnici and de vey Mestdagh (2005) who warn that "deciding what is 'harmful' and 'harmless' Internet content is a personal choice based on one's beliefs, preferences and social and cultural traditions" (p. 133). Although it is unclear whether UAE parents are aware of them all, five relevant internet risk areas are indeed summarised by Valcke, Bonte, De Wever, and Rots (2010):

- Negative impacts on social relations;
- Negative emotional impacts due to unwanted exposure to violence, explicit language, pornography etc;
- Negative effect on physical health, obesity, reduced concentration and muscle pain;
- Negative impact on time management, internet addiction, neglect of school tasks, lower involvement in family activities; and
- Increased risk of consumerism and commercial exploitation

However, Byron (2008) claims that young people are more likely to stay safe online if they have been given abilities to make their own appropriate and informed decisions about their use of the technologies that they use. The Byron Review refers to the need to increase children's resilience to harmful and inappropriate material to which they may be exposed, (Becta, 2010). Although most research focuses on the threats and oppor-

tunities about active Internet usage, Valcke et al.'s (2010) work focuses on the roles and impacts of parents styles relating to their children's Internet usage at home.

Although commonalities in approaches exist there is no singular model for Internet regulation. Every country appears to have its own specific approach to regulations, although Ang (1997) suggests that Western countries with a longer and stronger tradition of free press would tend to use the first three steps in the regulatory framework (see Table 3).

Asian and other countries with a less notable tradition of free press would be more inclined to use steps 4 and 5, where penal sanction is state-endorsed.

## RESEARCH METHODOLOGY

For this research, a single case study with an ethnographic data collection methodology is used. Yin (1994) suggests that when *'how'* or *'why'* questions are being asked in a primarily explanatory study, then a case study approach is favoured. A case study is considered a more relevant approach when no control is required over behavioural events and the study focuses on contemporary events. Yin summarises a case study as an empirical inquiry that: *"Investigates a contemporary phenomenon within its real-life context, especially when the boundaries between phenomenon and context are not clearly evident"* (p. 13).

Ethnography is *"the work of describing a culture"* and the goal of research of this type is *"to understand another way of life from the native point of view"* (Spradley, 1979, p. 3). Spradley suggests that it is a useful tool for *"understanding how other people see their experience"* (piv), but emphasizes that *"rather than studying people, ethnography means learning from people"* (p. 3).

*Table 3. Regulatory Framework (Adapted from Ellickson, 1991)*

| Regulator | Substantive Rules | Sanctions | Mechanism |
|---|---|---|---|
| The actor him/herself | Personal ethics | Self-sanction | Self |
| Second party controllers (i.e., the person acted upon) | Contractual provisions | Various self-help mechanisms | PICS, RSACi, filter software |
| Non hierarchically organized social forces | Social norms | Social sanctions | Code of conduct |
| Hierarchically organized nongovernmental organizations | Organization rules | Organization sanctions | Industry self-regulation |
| Governments | Law | State enforcement, coercive sanctions | Law |

Ethnography includes the following features (Atkinson & Hammersley, 1994, p. 248):

- An emphasis on exploring the nature of social phenomena rather than testing hypotheses about them;
- A tendency to work with unstructured data;
- Investigation of a small number of cases (even one) in detail;
- Analysis of data that involves explicit interpretation of meanings and functions of human actions and
- Quantification and statistical analysis plays a subordinate role at most.

In this case the ethnographic approach taken is one that the participant observer typology of what Gold (1958) and Junker (1960) referred to as 'participant as observer'. That is, although the authors all live in the UAE their observations are taken predominantly from other members of this society.

## The UAE Experience

This country's approach to harmful/illegal content is to take what we might call a primary safety approach and to (as far as possible) limit access to everything that might be considered harmful to any group of internet user (including minors).

Internet access in the UAE does however go through only two Internet service provider in the country Etisalat and Du, which blocks many sites on the Internet (see Figure 3) including the popular Skype text chat and voice over IP service (VOIP), as well as all other well-known VOIP services. Although Wu (2011) states it is still possible to work around Etisalat's VOIP block with a bit of extra work, there is still confusion by many Internet users in the country of precisely how the claim that Skype and other VOIP services contravene the prohibited content category of the UAE's Internet Access Management Policy. There is a widespread belief that these VOIP bans are not culturally driven at all, (as might reasonably be the case for pornographic or other potentially harmful or sensitive material), but indeed are commercially motivated. With this type of apparent inconsistency over what 'prohibited content' actually encompasses, it is not surprising that there may be a lack of confidence in precisely what types of content are being prohibited, leading to distrust in the regulator itself.

One female interviewee was recently quoted as saying that she did not intend allowing her children to have access to the internet, *"While my son is little everything is OK but when he gets older supervision will be difficult because of all the bad websites"*. When prompted to explain further she claimed that while she trusted the government to restrict access to these bad sites, she believed that children had the skills to 'break through' and find them. *"Clever children find a way of getting to bad sites and then they tell each*

*Figure 3. UAE site blocked banner*

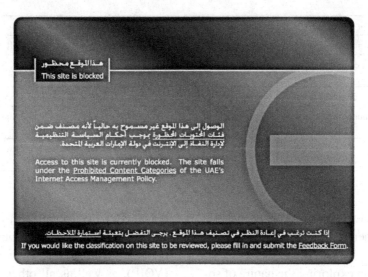

*other"*, she claimed, adding that she has friends who do these things.

Although the UAE has been classified as the fourth biggest Internet censor behind China, Iran and Saudi Arabia, its restrictions are mainly concerned with protecting the moral and religious values of the country; achieved through extensive filtering of websites that contain pornography, are related to alcohol and drug use, gay and lesbian issues, online dating and gambling (Nick, 2008).

The negative aspects that many people, especially parents, know and understand today include theft of personal information, spamming, virus threat, violation of privacy and pornography. These four categories play a role in the avoidance of the Internet within UAE society. Fear of these specific issues tends to make parents disregard the various benefits that the internet can provide to themselves and to their children.

In such a low crime society such as the UAE, it is still perfectly normal for individuals to deal in large sums of cash, the risks of being robbed being infinitesimal compared, for example, with many US cities or parts of South Africa. However, the Internet potentially allows undesirables from outside the country to also impact on UAE citizen's lives. The likelihood of citizens being

robbed from an internet fraud is thus likely to be genuinely higher than from traditional forms of trading. While there is no evidence of a greater degree of computer fraud in the UAE than anywhere else, because the amount of other types of crime is so low, the proportion of internet crime is much higher. From a traders perspective, there is similarly no evidence to think that MacGregor and Vrazalic's (2007) claim that security concerns are a primary reason for low adoption rates amongst small businesses throughout the world, should not also be valid for the UAE.

Many parents in the UAE, because of culture or religion, look at their daughters using social networks, or meeting other people (especially males) and uploading pictures as haram (forbidden). In the UAE culture, especially with traditional families' men are not generally supposed to see the local Emirati females unless they are religiously married. Additionally, parents look at talking to men on social networks such as MSN or Face book as bad behaviour since in this culture there is little association with the opposite sex unless they are related or married. All these aspects contribute to what makes UAE parents concerned for their children and thus they may prefer them, or in some cases forbid them from using the Internet.

A disconnect between two generations may exist, not simply relating to the technology itself but also to the influence and use of the technology. The e-generation use technology for almost everything and consider it to be a normal aspect of their daily lives, yet in the case of digital immigrants, it as if they are trying to learn a new language at an older age. Digital immigrants are likely to have more difficulties acquiring a language proficiency that an e-generation that has grown up. Examples of the differences of how different generations use technology include a parent's generation need to print out documents in order to write down notes or read and understand it better. The e-generation are less comfortable reading from papers or books, preferring to read documents online and more capable of easily highlighting and attaching notes to on-line versions. In today's world, digital immigrants struggle to understand this new language and these differences in views. Knowledge and capabilities of the two generations are thus believed to be yet one more reason for parent's unacceptance of their children's use of the internet.

There is widespread agreement amongst research subjects that the Internet brings a lot of benefits to the world that they live in while definitely making their lives a little easier. The gathering of information of any type is considered a major advantage because advanced search engines such as Yahoo or Google offers many opportunities for children to research and learn with ease. Some examples given included students able to look up information for school projects or even personal health issues. Another advantage would be entertainment, which is done through the downloading or uploading of videos and music or communication through social networks such as Facebook or Twitter. The numerous services which are provided online can be looked upon as other significant benefits. They include time and cost reduction items such as online banking, job seeking, purchasing tickets for movies, guidance services on an array of topics and hotel reserva-

tions. Time and cost are important factors that UAE users are beginning to better appreciate.

Internet analysts have determined that reasons for overall low Internet penetration in the Middle East region include (Julfar, 2006, p. 192):

- Weak infrastructure,
- Poor economic growth,
- High illiteracy levels,
- Lack of relevant language skills,
- Content and applications,
- Cultural factors

Certainly, the first two issues are irrelevant in the UAE as both a robust infrastructure exists and the country has maintained dynamic economic growth. The fact that the UAE does not have a traditional postal delivery service nor does it have specific residential addresses in the manner of US or European communities may very well contribute towards a higher level of e-business.

In February 2000, Dubai's then ruler, Sheikh Maktoum bin Rashid al-Maktoum issued a decree setting up a free trade zone, operating under the Dubai government, designed to spearhead the UAE's drive to become a regional centre for electronic commerce and technology. The decree established as an independent body, the Free Zone Authority electronic commerce, technology and information. In 2006 the Ministry of Economy issued two ministerial decisions (114 & 406) to establish a committee to oversee the implementation of the Electronic Commerce and Transactions Act, 2006 and recommended the appointment of a Telecommunications Regulatory Authority of the UAE (TRA) as the authority entrusted with overseeing certification services in the UAE pursuant to Article 20 of the Act. The mission of the Telecommunications Regulatory Authority (TRA) was to "support and enable the Information & Communication Technology (ICT) sector in the UAE by safeguarding competition, providing fair access to the domestic infrastructure, and ensuring the optimal use of natural resources through the implementation of best practice in every area," (Telecommunications Regulatory Authority, 2008). The key objectives of the TRA are to license, monitor, approve, and oversee the activities of Certification Service Providers and to continue providing strategic advice to current and new stakeholders who choose to conduct business on-line, while working towards fulfilling the objectives of Article 3 of the Electronic Commerce and Transactions Act (2006). Article 3's objectives include:

1. Protect the rights of persons doing business electronically and determine their obligations.
2. Encourage and facilitate Electronic Transactions and Communications by means of reliable Electronic Records.
3. Facilitate and eliminate barriers to Electronic Commerce and other Electronic Transactions resulting from uncertainties over writing and signature requirements, and promote the development of the legal and business infrastructure necessary to implement secure Electronic Commerce.
4. Facilitate the electronic filing of documents with governmental and non-governmental agencies and departments and promote efficient delivery of the services of such agencies and departments by means of reliable Electronic Communications.
5. Minimize the incidence of forged Electronic Communications, alteration of Communications and fraud in Electronic Commerce and other Electronic Transactions.
6. Establish uniform rules, regulations and standards for the authentication and validity of Electronic Communications.
7. Promote public confidence in the validity, integrity and reliability of Electronic Transactions, Communications and Records.
8. Promote the growth of Electronic Commerce and other transactions on the national and international level through the use of Electronic Signatures.

Dubai Internet City was set up to provide to the nation a world class environment with high bandwidth and low cost and secure high speed support infrastructure. Within a supportive government environment that backed e-business initiatives, business incubators, venture capital funds and e-education programs it provides a gateway to markets in the Middle East, North Africa, the Indian subcontinent and the Commonwealth of Independent States (CIS), covering previous Soviet republics (LowTax.net, 2008).

It should be noted that there are many elderly people in the UAE who are illiterate and would thus find it difficult conducting transactions on-line in any language. Respect for the elderly is so high that if these people suggest that conducting business on-line is unacceptable, it has a great influence on whether e-business is embraced by others. Also, without some external assistance people of all ages find difficulty engaging in e-commerce activities as they simply do not understand how to use computers, and there is little formalised help in teaching them how to do so. It has been regularly indicated by interviewees that significant numbers of people may now use the internet merely to get information about products prior to purchasing items in traditional marketplaces. This would appear to suggest that e-business usage while still at an early stage of evolution, predominantly as content providers providing information to customers in the form of on-line catalogues, is being used by increasing numbers of people. Many transactions are however still not being completed on-line, as many local sites are, in reality, difficult to navigate and contain little or no error checking facilities, making them difficult to use by even experienced users.

Interviewees reported that many UAE internet users avoid on-line shopping because they believe it is 'unsafe' and 'too risky'. This issue is exacerbated because in a collectivist society such as the UAE, details of a single incident of internet fraud will promptly and systematically be widely distributed, and this single incident may soon become regarded as the norm.

There appears however no doubt that the UAE has been successful in providing access to the Internet. It has a robust infrastructure and has maintained dynamic economic growth. The e-government services provided compares favorably with other advanced nations such as the US, Australia and the UK.

## SUMMARY

The need for digital literacy and its closely related digital competency of the United Arab Emirates people appears to be clearly understood; its role in the promotion and growth of the country has been identified and actions taken at various levels to create awareness of the need for local populations to be digitally literate.

Several important issues have emerged from the investigation of culture and digital literacy in the UAE. Firstly, a paradox emerged. The UAE has recognized the value and strategic potential of the Internet to its economic development but has not put sufficient systems in place to reconcile the culture of its people with accessing the internet. It appears that its young generation – the digital natives are somewhat curtailed in accessing the Internet in order to acquire the very skills or digital competencies required for the continued development of the country.

The government has recognized social and cultural issues related to the Internet and has set up systems to ban 'harmful' sites, minimize risk and protect all its citizens, including the younger generation, but in limiting access to sites they are also excluding access to the wider regional and global world. Banning sites was believed to have increased the confidence of its people yet this appears not to have significantly changed internet usage patterns. Parents, the key to using the In-

ternet and instilling confidence in their children, still appear reticent to embrace it. The continual business of banning sites surely indicates there are more harmful sites children can access, therefore confirming the parents unwillingness to allow their children to access the Internet.

The problem seems to lie in the use of the Internet and not its access as explained in the following short story. *Many years ago one of my friends was horizontally challenged? OK, without all the political correctness, he was fat, overweight, obese. His friends all contributed towards an annual membership of a fitness centre for him which was meant to help him lose some weight. After 12 months the results were very disappointing, if anything he had put on even more weight. We asked him why after 12 months membership of a fitness centre he had failed to lose a single Kg? He told us that the fitness centre had done no good whatsoever, a statement which surprised us all. We asked how many times a week he had visited the fitness centre? He then admitted that he had never actually been to the fitness centre during the past 12 months. The moral of this story is that access is only a starting point ... it is what you do with that access that is critical in attaining your goals.*

There appears to be an incomplete circle; a missing link to the government's ability to increase usage. To fully use the potential of technology and particularly the Internet, provision must be made in the education of its children for them to become digitally literate and competent. The four reasons Jewels et al.'s (2009) identified, in their investigation of e-business adoption, clearly identified why this circle was not closed. Further analyses of these reasons seem to pin point parents as being central in this missing link. Internet risk as identified by Valcke (2010) seems to reflect UAE parents fears, further emphasizing that if children are to become digitally literate parents must support their children and allow them to become skilled in consumption, evaluation, and creation of content in a future that seems to rely on the Internet as it becomes more globally connected. However, the cultural issues relating to accessing the Internet need to be better understood.

High illiteracy levels may influence parents curtailing access to the Internet because they are unable to read or understand information presented in any language. Poor navigation through sites may be manifest of something other than reading, possibly even the limited digital competency of some site designers. After all the measures and infrastructure the UAE government has developed, above all it comes down to the beliefs and attitudes parents have about the internet, which may impact on its adoption, high skill acquisition and usage. If parents were more supportive of children accessing the Internet would their digital literacy and competency increase? If parents were more informed and educated in the safety of the Internet would this impact on the use of the Internet? If these were also supported during their education would the two factors impact on the level of attainment and lead to increases of successful e-business and government initiatives? It is obvious that further research is required if the closing of the circle is to occur.

## FUTURE RESEARCH

The UAE has had the foresight to help formulate a way forward, ensuring the creation of digital literacy in its future generations. Although schools have in the past been seen as the primary educators in these matters, it may be of great benefit to the UAE to also invest in the education of parents. The strategic potential of the Internet to a country's development and prosperity may lie in parent's capacity to educate their children in digital literacy.

More information about the parenting approaches to children using the Internet is required if the UAE, or indeed any country, is to work strategically towards increasing the digital competency of its children. Facer (2003) has eloquently spelt out the types of skills all young people need

to learn in order to participate fully and safely in an increasingly digital world. Parents, as the first teachers of young children, appear to be the key in promoting, supporting and encouraging their children to function fully in the digital environment. UAE parents, with their own set of personal beliefs, preferences and social and cultural traditions are the parents of digital natives – children with hypertext minds who leap around (Prensky, 2001). Given schools are dominated by linear thought processes it seems essential that UAE parents are educated not only into the safe use, etiquette and benefits of the Internet but to promote the needed parallel thinking concomitant with the Internet and the information and knowledge age.

Although it seems that a relationship between the competency of its users in ICT and the experiences they have to become competent does exist, to what extent the Internet contributes to this competency is at this time speculative. Future research into the Internet use in the UAE will begin with the development of a survey to identify the extent of the use of the Internet in UAE homes.

Currently being distributed is a 10 item survey written in English and Arabic which seeks to investigate the beliefs, views, concerns and practices of parents regarding young children accessing the Internet. The time spent accessing the Internet, if this is done with or without supervision and a better idea of the types of sites that children access is being asked. Questions about parents experience and their own use of the Internet will illuminate their given description of such digital immigrants.

*Teach your parents well, their children's hell will slowly go by, and feed them on your dreams the one they picked, the one you'll know by (Nash, 1970).*

## REFERENCES

Ang, P. H. (1997). *How countries are regulating Internet content*. Retrieved from http://cad.ntu-kpi.kiev.ua/events/inet97/B1/B1_3.HTM

Atkinson, P., & Hammersley, M. (1994). Ethnography and participant observation. In Denzin, N. K., & Lincoln, Y. S. (Eds.), *Handbook of qualitative research*. Thousand Oaks, CA: Sage.

Becta. (2010). *Digital literacy: Teaching critical thinking for our digital world*. Retrieved from http://schools.becta.org.uk/upload-dir/downloads/digital_literacy_publication.pdf

Bonnici, J. P. M., & de vey Mestdagh, C. N. J. (2005). Right vision, wrong expectations: The European Union and self-regulation of harmful Internet content. *Information & Communications Technology Law, 14*(2), 133–149. doi:10.1080/13600830500042665

Bremer, J. (2005). The Internet and children: Advantages and disadvantages. *Child and Adolescent Psychiatric Clinics of North America, 14*(3). doi:10.1016/j.chc.2005.02.003

Byron, T. (2008). *Safer children in a digital world: The report of the Byron review*. Retrieved from http://webarchive.nationalarchives.gov.uk/tna/+/http://www.dcsf.gov.uk/byronreview/

Cartelli, A. (2005). Towards an information system making transparent teaching processes and applying informing science to education. *Journal of Issues in Informing Science and Information Technology, 2*, 369–381.

Electronic Commerce and Transactions Act. (2006). *Federal Law 1 442 Muhurram 1427*. Retrieved from http://www.rafed.net/en/index.php?option=com_content&view=category&id=164&Itemid=853

Ellickson, R. C. (1991). *Order without law: How neighbors settle disputes*. Cambridge, MA: Harvard University Press.

Facer, K. (2003). *Computer games and learning: Why do we think it's worth talking about computer games and learning in the same breath?* Retrieved from http://www.coulthard.com/library/Files/facer-futurelabs_2003_computergamesandlearning_discpaper.pdf

General Command of Abu Dhabi Police. (2008). *Internet and networks, and their effects on society and security*. Retrieved from http://www.alittihad.ae/print.php?id=52907&adate=2008

Gold, R. (1958). Roles in sociological field observations. *Social Forces, 36*, 217–223. doi:10.2307/2573808

Internet World Stats. (2011). *World Internet users and population stats*. Retrieved from http://www.internetworldstats.com/stats.htm

Jewels, T., Ghanem, A., Mongeal, A., Nuaimi, E., Aljaaidi, A., Al-Kaf, A., & Nuaimi, A. (2009, August 6-9). E-Business use in the United Arab Emirates: Lessons for evolving markets. In *Proceedings of the 15th Americas Conference on Information Systems*, San Francisco, CA.

Jones-Kavalier, B. R., & Flannigan, S. L. (2006). Connecting the digital dots: Literacy of the 21st century. *EDUCAUSE Quarterly, 29*(2).

Julfar, A. A. (2006). Empowering the Arab media through the Internet. In Emirates Center for Strategic Studies and Research (Ed.), *Arab media in the information age*. Abu Dhabi, United Arab Emirates: The Emirates Center for Strategic Studies and Research.

Junker, B. (1960). *Field work*. Chicago, IL: Chicago University Press.

LowTax.net. (2008). *Dubai e-commerce special feature - offshore e-commerce: Ready for action?* Retrieved from http://lowtax.net/lowtax/html/dubai/jdbecom.html

MacGregor, R., & Vrazalic, L. (2007). *E-Commerce in regional small to medium enterprises.* Hershey, PA: IGI Global. doi:10.4018/978-1-59904-123-0

Nash, G. (1970). Teach Your Children [Recorded by Crosby, Stills, Nash, & Young]. On *Déjà vu* [Record]. New York, NY: Atlantic Records.

Nick. (2008). *Top 10 countries censoring the Web.* Retrieved from http://www.dailybits.com/top-10-countries-censoring-the-web/

OECD. (1997). *Electronic commerce: Opportunities and challenges for government.* Paris, France: Organisation for Economic Co-operation and Development.

Prensky, M. (2001). Digital natives, digital immigrants, part II: Do they really think differently? *Horizon, 9*(6). doi:10.1108/10748120110424843

Prensky, M. (2009). H. sapiens digital: From digital immigrants and digital natives to digital wisdom. *Innovate, 5*(3).

Skiba, D. J. (2010). Digital wisdom: A necessary faculty competency? *Nursing Education Perspectives, 31*(4), 251–253.

Spradley, J. P. (1979). *The ethnographic interview.* New York, NY: Holt, Rinehart, and Winston.

Telecommunications Regulatory Authority. (2008). *eCommerce.* Retrieved from http://www.tra.gov.ae

Valcke, M., Bonte, S., De Wever, B., & Rots, I. (2010). Internet parenting styles and the impact on Internet use of primary school children. *Computers & Education, 55,* 454–464. doi:10.1016/j.compedu.2010.02.009

Wu, J. (2011). *How to make Skype work in UAE.* Retrieved from http://www.ehow.com/how_5006502_make-skype-work-uae.html

Yin, R. K. (1994). *Case study research: Design and methods* (2nd ed.). Thousand Oaks, CA: Sage.

*This work was previously published in the International Journal of Digital Literacy and Digital Competence, Volume 2, Issue 2, edited by Antonio Cartelli, pp. 27-39, copyright 2011 by IGI Publishing (an imprint of IGI Global).*

# Section 2
# Digital Literacy Evaluation and Development in Students, Teachers, and Adults

# Chapter 4

# Transformation of Individual Learning through Informatics and Information Technology Activities in Primary School

**Valentina Dagiene**
*Vilnius University, Lithuania*

**Vaiva Grabauskiene**
*Vilnius University, Lithuania*

## ABSTRACT

*The topic of the individual learning conditions creation can be analysed from the technological as well as pedagogical side. In both cases there is the same fundamental point: how to create valuable and as much as possible natural learning environment? The experience in the application of technologies for personalisation, analysed in scientific literature, reveals newer possibilities for the individual activities support. This encourages taking a different route in analysing individual learning – to interdisciplinary combine the content of close concepts. The paper deals with basic concepts of interdisciplinary content analysis – informatics and information technology impact to an individual learning in primary school.*

## INTRODUCTION

Learning is usually defined as a change in some-one's behaviour, knowledge, level of skill, or understanding which is long-lasting or permanent and is acquired through experiences rather than through the process of growth or ageing. Learning

DOI: 10.4018/978-1-4666-2943-1.ch004

is understood as the influence of the characteristic individual creative experience application to the individual himself. Changes in behaviour, knowledge, capabilities, understanding, determined by the experience, are individual to each person.

However, learning is inseparable from the social context. On the one hand, it is not the society, but the individual that creates knowledge (LaDuke, 2008). On the other hand, the intellectual potential of the social environment is reflected in the individual ideas and capabilities. In addition, ICT and alteration of the education priorities also change individual learning. Design of the optimum learning environment, realisation of the chosen learning/teaching aims, as well as organisation of the individual learning/teaching activities are becoming the objects of interdisciplinary discussion between the researchers of the pedagogy and information technology.

When talking about the individual learning through informatics and information technology activities in a primary school, the uniqueness of the individual has to be allowed for twofold: peculiarities common to all primary classes' children of common age as well as those unique to each of them have to be noticed. Therefore, the models of informatics teaching and information technology application created for the senior pupils do not fit for the primary school pupils. Further, it is noteworthy that the personalised learning environment design is burdened with the difficulty of matching the interdisciplinary pedagogical and technological positions.

The aim of this paper is to characterise individual learning through informatics and information technology activities in a primary school while analysing the notional nuances of technological and pedagogical concepts and going into the topic of the learning environment that fits to the primary school children.

The method of graphical visualisation of the concepts has been used in order to look at the content of adjustable concepts in more detail. Expressing the concept in a different form can help spotting extra similarities and differences of the concepts. From the cognitive standpoint the alteration of the visualisation method helps to understand better by discovering the foundation of the comprehension (Duval, 2002).

The means of visualisation has been chosen to be a metaphor of the geometric figure. This particular metaphor was chosen because of its functional similarity.

In order to reach the aim of the paper, personalisation types (Fan & Poole, 2006) have been used. This interdisciplinary personalisation typology, created based on ICT application, is grounded on a vast variety of personal individuals' requirements. Hence, such a typology could be valuable in elaborating the notion of the natural learning environment.

Main questions for which answers are sought in this paper: what interdisciplinary information fits into the concepts used for the description of individual learning? What informatics activities are topical in the primary classes? How can application of the informatics and information technologies transform individual learning in primary schools?

## FOCUS ON INDIVIDUAL LEARNING ACTIVITIES

The problem of individuality is topical for designing equipment and software, a learning, communication and dwelling environment, organizing markets and search for information.

The teaching is called individualised as a student has a possibility to apply the known matters going into depth of the matter he has to learn. In such sense, learning individualisation is the aim, which manifests in the practice through the form individual learning, face to face learning, differentiated learning, and personal learning.

Individual learning can be described as allowing students to learn at their own place and according to their own preferred learning style, and to cover those areas of the syllabus or lesson which are necessary to their learning. It is an approach which necessitates the teacher having a clear understanding of learning needs of a student. Such learning can be named as absolute individualisation. In theory, individual learning is also possible when teaching the whole class. It is an approach, in which all individual student's distinctions are taken into account while teaching the whole class, and in accordance with them the learning ways and contents are selected. In reality, individualisation expression in the form of face to face learning is bounded by the complexity of such learning process organisation. The modelling of the learning individualization process is a complex problem and it requires multidisciplinary knowledge (Aouag, 2007).

Conception of the learning differentiation analysed in the educational literature is somewhat similar to the expression of the individualisation's conception adjusted to real capabilities. Differentiated instruction is a pedagogical approach to teaching and learning for students of differing readiness levels, interests, and modes of learning within the same classroom (Koc, 2005). Differentiated instruction is designed to provide various learning opportunities for students who differ in their readiness levels (what they know, understand, and can do in relation to the content), their interests (affinity, curiosity, or passion for a topic), and their learning profiles (which may be shaped by their intelligence preferences, gender, culture, or learning style (Landrum & McDuffie, 2008).

Personalisation in virtual learning environments is the system ability to provide individualisation and a set of personalised services such as personalised content management, learner model, or adaptive instant interaction (Ashoori, Miao, & Cai, 2007).

In personalised learning the curriculum and teaching approaches are adapted to meet the unique needs of each child, enabling them to achieve the best results and participate at the highest level. On one hand, in such a way individualisation assumptions can be created. On the other hand in the case of personalisation, both common and individualised activity ideas are topical.

Theoretical bases of personalisation are marketing theory. Therefore personalisation can be called as an economy-oriented dialogue between a producer and a user.

Any individual learning is oriented to an individual's experience, capabilities and needs. It is related with the adaptivity of the learning activity to a particular situation of a learner.

Adaptable learning systems seek for the education quality by organising learning content according to the educational needs of individual student (Sonwalkar, 2008). Chosen method of the teaching content and process organisation is based on the individual's as well as learning system's capability to adapt.

Hence, individual learning activities are similar among themselves in their aim of individualisation; however, they differ in their capabilities of potential individualisation. Individual learning corresponds to absolute individualisation, which is hard to realise when learning in face to face method.

The concepts of differentiation and personalisation are based on the sorting of the individuals to the groups according to their needs, level and capabilities. Nevertheless, sorting, while differentiating education, is based on the educator's ability to cover narrow subset of special individual properties. Thence, differentiation is sort of a compromise between individuality and limited possibilities to individualise.

Personalisation means total adjustment of individualisation with the common education context. Hence, personalisation is a form of individualisation expression widened by the extra possibilities. On another side, if during personalisation, individualisation is sought after by automatically adjusting a set of personalised services, then the idea of differentiated learning can be realised using much more traditional measures.

## VISUAL CONCEPTUALISATION OF THE LEARNING INDIVIDUALISATION

The notions of individual, face-to-face, differentiated or personalised learning reflect the topic of organisation of individualised learning. In the narrow sense, it is as if other students do not exist to the person who is learning individually. In this instance, only two things are important: the person (circle metaphor, Figure 1) and the environment (everything except the circle, Figure 1). In the ideal case, learning environment is oriented to the person; therefore, conflict between the person and the environment which motivates learning simply never arises.

However, in fact, to realise such individual learning is quite difficult. Attempts to combine the requirements of the society and the great many individuals encourage learning, searching and coming of new, more economical attitudes towards the individual learning, as well as broader attitude to the individualisation of the education.

Classical learning in the classroom (face to face) environment is probably the most radical transformation of the individual learning. Individual is squeezed between some sort of frame common to everybody. Situation is vividly illustrated with the metaphor of the inscribed geometric figures (see Figure 2): some individuals fit nicely into the single suggested form, nevertheless there may be something that does not exactly fit their learning style; others, too different, become constrained and trapped.

Better conditions for individual learning are created when learning differentially. Situation is illustrated with the "parquet floor" constructed from geometric figures metaphor (see Figure 3). Individuals who study individually fit together quite well. Until there are not too many groups

composed by this method, it is quite simple to organise the learning process. Nonetheless, even here disregarding of "inconvenient" characteristics of an individual is not evaded.

Personalised learning can be understood as the possibility, provided by the information technology, to sort individual by personal characteristics; in such a way seeking the optimisation of the work results of individual and the person responsible for personalisation. The situation of personalised learning is illustrated by the "triangle set" metaphor (see Figure 4). Information technology application to learning allows firstly to simply "select all triangles", and further to consider "peculiarity of each triangle". Because of this last-mentioned reason precisely personalised learning can become the most contemporary transformation of the individual learning.

In this context it becomes relevant to harmonise the aspects of interdisciplinary personalisation concept.

Personalisation can be defined as a process, which alters functionality, interface, information accessibility and content, or as a property of the system to enhance personal suitability for individual or group of individuals (Fan & Poole, 2006).

Personalisation is a multidimensional product, designed, depending on the context, adjusting architectural, relational, instrumental and com-

*Figure 2. Classroom (face-to-face) learning*

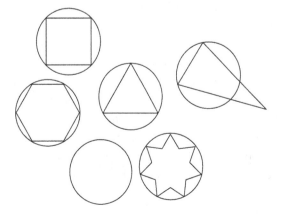

*Figure 1. Individual learning*

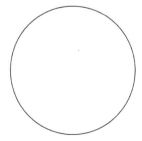

*Figure 3. Differentiated learning*

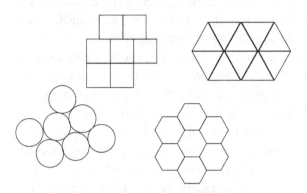

mercial aspects (Fan & Poole, 2006). Even though personalisation means different things to the people of different professions, separated, more general types of personalisation can provide extra information about the significant transformations of the individual learning.

General strategy of the architectural personalisation is individualisation while creating functional environment. Cognitive, emotional, social-cultural individual's aspects are taken into account (Fan & Poole, 2006). In such personalisation individuals are sorted as if indirectly. Allocation to a group is determined by vast amount of matches of characteristics and requirements. Architectural personalisation is illustrated by the "exceptional form" metaphor (see Figure 5). Even if such personalisation is based on vast supply of variants, still, essentially all "exceptional forms" are constructed from base elements. Expenditures are minimised, however, unique result can be achieved in such a way.

Such personalisation is similar to the construction of the microworld (Papert, 1987), compatible with the individual requirements. This personalisation strategy for the individual learning can provide a touch of natural functionality.

Relational personalisation can be defined as interpersonal relations mediator, suggesting convenient communication platforms, synchronised with the level of sociability and privacy (Fan &

Poole, 2006). In such personalisation individuals are usually sorted based on several foreknown criteria. Moreover, number of team members, as well as intersection of the individual sets constituting the teams, separated by such method, is not important for the personalisation result. Relational personalisation is illustrated by the "figure classes" metaphor (see Figure 6). Depending on the context, the same figure can be assigned to one or another class.

Relational personalisation becomes important for creating the conditions for learning to collaborate. This personalisation strategy can provide the touch of versatility to the individual learning.

Result of the instrumental personalisation is based on the harmony between the personal characteristics and context of activity. Efficiency and personal productivity is pursued by simplifying the usage of the tools. Work environment is designed specifically for each user (Fan & Poole, 2006). In such personalisation sorting process is continually proceeding since it is essential to constantly renew the connection individual-context. Instrumental personalisation is illustrated by the "figure construction tools" metaphor (see Figure 7). Every figure corresponds to special set of tools.

Instrumental personalisation strategy is important for the individual learning while choosing the components of the learning environment.

*Figure 4. Personalised learning*

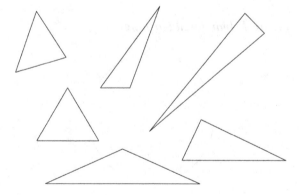

*Figure 5. Architectural personalisation*

Accent of commercial personalisation is the contents of the personalisation, user preference or demographic profiling, user online behaviour and user choices history. Differentiation of production, services and information is being done by adaptively personalizing (Fan & Poole, 2006). In such personalisation huge number of individuals is sorted according to very diverse entirety of features. Commercial personalisation is illustrated by the "relevant information about the figures" metaphor (see Figure 8). It reflects the possibility to discover repetition in the vast amount of variants.

Commercial personalisation strategy can give a touch of orderliness to the individual learning. It could be applicable for the process of relevant information searching.

## INFORMATICS ACTIVITIES IN PRIMARY SCHOOL

Informatics or some elements of understanding digital world and devices are more and more important in today's education. The process of informatisation of the whole learning process has been started in many countries. New space is created for quality development not only of digital literacy, but also of other important components of informatics and competencies such as program-

ming, problem solving and data handling (Kalas, 2006; Dagiene, 2008; Drenoyianni, Stergioulas, & Dagiene, 2008).

The research of ICT application and elements of informatics learning in the primary classes reveals quite a big variety of suitable activities. Quite a bit of attention in the primary schools is devoted to the formation of the technical skills (Tondeur, vanBraak, &Valck, 2007). ICT is used for the familiarisation with the informatics' concepts (Mittermeir, Bischof, & Hodnigg, 2010; Keller, Komm, Serafini, Sprock, & Steffen, 2010), training algorithmic thinking and creativity (Papert, 1987; Wheeler, Waite, & Bromfield, 2002), information searching, arrangement, presentation and discussion (Selwyn, Potter, & Cranmer, 2009). Taking deeper interest into the informatics education at the lower secondary level (Kalas & Winczer, 2008) topic, it could be spotted that more attention could also be devoted to the social, ethical and legal aspects of informatics and the information society.

There are also other constantly performed activities by the primary classes' children that can be tagged as topical informatics activities, i.e., matching of various methods of information expression, object grouping, investigation of the objects and data groups properties, information collection and structurisation, comprehension of

*Figure 6. Relational personalisation*

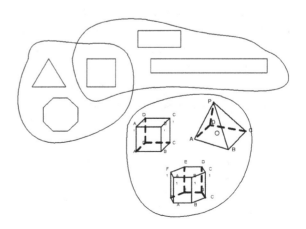

*Figure 7. Instrumental personalisation*

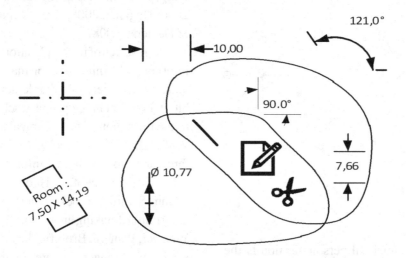

instructions, exact execution and creation is frequent in the mathematics lessons (Grabauskiene, 2005; Carreira, 2001). Some of these activities, some more, some less can also be found in other (language, world knowledge, arts, and technologies) lessons.

Nevertheless, it is important to emphasise some aspects of such activity topical to precisely informatics. When learning informatics, analysis of objects and processes by deliberately "looking from outside" becomes particularly important. Even though it is possible only after gaining enough experience of practical manipulation, construction, visual expression methods alterations (Grabauskiene, 2005), it still seems that early orientation to the conscious investigation of causes and results, discussion about the difficulties to match elements, corrections of instructions could be the priority of learning informatics' essentials in the primary schools.

Application of last mentioned activities in the primary classes is based on the younger school-age children psychological peculiarities. Thus, the aims of learning informatics are sought through playful construction, creation, communication and cooperation.

The change of the learning environment has changed the learning motivation most of all. Following many researchers the most common barriers to learners' motivation are fear, boredom, previous negative experiences of education, and lack of hope about future prospects. Naturalness of the learning environment of an individual remains an objective aspiration, because in this way a contradiction between individuality and societal necessity to provide an individual the knowledge basis can be diminished (Chatti, Jarke, & Specht, 2010; Hartley, 2009).

*Figure 8. Commercial personalisation*

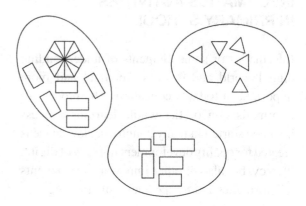

An environment is considered as the natural learning environment, in which the learning process is attractive for individual and as if invisible. The learning environment of this kind establishes conditions for individuals to investigate "it is like a construction kit, an erector set, mud pies, and building with blocks <...>. They are able to play with motion in this and other microworlds, in ways, that have only been possible with static forces in the past. So this microworld is not just mathematical, it is physics as well. It allows children to develop both intuitive and formal experience with motion in an integrated way (Papert, 1987).

The natural learning environment stimulates motivation through the versatility of learning activities as well. Note that much versatility is usually deliberately endeavoured by theoretically founding the models of designed learning environments.

Students play an active role rather than a passive when they are involved in a project-based work. They become eager recipients of information transmitted by a teacher, textbook, or broadcast. The students actively make decisions how to generate, obtain, manipulate, and display information. The project-based methodology stimulates students to deal with information, make choices, and develop executing skills much more actively than it is happens in instructional lessons. Each student could work independently or within a small group on a problem interesting to him.

Seymour Papert (1987, 1993) talked about a computer making possible to create microworlds, which can transform rather a clumsy educational process into a more natural and spontaneous one. The protean quality of computer as an intellectual medium means that every child can find a rich intellectual activity, with which to fall in love. It is through such "intellectual love affairs" that people acquire the taste for rigour and creativity" (Papert, 1987).

Therefore, several kinds of informatics activities in primary education can be singled out. These are activities, directly connected to the computer application to the learning, also, those oriented to the main informatics ideas and principles. In the first case application of various personalisation strategies in the primary classes is topical. In the second case, informatics learning aims can be sought after even by not emphasising the exceptionality of the informatics science; and the support of the individual learning is as if not connected with the facilities provided by ICT. In both cases it is important to create a natural learning environment.

## INDIVIDUALISATION THROUGH INFORMATICS ACTIVITIES IN PRIMARY SCHOOL

Possibilities of learning individuality maintenance in modern learning environments can be specified by the Kolb learning style typology (Kolb & Kolb, 1984). Perception continuing (concrete experience and abstract conceptualisation), as well as processing continuing (active experimentation and reflective observation) make up the main part of learning environments.

A Kolb learning style typology (Kolb & Kolb, 1984; Kolb, 1984) interpretation, chosen by us, lays the main stress on the learning environment component alternation – learning abilities. The classic learning environment and ICT-based learning environment potentially differ by the volume of learning style applications, agreeable to individuals. The statements on coordination of different learning activities in ICT-based learning environment make the basis of the Kolb learning theory. The ICT-based learning environment potentially gives better learning conditions to an individual which is relevant in various education stages, especially in primary education when a unique learning style of an individual starts forming.

A typical presentation of Kolb's two continuums (Kolb & Kolb, 1984) is that the east-west axis is called the Processing Continuum (how we approach a task), and the north-south axis is called the Perception Continuum (our emotional response, or how we think or feel about it).

These learning styles are the combination of two lines of axis (continuums) each formed between what Kolb (Kolb & Kolb, 1984) calls 'dialectically related modes' of 'grasping experience' (doing or watching), and 'transforming experience' (feeling or thinking).

Interdisciplinary personalisation typology can transform the conception of individual learning. In the extreme case, when individual learning is exclusively based on the application of information technologies, such transformation can be likewise represented by the scheme constructed based on basis of Kolb learning style (see Figure 9). Each learning stage corresponds with one personalisation strategy.

The stage of active experimentation is best corresponded by the instrumental personalisation

strategy, oriented to the optimisation of work tools. Reflective observation stage corresponds to the relational personalisation strategy, intended for boosting communication about topics interesting to the individual. Concrete Experience stage corresponds to Commercial Personalisation strategy, since especially in this stage individual finds a lot of various information, which needs to be sorted, so that it would be easier to understand it. Abstract Conceptualisation stage corresponds to Architectural Personalisation strategy, because abstract understanding is inseparable from the pure functionality.

Primary schools' children individual learning activities are illustrated by slightly different scheme (see Figure 10). The structure of the scheme remains the same; however, the accents of the informatics teaching and information technologies application change.

*Figure 9. Expression of the personalisation type in Kolb learning conception, the case of the whole information technology application*

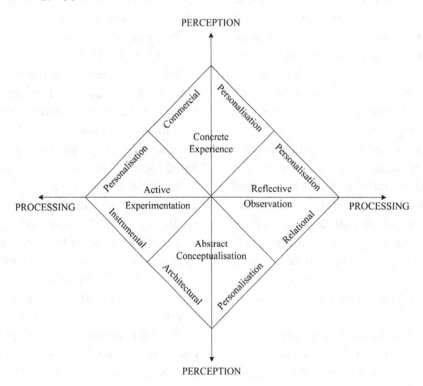

*Figure 10. Expression of the personalisation types in Kolb learning conception, information technologies application to the primary education case*

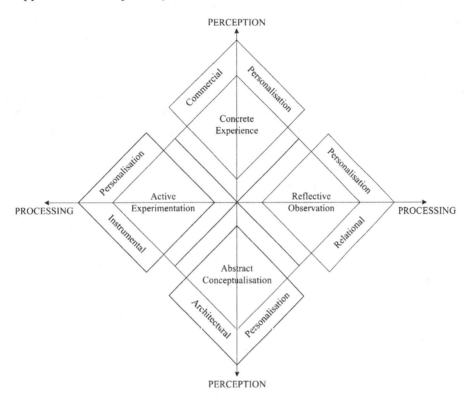

Because of the psychological and physical specifics of the younger school-age children, the extent of direct information technologies application has to inevitably decrease.

Since in this age main knowledge and abilities important for the further learning are gained, respectively the extent of the activity which would stimulate the understanding of informatics basis, is increasing.

On the one hand, the same continuums (concrete experience and abstract conceptualisation; active experimentation and reflective observation) described by Kolb and Kolb (1984) are appropriate to the primary classes' children learning environment. On the other hand, the appeasement of the individuals' perception and processing needs is based more on the real and virtual environments' synergetic influence.

This situation is imaged in Figure 10 by the four "mobile squares" compositions. Mobility is here understood as a possibility to choose the ratio of real and virtual environments needed for particular learning situation. Small squares more removed from the centre of the scheme symbolise the application of special personalisation strategies. About the centre of the scheme other four small squares which make up the bigger square symbolise the variety of the learning activities.

The intersections of the squares in the mentioned compositions symbolise the extent of the particular personalisation strategy when used for individual learning. Such extend depends on the parameters which characterise the student. This means that for every particular student, the scheme shown in Figure 10 will be more or less asymmetric. The part of external square not belonging to the intersection represents personalisation's possibilities which are topical to individual learning, though not applied to the primary class children.

Analysing the possibilities of individual education from particular positions of informatics activities in primary education it can be seen that personalisation strategies based on the application of information technologies are acceptable in primary education only to some extent. However the main architectural, relational, instrumental and commercial strategic ideas (respectively – functionality, openness, practicality, orderliness) are basically only different accents of individualisation, therefore can be applied to any individual learning activity.

## CONCLUSION

The context of information technologies application to learning firstly shows the possibility of transferring the personalisation concept's content to the educology topic. The application of the personalisation strategies to a learning environment can give functionality, openness, practicality and orderliness. Activities of informatics provide a possibility for the student to faster become a citizen of modern world, comprehend technologies, and acquire digital literacy.

For the primary classes important activities are directly related to the computer usage, also, activities directed to the basic informatics ideas and principles. In the first case, application of various personalisation strategies is especially important. In the second case, informatics learning aims can be sought after even by not emphasising the exceptionality of the informatics science; and the support of the individual learning is as if not related to the facilities provided by ICT. However, it seems that even then it is meaningful to use personalisation ideas in order to realise aspects of individual's activity particularly important to informatics. When learning informatics, analysis

of objects and processes by deliberately "looking from outside" becomes particularly important. Thus individual learning, as well as personalisation have to be based by versatile research.

Design of conscious and versatile application of personalisation strategies in primary classes reveals asymmetrical nature of various individual's learning activities. This way the possibility to choose advisable ratio of real and virtual environments, suitable for particular learning situation, is realised.

In conclusion, it can be said that thanks to the informatics and IT, individual learning is transforming much faster. It becomes more versatile and optimally organised. Hence, better learning achievements can be expected.

## ACKNOWLEDGMENT

This paper has been developed under the European Union Structural Funds project "Postdoctoral Fellowship Implementation in Lithuania" within the framework of the Measure for Enhancing Mobility of Scholars and Other Researchers and the Promotion of Student Research (VP1-3.1-ŠMM-01) of the Program of Human Resources Development Action Plan.

## REFERENCES

Aouag, S. (2007). Designing learning activity to be individualized. In *Proceedings of the International Conference on Web Information Systems and Technologies.*

Ashoori, M., Miao, C., & Cai, Y. (2007, November 2-5). Socializing pedagogical agents for personalization in virtual learning environments. In *Proceedings of the IEEE/WIC/ACM International Conferences on Web Intelligence and Intelligent Agent Technology*, Silicon Valley, CA.

Carreira, S. (2001). Where there's a model, there's a metaphor: Metaphorical thinking in students' understanding of a mathematical model. *Mathematical Thinking and Learning, 3*(4), 261–287. doi:10.1207/S15327833MTL0304_02

Chatti, M. A., Jarke, M., & Specht, M. (2010). The 3P learning model. *Journal of Educational Technology & Society, 13*(4), 74–85.

Dagienė, V. (2008). Teaching information technology and elements of informatics in lower secondary schools: Curricula, didactic provision and implementation. In R. T. Mittermeir & M. M. Syslo (Eds.), *Proceedings of the International Conference on Informatics Education: Supporting Computational Thinking* (LNCS 5090, pp. 293-304).

Drenoyianni, H., Stergioulas, L. K., & Dagiene, V. (2008). The pedagogical challenge of digital literacy: Reconsidering the concept – envisioning the curriculum' – reconstructing the school. *International Journal on Social and Humanistic Computing, 1*(1), 53–66. doi:10.1504/IJSHC.2008.020480

Duval, R. (2002). The cognitive analysis of problems of comprehension in the learning of mathematics. *Mediterranean Journal for Research in Mathematics Education, 1*(2), 1–16.

Fan, H., & Poole, M. S. (2006). What is personalisation? Perspectives on the design and implementation of personalisation in information systems. *Journal of Organizational Computing and Electronic Commerce, 16*(3-4), 179–202. doi:10.1080/10919392.2006.9681199

Grabauskiene, V. (2005). *Formation of geometric images at primary school stage.* Unpublished doctoral dissertation, Vilnius Pedagogical University, Studentu, Lithuania.

Hartley, D. (2009). Personalisation: The nostalgic revival of child-centred education? *Journal of Education Policy, 24*(4), 423–434. doi:10.1080/02680930802669318

Kalas, I. (2006). Discovering informatics fundamentals through interactive interfaces for learning. In R. T. Mittermeir (Ed.), *Proceedings of the International Conference on Informatics Education: The Bridge between Using and Understanding Computers* (LNCS 4226, pp. 13-24).

Kalas, I., & Winczer, M. (2008). Informatics as a contribution to the modern constructivist education. In R. T. Mittermeir & M. M. Syslo (Eds.), *Proceedings of the Third International Conference on Informatics Education: Supporting Computational Thinking* (LNCS 5090, pp. 229-240).

Keller, L., Komm, D., Serafini, G., Sprock, A., & Steffen, B. (2010). Teaching public-key cryptography in school. In J. Hromkovic, R. Kralovic, & J. Vahrenhold (Eds.), *Proceedings of the 4th International Conference on Teaching Fundamentals Concepts of Informatics* (LNCS 5941, pp. 112-123).

Koc, M. (2005). Individual learner differences in web-based learning environments: From cognitive, affective and social-cultural perspectives. *Turkish Online Journal of Distance Education, 6*(4), 12–22.

Kolb, A. Y., & Kolb, D. A. (1984). Learning styles and learning spaces. Enhancing experiential learning in higher education. *Academy of Management Learning & Education, 4*(2), 193–212. doi:10.5465/AMLE.2005.17268566

Kolb, D. A. (1984). *Experiential learning: Experience as the source of learning and development.* Upper Saddle River, NJ: Prentice Hall.

LaDuke, B. (2008). Knowledge creation in collective intelligence. In Tovey, M. (Ed.), *Collective intelligence: Creating a prosperous world at peace* (pp. 65–74). Oakton, VA: Earth Intelligence Network.

Landrum, T. J., & McDuffie, K. A. (2008). Learning styles in the age of differentiated instruction. *Exceptionality*, *8*, 6–17.

Mittermeir, R. T., Bischof, E., & Hodnigg, K. (2010). Teaching kids to teach their teachers. In J. Hromkovic, R. Kralovic, & J. Vahrenhold (Eds.), *Proceedings of the Fourth International Conference on Teaching Fundamentals Concepts of Informatics* (LNCS 5941, pp. 143-154).

Papert, S. (1993). *Mindstorms: Children, computers and powerful ideas*. Boston, MA: Basic Books.

Papert, S. (1987). Microworlds: Transforming education. In R. W. Lawler & M. Yazdani (Eds.), *Artificial intelligence and education, vol. 1: Learning environments & tutoring systems* (pp. 79-95). Norwood, NJ: Ablex.

Selwyn, N., Potter, J., & Cranmer, S. (2009). Primary pupils' use of information and communication technologies at school and home. *British Journal of Educational Technology*, *40*(5), 919–932. doi:10.1111/j.1467-8535.2008.00876.x

Sonwalkar, N. (2008). Adaptive individualisation: The next generation of online education. *Horizon*, *16*(1), 44–47. doi:10.1108/10748120810853345

Tondeur, J., van Braak, J., & Valcke, M. (2007). Curricula and the use of ICT in education: Two worlds apart? *British Journal of Educational Technology*, *38*(6), 962–976. doi:10.1111/j.1467-8535.2006.00680.x

Wheeler, S., Waite, S. J., & Bromfield, C. (2002). Promoting creative thinking through the use of ICT. *Journal of Computer Assisted Learning*, *18*, 367–378. doi:10.1046/j.0266-4909.2002.00247.x

*This work was previously published in the International Journal of Digital Literacy and Digital Competence, Volume 2, Issue 3, edited by Antonio Cartelli, pp. 1-14, copyright 2011 by IGI Publishing (an imprint of IGI Global).*

# Chapter 5
# Digital Literacy and Competence in Students Attending a Faculty of Humanities

**Antonio Cartelli**
*University of Cassino, Italy*

**Angela Di Nuzzo**
*University of Cassino, Italy*

## ABSTRACT

*In this paper the behaviors and tendencies in the use of digital technologies by university students are analyzed. After a short discussion of former studies and the presentation of the model for digital literacy structure and assessment in students attending compulsory school, the investigation carried out by the authors is described and the results obtained from the analysis of the university students' answers is reported. The survey was submitted to 331 students in the Faculty of Humanities at the University of Cassino, Italy, and the students' answers show a contradictory reality: on one side, digital technologies are mainly used to communicate in social networks or to play music and movies, on another side it is evident the students' interest for the most recent aspects of the application of digital technology and for the improvement in the quality of their use.*

## INTRODUCTION

Undoubtedly today society, usually defined *knowledge society*, has significant different features with respect to industrial, post-industrial and information society, which preceded it. Among the various

DOI: 10.4018/978-1-4666-2943-1.ch005

aspects to be considered for the understanding of the changes affecting today society, those reported below have a special relevance for the effects they have on what follows:

- The gap between "digital natives" and "digital immigrants" (both in learning styles and knowledge development) (Prensky,

2001), which is the basis for the better relationship between young generations and digital technologies in the management of information, with respect to the elders,

- The skills and competences for lifelong learning, which are considered essential for people to be good citizens in the knowledge society. Digital competences, among them, are especially important for their cross cultural features with respect to language (reading / writing) and calculus (Council of European Parliament, 2005).

Otherwise stated, today more than in the past, knowledge construction and development, and meta-cognitive features, go hand in hand with the development of digital equipments and their effects on mankind, and especially with the ability of human beings to use them as prostheses of their minds, more than of their bodies (de Kerckhove, 2000).

Starting from a research project guided by Calvani (2010), frameworks for the assessment of digital competences have been developed, which recently led (Cartelli et al., 2010; Cartelli, 2010) to hypothesize a model for the structure of digital competences and their development.

Starting point for the construction of the model has been the subject in its evolution, as reported in the psycho-pedagogical literature and in the taxonomies used for its assessment (Anderson & Krathwohl, 2001; Bloom, 1956; Brandhorst, 1976).

The human dimensions especially affected by digital revolution, as reported in the final model are the *cognitive*, the *affective* and the *social-relational* (due to the multiple effects of IT/ICT and virtual worlds on mankind). Cognitive dimension is a special case among them, for the influence of digital world on human languages and intelligences; as a consequence, three sections in this dimension have been identified: technological, verbal-linguistic and logical-mathematical, the last two being inherited by Gardner idea of multiple intelligences (Gardner, 1993). At last, the same cognitive dimension, has been seen under the umbrella of space, time and causality categories (the ones studied by Piaget in individuals' knowledge construction, for their dependencies from history of science, or, to use Piaget words, for the genetic epistemology underlying subjects' evolution); this last hypothesis is derived from the reality and especially from the effects that virtual environments have on the perception of reality and on the above categories. In Figure 1, the above considerations are synthesized, together with the representation of the affective and the social-relational dimensions, where the *ethical/moral behavior – judgment* is proposed as a meta-category, crossing over the affective and the social-relational dimensions, both affected by digital world and especially by its virtual environments.

When passing to the assessment of digital competences, old taxonomies confirm their value and for each dimension is possible to draw a rising scale. In Table 1 they are shown, side by side, as they appear in the literature.

The above model and the correspondent framework have been positively verified by means of different questionnaires submitted to students in almost all educational levels, from Primary to High School. Some problems, mostly concerning the highest levels of the taxonomies, still remain open, due to the difficulty of finding adequate instruments for the assessment of creativity, wisdom and all human functions not directly connected with the measurement of knowledge and skills. Furthermore, whether the framework structure will be confirmed by deepen analysis, it cannot be immediately deduced that an identical or similar model can be applied to elders and especially to university students.

Main questions guiding the development of the study reported below have been in fact:

- How much the above model is applicable to university students?

*Figure 1. The final framework for digital competence assessment*

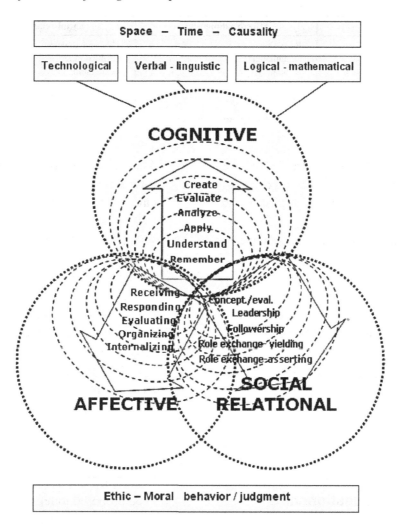

- Are there instruments helping the development of digital competences in university students?

Starting point for this study has been the research by Ferri and Pozzali (2010), who found that university students have special digital diets, in terms of use and application of digital equipments. On the basis of the above hypotheses the authors decided to conduct a survey to investigate both the perceived knowledge of digital instruments (i.e., how much students thought they were able in the use of computers, and more generally digital

equipments) and the students' ability in making simple operations with them.

## THE SURVEY: QUESTIONNAIRE BUILDING AND DATA ANALYSIS

The main problem with the analysis of digital competence in university students concerned the idea that even if the structure of the framework was the same as in the above model, the width of the different languages and the dependencies between dimensions and categories were different.

*Table 1. Taxonomies of education with a special attention to digital influence*

| Cognitive dimension | Affective dimension | Social-relational dimension |
|---|---|---|
| – Remember,<br>– Understand,<br>– Apply,<br>– Analyze,<br>– Evaluate,<br>– Create | – Receiving,<br>– Organizing,<br>– Evaluating,<br>– Organizing,<br>– Internalizing | – Conceptualization<br>– Evaluation,<br>– Leadership,<br>– Followership,<br>– Role exchange in a yielding direction,<br>– Role exchange in an assertive direction |

As a consequence the authors decided to have a first approach to students' digital competences by means of a survey involving the students in the Faculty of Humanities.

The survey was based on a questionnaire to acquire information on the following issues:

• Education and training to computer use,
• Students' computer practices and skills,
• How computer use can influence the way of studying and the relationship/communication the students performed with lecturers and professors.

In what follows the structure of the questionnaire and the answers of the students are better described.

## Structure of the Questionnaire

The questionnaire provided for the investigation emerges from two opposite needs, the analysis of the influence that former education and the environment had and has on students' use of digital equipments and the development of digital competences.

The consideration of the above requirements influenced the structure of the questionnaire, which was made of four sections:

1. **The first section is devoted to general information:** The students gender, the place he/she lives in, the high school he/she attended before university, the graduating course he/she is attending within the Faculty,

2. **The second section analyzes students' interaction with IT/ICT tools, and especially:** The time spent at the computer, the training had in computer use, the use of the Internet at home (if they have the connection at home), which tools are used when connected to the Internet, the participation in *social networks*, the use of search engines, the use of the Internet in accessing university information and contacting lecturers/professors,

3. The third section, which has been called *technological*, contains technical questions about computer use, and more generally IT/ICT use; it aims at evaluating students' basic knowledge of digital instruments and their use and application in simple situations,

4. In the fourth and last section *free spaces* have been proposed to let students comment the questionnaire, discuss their experiences and suggest further digital competence issues.

Due to organizational and temporal reasons (i.e., the number of persons charged of carrying out the investigation and the period which could be used for the submission of the questionnaires to the students before the end of the lessons), the following elements were pre-defined:

• The universe of the survey was the whole population of the students of the Faculty of Humanities,
• The questionnaire, to be submitted to the volunteers who would have accepted to answer to its questions, was the instrument of the investigation.

The questionnaire is made of closed-answer questions with one or more items to be chosen among different ones (depending on the questions). Only the last section of the questionnaire has two open-answer questions.

The submission of the questionnaire has come after an organization phase based on three different steps:

1. The authorization by the Dean of the faculty to make the survey and the contact of the Heads of all graduating courses for the description of the initiative and the support in carrying out it;
2. The communication and explanation of the reasons and the structure of the investigation to the students' representatives in the Faculty, to let them contact the other students and persuade as many students as possible to participate in the survey;
3. The finding of the submission times, usually 15-20 minutes at the beginning of the lessons, to allow students answer the questionnaire.

The submission of the questionnaire took seven days and no special problem happened during the proposal of the questionnaire to the students.

## Analysis of Students' Answers

### Section A: General Information

Of 3.125 (694 males and 2.431 females) students enrolling the Triennial Graduation Courses and of 775 (117 males and 658 females) students[*1] enrolling the Post Graduation Biennial Courses in the Faculty of Humanities at the University of Cassino, 331 students took part into the survey. They distributed among the graduation courses as specified in Table 2.

In terms of percentages the participation into the investigation was as follows:

- Quite 9% of the students in the first graduation triennial courses,
- Quite 7% of the students in the final graduation biennial courses.

The above results, which could look as a partial result (i.e., the results were limited to the students who answered the questionnaire), were much more general and could be applied to all the students in the Faculty, when the comparison with global students' data was made.

The above result was mainly deduced from the considerations below:

1. Students' attendance to the courses in the Faculty of Humanities, which is usually

*Table 2. Distribution of the students who took part into the survey (L = triennial course, S = biennial post-graduation course)*

| Graduation course | N. of students |
|---|---|
| Literature and history (L) | 46 |
| Philosophy (L) | 4 |
| Modern Languages and Literature (L) | 56 |
| Educational Sciences (L) | 96 |
| Social Service Sciences (L) | 71 |
| Communication Sciences (L) | 1 |
| **Total amount of triennial graduation students** | **274** |
| Greek and Latin Philology (S) | 1 |
| Modern Philology (S) | 5 |
| Planning and Management of Educational Services (S) | 18 |
| Planning and Management of Social Services (S) | 4 |
| History and Analysis of Philosophical Ideas (S) | 2 |
| Literature, history and philology from ancient to contemporary age (S) | 2 |
| European and American Modern Languages and Literature (S) | 16 |
| Education and E-learning Sciences (S) | 8 |
| Communication Theories and Methods (S) | 1 |
| **Total amount of post-graduation students** | **57** |
| **Grand Total** | **331** |

based on 10% of the students participating at final examinations (i.e., the students having that course in their study plan),

2. The features of the students' sample, as deduced from the answers to the questions in the first section of the questionnaire, which are summarized in Figure 1. The correlation analysis of the data reported in the figure with those coming from the students' offices (i.e., concerning all the students in the faculty), led to high correlation values (i.e., more than 9.6). Otherwise stated, at least for the general features reported (see Figure 2), the sample of the students investigated differs from the universe from less than 10%; this value has been assumed as the error to be accepted when the answers to the other questions in the survey are considered to belong to all the students.

## Section B: The Students' Interaction with IT/ICT Tools

When looking at how long the students used the computer, the following data have been obtained:

- 1.82% never used it,
- 6.38% began to use it in the last year,
- 91.80% are using it for a long time, which is more than one year.

Differently from the above data, when the students' training on computer use has been investigated, a relevant quantity of students (40.12%) said that they didn't train at all. Those who were enrolled in training courses on computer distributed as follows:

- 24.01% had less than 8 hours training,

*Figure 2. Features of the student sample*

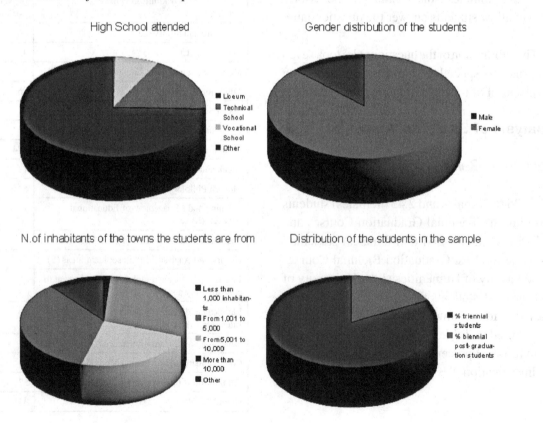

- 13.08% had training for a time going from 8 to 20 hours,
- 8.81% trained from 21 to 40 hours,
- 13.98% attended courses for more than 40 hours.

It is interesting to note that may be 50% of the students did train on computer use before entering the University or outside institutional courses.

Furthermore it has been analyzed the numbers of hours the students sit daily at the computer:

- 2.42% never use it,
- 24.47% uses the PC less than one hour,
- 57.40% works on the PC from one hour to four hours,
- 15.71% stay at the PC more than four hours.

Whether questioning on the use of the computer, and especially if it was limited to the use of special tools or extended to Internet connection the following situation emerged:

- 2.41% of the students had the connection at home but have discarded it,
- 92.14% have Internet connection at home and use it,
- 4.53% haven't it,
- 0.92% plan to install it.

From the investigation on Internet use emerged that students retrieve documents, search for information, communicate with friends and colleagues. Furthermore, when asked to say if they knew and used the services of a social network they gave the following answers:

- 2.16% didn't know them at all,
- 4.32% were registered in a social network but visited it rarely,
- 26.85% knew different social network but were not registered on them,
- 66.67% were enrolled in a social network and visited it regularly.

Leading activities performed by students at their PC are:

- To listen music (31.43%), while standing alone,
- To be in a social network (36.57%), to exchange messages and chat with friends.

The data reported above agree with the Italian statistical results on PC possession and use and on the access to the Internet by Italian students; furthermore they confirm the results of similar inquires (Pozzali & Ferri, 2010), made on students in a Northern Italian University (Milan):

- 60.0% of the investigated students said that they constantly access Facebook and put messages on it,
- 2.2% didn't know what Facebook was.

At last, it is interesting to remark how students use computers and the Internet to be in touch with lecturers and professors:

- 41.12% of the students directly go to professors' rooms when they need explanations,
- 32.41% send an e-mail to professors when they don't succeed in talking with them,
- 25.23% send an e-mail to professors before going to their rooms,
- 1.25% like much to ask to colleagues and friends for suggestions.

## Section C: Technological Area

In regards to the technological area of the questionnaire the main aspects to be remarked concerns the set of the topics analyzed and the levels of knowledge and skills under analysis (see Tables 3 through 6):

- Computer general administration, use of software tools (i.e., office automation, image editing, video editing etc.) and connection to the Internet,

*Table 3. Computer administration (management of files and folders, backup copies, cleaning the hard disk, making the computer faster etc.)*

| Operation | Right answers |
|---|---|
| Copy and/or transfer of a file from folder to folder and device to device | 50.00% |
| Deletion of information in different situations | 77.80% |
| Cleaning of an hard drive and its defragmenting | 12.85% |
| Writing of information on a CD/DVD-ROM | 11.44% |

*Table 4. Use of programs belonging to a suite of office automation*

| Program | Right use |
|---|---|
| Word processor | 22.70% |
| Spread sheet | 20.85% |
| Presentation manager | 19.31% |
| Database manager | 13.33% |

- For each topic there were questions of at least two different levels of difficulty.

Furthermore, problems were posed on the same topics, so that not only the knowledge of the single arguments was evaluated, but also the students' ability in finding solutions when involved in simple problematic situations.

It can be easily deduced from the reported data that students:

- Are not very familiar with programs in a suite of office automation with respect to what it could be initially hypothesized,
- Have a little or no familiarity with image processing and editing,
- When involved in more complicated tasks, they usually don't succeed in applying their knowledge and fail in finding the right solutions to the problems they are facing.

## Section D: Suggestions and Comments

This section had a poor adhesion. The main answers have been:

- "The questionnaire contains too many questions; so to focus on it is hard" (2 students);
- "The questionnaire is too easy";
- "It is interesting and I hope that we will have other questionnaires of this kind in the future" (3 students);
- "It is executable, but I made some mistakes because I have a poor knowledge about technological tools" (3 students);
- "The questionnaire contains questions too difficult" (3 students);
- "It concerns only computer and it ignores other technologies" (1 student).

At last, some students expressed the desire that University, and especially the Faculty, could organize free computer courses of higher level (4 students).

*Table 5. Use of a drawing program and/or an image editor*

| Program | Use |
|---|---|
| Painting program | 9.23% |
| Image editing | 6.73% |

*Table 6. Connection to the Internet and use of online services*

| Program | Use |
|---|---|
| Web browsing, e-mail management | 42.12% |
| Making good queries with a search engine (i.e., being satisfied of the results of a query) | 31.75% |
| Using online databases | 28.77% |

## CONCLUSION

The first datum which emerges from the analysis of students' answers concerns the impact that computer use has on the development of digital competences in university students (at least in the investigated Faculty of Humanities). Computers appear in fact as equipments devoted to the transmission of information and to the acquisition of "technical skills", more than instruments for the development of *problem solving* skills (i.e., students learn specific topics on computer structure and administration if they have to attend examinations where these topics are integral part of the curriculum, otherwise they limit to simpler operations and don't care of information and skills which are not in their everyday experience). A phenomenon to be better investigated is the diffidence that students have towards practices and skills which could make their life easier and help them to communicate with lecturers and professors; probably the following sentence can give a first explanation to the observed phenomena: "for effective use of digital technologies, students must have basic skills. Unfortunately they can't achieve these skills by books or being helped to find web information, to use a word processor, or to send an e-mail: this isn't the way that allows students to become competent" (Radoslav & Wechtersbach, 2008).

To be more precise, from a detailed analysis of the collected data emerge the following trends:

- Demographic factors do not seem to affect the students' answers in the technological section of the questionnaire; this result has two different origins: first, training do not seem to affect students performances at all, because those who attended more than 40 hours of computer training obtained lower scores than those who didn't attended any course; second, no significant connection could be detected between geographic distribution and positive answers to the questionnaire in the technological section;

- A "poor perception" of students' own digital competences has been detected; otherwise stated, students are persuaded that their use of the programs in a suite of Office automation (i.e., Word, Excel, Power Point and Access), is sufficient to state that they are digitally competent, but the low level of positive answers in the technological section of the questionnaire contradicts their ideas;

- Notwithstanding the general datum, by which students mostly *visit social networks* (36.57%) and *play music* (31.43%), the great majority of students use the Internet to find materials connected to the topics they are studying and only seldom go to the library in the Faculty.

Final remark of the investigation is the need of a wider presence and a more specific role of technology in teaching and education. Otherwise stated a paradigmatic change is needed in teaching, because more than train students *to use* IT/ICT, lecturers and professors must teach *using* IT/ICT and, what's more, they must teach *in a* context rich of digital technologies.

## AUTHOR'S NOTE

The authors worked together on all of the paper but especially wrote specific parts. A. Cartelli prepared and wrote the introduction and the conclusion, A. Di Nuzzo carried out the investigation, collected the data and wrote the corresponding part of the paper. The numbers on the global amount of students attending the Courses in the Faculty of Humanities were obtained from the Ministry of Education.

# REFERENCES

Anderson, L. W., & Krathwohl, D. (2001). *A taxonomy for learning, teaching and assessing: A revision of bloom's taxonomy of educational objectives*. New York, NY: Longman.

Bloom, B. S. (1956). *Taxonomy of educational objectives, Handbook I: The cognitive domain*. New York, NY: David McKay.

Brandhorst, A. R. (1976). Toward a taxonomy of educational objectives in the relational domain. In *Proceedings of the Annual Meeting of the National Council for Social Studies*. Washington, DC. Retrieved August 4, 2010, from http://www.eric.ed.gov/ERICWebPortal/search/detailmini.jsp?_nfpb=true&_&ERICExtSearch_SearchValue_0=ED134505&ERICExtSearch_SearchType_0=no&accno=ED134505

Calvani, A., Fini, A., & Ranieri, M. (2010). *La competenza digitale nella scuola*. Trento, Italy: Erickson.

Cartelli, A. (2010). Theory and practice in digital competence assessment. *International Journal of Digital Literacy and Digital Competence, 1*(3), 24–39. doi:10.4018/jdldc.2010101902

Cartelli, A., Dagiene, V., & Futschek, G. (2010). Bebras contest and digital competence assessment: Analysis of frameworks. *International Journal of Digital Literacy and Digital Competence, 1*(1), 24–39. doi:10.4018/jdldc.2010101902

Council of European Parliament. (2005). *Recommendation of the European Parliament and of the Council on key competences for lifelong learning*. Retrieved December 3, 2010, from http://ec.europa.eu/education/policies/2010/doc/keyrec_en.pdf

De Kerckhove, D. (2000). *La pelle della cultura*. Genoa, Italy: Costa & Nolan.

Gardner, H. (1993). *Multiple intelligences: The theory in practice*. New York, NY: Basic Books.

Pozzali, A., & Ferri, P. (2010). The media diet of university students in Italy: An exploratory research. *International Journal of Digital Literacy and Digital Competence, 1*(2), 1–10. doi:10.4018/jdldc.2010040101

Prensky, M. (2001). Digital natives, digital immigrants. *Horizon, 9*(6), 1–6. doi:10.1108/10748120110424843

Wechtersbach, R. (2008). Lo sviluppo delle competenze digitali nella scuola slovena. *Tecnologie Didattiche, 43*, 17–22.

*This work was previously published in the International Journal of Digital Literacy and Digital Competence, Volume 2, Issue 1, edited by Antonio Cartelli, pp. 27-36, copyright 2011 by IGI Publishing (an imprint of IGI Global).*

# Chapter 6
# Development of ICT Competency in Pre-Service Teacher Education

**Valentina Dagienė**
*Vilnius University, Lithuania*

## ABSTRACT

*Starting from the key competencies for a knowledge society, this paper examines the information and communication technology (ICT) competency needed by teachers for effective teaching in the 21st-century. The paper analyzes the existing pre-service education programmes for teachers' ICT competency in Lithuanian universities and colleges, self-evaluation of future teachers of their technological and pedagogical ICT competency, and comparison of these results with the course requirements for the teachers' educational ICT literacy, based on the existing Lithuanian requirements for teachers' pedagogical ICT literacy programmes. The paper is based on the data of the research study "Teachers' Training on ICT Application in Education" developed by the Institute of Mathematics and Informatics in 2009. Conclusions and recommendations of the study have been proposed to implement deeper content-based modules for pedagogical ICT competency and skills in all-level pre-service teacher education as well as in-service training courses.*

## 1. INTRODUCTION

Educational systems of various countries need to effect changes in the preparation of their citizens for lifelong learning in a 21st Century Knowledge-based or Information Society. Preparation of young people to successfully face the challenges of the modern society has become an increasingly important objective of educational systems all over the world. Numerous international and national initiatives reflect the growing interest. A detailed work programme on future objectives of education and training systems up to 2010 has been elaborated (Commission of the European Communities, 2008).

DOI: 10.4018/978-1-4666-2943-1.ch006

Predominant theories of the development of formal education (at least in the industrialised world) are based on the premise that learning is an epistemological problem involving individual psychological processes that lead to the acquisition of knowledge (Lave, 2008). Thus, an individual constructive view sees learners as active agents who construct knowledge in the form of their own internal model of 'the world', as a result of interactions within it.

There are many variations on how to define 21st century skills. A group of business leaders, educators and lawmakers in Massachusetts have elaborated five areas for the 21st century learner's education (Massachusetts Department of Elementary & Secondary Education, 2008):

1.  *Core Academic Subjects*, reading, world languages, arts, math, economics, science, geography, history, government, and civics.
2.  *Interdisciplinary Themes* to be woven into each subject include global awareness, financial, economic, business and entrepreneur literacy, civic literacy, and health literacy.
3.  *Learning and Innovation Skills* including creativity, innovation, critical thinking, problem solving, communication, and collaboration.
4.  *Information, Media and Technology Skills* required by today's students include information and media literacy, communications and technology literacy.
5.  *Life and Career Skills*, needed to navigate in today's world, include flexibility, adaptability, initiative and self-direction, social and cross-cultural skills, productivity, accountability, leadership, and responsibility.

In order to summarize the debates on key competencies, the world institutions, such as OECD (Ananiadou & Claro, 2009), UNESCO (2008a, 2008b, 2008c), and European Commission (2005, 2007) launched surveys and settled several recommendations.

We have discussed the idea that 21st century students will learn to think both critically and creatively, be skilled at working collaboratively, and understand how to take risks constructively. They will learn and understand their connection to the world around them, use technology to pursue research and communicate with others, feel comfortable working in teams and will develop the strength and skills to assume leadership responsibilities.

Digital literacy, media, ICT and other modern technology-based skills are essential requirements for the 21st century learner's education. ICT competency and skills are important for every citizen in a modern society.

The fact that these skills have never been the focus in traditional education is a serious problem. Delivery and acquisition of these skills in teaching and learning to students of primary and secondary education will require a shift in what we teach, how we teach it, the tools we use and how we educate, train, nurture and retain our teachers and school leaders. The overarching challenge for all educators today is to rethink not only what they teach, but "how they empower students to use that information" (Murnane & Levy, 2004).

We cannot change how our students learn unless our teachers are equipped to teach in new ways. Research shows that a teacher's qualification has a significant effect on student's performance, more than any other variable (Barber & Moursched, 2007). It is unreasonable to expect that our students will ever gain the skills and knowledge to succeed in the 21st century, if they are taught primarily by educators trained using a model developed in the 19th century. It is necessary to rethink and overhaul the teacher training and professional development programs, in order to recruit and retain high achieving educators who have up-to-date knowledge of [omit –the] 21st century skills.

A recent study by McKinsey & Co. on the common characteristics of the most successful school systems highlights the central role of teachers, asserting that 'the quality of an education system cannot exceed the quality of its teachers' and that 'the only way to improve outcomes is to improve instruction' (Barber & Mourtsched, 2007).

21st century teachers should be high achievers who model the behaviour they expect their students to learn. Through the use of team projects and the latest technology they will maintain a focus on core academic skills and use their classrooms as labs for students to explore, create and work together. They will participate in professional development opportunities to keep their skills up-to-date, and collaborate with their colleagues to share the best practices.

This paper deals with teachers' ICT competence today in Lithuanian higher education and how we can move them forward. We are going to focus on the role of ICT in pre-service teacher education – the education and training provided for student teachers (future teachers) before they have undertaken any kind of teaching.

## 2. THE 21ST CENTURY TEACHERS' ICT COMPETENCY AND SKILLS

The problems of teachers' ICT competence as well as the content, teaching and assessment methods of the teacher training programmes are very relevant to education worldwide. Let us begin with the definition of the terms 'skills' and 'competency'. The European Commission's Cedefop glossary (Cedefop, 2008) defines a skill as the "ability to perform tasks and solve problems", while a competency is the ability to apply learning outcomes adequately in a defined context (education, work etc.). It is clear that a competency is more than a skill; actually, it comprises skills as well as attitudes and knowledge. ICT competency can be considered as having many components, e.g., technical and pedagogical components.

The UNESCO ICT-Competency Standards for Teachers Project (UNESCO, 2008a, 2008b, 2008c) was launched marking the culmination of many attempts made by governments, academia,

and the private sector to establish a universal terminology or standards for ICT integration into teachers' professional development. Most of the sixteen OECD countries or regions that responded to the questionnaire have guidelines or regulations regarding the teaching and/or assessment of what is considered to be 21st century skills.

The ICT-Competency Standards for Teachers provide guidelines for all teachers, specifically for planning teacher education programs and training offerings that will prepare them to play an essential role in producing technologically capable students. To live, learn, and work successfully in an information and knowledge-based society, students and teachers must utilize the technology effectively.

A framework for conceptualising the teachers' competencies in the OECD study can be thought of in terms of three dimensions: information, communication and ethics and social impact (Ananiadau & Claro, 2009).

In developing the ICT Competency Standards for Teachers, UNESCO identified three productivity factors that lead to growth based on an increased human capacity (UNESCO, 2008c):

- **Technology literacy, e.g. capital deepening:** The ability of the workforce to use equipment that is more productive than earlier versions;
- **Knowledge deepening, e.g. higher quality labour:** A more knowledgeable workforce that is able to add value to economic output;
- **Knowledge creation, e.g. technological innovation:** The ability of the workforce to create, distribute, share and use the new knowledge.

Productivity factors serve as the basis for all the three complementary, somewhat overlapping, approaches to both pre-service and in-service teacher education: to increase the technological mastering skills of all kinds of educators, to increase their ability to use knowledge to add value to the society and economy by applying it in solving complex, real-world problems, to increase the ability of educators in innovating and producing new knowledge and to benefit from that new knowledge.

21st century educators are challenged to acquire various skills such as a deep understanding of the content and relevance for today's global economy of the subject(s) they teach, as well as reasoning, problem-solving, critical thinking, and technological competence. These educators should also develop their ability to help students use the technology effectively as well as to collaborate successfully. Finally, they must be committed to improve instructional practice

The successful integration of ICT into the classroom will depend on the ability of teachers to structure the learning environment in non-traditional ways, to merge the new technology with new pedagogy, and to develop socially active classrooms by encouraging a cooperative interaction, collaborative learning, and group work.

Teachers' professional development and the educational reform of new technologies demand new teacher roles, new pedagogies, and new approaches to teacher education and training. This requires the development of a different set of classroom management skills. The main key skills of the future will include the ability to develop innovative ways of using technology to enhance the learning environment, and to encourage technology literacy, knowledge deepening and knowledge creation.

During our national discussions on the UNESCO ICT Competency Standards for Teachers project with policy makers, researchers and teachers, we have noticed that:

1. We focus too much on the technological use of ICT, however, in some areas, many teachers have not attained a sufficient level of technology literacy as yet.

2. We need to rethink our national ICT Competency Standards for Teachers, using the UNESCO standards as a framework.
3. Major goals should be to concentrate on reaching Knowledge Deepening and, in some components, Knowledge Creation levels in the 10-year development for 2010–2020.

## 3. PEDAGOGICAL COMPONENT OF THE TEACHERS' ICT COMPETENCY

OECD proposed three different categories for grouping skills and competencies (Ananiadou & Claro, 2009):

- *ICT functional skills* that include the skills relevant to mastering the use of different ICT applications;
- *ICT skills for learning* which include the skills that combine both cognitive abilities and higher-order thinking skills as well as the functional skills for the use and management of ICT applications;
- *21st century skills* which bring together the skills considered necessary in a knowledge society, but where the use of ICT is not a necessary condition.

The ICT functional skills are more like content-based academic subjects such as history or chemistry and could be taught as such, while the ICT skills for learning pay more attention to learning outcomes.

Research suggests that countries that have reached a certain level of 'ICT-maturity', the Nordic countries, for example, where ICT has penetrated people's lives, including schools, are moving away from teaching ICT as a separate school subject.

For developing the teachers' ICT competency in Lithuania the Standard Requirements are elaborated in 2007 (Emokykla, 2007). In conformity with the approved requirements, an ICT literate teacher, while participating in the teaching and learning process and using technology, should know and be able to:

1. Creatively individualise their subject's teaching and learning content;
2. Purposefully use ICT tools;
3. Systematically and reasonably apply teaching and learning approaches;
4. Plan the use of today's technologies;
5. Manage the resources in the teaching and learning process;
6. Evaluate and reflect on topics regarding the use of ICT.

The general model of teachers' ICT competency has been elaborated mainly focusing on the pedagogical component of ICT competency (see Figure 1).

The model of teachers' pedagogical ICT competency consists of the three-level skills as well as assessments of ICT competency:

**Level I:** Teachers know ICT tools and are able to use them in order to enrich the traditional educational process;

**Level II:** Teachers purposefully plan, organise and evaluate their own activities while applying ICT, improve the educational process by purposefully using ICT, and pay enhanced attention to computer networks and a constructivist learning paradigm (integrated learning, project-based learning, and collaborative learning);

**Level III:** Teachers help their colleagues actively participate in the dissemination of the experience of ICT application in education in their schools, towns, regions and country.

In order to train the pedagogical component of ICT competency a particular course has been prepared for Lithuanian teachers by the researchers of the Institute of Mathematics and Informatics (Dagienė, Zajančkauskienė, & Žilinskienė, 2008). The course consists of three main components: 1) competencies (goals); 2) topics and explanations (content); 3) learning activities (teaching, learning and assessment methods) delivered through six modules (see Figure 2).

In order to improve teachers' pedagogical ICT competency, it is proposed that teachers prepare their own electronic portfolio (e-portfolio) where

*Figure 1. Teachers' ICT competency model in Lithuania*

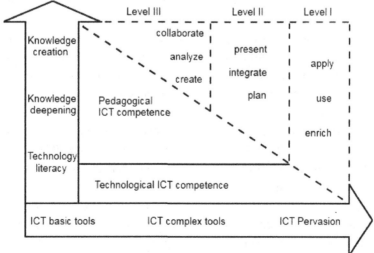

*Figure 2. Modules for developing teachers' pedagogical ICT competency*

| Module | Competence | Level I | Level II | Level III |
|---|---|---|---|---|
| Use of ICT in primary and special education | individualize the contest creatively | enrich | integrate | apply |
| Use of ICT in primary and special education: presentation | use ICT purposively | apply | use | help others |
| Innovative teaching approaches | apply learning approaches reasonably | use | apply, select | help others |
| Working with Learning Objects | plan ICT activities | | evaluate | plan, systemize |
| Application of Learning Objects | manage the resources | | organize | work virtually |
| Virtual Learning Environment | evaluate and reflect the use of ICT | | make presentation | reflect |

they are able to collect activity documents that corroborate the ICT application experience.

The following Section is aimed at analysing the pre-service teachers' opinion survey on the implementation of teachers' ICT competency model in their universities and colleges.

## 4. SURVEY ON PRE-SERVICE TEACHER EDUCATION OF ICT IN LITHUANIAN UNIVERSITIES AND COLLEGES

The re-design of the pre-service teacher education, license and professional development systems is aimed at attracting, retaining and nurturing high-achieving educators. It is important to enable them to obtain a rigorous, technology-rich education, supplemented by a high-quality pedagogical experience and training from instructors with broad, recent applications in a modern society. Our goal is to create a system to ensure that all teacher education professional development programs include appropriate 21st century skills.

To this end, the scientists of the Institute of Mathematics and Informatics conducted research on the analysis of problems, called "Teachers' Training on ICT Applications in Education" (Emokykla, 2009).

The research methodology consists of the following: (1) the processing of the origins, data analysis (including the analysis of ICT-related study programmes of Lithuanian higher education institutions); (2) a written questionnaire-based survey of educational specialty students; (3) statistical analysis of the data; (4) insight – formulation of conclusions and recommendations, based on the qualitative data analysis.

The structure of the research attributes in the questionnaire to measure the teacher's ICT competency was as follows: socio-demographic attributes – 5; ICT literacy (technological, informational, social) – 27; the content of the teachers' training programmes – 28; ICT application methods for competency teaching and assessment– 26; the direct conformance of ICT competency with the skills indicated in the approved requirements on teachers' computer literacy programmes – 16; integral educational ICT competency (pedagogical and managerial) – 34. The total number of the attributes analysed is 136.

Sixteen Lithuanian higher education institutions have been selected for the research. All have a pre-service teacher education strand, (bachelor's and master's degree, and special pedagogical studies). Last year, 648 education strand students were examined during the research. The number of examined students was chosen pro rata with the number of the students in the pedagogical strand studies in higher schools. The research sample is purposive, stochastic and criteria-based.

84% of women and 16% of men have participated in the research. According to the survey results 49% of the respondents plan to do a teacher's job in schools, 23% do not plan to be teachers, and 27% have not yet decided. 81% of the respondents have a laptop or a table computer at home.

## 4.1. The Existing Pre-Service Programmes on the Teachers' ICT Competency

During the research, 190 university and 39 college pedagogical study programmes were analysed. Usually only two or three credits are scheduled for ICT-based learning (excluding informatics study programmes). This is obviously an insufficient number. Almost all the programmes are similar to that of the other (non-pedagogical) specialties, i.e., the students are trained in the general skills of how to use the computer and application software. Only a few of the study programmes have been prepared as courses especially for ICT application in education, regarding the topic specificity, didactical attitudes, teaching methods and methodology. The majority of the study programmes are quite obsolete and not renewable.

## 4.2. The Technological part of ICT literacy

In conformity with the requirements (Emokykla, 2007), before taking the course on ICT pedagogical issues, teachers have to pass the course on the ICT technological part. According to the survey, the technological component of ICT competency is quite good in pre-service teacher preparation in the higher institutions of Lithuania.

Our pre-service teachers have mastered mostly all of the essential technology-based ICT knowledge and skills (see Figure 3).

According to the survey, the best indicators deal with the general activities of working with a computer: text processing, surfing the internet, emailing and using other communication tools as well as file processing, printing, etc. The worst indicators refer to the understanding of authors' (intellectual property) rights, and knowledge about the viruses.

## 4.3. Pedagogical ICT Competency

An important question to be answered is whether the concept of pedagogical orientation could help us better conceive how to use ICT in learning and teaching. In particular, whether pedagogical orientation matters in terms of the impact of ICT use on students' learning outcomes. Investigation of the teachers' pedagogical ICT competency showed significantly positive findings in students' performance especially in math and science (Emokykla, 2008).

Pedagogical ICT competency can be understood as comprised of many components (features), e. g., preparations of lessons where students use ICT; knowledge of pedagogical situations suitable for ICT use; finding useful curriculum resources on the internet; using the internet to support student learning; using ICT to monitor students' progress and evaluate students' learning outcomes; using ICT to give effective presentations; using ICT to collaborate with others.

The survey indicates that most Lithuanian pre-service teachers evaluate their pedagogical ICT competency level very high or high (see Figure 4).

The teacher-respondents believe that the importance of rating ITC applications for educational competency is as follows: (1) to systematically and reasonably apply teaching and learning methods (80%); (2) to evaluate and reflect on topics regarding the use of ICT (79%); (3) to purposefully use ICT tools in the teaching and

*Figure 3. Basic computer literacy skill levels as self-estimated by pre-service teachers*

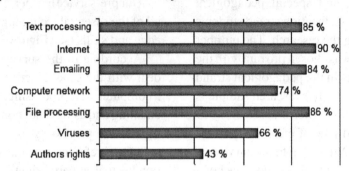

learning process (77%); (4) to plan the use of ICT (76%); (5) to creatively individualise their subject's teaching and learning content (75%); (6) to organise the technological resource management in the teaching and learning process (63%).

In the respondents' opinion, they have obtained the following high ICT competency level during their study: (1) to creatively individualise their subject's teaching and learning content (56%); (2) to systematically and reasonably apply teaching and learning methods (50%); (3) to evaluate and reflect on topics regarding the use of ICT (50%); (4) to purposefully use ICT tools in the teaching and learning process (50%); (5) to organise the technological resource management in the teaching and learning process (38%); (6) to plan the use of ICT (38%).

## 4.4. Self-Evaluation for Future Work at Schools

Lithuanian pre-service teachers believe that: (1) the level of their knowledge on ICT application in the teaching and learning process is enough to work at school (58%); (2) educational ICT training programmes in their higher schools are high quality (46%); (3) they are acquainted with the main methods of ICT application in education (44%); (4) they are acquainted with LOs, their repositories and VLEs (39%); (5) they know enough about the main ICT tools and software

(38%); (6) they know well what Semantic Web technologies are (36%).

During the survey, respondents were asked to think about their future work at school. The respondents estimated that they are most able to do the following jobs after they begin teaching in the schools: (1) they are able to prepare the presentations containing not only the text, but also multimedia information; (2) to work with the students in the class using the digital lesson plans prepared by them; (3) to evaluate and reflect by using ICT in the teaching and learning process.

The respondents also judged that they would not be able to do the following jobs well after returning to their schools: to find ICT application shortages and problems, to learn how to avoid these problems and to teach their colleagues on these topics; to manage the class work using Web 2.0 technologies; to help their colleagues apply ICT in teaching students with special needs. (see more details in Figure 5).

*Figure 4. The level of ICT competency as estimated by pre-service teachers*

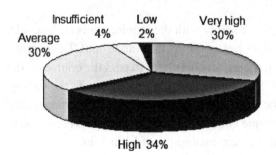

*Figure 5. How pre-service teachers estimate their ICT competency for future work at school*

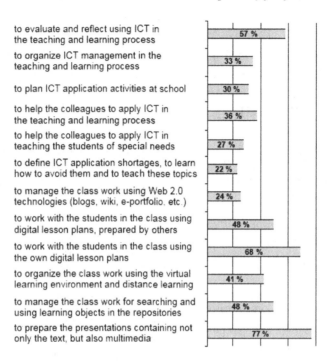

# 5. CONCLUSION AND RECOMMENDATIONS FOR IMPROVING TEACHERS PEDAGOGICAL ICT COMPETENCY

Using technology for teaching is a necessary but not sufficient requirement for developing the knowledge and skills needed in the 21st century. It has to be accompanied by curriculum reform (the content), by changes in teaching methods that facilitate the development of skills in a particular subject area, as well as changes in assessment.

There are few teacher training programmes, beginning or in-service that targets the teaching or development of 21st century skills. There exist several teacher training initiatives that focus on developing teachers' ICT pedagogical skills, however, most of them are optional.

After the survey in Lithuanian higher education for initial teacher education, the recommendations

to higher schools have been formulated. The most important is the staff ability to organise ICT application in education programmes so that future teachers will be able: (1) to estimate ICT application shortages and problems; to learn how to avoid these problems and to teach colleagues on these topics and (2) to manage class work using Web 2.0 technologies; to help colleagues to apply ICT in teaching students with special needs.

We would also like to recommend strong consideration of the following components of teachers ICT pedagogical competency: (1) to creatively individualise the teaching and learning content of their subjects; (2) to purposefully use ICT tools in the teaching and learning process; (3) to plan the use of ICT; (4) to organise the technologic resources management in the teaching and learning process.

# REFERENCES

Ananiadou, K., & Claro, M. (2009). *21st Century skills and competencies for new millennium learners in OECD countries.* Retrieved from http://www.oecd.org/LongAbstract/0,3425,en_2649_35845581_44303186_119684_1_1_1,00.html

Barber, M., & Moursched, M. (2007). *How the world's best-performing school systems come out on top.* London, UK: McKinsey & Co.

Cedefop. (2008). *Terminology of European education and training policy: A selection of 100 key terms.* Luxembourg: Office for Official Publications of the European Communities.

Commission of the European Communities. (2008). *Improving competences for the 21st century: An agenda for European cooperation on schools.* Retrieved from http://ec.europa.eu/education/school21/sec2177_en.pdf

Dagienė, V., Zajančkauskienė, L., & Žilinskienė, I. (2008). Distance learning course for training teachers' ICT competence. In R. T. Mittermeir & M. M. Syslo (Eds.), *Proceedings of the Third International Conference on Informatics Education–Supporting Computational Thinking* (LNCS 5090, pp. 282-292).

Emokykla. (2007). *Reikalavimai mokytojų kompiuterinio raštingumo programoms: Patvirtinta švietimo ir mokslo ministro 2007 m. kovo 29d. įsakymu ISAK-555.* Retrieved from http://www.emokykla.lt/

Emokykla. (2008). *Pedagogų rengimas IKT taikymo aspektu: Mokslinio tyrimo ataskaita.* Retrieved from http://www.emokykla.lt

European Commission. (2005). *Common European principles for teacher competences and qualifications.* Retrieved from http://ec.europa.eu/education/policies/2010/doc/principles_en.pdf

European Commission. (2007). *Key competencies: A developing concept in general compulsory education.* Retrieved from http://www.eurydice.org

International Society for Technology in Education. (2000). *Educational technology standards and performance indicators for all teachers.* Retrieved from http://cnets.iste.org/

Kurilovas, E. (2007). Digital library of educational resources and services: Evaluation of components. *Informacijos Mokslai, 42-43,* 69–77.

Lave, J. (2008). Everyday life and learning. In Murphy, P., & McCormick, R. (Eds.), *Knowledge and practice: Representations and identities* (pp. 3–14). London, UK: Sage.

Law, N., Pelgrum, W. J., & Plomp, T. (2008). *Pedagogy and ICT use in schools around the world.* New York, NY: Springer. doi:10.1007/978-1-4020-8928-2

Massachusetts Department of Elementary & Secondary Education. (2008). *School reform in the new millennium: Preparing all children for 21st century success: Recommendations of the 21st century skills task force.* Malden, MA: Massachusetts Department of Elementary & Secondary Education.

Murnane, R., & Levy, F. (2004). *The new division of labor: How computers are changing the way we work.* Princeton, NJ: Princeton University Press and Russell Sage Foundation.

UNESCO. (2008a). *ICT competency standards for teachers: Competency standard modules.* Retrieved from http://unesdoc.unesco.org/images/0015/001562/156207e.pdf

UNESCO. (2008b). *ICT competency standards for teachers: Implementation guidelines.* Retrieved from http://unesdoc.unesco.org/images/0015/001562/156209E.pdf

UNESCO. (2008c). *ICT competency standards for teachers: Policy framework.* Retrieved from http://unesdoc.unesco.org/images/0015/001562/156210E.pdf

*This work was previously published in the International Journal of Digital Literacy and Digital Competence, Volume 2, Issue 2, edited by Antonio Cartelli, pp. 1-10, copyright 2011 by IGI Publishing (an imprint of IGI Global).*

# Chapter 7
# Technological Literacy in the Profile of Skills of University Professor in the New European Higher Education System

**Antonella Nuzzaci**
*University of Valle d'Aosta, Italy*

## ABSTRACT

*This article describes the new requirements of the European Higher Education Area (EHEA) - international and cross-cultural, Information and Communication Technologies (ICTs) that are important in all fields of university studies and take on a central role for learning and teaching. The literature review showed that, despite the considerable attention focused on the technological know-how of university teaching, few studies have examined the characteristics of these actors. The purpose is to focus more on teachers, clearly defining the technological skills necessary to develop the new European System of Higher Education in order to facilitate the development of skills, general learning, disciplinary, and professional digital education. This paper analyzes why this adaptation is necessary, the difficulties encountered, the objectives, and the response of teachers to these changes. On the other hand, university education acts on three fronts: the integration and use of new educational technologies in universities, the European convergence and application of ICT, the innovation and education needed to bridge the gap between universities, and teachers facing reality, both socially and professionally. This study contributes to the debate on the interactions between academic literacy, technological skills, and employment prospects for university teachers.*

DOI: 10.4018/978-1-4666-2943-1.ch007

## 1. THE ROLE OF TECHNOLOGIES IN THE NEW INTERNATIONAL AND CROSS-CULTURAL UNIVERSITY

The key challenge for universities today is to respond effectively to all the social changes and developments required by the new European higher education system, both in terms of governance and, cultural policy, which involves a gradual process of integration of a perspective, international, intercultural and/or global in scopes, functions (teaching, research and services) and universities' mission (Knight, 1997). The forces behind this transformation, clearly illustrated by Ward (2000), oblige the various institutions to question tasks, roles, and academic skills and to create learning environments that foster innovative educational and professional perspectives which produce new guidelines, standards, objectives and practices which attempt to secure the interests of all stakeholders and meet the needs of increasingly diversified student populations.

For example, the rapid increase in demand from senior students to access higher education is forcing universities across Europe, often located in a trans-national and trans-cultural region, to confront themselves with cross-curricular courses and unusual educational strategies aimed at curbing the current forms of social exclusion (Ribble & Bailey, 2005; Ribble, Bailey, & Ross, 2004; Underwood & Szabo, 2003, 2004; Van Soest, Canon, & Grant, 2000). On the other hand, the emergence, alongside the more traditional functions, such as education (construction of knowledge and skills) and research (production of knowledge and competence), of lifelong learning, perceived as a "continuous process by which every human being may extend and adapt his/her knowledge and skills, the ability to give an opinion and act on it" (Knežević-Floric, 2008, p. 201), should enable individuals throughout their lives to pursue virtuous learning paths and continuously update their cultural and professional profiles (Cranton, 1996). According to Knezevic-Floric (2008), in

fact, the first step in lifelong learning is made when a more flexible understanding, assessment and enhancement of various forms of education and training is obtained.

In this sense, the technologies from an educational point of view are considered appropriate means to provide university teaching staff with the opportunity to prepare appropriate educational activities and actions to ensure a quality education to all categories of subjects (Alkan, 2005). For this reason, Europe has made a long-term commitment to press universities for technological innovation (Distance Education Report, 2000), especially with reference to teachers' competences (Aho Report, 2008) that could determine a multiple access to higher education by those segments of the population traditionally excluded from the university (Galliani, Zaggia, & Serbati, 2011), that obliges us to rethink teaching and research in a new way. However, if it is true that learning is the prevailing paradigm of the new cyber communities (Haterick, 2000), it is unthinkable that, as a consequence, teaching does not need to develop multimodal strategic interventions intended to effectively meet the emerging training needs of those populations, thus allowing academics to take charge of specific responsibilities towards the teaching offer.

It is well known, however, how the new technological equipment and infrastructure require highly qualified personnel both from a technical and pedagogical point of view ; in higher education contexts which are constantly evolving, this would necessarily shift the "teaching mediation" paradigm with a direct fallout on the development of cognitive processes, the reflection of the conditions that characterize the teaching-learning processes, assessment of learning contexts (Quellmalz & Kozma, 2003) or educational equipment, with the prospect of matching the new trans-national needs in terms of means and tools, for the development and coordination of the ever- increasing activities at different academic, educational and research levels.

In many cases, these activities involve not only teachers and students from universities in different European countries, but also require the creation of links with businesses, public and private institutions, local and national governments, international organizations and bodies that have a significant impact on educational and research purposes, producing a reflection on the characteristics of culture, their elements, constitution and nature of their relations, as well as the modes of its construction.

Faculties, Departments, Courses, Inter-University Centers etc. of several European universities are facing issues, such as the need to create structures of trans-national assessment, transversal information and communication strategies and cross-culturally comprehensive curricula that encourage institutions to provide the academic communities not only with technological instruments, but also the effective capacity to use them productively, taking into account the emerging trends, such as those related to the size of the gradual "techno-methodological half-casting" process, "interculturalizing" and educational technology.

Since then, the new "internationalized university" promoted by the Bologna Process (1999) incorporates a set of institutions, disciplines, organizations (private and public), etc. both locally and internationally, which are constantly re-arranging the European Higher Education System and must ensure the cooperation among all stakeholders (teachers, students, administrators, etc.). In all stages of the process, from the conception of the educational and scientific knowledge, to its design, dissemination and implementation at trans-national level, technologies point to the possibility of bringing about such a collaboration in a short time and accounting for the transparency of the offer stated in the courses and programs, and in the structuring of curricula, the harmonization of credits, the choice of investments in education and research resources, and so on, establishing themselves as agents of change involving those primarily responsible for this cultural system, i.e. university professors.

But to hit the above target we should consider a profile of the university professor closer to the new roles he/she's called to play, not least that of teaching students to review the cognitive experiences, including the technological ones which they could face. As an example, we may consider that in order to improve teaching methods and develop more appropriate means of intervention, it would be appropriate for institutions, before planning the deployment of e-learning training programs, the recruitment of competent and knowledgeable staff in order to manage their teaching activities correctly, so as to improve the quality of the educational offer.

In fact, it is well known how technology helps to build and share knowledge, improving and enhancing the learning of university professors and their teaching in all subject areas and forms of experience. In this sense, the collaboration among European universities is working to provide educational and international research services, able to go beyond the national rationale with implications for study abroad programs, for the types of mobility enabled, the definition of curricular activities, the mapping of new professional profiles, etc. and for a wide range of issues related to certification and recognition of credits among different countries.

Therefore a realignment of the European institutional missions and visions of technology may be necessary, in order to govern the transnational flow of teachers and students and the different types of partnership among the institutions, also calling for a rethinking of the relationships between teaching and learning, discipline and professional practice, research and social commitment, which could be enhanced by an attitude of awareness and responsibility in choosing and using different technologies, both in terms of technological literacy (knowledge of technology) and technology integration (teaching with technology).

A development of the European higher education system in fact, must ensure full access to information and communication technologies to both the student and the teaching population (Dani & Koenig, 2008). In fact, the increasing of educational and professional opportunities and the modification or innovation of the educational instruments becomes impossible to attain without such access, as does the opportunity to ensure an ever growing and authentic participation of the different national academic communities in the international scientific activities.

## 2. THE RELATIONSHIP BETWEEN "CORE COMPETENCIES" OF THE TEACHING PROFESSION AND "TECHNOLOGICAL LITERACY"

ICTs are thus playing a key role in helping to rewrite the teaching, learning and research environments, and in redefining the new dynamics of intellectual work in an information society which is constantly changing the institutions and reshaping the contours of their educational, organizational and managerial forms. They are therefore an increasingly strong "lever", even though much advertised but little practiced, which may act to make qualitatively relevant both the teaching and learning experience.

However, a serious effort to become integrated within the university, entails not only an investment in educational research on learning "with and through" technology, which accepts the idea that it helps to de-construct and re-conceptualize the pedagogical and scientific discourse and meta-discourse, but also the very manner of learning and teaching. This inevitably leads to the development and increase of specific skills, to a change in teaching methodologies, the sense of design and co-design, the planning and methods for providing education, tools to support the students' ability to search, organize, manage, evaluate and communicate information, and the practices of assessment.

This happens because the technologies have created the need for new skills such as those necessary to gather, analyze and use information resources, in order to answer questions, solve problems and make decisions (Kasper, 2000a, 2000b). To find, to understand and to use the information on the web, for example, together with searching and navigating strategies, as well as summarizing and critically thinking (Reinking, 1998; Laddo & Reinking, 1999), are "cognitive and action systems" which increase the repertoires of skills within a classical concept of "literacy", which will continue to change dynamically in the future because of the interdependence between technology and teaching.

Therefore the extension of the meaning of literacy over time (Lankshear & Knobel, 2003), which has come to include in its different acceptations a variety of contexts (Burkhardt et al., 2003), not only the technological ones (Leu, 2002), compels a re-conceptualization of educational knowledge, implying an interdisciplinary crossing that clearly requires the possession of transversal skills such as interpersonal abilities. The relevant agreement that seems to exist regarding the definition of "technological literacy", the broad concept of which includes it in what is defined as "the age of digital literacy" (International Technology Education Association, 2000) and involves considerations on basic scientific, economic, and visual literacy, information, multicultural and global awareness, depends on the fact that the range of available technologies, from an educational point of view is today quite extensive, as is the spectrum of educational issues that it is able to solve. Thus the creation of new technologies and their expansion will require a continuous enhancement of skills in both these areas.

Gagel (1997) suggested that some common elements of "technological literacy" include the knowledge of specific details which belong to the individual technologies and their development process as well as to at least four kinds of expertise, "hosting and managing the rapid and continuous technological change; generating creative and innovative solutions to technological problems, working through technological knowledge to be effective and efficient; assessing technology and its presence in the human world wisely" (p. 25). In this regard, Prime (1998) defines technological literacy as a set of knowledge and expertise that contains those knowledge areas which revolve around problems that could be solved by technology, the social and cultural effects that the latter produces, the prerequisites required for the other disciplines (e.g. mathematics) and the shape or structure of technological knowledge.

This involves the acquisition of skills which are both manipulative and cognitive (e.g., evaluation, analytical thinking, creativity, problem solving, research, analysis, design), as well as emotional skills, recalling their ability to act technologically in an adequate and proper manner, making appropriate technology choices, considering the ethical implications that these decisions have on educational outcomes, as well as the attitudes of independence and interdependence, care, concern for the environment-technology training, social responsibility, habits and technological behaviour which produce a positive effect. As a result of this assertion, university professors will need more than just knowledge and technical ability to use these technologies, they will be asked to reflect on the set of knowledge and skills necessary to receive and implement the technologies of tomorrow.

Clearly, in an internationalized university the "state of teaching" changes, because the way we write, design and use technology resources, included in teacher training, also changes (Baylor & Ritchie, 2002) by means of the acquisition of specific skills, a fundamental factor to understand and be aware of is the importance of such integration. In this sense, the technologies used in the processes of internationalization of the university system are forcing teachers to adopt new ways of conceiving their discipline and teaching methods,

producing epistemological implications among which we find:

- Alternative ways of knowing and validating what we know, which is the meaning of truth and reality;
- Expansion and infusion of unknown ways of understanding the formulation and implementation of curricula, learning objectives, methodologies and teaching strategies;
- The definition of areas of research and disciplinary issues, with undoubted influence on society, culture and goals of the organizations themselves;
- The acquisition of new knowledge of a certain culture and its educational practices;
- Operability on cultural knowledge teaching in relation to certain constraints and interactive communication;
- The identification and comparison of symbols, objects or products of their own educational culture with those of another country to achieve integration;
- Critical evaluation (critical cultural awareness) on the basis of clearly identified criteria, perspectives, practices and educational products of a culture with those of other cultures in other countries;
- Examination of the educational aspects of the disciplines inherent to the view of researchers and teachers from other countries.

These elements upgrade the "academic expertise" to a stronger educational role, since the process of infusion technology transforms the teachers' mental processes and their actions (Gimbert & Cristol, 2004. pp. 207-216). Able to act when there is a lack of homogeneity in terms of professional development, difficult conditions in the classroom, asset management support and feedback to students, a lack of alignment with the practices of teaching methods and classroom research, technology supports the "academic literacy" of the teacher and his professional device when he/she is able to apply it in concrete situations in carrying out its functions of research and education contexts and different teaching-learning process, when he/she is able to modify and adapt to technological change and to diversify his/her approach and use of new technologies to fulfill the needs and to adapt to the emerging interests of students and those working in field of study and research. Chickering and Ehrmann (1996) suggest that teaching methods are at the center of this discourse rather than the technological aspects. These methods seem to increase learning more than technology itself.

Obviously for the purposes of an internationalized university, technology certainly becomes something more than just a "learning tool" to evolve into a true "professional style of teaching". Therefore, the fundamental problem for the teacher is tied to the type of design adopted and the way they support students' with and through technology, as in the case of blended learning, e-learning, distance learning, etc. Because the technologies to communicate and disseminate information have a great potential impact on teaching practice, it is unlikely that the concern, more or less widely implied that teaching methods will drop in quality, will prove to be justified.

Technological innovation may be able to produce more efficient and effective teaching and learning activities at a local, national and international level, when used for strategic purposes, in particular contexts and areas (Valdez, McNabb, Foertsch, Anderson, Hawkes, & Raack, 2000) and if conceived as a "keystone" to increase the quality of teaching and learning, as well as research, in a situation where European higher education is currently experiencing a state of "stalemate" and a continuing reduction of resources for teaching and research facilities. However, the current debate on the role and use of new technologies in the higher education system, both in terms of teaching and research, on what leads to the discussion of the

criteria that the university community processes to define what qualifies something (in terms of technology) as being of high academic quality, and currently indicates the need for empirical evidence and research methods with a scientific basis (Ehrmann, 1997, 1999) that confirms the usefulness of technology (Roblyer & Knezek, 2003; Dede, 2004; Hostetler, 2005; Thompson, 2005), as has been happening since 2001 in the United States for the No Child Left Behind Act (NCBL), the SBR, which is trying to conduct analysis and measurements which examine the relationship between technology and teaching-learning processes. This debate will surely advance the 'high quality' of educational research in terms of technology, but is raising questions about the application of these devices both in the classroom and in the laboratory. In this sense the "intercultural academic territory technologized/internationalized" reveals the emerging challenges that educational research must address, that is to say, how to:

- Reflect on the meaning of an educational-programming technology;
- Explore ways of coordinating programs, activities and educational technological trans-cultural interventions
- Study how to incorporate technology issues in the design of cross-cultural curricula and courses and integrate new skills and knowledge in academic practices (Byram & Zarate 1997);
- Study the way teachers teach and learn to teach technology in the sense of cultural diversity;
- Describe technological skills and knowledge of past teachers, their level of literacy and academic multiliteracy, as well as technological multilingual mastery;
- Describe the outfits of professional skills necessary to make a technologically competent teacher;

- Study the relationship between trans-cultural and technological forms of access and use them with respect to other forms of knowledge;
- Find ways of developing learning environments and situations which promote technological forms of intercultural communication and quality relationships in heterogeneous environments with diverse groups;
- Identify valid ways of facilitating teaching methods which meet the students' technological, cultural, linguistic and academic needs and the devices required to support them effectively;
- Understand how teachers learn and implement teaching practices and assessment supported by technology and take into proper account the cross-cultural dimension of European higher education system;
- Understand how explicit and implicit reference models of technological, institutional and social norms, values, beliefs, meanings, conventions, practices, are at a didactic level.
- Define the levels and areas of ambiguity in the language of academic discourse technology and its mode of operation in a trans-cultural context.

The numerous magazines and international organizations that demonstrate the interest which exists in Europe for the extensive use and application of ICT, both as a means of training and research, have revealed new issues about mechanisms of the professionalization of academics, as their unequal preparation requires us to reconsider how they participate in university community life, which is of concern, as the gap widens between those who possess the necessary skills and those who do not. The fact that some teachers are able to use technology while others are not, forces us to ask specific questions about the precise iter of "training for teaching and research", particularly

for those who are to work in the field of educational research. And although it is understandable that this question cannot be addressed only at a scientific level but also needs to be interpreted in terms of the financing of ICT policies, the problem of the technological professionalization of university teachers throughout their career is now a discussion which cannot be postponed.

## THE ICT FOR QUALITY EDUCATION: MULTILITERACY, TEACHING SKILLS AND TECHNOLOGY

As we have said before, what concerns us here is to discuss in particular the use of ICT for the improvement of teaching, dealing with the problem of its use and aims, according to the needs and skills of the university professor that is to live in an internationalized university. In general, the various surveys indicate that most academics are favorable to the integration of ICT in teaching, but at the same time, stress the lack of instrumentation and skills necessary to its exploitation for educational purposes. It follows that we need to refine the objectives and policies for ICT integration in the domain of higher education, which, even if currently heavily promoted in all disciplines, models of teaching and research, is not always able to function as a powerful driver of development in university, or in cultural and socio-economic contexts. However, it is well known that the development of skills of university teachers in this area remains long overdue, as the training methods are not always suitable to meet the technical needs of teaching and research (the Bologna Process has given great importance to the 3rd cycle - postgraduate studies/students - Research and Doctoral degree program), it is clear that such training involves all levels of education with the task of preparing individuals and communities to cope with this new way of providing information and knowledge. The University is required to equip the teachers, first and foremost, with the technological skills that enable them to develop, produce and disseminate knowledge in new ways and thus, facilitate the adjustment of their action to the academic, socio-economic and professional requirements, in a society which is increasingly global in nature. Already in 1999 Arnold stated that the new technologies were able to create appropriate learning environments in science and in the knowledge society and in his book "Virtual University" he provided an overview of ICT in the European system, concluding that the impact of information technology on teaching and university research would have probably been profound, swift, but also discontinuous. New technologies not only influence the intellectual activities of the university (learning, teaching and research), but also change the way in which these are organized, financed and governed, acting on the operation of universities themselves and the ways in which knowledge is generated, processed and distributed, and this does not happen, as is generally believed, only within the university campus and in the contexts of distance or virtual education. The achievement of these goals is a priority for the involvement and motivation of university teachers, as outlined in the Aho report by the European Community (2008) which finds the teachers obliged to deal with the rapid evolution of technology (Weisbord, 1987) to understand the nature and significance of technological change (the ability to read and understand the technical language of technology and its symbols), in contextualising (Ruml & Brache, 1988) and controlling the emerging technology. A key aspect however is given by the educational policies which a university professor adopts when using technology, these policies create a series of conditions which characterize authentic learning activities (Newman & Wehlage, 1993): an analysis based on an in-depth knowledge, dependence on higher order thinking, substantive dialogue, social support for learners and the applicability of learning to the real professional world. The university is the place where, within specific "fields and scientific

thought, students are taught to develop and produce knowledge, to demonstrate, to monitor, and to give positive feedback which has an impact on the students' capabilities (Chen & Shaw, 2006). Kester, Kirschner, and Corbalan (2005) describe them as a place of learning in which tasks are complex, students' motivation is intrinsic, and dialogue and debate play an integral part. In this direction, several researchers such as Biggs (1999) and Onwuegbuzie, Witcher, Collins, Filer, Wiedmaier and Moore (2007) addressed the issue of quality in university education (Norton, Richardson, Hartley, Newstead, & Mayes, 2005), noting, for example, that college students believe teachers are effective when they prove to be professional and experienced, when they show reactivity and enthusiasm, when they focus on students, when they provide multiple opportunities to interact and communicate critical information clearly and accurately, when they organize the learning environment so that time is spent productively and the environment is functional, but also when teachers:

- Encourage the student-faculty contact;
- Nurture cooperation among students;
- Support active learning;
- Provide rapid feedback to students;
- Stress the importance of "time" with respect to the learning task;
- Communicate expectations with respect to the characteristics and ways of learning.

The extent to which these dimensions of effectiveness of education are met, is influenced not only by the teacher's characteristics, but also the techniques and means by which the proposal is provided, some of which may work well for some tasks but not for others, permitting the students to decide whether or not to proceed autonomously with their own learning tasks (Ormrod, 2004). While there is a clear and widespread agreement about the fact that today both teachers and students need to be experienced users of technology, 'technological literacy' is one of the terms that most frequently appear among the mapping skills profiles of university teachers (Nuzzaci, 2011), because it constitutes a form of cultural literacy required to operate in the international academic community which exists in a culturally diverse and pluralistic society. Even if there are other elements which are invoked as essential, such as the ability to capitalize on the educational potential offered by technological resources that links two aspects of the growing cultural complexity of the teaching and learning processes, namely: the proliferation of ways of reading and building multimodal meaning where language (verbal and written) is increasingly an integral part of visual and audio communication and of spatial patterns and on the other hand, the growing importance of cultural and linguistic diversity characterized by local diversity and global connectedness.

In response to this phenomenon, however, describing the responsibilities of "technological literacy" (Siegle, 2004) is merely a first step to ensure that all teachers become competent users of technology, because beside it, a new literacy for teachers must be supported (New London Group, 1996) to ensure that the university professor is able to really take advantage of the growing variety of new information technologies and media and become "multi-literate", or in other words, a professional socially and cognitively literate in all modes of communication (Anstey & Bull, 2006). This is necessary in order to choose appropriate forms to define the knowledge to teach, to express them in concrete ways, to involve students in the process of the elaboration of meaning, leadership and guidance in the construction of meaning, which lead to the acquisition of skills and gradually allow students to self-orient themselves and to gain the ability to manage personal and self-knowledge.

The interest and the value of this approach lies in its flexibility and the huge possibilities for using technology, according to the characteristics, needs, skills, etc. thus gradually changing the ways the teacher has to read the academic world, which continues to grow and change. As literary forms change, so too does technology, thus requiring new modes of approaching teaching and science. Recognizing the importance of providing technology tools and programs that work effectively to improve learning outcomes for students (Huerta-Macias, 2002; Bucker & Lamboy, 2002, 2003; Monroe, 2004; Moran & Payne, 1998) now becomes indispensable, as does the improvement and maintenance of a strong link between technology and pedagogy, that link requires much more than just providing infrastructure for technology literacy, as this regularly alters the rules of academic culture by requiring universities to have a faculty, capable of expressing technological and complex cognitive skills of a higher order (Kirkwood & Price, 2005). It happens all too often, that the ability of teachers is even lower than that of the students and the institutions, even though in some cases, these institutions are physically equipped with advanced technological systems, they still fail to achieve integrated policies in support of the faculty because of the teachers' lack of appropriate technological skills, they fail to support the students adequately (Anderson & Dexter, 2005; Donlevy, 2003; Hartnell-Young, 2006). However, to detect and assess the academics' need for technology is not an easy task: it is expensive to measure their "professional status" and the progress made so far.

This new vision of literacy which today is becoming more and more the object of approval is central to the orientation of the process of the university teacher's professionalization. This new conception implies a view of learning and teaching which must be closely intertwined and socially distributed. The transformation of "literacy" will help, with the contribution of technology, to become a "multiliteracy" social construction that forces the teacher to evolve into a "multi-literate" subject, capable of understanding the differentiation of distinctive forms of literacy in the different areas where it is expressed in the curriculum and to determine the distinction between practical forms of the reproductive type of literacy and those of the critical reflexive kind. To become multi-literate, the teacher needs to understand how language resources, visual and digital, can be deployed independently and in an interactive way, in the construction of different types of meaning. This means increasing the types of knowledge, relying on the different systems of meaning, require meta-linguistic ability to describe languages, images, and elaborate the meaning of the decision-making processes that occur in the interactive intermodal processes of teaching-learning, meta-linguistic forms in a wide range of "grammars", inextricably intertwined with modes of learning. Changing the size and role of forms of "academic literacy" and the nature of its practice, demands a realistic contextualization of these forms of complexity and influence, teaching new models of interpretation and perspective to handle spaces and to maximize learning and teaching. The barriers of this kind are now well known, as are many others which prevent or restrict the use of technology by teachers (BECTA, 2003, 2004; Ertmer, 1999) and affect the possibility of their integration in the classroom. Barriers may exist in four main categories of factors: the institutional resources and administrative support, training and experience, individual factors, which are naturally influenced by the interaction of a multitude of complex social and individual elements within the institutions, the scientific community and the broader cultural context, and national politicians. Technologizing the teaching-learning environments of the learning society assumes that technical systems are adopted in order to provide real learning, highlighting the growing need to increase investment in technology in higher education that involves the use of a coherent framework for the conceptualization of educational practices and raises many questions that have to deal with the characteristics of existing structures.

Research has shown a gradual adjustment, both by teachers and students, to embrace the use of ICT during teaching activities (Baron & Bruil-

lard, 2000). Hence the need for the preparation of university teachers in the field of educational ICT innovation, which concerns the re-shaping of their sense of professionalism in technology, especially compared to the percentage of time, the use of ICT, the focus and the objectives being pursued by their use, the procedures, and so on., ie the overall impact on their professional activities (teaching and research). This is due to the fact that the university professors technologically competent, spontaneously introduce technology into their teaching practices (National Center for Education Statistics, 2000), while those who are technologically weaker are unable to do so (Market Data Retrieval, 2001), so much so that in most cases the technology is used almost exclusively to support the actions of traditional teaching or a "special event" within the curriculum (Pedersen & Yerrick, 2000) that, as such, loses its potential as an agent for promoting the reform of science and its teaching (Settlage, Odom, & Pedersen, 2004). The goal is to exploit technology in order to support the student's conceptual way of learning science and to achieve teaching skills which permit continuous high quality contamination of disciplinary skills and teaching skills, between science and the science of teaching, because technology can be used to facilitate a deep understanding of the concepts and the use of science as a means of investigation for an exploration and reflection focused on and driven by and aware of the objectives of acquisition and the heritage of authentic experiences with which we can collect, analyze and interpret data, identify assumptions and consider alternative explanations. This is because technology can help to strengthen the central goals of higher learning, namely:

- To raise awareness;
- To develop the ability to use ideas and information;
- To develop in students critical thinking skills;

- To develop the students' ability to generate ideas and evidence;
- To facilitate their personal development;
- To develop the students' ability to plan and manage their own learning. Offering a range of different application contexts, technology allows teachers to expand their "territory occupation" and their ability to use them to support and enhance the quality of teaching by strengthening results, and at the same time, their kit of professional knowledge, and inserting expertise within specific learning environments. If it is true, then, that technologies fuel the ability to learn to master the process of teaching and the critical knowledge of it, the university professor, by becoming a " technology literate", is able to understand what "technology" is, how it is created, how to use it, how it affects society, how it develops, following training programs that gradually make him/her able to use it as a teaching tool which can create contexts of study for students that encourage them to understand and create meanings through personal reflection and to provide them with an opportunity to apply knowledge and skills in real life settings. To this aim, in terms of *key ICT skills*, the university professor is asked to:
  - Evaluate technology resources and recognize their potential and limitations for educational innovation and research;
  - Understand and learn how to use new ICT resources;
  - Explain students how and why to use certain technologies to achieve specific learning goals;
  - Be willing to use different types of technology;
  - Be willing to learn to maintain and increase the temporal learning technology;

  - Be willing to change the type of technology used if the first is not suitable for educational purposes or proves ineffective.

For that reason, the teachers in their repertoire of technology skills will inevitably cover the techniques of self-reflection, such as:

- Their technological knowledge as action learning to improve the quality of education practices;
- The process of change through educational intervention techniques;
- The different contexts in which they teach and assess the technologies;

The tools and resources specific technology that really validate the progress made in relation to their professional skills and those of the students;

The mechanisms and support mechanisms put in place throughout the process of teaching-learning and instructional design and as the technological culture of a certain academic community has an impact on values, communication styles, perception of time, the meaning of success and other important concepts of culture teaching (such as the objectives of university education, the discipline, research and its focus etc..), the teacher, in skills, must be able to:

- The identification of those aspects of technological culture that promote educational achievement of significant learning ("deep culture") in culturally and linguistically diverse students;
- The correct identification of the role of technology and cultural factors in determining social and behavioural management of teaching activities;
- The implementation of appropriate educational interventions and use technology in a way which supports students from cultural and linguistic different realities;

- The consideration on the impact of technology on assessment procedures (such as environment, contexts, social and cultural issues, languages, second language acquisition, acculturation process, the medical history, quality educational programs, the curriculum);
- The use of technological teaching methods appropriate to interact effectively and professionally with students from different cultural, socio-economic, educational and ethnic backgrounds;
- The development of new approaches suitable to address technological problems and taking into account the characteristics of the subjects and their cultural differences;
- The encouragement given to students to choose technological and cultural exchange activities for the resolution of disciplinary matters;
- The use of practical technology-teaching systems, including guidelines for the management of the teaching-learning processes.

## In Terms of Attitudes

The identification and understanding of the dynamics involved in the activities related to technology and education that contribute to ambiguity (semantic interpretation etc.).

The creation of an emotional disposition which favors the use of technology;

The establishment of a positive interaction with the different technologies, so that students can develop positive perceptions of both their own capabilities and the technology used ;

The demonstration that learning through technology is useful in terms of cultural and disciplinary action and that this means can greatly improve the learning experience at a cognitive and emotional level

These components are intertwined with their teaching skills, i.e.

- The ability to recognize the different technological and cultural elements (traditions and models) that constitute the description of science and its teaching, as well as aspects of their work (teaching practices);
- The ability to observe, analyze and understand facts, events and phenomena relating to the use of educational technology;
- The ability to understand their own conception of technology and teaching and to recognize the ways in which these affect the different communications and interactions involved in the processes of education;
- The awareness of the dynamics inherent to the technological elements and the effects they produce at a cultural level and learning and how they work within teaching cultures;
- A mastery of a pedagogical type of technology covering an accredited family of teaching skills and methodologies that enable them to represent different paradigms and approaches to teaching with technology, and the provision of individualized instruction to meet the social, cultural and linguistic diversity of students.

In this sense, we can draw up three areas of technological competence of teachers:

1. The ability to identify what ICT can be used for in teaching by the definition of certain learning objectives (awareness);
2. The possession of skills required for an effective and efficient use of hardware and software (use);
3. The knowledge of the principles and use of ICT in teaching-learning education (applications) (Awouters, Jans, & Jans, 2008).

Thus a conscious and responsible approach by the teachers in the teaching of technology becomes a necessity in order to control such use as reported in Table 1.

*Table 1. The controlled use of educational technology in the teaching plan*

| | Before<br>guidance in the use | During<br>regulating the use | After<br>assessment of the use |
|---|---|---|---|
| **Technical role and function** | Take account of the anticipated effects of the use of a specific technology | Correct continuously unanticipated disturbances by the use of a certain technology | To study the relevance of technology in order to function |
| **Function** | Prerequisites of use | Control of use | Cap use |
| **Educational role** | Improve teaching conditions | Improve processes of teaching | Improving learning outcomes |

University teachers can then hope for a deeper understanding of the technology if a closer relationship is established between action planning, pedagogical principles and teaching practices that are likely to reflect in terms of changes in the "teacher's behaviour". It follows that, the meaning and the professional qualities of a "good teacher" consist in the ability to be a "technology-multi-literate" figure who comprehends the integration and interaction between families of different area of expertise: technology, education and multidisciplinary (see Tables 2 and 3).

The first issue regarding the use of ICT in education in fact, is the problem of the redefinition of teaching strategies, both "macro" and "micro", designed to plan and coordinate a series of operations with the aim of effectively reaching an objective (Tardif, 1992): at a micro level, they are based on an idea, a concept, a principle or procedure, while at a macro level, they are used to organize a series of skills and knowledge, linked together in such a way as to join a number of different ideas within the same path (Van Patten, Chao, & Reigeluth, 1986). This distinction is particularly important in e-learning, for example, because it recalls the utility of appropriate interventions which will foster global (macro) and micro (local) information. It is a matter of achieving that 'deep education' (Biggs, 1999), that is to say, education which is governed by independent critical thinking and critical reflection that refer to the awareness of cultural criticism, in which technology becomes the scope and the learning tool, and it has the responsibility to insert itself trasversally respect to the powers of the teaching profession and to all areas of teaching and learning, guaranteeing and strengthening the ability of families' input together with the other ones (disciplinary, cross-cultural, etc.) and the overall cultural profile of the subjects. If it is true, then, that the essential capabilities of the teaching profession are the basis of a "technological literacy" broad, deep, lasting and critical, it is equally certain that it will bring more accountability and will strengthen the role of the teacher if accompanied by "awareness and reflexivity"

*Table 2. Areas of expertise of the teaching profession*

| **Define the educational role** | take into account the individual learning needs within a group, create a positive attitude towards learning, discuss how to manage groups, start the self-assessment of teaching |
|---|---|
| **Plan and organize the processes of teaching-learning** | identify learning outcomes, define contents, structure, plans and learn sequences and identify ways in which learning is recognized, use resources productively |
| **Managing the teaching-learning processes** | use appropriate methods and strategies, establish the conditions and learning environment, organize assistance and compensation, use language resources and assessment tools appropriate to encourage feedback and so on. |
| **Evaluate the learning and teaching** | assess the prerequisites, identify and analyze the strengths and weaknesses, provide feedback, make an assessment of learning and teaching |

*Table 3. Transversal skills*

| Conceptual skills | analyze, understand and manage problems of intercultural learning |
|---|---|
| Technical Skills | define methods, processes, procedures and technical specifications in order to make the experience of intercultural learning valuable qualitatively |
| Organisational skills | develop and build cultural activities consistent with the objectives of an intercultural learning in different segments of university education |
| Relational skills | relate to the ability of teachers to establish appropriate forms of intercultural communication with all students |

regarding the use of specific ontological and epistemological tools of learning and teaching trans-cultural technology, giving shape to a process of acquisition that recognizes the changes in meaning and understanding, involved in the interpretative approach of culture, paving the way for changes and opportunities, to build new modes of understanding phenomena and meanings. To sum up, technologies trigger the change in the cultural contexts of higher education by helping to identify new solutions to be implemented with respect to emerging issues, while opening up at the same time to other areas of uncertainty, both in terms of learning and teaching, concerning the transformation of populations of culturally diverse students and teachers into a real asset for the activation of processes of social and international connectivity and of transactional learning, but today this is still only an aspiration.

# REFERENCES

Alkan, C. (2005). *Educational technology*. Ankara, Turkey: Ani Publishers.

Anderson, R. E., & Dexter, S. (2005). Technology leadership: Its incidence and impact. *Educational Administration Quarterly, 41*(1), 49–82. doi:10.1177/0013161X04269517

Anstey, M., & Bull, G. (2006). *Teaching and learning multiliteracies*. Newark, DE: International Reading Association.

Arnold, M. (1999). The virtual university. *Arena Journal, 13*, 85–100.

Awouters, V., Jans, R., & Jans, S. (2008, April). E-learning competencies for teachers in secondary and higher education. In *Proceedings of the International Conference on E-Learning*, Saragossa, Spain.

Baron, G.-L., & Bruillard, É. (2000). Technologies de l'information et de la communication dans l'éducation: Quelles compétences pour les enseignants? *Educations & Formations, 56*, 69–76.

Baylor, A. L., & Ritchie, D. (2002). What factors facilitate teacher skill, teacher morale, and perceived student learning in technology-using classrooms? *Computers & Education, 39*(4), 395–414. doi:10.1016/S0360-1315(02)00075-1

BECTA. (2003). *What the research says about barriers to the use of ICT in teaching*. Coventry, UK: British Educational Communications and Technology Agency.

BECTA. (2004). *Barriers to the uptake of ICT by teachers*. Coventry, UK: British Educational Communications and Technology Agency.

Biggs, J. (1999). *Teaching for quality learning at university*. Philadelphia, PA: The Society for Research into Higher Education and Open University Press.

Bucker, A. J., & Lamboy, C. (2002). Are professors ready for the technology age? In *Proceedings of the Selected Papers on the Research of Educational Communications and Technology Presented at the National Convention of the Association for Educational Communications and Technology Sponsored by the Research and Theory Division*, Dallas, TX.

Bucker, A. J., & Lamboy, C. L. (2003). An investigation of faculty technology skills in a Puerto Rican university. *Quarterly Review of Distance Education*, *4*(2), 143–152.

Burkhardt, G., Monsour, M., Valdez, G., Gunn, C., Dawson, M., & Lemke, C. (2003). *21st century skills: Literacy in the digital age* (pp. 42–83). Naperville, IL: North Central Regional Educational Laboratory.

Byram, M., & Zarate, G. (1997). *The sociocultural and intercultural dimension of language learning and teaching*. Strasbourg, France: Council of Europe.

Chen, C., & Shaw, R. (2006). Online synchronous vs. asynchronous software training through the behavioral modeling approach: A longitudinal field experiment. *International Journal of Distance Education Technologies*, *4*(4), 88–102. doi:10.4018/jdet.2006100107

Chickering, A. W., & Ehrmann, S. (1996). Implementing the seven principles: Technology as lever. *AAHE Bulletin*, *49*(2), 3–6.

Cranton, P. (1996). *Professional development as transformative learning: New perspectives for teachers of adults*. San Francisco, CA: Jossey-Bass.

Dani, D. E., & Koenig, K. M. (2008). Technology and reform-based science education. *Theory into Practice*, *47*(3), 204–211. doi:10.1080/00405840802153825

Dede, C. (2004). If design-based research is the answer, what is the question? *Journal of the Learning Sciences*, *13*(1), 105–114. doi:10.1207/s15327809jls1301_5

Distance Education Report. (2000). *Global village: Focus on Europe*. Madison, WI: Magna Publications.

Donlevy, J. (2003). Teachers, technology and training. *International Journal of Instructional Media*, *30*(2), 117–121.

Ehrmann, S. C. (1997). *Asking the right question: What does research tell us about technology and higher learning?* Retrieved from http://www.tltgroup.org/resources/Flashlight/AskingRightQuestion.htm

Ehrmann, S. C. (1999). Asking the hard questions about technology use and education. *Change*, *31*(2), 25–29. doi:10.1080/00091389909602676

Ertmer, P. A. (1999). Addressing first- and second-order barriers to change: Strategies for technology integration. *Educational Technology Research and Development*, *47*(4), 47–61. doi:10.1007/BF02299597

Gagel, C. W. (1997). Literacy and technology: Reflections and insights for technological literacy. *Journal of Industrial Teacher Education*, *34*(3), 6–34.

Galliani, L., Zaggia, C., & Serbati, A. (Eds.). (2011). *Adulti all'Università*. Lecce, Italy: Pensa Multimedia.

Gimbert, B., & Cristol, D. (2004). Teaching curriculum with technology: Enhancing young children's technological competence during early childhood. *Early Childhood Education Journal*, *31*(3), 209–218.

Hartnell-Young, E. (2006). Teachers' roles and professional learning in communities of practice supported by technology in schools. *Journal of Technology and Teacher Education*, *14*(3), 461–480.

Haterick, R. (2000). Time is nature's way of making sure everything doesn't happen at once. In Haterick, R. (Ed.), *The learning market space: A publication of the leadership forum at the center for academic transformation*. Troy, NY: Renssalaer Polytechnic.

Hostetler, K. (2005). What is "good" education research? *Educational Researcher*, *34*(6), 16–21. doi:10.3102/0013189X034006016

International Technology Education Association. (2000). *Standards for technological literacy: Content for the study of technology*. Reston, VA: Virginia.

Kasper, L. F. (2000a). The role of information technology in the future of content-based ESL instruction. In Kasper, L. K. F., Babbitt, M., Mlynarczyk, R. W., Brinton, D. M., Rosenthal, J. W., & Master, P.,(Eds.), *Content-based college ESL instruction* (pp. 202–212). Mahwah, NJ: Lawrence Erlbaum.

Kasper, L. F. (2000b). New technologies, new literacies: Focus discipline research and ESL learning communities. *Language Learning & Technology, 4*(2), 105–128.

Kester, L., Kirschner, P., & Corbalan, G. (2005). Learner control over information presentation in powerful electronic learning environments. In Verschaffel, L., De Corte, E., Kanselaar, G., & Valcke, M. (Eds.), *Powerful environments for promoting deep conceptual and strategic learning* (pp. 199–212). Leuven, Belgium: Leuven University Press.

Kirkwood, A., & Price, L. (2005). Learners and learning in the 21st century: What do we know about students' attitudes and experiences of ICT that will help us design courses? *Studies in Higher Education, 30*(3), 257–274. doi:10.1080/03075070500095689

Knežević-Florić, O. (2008). Lifelong leaning as a basis of the sustainable development concept. In Popov, J., Wolhuter, C., Leutwyler, B., Kysilka, M., & Ogunleye, J. (Eds.), *Comparative education, teacher training, education policy and social inclusion* (pp. 199–203). Sofia, Bulgaria: Bureau for Educational Services, Bulgarian Comparative Education Society.

Knight, J. (1997). Internationalisation of higher education: A conceptual framework. In Knight, J., & de Wit, H. (Eds.), *Internationalisation of higher education in Asia Pacific countries* (pp. 5–19). Amsterdam, The Netherlands: European Association for International Education.

Labbo, L. D., & Reinking, D. (1999). Negotiating the multiple realities of technology in literacy research and instruction. *Reading Research Quarterly, 34*(4), 478–492. doi:10.1598/RRQ.34.4.5

Lankshear, C., & Knobel, M. (2003). *New literacies: Changing knowledge and classroom learning*. Buckingham, UK: Open University Press.

Leu, D. J. (2002). The new literacies: Research on reading instruction with the Internet and other digital technologies. In Farstrup, A. E., & Samuels, S. J. (Eds.), *What research has to say about reading instruction* (3rd ed., pp. 310–337). Newark, DE: International Reading Association.

Monroe, B. (2004). *Crossing the digital divide: Race, writing, and technology in the classroom*. New York, NY: Teachers College Press.

Moran, T. J., & Payne, M. (1998). Humanizing the integration of technology. *New Directions for Community Colleges, 101*, 43–47. doi:10.1002/cc.10105

New London Group. (1996). A pedagogy of multiliteracies: Designing social futures. *Harvard Educational Review, 66*(1), 60–92.

Newmann, F., & Wehlage, G. (1993). Five standards of authentic instruction. *Educational Leadership, 55*(2), 72–75.

Norton, L., Richardson, J. T. E., Hartley, J., Newstead, S., & Mayes, J. (2005). Teachers' beliefs and practices concerning teaching in higher education. *Higher Education, 50*(4), 537–571. doi:10.1007/s10734-004-6363-z

Nuzzaci, A. (2004). *Profili di competenza e trasformazioni sociali. Insegnare ed apprendere*, Cosenza, Italy: Lionello Giordano.

Nuzzaci, A. (2006). Per la costruzione di una banca dati italiana dei progetti di ricerca internazionali. In C. LANEVE, C. GEMMA (EDS.), *La ricerca pedagogica in Europa. Modelli e temi a confronto* (pp. 375-387). Atti del XXII Convegno Nazionale della Società Italiana di Pedagogia (SIPED), Cassino, 24-26 maggio 2006, Lecce. Italy: Pensa Multimedia.

Nuzzaci, A. (2011, December 2-3). La dimensione trans-culturale della didattica (e della ricerca). In L. Galliani (Ed.), *Il docente universitario: Una professione tra ricerca, didattica e governance degli Atenei: Atti dell'VIII Biennale Internazionale sulla Didattica Universitaria* (Vol. 2, pp. 263-286). Lecce, Italy: Pensa Multimedia.

Onwuegbuzie, A. J., Witcher, A. E., Collins, K. M. T., Filer, J. D., Wiedmaier, C. D., & Moore, C. W. (2007). Students' perceptions of characteristics of effective college teachers: A validity study of a teaching evaluation form using a mixed-methods analysis. *American Educational Research Journal, 44*(1), 113–160. doi:10.3102/0002831206298169

Ormrod, J. (2004). *Human learning* (4th ed., p. 456). Upper Saddle River, NJ: Prentice Hall.

Pedersen, J. E., & Yerrick, R. K. (2000). Technology in science teacher education: A survey of current uses and desired knowledge among science educators. *Journal of Science Teacher Education, 11*(2), 131–153. doi:10.1023/A:1009468808876

Prime, G. (1998). Tailoring assessment of technological literacy learning. *Journal of Technology Studies, 24*(1), 18–23.

Process, B. (1999). *European higher education area*. Retrieved from http://www.bolognaprocess.it

Quellmalz, E. S., & Kozma, R. (2003). Designing assessments of learning with technology. *Assessment in Education, 10*(3), 389–405. doi:10.1080/0969594032000148208

Reinking, D. (1998). Synthesizing technological transformations of literacy in a post-typographic world. In Reinking, D., McKenna, M. C., Labbo, L. D., & Kieffer, R. D. (Eds.), *Handbook of literacy and technology: Transformations in a post-typographic world* (pp. xi–xxx). Mahwah, NJ: Lawrence Erlbaum.

Report, A. (2008). *Aho report on EU high-tech research: A wake-up call for innovation in Europe*. Brussels, Belgium: European Commission.

Ribble, M. S., & Bailey, G. (2005). Developing ethical direction. *Learning and Leading with Technology, 32*(7), 36–38.

Ribble, M. S., Bailey, G. D., & Ross, T. W. (2004). Digital citizenship: Addressing appropriate technology behavior. *Learning and Leading with Technology, 32*(1), 6–12.

Roblyer, M. D., & Knezek, G. A. (2003). New millennium research for educational technology: A call for a national research agenda. *Journal of Research on Technology in Education, 36*(1), 60–71.

Rummler, G. A., & Brache, A. P. (1988). The systems view of human performance. *Training (New York, N.Y.), 25*(9), 45–53.

Settlage, J., Odom, A. L., & Pedersen, J. E. (2004). Uses of technology by science education professors: Comparisons with teachers: Uses and the current versus desired technology knowledge gap. *Contemporary Issues in Technology & Teacher Education, 4*(3).

Siegle, D. (2004). The merging of literacy and technology in the 21st century: A bonus for gifted education. *Technology (Elmsford, N.Y.), 27*(2), 32–35.

Tardif, J. (1992). *Pour un enseignement stratégique: L'apport de la psychologie cognitive.* Montréal, QC, Canada: Éditions Logiques.

Thompson, A. (2005). Scientifically based research: Establishing a research agenda for the technology in teacher education community. *Journal of Research on Technology in Education, 37*(4), 331–337.

Underwood, J., & Szabo, A. (2003). Academic offences and e-learning: Individual propensities in cheating. *British Journal of Educational Technology, 34*(4), 467–478. doi:10.1111/1467-8535.00343

Underwood, J., & Szabo, A. (2004). Cybercheats: Is information and communication technology fuelling academic dishonesty? *Active Learning in Higher Education, 5*(2), 180–199. doi:10.1177/1469787404043815

Valdez, G., McNabb, M., Foertsch, M., Anderson, M., Hawkes, M., & Raack, L. (2000). *Computer-based technology and learning: Evolving uses and expectations.* Oak Brook, IL: North Central Regional Educational Laboratory.

Van Patten, J. R., Chao, C. I., & Reigeluth, C. M. (1986). A review of strategies for sequencing and synthesizing information. *Review of Educational Research, 56*(4), 437–472. doi:10.3102/00346543056004437

Van Soest, D., Canon, R., & Grant, D. (2000). Using an interactive website to educate about cultural diversity and societal oppression. *Journal of Social Work Education, 36*(3), 463–479.

Ward, D. (2000). Catching the wave of change in American higher education. *EDUCAUSE Review, 35*(1), 22–30.

Weisbord, M. R. (1987). *Productive workplaces.* San Francisco, CA: Jossey-Bass.

*This work was previously published in the International Journal of Digital Literacy and Digital Competence, Volume 2, Issue 2, edited by Antonio Cartelli, pp. 11-26, copyright 2011 by IGI Publishing (an imprint of IGI Global).*

# Chapter 8
# Developing and Managing Digital/Technology Literacy and Effective Learning Skills in Adult Learners

**Jeffrey Hsu**
*Fairleigh Dickinson University, USA*

**Zhongxian Wang**
*Montclair State University, USA*

**Karin Hamilton**
*Fairleigh Dickinson University, USA*

## ABSTRACT

*The needs of adult learners are different from those of traditional undergraduate students, and programs must be designed to meet this need. In particular, digital and technology literacy needs, including general computing skills, computerized communications, online and distance learning, and Web 2.0 tools make navigating coursework an additional challenge. In this paper, the authors examine the technology and digital literacy needs and backgrounds of adult learner students and discuss research on the interaction between technology and adult learner education. Using the features of intensive weekend classroom sessions, on-line distance learning, and specialized teaching methods, an improved learning environment tailored to unique needs and career goals can be offered to business undergraduate adults. An important component is the development of technology and digital literacy skills to "fill the gaps" of students who may have extensive business or working experience, but are less than proficient in the use of technology. More depth and analysis is given to the following areas: digital and technology skills and knowledge improvement, pedagogical features, the use of intensive weekend and evening sessions, and the role of distance learning to supplement the classroom sessions.*

DOI: 10.4018/978-1-4666-2943-1.ch008

## INTRODUCTION

To meet the needs of students in the 21st century, it is critical to examine not only the state of the educational market in terms of student type, but also to isolate the unique needs of each population who will be enrolling in and graduating from degree-based programs. Since the dynamics and demographics of college students are changing, the need to change and adapt to meet their needs and requirements is paramount.

Adult learners are forming an important segment of the educational market, and their increasing numbers now comprise a solid portion of the overall undergraduate population. It has been noted that almost 50% of undergraduate students can be classified under the categories of "non-traditional" or "adult learners" (Calvin & Freeburg, 2010; National Center for Education Statistics, 2002). The number is growing, and it is conceivable that very soon the majority of students will fall into this category, according to the National Center for Education Statistics (Calvin & Freeburg, 2010; Horn, 1996). Some of the core characteristics of non-traditional students are that they delayed enrollment (did not enter college after high school), are likely to attend part time, have full-time jobs, and are likely to be married with dependents (National Center for Education Statistics, 2002).

There are a number of characteristics common to adult, non-traditional students. While many possess significant professional experience and knowledge (many are or have been working full time), adult students may frequently lack a firm grounding in a variety of business and other theoretical knowledge areas which an undergraduate college business degree provides. In addition, work and home responsibilities often make it more difficult for adults to attend classes scheduled in the daytime or on weekday evenings. Many may also have had negative experiences in their previous educational work which may impact new attempts at completing their educations (Knowles, 1984; National Center for Research in Vocational Education, 1987).

Because of a more highly developed career focus, adults tend to view their studies as being more closely linked to career-oriented goals and orientations. As a result, adult learners are generally more engaged and involved in the learning process and seek to master a subject (especially the applied and practical aspects) because they understand the benefits provided by enhanced knowledge towards improved career performance and advancement. For instance, adults tend to ask more questions, demand more class discussion, and seek connections between the material and practical applications from work. The result is a need for more dynamic and real-time learning, focused toward specific goals or agendas related to improving careers and lives (Hamilton, 2002). In fact, 73% of adult non-traditional students attend college for the purposes of career advancement, to improve their knowledge in a subject area, and/or to complete a degree to add to their credentials (U.S. Department of Education, 2002).

This is in stark contrast to traditional undergraduates who are more focused towards social aspects of college life and strive toward better grades more often to maintain satisfactory standing, and to meet the expectations and demands of parents. To compensate for youth and lack of experience, one of the important benefits of a traditional undergraduate education is to create context using social and professional experiences from which young students can attach and build the educational knowledge learned. As a result, many traditional students exhibit a more passive approach to learning; with emphasis on absorbing and memorizing what "experts" (teachers) profess (Huang, 2002).

The number and influence of adult learners has brought about the development of a different set of teaching skills and methodologies, including andragogy which is defined as the "method of teaching adults." This contrasts to the more common and widely-used term, pedagogy, which is focused primarily on the teaching of children and young persons. Important aspects relating to andragogy include incorporation of prior experience in educating the learner, a greater sense of readiness and need for applied learning, greater motivation, and also a problem-solving orientation (Knowles, 1998, 1992; Huang, 2002).

Other theories and methods that relate to teaching adult learners include constructivism, social context of learning, self-directed learning, critical reflection, experiential learning, and situated cognition. Constructivism is based on earlier theories by Piaget (1973) and Dewey (1916) and was designed to help improve reasoning processes, by allowing students to solve real life problems and emphasizing experiences from one's environment (Huang, 2002; Ornsten & Hunkins, 1998). The social context of learning is concerned with the role of interpersonal interaction between learners and both other students and the instructor during the learning process (Maddux, Johnson, & Willis, 1997; Vygotsky, 1978). Situated cognition is the belief that adult learning is closely related to the context in which it is located, and so learning should be done within that context, not separated from it (Merriam & Caffarella, 1999).

Self directed learning is concerned with a learner taking control of one's learning, setting goals, and evaluating one's progress (Brookfield, 1995). Other important learning approaches include that of critical reflection and thinking and experiential learning. These are found to be approaches developed in, and used by adults in their learning, all of which are connected to what can be termed "learning to learn." The ability to learn in various contexts and ways includes the valuable ability to learn outside of specific classroom and course contexts, which is termed informal learning (Milheim, 2007). The employment of these in various ways can lead to the positive outcomes associated with lifelong learning (Huang, 2002; Brookfield, 1995).

## ADULT LEARNERS AND TECHNOLOGY

The importance of technology skills and knowledge to adult learners cannot be overemphasized. Adult learners already have experience in the workplace and are intending to continue or return to it during or after one's studies (Jimoyiannis & Gravani, 2010).

The rapid growth of technology and the widespread use of it in the workplace has made it paramount that college programs, especially those in business, include technology and computing as a part of its curriculum and ensure that students are fully equipped to make effective use of technology in their work (Lawson, 2005).

Advancement of communication technology is now proceeding at a fast pace, with e-mail, Web 2.0 and social networking replacing or supplementing the traditional modes of mail or telephone. Growth of e-commerce has resulted in an increased need to effectively use and understand the underlying logic of communication technologies. Many of the processes (ordering, buying, giving and receiving quotes, reservations) are now being done online rather than using more manual means (Turban et al., 2010).

Education is one area that has been strongly linked with computing and technology, and the link has been widespread, going beyond computer science and information systems to all areas of business, the sciences, and the humanities. Aside from computing and technology support for administrative functions, there is a significant level of technology associated with teaching and learning. Internet-based tools including course management systems (CMS) such as Blackboard are used to support courses and provide both delivery and communications features. The use of Web 2.0 tools is expanding to include blogs, wikis, and social networking. Many of the tools now available online through the Internet support communications in the form of discussions, collaborative sharing, video and real-time conferencing, and developments for better engagement and critical thinking (Hsu, 2008).

Since adult learners comprise a different category of undergraduate student, and technology, including learning technologies, have become an important component of the educational process, it is important to examine the digital and technology skills of adult learner students. Questions arise on the role and applicability of employing technology in the education of adult students. This section examines how adept adult learners react to and engage in the use of new technological tools. The prevalence of a larger "digital divide" among adult learners vs. traditional students is also examined, followed by some other related issues.

The role technology plays in adult learning is important in that it is closely linked with the teaching of classes, and in applications and problems which are used in courses. While the traditional textbook and blackboard are still being used, the influence of technology is increasingly playing a key role in the teaching and learning process. Thus, ability to effectively use technology, particularly computer and communications technologies, can impact success in college and perhaps more importantly, in one's career.

A first issue that can be examined is the background of adult learners in terms of technological expertise and experience. It may be assumed that adult learners have a solid level of technological skill related to work experience and that the use of certain job-related technologies (e-mail, advanced cell phones, corporate intranets and websites, etc.) translates to a broader overall knowledge of how to use computers for their studies. Yet, some studies have shown that many adult learners lack basic computer skills (Yang et al., 2007), and in fact may be fearful of using computers (Saade & Kira, 2007). Other studies indicate that there is no clear answer to how well-versed adult learners are with technology (Broady et al., 2010; Calvin & Freeburg, 2010).

Even among adult learners, there appears to be a digital divide based on a number of factors (Rao, 2009) including age, gender, income, and language use. In general, older students tended to have lower levels of technology assimilation than younger persons, however adult students tended to be able to pick up and retain knowledge better on their own, without the need of an instructor, compared with younger, traditional students (Broady et al., 2010; Li & Edmonds, 2005; Morris & Venkatesh, 2000).

Gender, not surprisingly, also fits into this. Studies have shown that males tended to have a more positive view of technology than females (McKinney et al., 2008; Bain & Rice, 2007). Income level is a factor that varies a great deal, and in general the higher the income level, the greater the likelihood that someone would have the funds to acquire, learn, and use computer and related technologies.

Focusing on technology can also help to improve persistence and retention in adult learner programs. This can be the case when the program is hybrid or more fully online, however the situation is more critical in the case of the latter. Studies have shown that problems in completing a course (or program) are frequently linked as much to the inability to navigate the technological aspects, as to an ability to understand and apply the actual course content. Fisher (2007) discussed computer phobia in adult learners, which can have an impact on how well a student works with technology. Computer phobia arises when a person experiences fear, avoidance, or other adverse effects when using technology. An online distance learning course, for instance, may be subject to a large number of dropouts and failures if there is inadequate background, training, or exposure to the skills and techniques needed to access content, participate in discussion boards, and submit assignments/communicate effectively (Tyler-Smith, 2006; Hsu & Hamilton, 2010).

Regardless of the background of students which may vary in terms of their differing levels and uses of technology based on socioeconomic background (digital divide or DD), the goal is to achieve digital equity (DE) where all students have the same level of access to technology in their learning (Judge, Puckett, & Cabuk, 2004). The role of providing varying and different levels of support, as suggested by the concept of instructional scaffolding, is discussed in the educational literature (Hurt, 2007; Hughes, 1998).

Technology use by adult learners pursuing an educational course or program can be segmented into three categories. The first concerns general technology use, which can include many of the skills and tasks involved in everyday computing use in a business setting. The second concerns the use of more specialized educational and communication tools, including learning management systems (LMSs), computer conferencing and teleconferencing, and facilities designed to enhance the classroom experience. The third is related to the second, in that it involves computer communications; however it centers on systems and technologies related to distance and online learning.

The goal of most adult learners in pursuing their education is to improve job performance and employment prospects. Command of technology can be an important part of career advancement. Necessary skills could include general computer and Internet proficiency, effective Internet research and the use of social media to communicate and send/receive information effectively and efficiently. Effective use of technology can enhance the learning process, including group and collaborative work, simulations, both real-time and asynchronous communications, and the ability to conduct discussions and access content remotely. In terms of collaboration, some of the new Internet based tools, such as Google Docs, allow for students to work together on the same document, with real-time changes being reflected for all members to see and respond to. The use of a wiki, for example, allows review and editing to be done by a group of users on the same document. This same level of engagement may not easily be accomplished using paper, pencil,

blackboard/whiteboard, or even a single computer being shared by a group (Hsu, 2008).

Technology can allow people to form an "online community" where ideas, thoughts, development, and even personal events can be shared, allowing for a greater "sense of community" among adult learner students in a program (Stein et al., 2009).

The third category, and one that is closely related to (and in some ways, overlapping with) the second, is the use of distance and online learning tools to extend the course outside of the classroom, or to conduct portions of the entire course online, without the need for face-to-face classroom sessions. The use of distance learning can help to alleviate the need to travel to class, and also can continue interaction when the class is not in session (Calvin & Freeburg, 2010). The "virtual classroom" (Hiltz, 1994) can be invaluable in extending beyond the classroom to allow for learning to continue throughout the week and semester.

## TECHNOLOGY AND ADULT LEARNER CLASS ENVIRONMENTS

As mentioned, adult learners actively seek out practical learning that is relevant to career goals and objectives. Providing assignments and exercises which allow students to bring life and work experiences into the learning process would therefore help to improve motivation and interest in the course, while enriching the learning process. Effective use of self-directed and active learning assignments would have the benefit of making projects more relevant to student work responsibilities and challenges, as well as emphasize critical thinking skills rather than the accumulation of information (Huang, 2002).

The goals and objectives of adult students also relate to classroom and course situations which employ distance learning and the use of technologies to supplement the classroom process (Knowles, Holton, & Swanson, 1998; Brookfield,

1991). These include active learning, cooperation, and collaboration; real-world problems and work-related applications; problem solving; decision making; applied experience; and a strong emphasis on practice. In connection with this the roles of interactive activities, critical thinking, and discussion are also important.

Support for these kinds of activities can be accomplished (or enhanced or supported) by the use of e-mail, the web and Internet, course management systems, computer conferencing systems, and various tools designed to support a specific application area.

Because of the critical role of computer related technologies in industry, the professional world, and education, the use of various methods, techniques, and approaches can help to bring about, encourage, strengthen, and further reinforce the ability to use technology effectively. This can be employed both in the classroom, and in online sessions conducted outside of class. Examples include the use of electronic submissions and communications (e-mail, CMS), the use of digital libraries for research, the requirement for use of certain software, and the maintenance of regular communications with the instructor and other students online. There can also be regular assignments linked to finding current news and information using various resources using the web (Hsu, 2008).

While students may tend to prefer and find value in practical assignments, an effective adult learning course and program should also incorporate aspects of theory. This differentiates a well-rounded college education from that of a trade or vocational school and provides important background knowledge to enhance and validate student perspectives. As a result, a different kind of class environment should be developed for adult learner students.

In traditional classes, the instructor is an authority figure, taking on the role of "sage on a stage." Students are lectured to and presented information ("chalk and talk"), and are then expected to

memorize facts for tests. There is frequently an emphasis on the one "right" answer, and most learning outside of class lectures comes from textbooks and other printed materials. There is less of an emphasis on group work, and students typically listen and take notes during class (Huang, 2002; Hamilton, 2002).

This contrasts significantly to effective adult learner class environments, which should be designed to facilitate and support more active individuals who will participate, offer arguments, debate issues, and benefit from working with peers in groups to solve problems for which there may be multiple solutions. To improve relevance and injection of "real-time" assignments, project ideas may be initiated by students, rather than assigned by the instructor. Primary assessment would remain the responsibility of the instructor, but can be supplemented by assessments from other students, team members, or the like. Group work is typical, and there is a level of engagement and interest conducted at higher levels of critical thinking (Hamilton, 2002). The use of online message boards can help to promote active communications between the instructor and the students. The ability to conduct an e-mail discussion can also provide a means for helping to maintain communication flows outside of the classroom.

Critical thinking is another aspect which is relevant to adult learners (Huang, 2002). Perry (1970) discussed the levels or stages from which students develop critical thinking skills. Espana (2004) found that adults tend to have higher levels of thinking, emphasizing contextual relativism (needing supporting information to confirm validity), and the dialectic (handling a problem from different perspectives with answers varying by context). This is in contrast to lower levels such as dualism (choosing between right/wrong answers), and multiplicity (considering multiple answers), which may be associated with younger students. Consequently, professors and instructors of adults are often pressed by them to function more as a coach or facilitator rather than an expert who lectures acting as a "sage on a stage."

As a result of these distinctions, teaching adult learners can be both interesting and challenging. Some of the pedagogical needs of the adult learner which come into play include replacing lecture with dialog, using structured assignments, replacing case studies with "present time" assignments, and emphasizing application of concepts over memorization. The use of project-based assignments rather than objective tests in assessing learning is also suggested to be more appropriate for adult students (Huang, 2002; Hamilton, 2002).

This can be accomplished by presenting material from which an online discussion can be employed. Or, a problem or issue can be posed to the class from which solutions can be proposed by the students. The use of group projects, where students need to collaborate to come up with a solution, can be also implemented and supported online.

## DISTANCE LEARNING AND ADULT LEARNERS

While there are numerous means to support work being done in the classroom and for assignment completion in conjunction with class, the ability to conduct classes online is another approach to consider, especially given the time constraints of adult learner students. The effectiveness of online courses and programs is currently a topic which has been debated and analyzed, eliciting both positive and negative characteristics and outcomes (Ahn, Han, & Han, 2005; Beck et al., 2004).

Distance learning (DL) can play a significant and critical role for adult learner programs, due to several main factors. First, adult students have more experience, maturity, and career orientation, and therefore would be better able to take advantage of the flexibility and convenience which DL offers. At the same time, their maturity and desire to succeed and to successfully complete their college educations would facilitate the proper and focused use of online tools, which often require initiative and self-directed focus and concentration. The fact that class contact hours are limited makes the ability for anytime-anywhere communications to be conducive and suitable to the scheduling needs of adult students.

There is a fundamental difference between traditional classroom learning formats and Internet-based asynchronous learning. Lectures, discussions, and some in-class exercises are the basic elements of traditional classroom learning, and in general students receive direct face-to-face communication from his or her instructor. This is in direct contrast to asynchronous learning, where online technologies and the Internet are used, and the instructor and students are not necessarily interacting in the same place and time. Instead, both instructors and students can log in when needed to enter or retrieve information, respond to other posts, and otherwise participate in the course.

The application of distance learning to adult learner/non-traditional programs has been found to be useful and appropriate. Many courses are being offered through the Internet and other means, which results in the student-instructor-class interaction to be conducted in whole, or in part, without physical face-to-face interaction in a classroom on campus. According to Chaffee (1998), adult students tend to have expectations in terms of flexibility, convenience, and responsiveness, and have no qualms about seeking out these in educational programs.

Distance learning can be implemented in a number of ways. Some courses and programs can be run completely online with no face-to-face sessions. The course content is presented in various formats online, and communication can be conducted through e-mail, real-time messaging, and through threaded message boards. This option is best for students who are geographically dispersed, and have difficulty attending on-campus sessions.

For courses where some classroom interaction is desired, hybrid distance learning provides an option that combines face-to-face instruction with interaction outside of class through the Internet. Although considerable variation in terms of format and implementation can occur across courses and programs, hybrid distance learning typically deploys some introductory class sessions in a traditional face-to-face format, followed by interaction to be conducted online. As an option, both modes could alternate throughout the course. The use of an online portal such as Blackboard is frequently used to support the online portion, since both offer course workspaces from which instructors and students can run their course activities and present information online. The specific tools used may include e-mail, synchronous chat, threaded discussions, message boards, and also online lectures, tutorials, and quizzes (Martyn & Bash, 2002).

Distance learning offers students the flexibility of interaction at more convenient times, which can help balance school, work and family responsibilities. Working adults may adapt well to online assignments, since they are likely to be accustomed to technology through their jobs. Online applications can also include m-learning (mobile learning), which supports learning using mobile hand-held devices, and b-learning (business learning) which employs transactional data in the learning process. The use of learning management systems (LMS) also can be integrated into the process (Seng & Lin, 2004).

While there are a number of benefits for online and distance learning, especially when it is done properly with proper instructor training and support, there is also potential for less than optimal results. In fact, studies have been quite varied in terms of the attrition and drop-out rate of distance/online learning courses and programs, ranging from 10% to 80%, which clearly reflects the challenges that e-learning students face, especially for first-timers (Tyler-Smith, 2006; Flood, 2002).

The reasons are complex, and even narrowed within the context of adult learners, a number of

variables and considerations may affect the ability of a student to persist and succeed. Kember (1989) examined this issue and suggested that social, work, and family commitments may have a significant impact, together with income, gender, and distance from the institution as relevant variables. More generally, personal, institutional, and circumstantial variables were cited as reasons affecting attrition and retention (Berge & Huang, 2004). The influence of "locus of control" and self-efficacy are also relevant (Martinez, 2003; Bandura, 1986), as well as a technology-skill factor, termed "readiness for online learning" which included well-developed online skills and a good level of online interaction (Bernard et al., 2004).

Cognitive load theory also supports the need for technology training and skill development prior to starting a course employing online/distance learning. This theory states that there is a limit to the amount of short- term working memory that can process new information at any given time. Processed information is added into one's mental models/schemes in long-term memory, allowing one to handle problems and situations previously encountered. However, for a technology or online learning novice, these schemes are either non-existent or not well developed. In the case of an online learning course, the numerous and conflicting demands of accessing the site, understanding how to access material, uploading and downloading files and assignments, and participating in message board discussions can quickly overload one's working memory, causing stress, anxiety, loss of confidence, and perhaps dropping out (Whipp & Chiarelli, 2004; Eshet-Alkalaim, 2004; Paas, Renkl, & Sweller, 2004; Sweller & Chandler, 1994).

Clearly, providing technology training, support, and scaffolding would help adult learner students challenged by the multiple demands placed on them by the online course and its associated technologies.

## INTENSIVE COURSE SCHEDULING SUPPORTED BY TECHNOLOGY

Unlike traditional undergraduates, who are on campus full-time and can attend classes at any time, adults often face time limitations and constraints. There is both a shortage of time available for class meetings (and study), a limitation in terms of when adult students are available for class (usually evenings and weekends) and also a desire to complete a course in shorter, rather than longer, time frames.

Intensive class formats are accelerated and compressed, resulting in shorter course calendar terms with equivalent instruction time. Initially, it was thought by some faculty that a lower quality pedagogical outcome would result for students taking an intensive course compared to a course delivered over the span of a semester or quarter, since there would be less time allocated to process the material. Intensive courses were thought to sacrifice effective learning and academic standards in the interest of student preferences and convenience (Daniel, 2001; Scott & Conrad, 1991; Scott, 1994, 1995, 1996).

Research conducted on this suggests otherwise. Serdyukov et al. (2003) found that compressed formats, starting with courses as short as one month, produced learning outcomes comparable, or even superior to, longer courses lasting several months in length (such as full semester courses).

One important difference when using most compressed formats is that a sequential, rather than a parallel format, is deployed. Students would take one intensive course at a time, followed by another one, rather than having several longer-term courses taken simultaneously. A new course is not started until the first one is completed, allowing for greater concentration and focus, rather than the dilution and multitasking required to manage several different courses simultaneously. Some of the argued benefits of this approach include better understanding, skill development, as well as higher levels of immersion and concentration (Espana, 2004; Scott & Conrad, 1992; Csikszentmihalyi, 1982).

Another difference is that compressed courses tend to employ certain types of pedagogical methods, procedures, and processes. To be effective, instructors of intensive courses must provide clearly identified expectations and requirements, prompt feedback, and detailed schedules for assignments and course activities (Espana, 2004; Serdyukov et al., 2003). Group projects and collaboration are also found to be effective for intensive courses as they provide opportunities for additional discussion, reinforcement and multiple perspectives in mastering concepts (Singh & Martin, 2004). To enable communication, supplement the classroom experience and extend the learning process outside of the classroom, communication technologies, such as e-mail, computer software, and Internet based course portals such as Blackboard are used (Wlodkowski, 2003).

One of the critical supports for intensive course scheduling is the use of course management systems (CMS), and also communications technologies (e-mail, Web 2.0) to support the courses which can only meet for limited hours on weekends. Since it is difficult to conduct all of the teaching and learning during the limited face to face time, the use of the CMS or web tool is used to extend the course interaction time to outside of the classroom. This would include the use of discussion boards, online real-time chat, collaborative exercises, and online, asynchronous communications with both other students and the instructor. The use of these helps to alleviate the problems of adult students who have difficulty attending class but may have time throughout the week that they can devote to their studies.

## MODULAR/PROJECT-BASED LEARNING SUPPORTED BY TECHNOLOGY

In addition to having a practical emphasis in their programs, it was also found that packaging lessons and presenting information and concepts in the form of modules facilitates adult student learning. Modules typically present a specific theory, topic, or learning unit which is supplemented with a practical application-based exercise (Huang, 2002).

An important element of project-based assignments would be to encourage or require teams or groups to work collaboratively. Previous research has indicated that collaborative project-based assignments can bring about active engagement in learning, develop higher-order learning skills, and enable students to better synthesize various parts into a cohesive whole. In terms of learning in general, collaborative group work helps to improve information retention, since there is higher level of engagement in the learning experience (Hafner & Ellis, 2004; Sloffer et al., 1999; Dillenbourg et al., 1996). The use of collaborative features found in course management systems, computer conferencing systems, and also in new Web 2.0 features including Google Docs, can be used to support collaborative group projects.

## ADULT LEARNER TECHNOLOGY INTEGRATION

The authors have been involved with adult learner programs, including a program that was intended for adult learners to complete a business undergraduate degree in four years, while taking classes only on Friday evenings and weekends. The courses were created and designed with the adult learner in mind and enrollment was only allowed for students classified for this program/scheduling option.

The intensive nature of the program is designed to allow students to complete within a time frame comparable to traditional students attending full-time, however class schedules are limited to evening and weekend classes. The courses are arranged using a modular approach, which allows for both focused classroom sessions, as well as projects and assignments that include individual, group, and critical thinking work.

Support in the form of both technology and program/course related resources (written, online, live) was also provided to students throughout the program. The insights gained from this program, and also from research and surveys of other adult learner programs and related literature, are used to propose this model/framework of adult learner technology integration. Please see Table 1 for a diagram of this model.

The model comprises two dimensions; the Levels and the Components. The Levels (or views) look at whether the technology education and support are addressing the needs of the students in a program, or for the courses in general; or if they are focused on the needs of a specific course. The Macro view examines which features and support would benefit all students and instructors, regardless of the courses being taken. The Micro view examines training and use of technology from the perspective of an individual course and instructor.

The various technology integration perspectives are deconstructed into several component parts:

- Basic Technology Skills Support,
- Course Technology Support,
- Distance Learning Support, and
- Continuing Support.

### A. Basic Technology Skills Support

This component is designed to address basic computing and technology skills that are expected of adult students, particularly those likely to be used in their studies. Aside from general computing skills, such as using a Windows or Mac

*Table 1. Model of adult learner technology integration*

| | Basic Tech. Skills | Course Technology | Distance Learn Tech | Continuing Support |
|---|---|---|---|---|
| Macro Level (Program, administrative level) | Orientation/ Diagnostic Technology Survey Personal Interview; recommendations Online Tutorials Online library tutorial Seminars Self-Study resources Institutional support for Basic Technology Initiatives Guidelines and advocacy for basic technology skill development. | Faculty Training, Workshops, Seminars on use of new media tools. Institutional support for course technology resources. Guidelines and advocacy for course technology skill development. | Faculty Training, Workshops, Seminars on use of CMS and online course delivery tools and resources. Assistance to faculty developing online courses. Support for online course initiatives Guidelines and advocacy for online course development. | Support for technical problems, including Help Desk, tutorials, reference documents, Support for course technology- related problems, including help desk, tutorials, reference documents, Support for both technical and course-related online learning resources. |
| Micro Level (Course /Instructor Level) | Course-specific basic technology review/self-study/support Review of specific basic technology skills needed in a course (if not commonly used). | Course-specific specialized technology tutorial before use in the course. Electronic assignment submission Online Research required in the course. Message Board discussions in the course. Group work and collaboration done in the course (including tools to be used). Web 2.0 tools used in the course. | Develop a sense of community. Develop a learning community for the course. Attention to main skills used in the online/hybrid course. | Availability of help desk, tutorial, reference materials (phone, e-mail web, in person) Webinars on relevant topics. Self-service website. |

computer, the basics of using the Internet, office productivity software such as Office or a similar package, are emphasized.

## B. Course Technology Support

The next component considers the support for technology knowledge within a course. This is primarily focused on those technologies which are used in the class, aside from tools used to deliver courses online. This is a broad area, and one that can span everything from e-mail to specialized software or tools for applications in certain areas.

*Productivity Tool Support:* These include tools which are normally found in the workplace, including word processors, spreadsheets, presentation software, e-mail, etc.

*Application Tool Support:* These include tools designed for specific applications, but not general productivity tools outlined in the previ-

ous categories. Examples could be software for project management, CASE systems development, statistics, or graphics.

*Collaboration Tool Support:* These include programs, websites, or specific components of other tools that support collaborative work by a group. Course management systems, a specific collaboration-focused application, or a web 2.0 based tool such as documents and spreadsheets shared using Google Docs, or wikis, are all examples.

## C. Distance Learning Support

Distance Learning support can serve one of two main purposes: to support and complement the learning experience outside of the classroom, and/or to provide access to the course, without requiring the need to have face- to- face classroom sessions.

Hybrid distance learning was found in our experience to be the preferred mode for adult-centered classes. This involves the employment of both classroom sessions and online sessions in a course.

Online course support requires a greater instructor commitment, in that assignments must replace the face to face instructor support existing in the classroom. Additional materials may need to be presented as context for learning, and instructors need to be trained in, and prepared for the task of managing the course, including how the course will be run, managing online interactions, and monitoring student performance.

## D. Continuing Support

Support can be provided through a "self-service" website made available to students, or through a help desk.

Now that the various components and levels have been explained, the model itself can be discussed.

## THE ADULT LEARNER TECHNOLOGY INTEGRATION MODEL

### Macro-Basic Technology Skills

The first major component of adult learner technology integration is to assess incoming student skills and expertise in computing and technology. This can be accomplished using a survey that identifies prior use and perceived expertise in terms of knowledge of various software tools, online tools, and other technologies commonly used in the courses to be taken, the workplace, and for everyday personal use.

This is followed by a personal interview with an advisor, who can review survey results and make recommendations for areas in which technology skills and knowledge could and should

be improved. From there, a prescriptive set of recommendations are presented and the student is pointed towards one or more of the following options in order to strengthen the student's technology skills:

*Online Tutorials (provided by the university):* There are online tutorials, information sheets, and other resources provided by the computing services department. There are also tutorials and printed information provided by the "teaching and learning with technology" department. In general, these are likely to include the software and tools provided by the university in its labs, networks, and public computers on campus.

*Online Tutorials (external):* There are external online tutorials provided by outside sources which can provide the knowledge needed for self-study. If logins and accounts need to be set up, information should be provided to students.

*Seminars (provided by the university):* There are classes/seminars offered to students that can provide the basis of using various programs and allow for hands-on instruction for these programs and resources.

*Resources for self study:* Books, Internet sites, and other places for further study are provided for those students who need to strengthen their background in a specific area. An awareness of the importance of basic technology skills, together with institutional support (and funding) is also an important part of basic technology support.

### Macro – Course Technology

The major focus of this area would be to educate faculty on the effectiveness of the various tools for use in courses, including course management systems, Web 2.0, Internet-based tools, and options including video conferencing, real-time interaction, and exploration of using clickers, mobile devices, and other educational technologies.

The initiatives in the area should be to encourage awareness, provide support in terms of funding and personnel, providing training and seminars for faculty, and making the technologies available for use on campus (and by students and faculty remotely). Opportunities for self-study and other resources should be made available, as well as personal help from an instructional technology specialist in the case where a tool is being used for one's course.

If a university has a course management system available to all instructors, then training, materials, and other forms of support should be provided for those who want to use this in their courses.

## Macro – Distance Learning Technology

The approaches and focus for this are similar to that for course technologies; however the focus is on developing content, course structures, assignments, and methods of interaction for both hybrid and fully online courses. Attention should be given not only to the development of the course materials to be usable and appropriate for an online format, but also looking at the proper ways to encourage participation and interaction once the course is up and running.

Because designing for online courses can be involved and time-consuming, the availability of help from the instructional design staff would be helpful.

## Macro – Continuing Support

Follow ups with students and providing support in multiple ways on an ongoing basis would also be helpful to assure students that help is available if they need it.

The need to establish a means to stay in touch with students or for them to get any needed information should be implemented, and should not be exclusively course-specific.

## Micro – Basic Technology Skills

Technology should be used, wherever possible and appropriate, as an everyday tool.

It would be helpful for instructors to specify the technologies and software used in a certain course so that plans to receive upfront and/or additional help can be undertaken. In a writing course, for example, the ability to use word processing and the Internet is essential. In the case of an accounting or finance course, the need to use a spreadsheet such as Excel should be clearly mentioned, otherwise some students may find themselves struggling with how to use the software, rather than mastering content.

## Micro – Course Technology Skills

Given a wide range of options, the instructor can choose those technologies that fit the course, subject matter, and content/assignments. Examples of common ways that technology can be integrated into a course include electronic assignments and submissions, doing research online, holding discussions using a threaded message board, or having a group work on a project, while being supported by a tool that allows viewing and contributions by all group members. Technology can also be used to support peer reviews of a documents such as a writing assignment given to a class.

## Micro – Distance Learning

There are two main goals for distance learning on the individual course level. The first is assuring that both the instructor and student are well versed in the use of the course management system or tool being used by the class. This is often an obstacle since students may think they are technologically adept due to a general knowledge of computers and the Internet from personal or recreational use. However, due to the different tasks required when taking a distance learning course, the experience may prove to be daunting once the course begins and constant demands are placed on the student.

A second issue involves interaction. A course can be solid and properly run from the perspectives of delivery of material, a logical structure, and reasonable course requirements; however, if the students have difficulty becoming engaged in the course (such as online discussions) then the course may suffer from the effects of transactional distance. This describes the perceived "separation" of the instructor from the other students (and also students from each other), and may cause students to become isolated, frustrated, and "lost." (Stein et al., 2009). The ability of the instructor to recognize these pitfalls and to make attempts to engage students and create a "sense of community" is critical. Providing assignments which promote group work and collaboration among students can also be valuable.

## Micro – Continuing Support

The ability to obtain help 24 hours a day, 7 days a week, should be the goal of any continuing support operation. A help desk, e/mail or online chat, or self-service website is essential.

To illustrate the impact of technology, examples of technology use in a business and a General Education course are described below:

## Upper Level Business – Marketing

A course on Interactive Marketing is one type which would make effective use of technology. Use of the Internet as a marketing medium and the means of communicating and interacting with buyers are explored. The course builds upon theories of how one might effectively frame a message, communicate it, target and reach a specific audience, while at the same time use and understand the Web in the process. The focal point of instruction is use of the Internet to accomplish the traditional advertising and public relations functions of creating an image, as well as building a website to

achieve a specific function such as the sale of a product. Utilizing a modular course structure, a typical assignment for the course would progress as follows:

Students start with an individual assignment. This focuses on an actual problem or obstacle experienced by a client, and students must recommend a solution to the given problem or obstacle. This can be submitted online, and posted for instructor access. The instructor may select several of these for posting to elicit comments and discussion from the class.

Later, students are grouped in teams (which may or may not be different each class) and instructed to discuss and share their solutions/insights. Solutions are written up and displayed in the classroom. This can be supported by Google Docs, or a wiki, to help enhance collaboration.

Solutions are critiqued by the instructor by challenging the thinking of each group. Questions might be along the lines of, "Why do you think this will work?" or "What theory is this based on?" and so forth, accompanied by lectures or posting online content as needed. The instructor would receive feedback as to whether students are reading and absorbing the assigned materials in building solutions, or are applying inappropriate or incomplete solutions to the problem. Knowledge gaps could be a viable topic for a threaded message board discussion.

The next step has students reviewing solutions and data recommended by a PR firm. This is followed by a class discussion where student solutions are compared and contrasted with the actual solution. Class interaction may include students defending their solutions and positions, debating relevant issues, seeking clarification, and probing for additional insights regarding the solutions. If done outside of class, a message board or real-time discussion could be used.

Another assignment was to develop a web site concept and marketing plan for a local start-up firm. The requirements of the assignment included designing a flowchart diagram that fully described site navigation and functionality, together with creating an online research questionnaire. Also required was a marketing plan which included such elements as objectives, target audience, brand position/message, market trends and life-cycles (SWOT analysis), strategic partners (offline or online), campaign benchmarks, and program schedules. Software to help prepare flowcharts and diagrams, creating an online questionnaire that can be taken, and perhaps even designing a running prototype hosted on a web server would be useful.

## Lower Level General Course – English (General Education: College Writing)

For a college level writing course, the focus is on academic essay writing while helping to move students to the higher-order critical thinking required to successfully complete college-level work.

One of the goals leading to success in college-level study is to become a more critical reader, thinker, and writer. At their workplace, many adult learners typically undertake limited to no analytical work as part of their daily job content. To build analytical capability, several skills must be mastered including the ability to separate opinion from fact.

To gain competency in this skill utilizing a modular assignment, the following approach is employed:

Students are first required to find and email to the instructor (through the course management system or via e-email) an article having an unfamiliar subject matter, a more challenging vocabulary, a lengthier sentence structure, or an advanced writing style.

The instructor then previews the articles received, selects one, and emails/posts it to the entire class. Students read the assigned article in advance of class, and in the next meeting or online, engage in discussion, where students are challenged students to explain/evaluate/question/analyze critically what was written.

Students are shown how to move from factual to more complex thinking using the following stages: knowledge, comprehension, application, analysis, synthesis and evaluation. The main assignment is to write an expository/reflective essay incorporating the readings, discussion in class, online discussion, and experiences shared with others in class.

Prior to each class, students use the asynchronous conferencing feature in Blackboard (distance learning) to ask for assignment clarification, vent frustration when confronted with obstacles (typically arising from vocabulary and reading deficiencies), and help peers in need of support. The instructor utilizes the asynchronous conferencing feature in Blackboard to check student progress, answer questions, engage critical thinking, provide encouragement, and keep students on track.

## CONCLUSION AND DISCUSSION

Significant growth of adult non-traditional students within the undergraduate student population is noteworthy. Critical to the success of these students and to those seeking to enter the workforce after graduation is an ability to use, apply, and to make effective use of computers and related technologies. While there are no definitive indications as to the level of technology skills and knowledge among adult learners, sufficient evidence exists to indicate that at least a portion of adult learners have weak, or need updated skills, in using computing and related technologies. This deficiency can have an impact on performance, self-esteem, and persistence in completing an academic program.

Based on a review of literature, theories, and our experience with an adult learner program for business undergraduates, a model of Adult Learner Technology Integration was developed, suggesting effective methods and practices that can help to improve basic, course-related, and distance learning technology skills, on both the macro (institutional/program) and micro (course/instructor) levels. Aside from descriptions of all components of the model, the application of the micro-level, in implementing technology throughout parts of both an upper level, and basic requirement course, are described.

Certainly, more work needs to be done in the area of adult learners and technology. Web 2.0, social networking, and collaborative "cloud computing" tools are rapidly changing the face of education and computing on a rapid and dramatic basis. The need to be continually updated and current on the latest technology remains paramount, and thus a plan or framework for technology integration should be incorporated into any adult learner educational program.

Additional research is needed to further examine and validate new techniques for effectively teaching and supporting adult learners relative to technology. This paper offered a number of methods and techniques to consider with the understanding that additional work still needs to be done to fully understand the potential impact derived from offering program-wide enhancements, varying instructional methods, and exploring the use of distance learning (and related Web 2.0 and social networking), and support tools, to help foster proactive faculty and adult student involvement in the learning process.

# REFERENCES

Ahn, J., Han, K., & Han, B. (2005). Web-based education: Characteristics, problems, and some solutions. *International Journal of Innovation and Learning*, *2*(3), 274–282. doi:10.1504/IJIL.2005.006370

Bain, C. D., & Rice, L. (2007). The influence of gender on attitudes, perceptions, and uses of technology. *International Journal of Research on Technology in Education*, *39*(2), 119–132.

Bandura, A. (1986). *The social foundations of thought and action: A social cognitive theory*. Englewood Cliffs, NJ: Prentice Hall.

Beck, P., Kung, M., Park, Y., & Yang, S. (2004). E-learning architecture: Challenges and mapping of individuals in an internet-based pedagogical interface. *International Journal of Innovation and Learning*, *1*(3), 279–292. doi:10.1504/IJIL.2004.004884

Berge, Z., & Huang, Y. (2004). A model for sustainable student retention: A holistic perspective on the student dropout problem with special attention to e-learning. *DEOSNEWS*, *13*(5).

Bernard, R. M., Brauer, A., Abrami, S., & Surkes, M. (2004). The development of a questionnaire for predicting online learning achievement. *Distance Education*, *25*(1), 31–47. doi:10.1080/0158791042000212440

Broady, T., Chan, A., & Caputi, P. (2010). Comparison of older and younger adult' attitudes towards and abilities with computers: implications for training and learning. *British Journal of Educational Technology*, *41*(3), 473–485. doi:10.1111/j.1467-8535.2008.00914.x

Brookfield, S. (1991). The development of critical reflection in adulthood. *New Education*, *13*(1), 39–48.

Brookfield, S. (1995) *Adult learning: An overview*. Retrieved from http://nlu.nl.edu/ace/resources/documents/adultlearning.html

Calvin, J., & Freeburg, B. W. (2010). Exploring adult learners' perceptions of technology competence and retention in web-based courses. *Quarterly Review of Distance Education*, *11*(2), 63–72.

Canady, R., & Rettig, M. (1995). The power of innovative scheduling. *Educational Leadership*, *53*(3), 4–10.

Cawelti, G. (1994). *High school restructuring: A national study*. Arlington, VA: Educational Research Service. (ERIC Document Reproduction Service No. ED366070).

Chaffee, J. (1998). *Critical thinking: The cornerstone of remedial education*. Paper presented at the Conference on Replacing Remediation in Higher Education, Stanford, CA.

Choy, S. (2002). *Nontraditional undergraduates (Tech. Rep. No. NCES 2002-012)*. Washington, DC: National Center for Education Statistics.

Csikszentmihalyi, M. (1982). *Beyond boredom and anxiety*. San Francisco, CA: Jossey-Bass.

Daniel, E. L. (2000). A review of time shortened courses across disciplines. *College Student Journal*. Retrieved from http://findarticles.com/p/articles/mi_m0FCR/is_2_34/ai_63365186/

Dewey, J. (1916). *Democracy and Education*. New York, NY: The Free Press.

Dillenbourg, P., Baker, M., Blaye, A., & O'Malley, C. (1996). The evolution of research on collaborative learning. In Spada, E., & Reiman, P. (Eds.), *Learning in humans and machine: Towards an interdisciplinary learning science* (pp. 189–221). Oxford, UK: Elsevier.

Eshet-Alkalai, Y. (2004). Digital literacy: A conceptual framework for survival skills in the digital era. *Journal of Educational Multimedia and Hypermedia, 13*(1), 93–106.

Espana, J. (2004). Teaching a Research-Oriented, Graduate Global marketing Course to Adult Learners in a One-Month Format. *Journal of American Academy of Business, 4*(1-2), 418.

Fisher, M. (2007). Computerphobia in adult learners. *Computers & Education*, 14–19.

Garnham, C., & Kaleta, R. (2002). Introduction to hybrid courses. *Teaching with Technology Today, 8*(6). Retrieved from http://www.uwsa.edu/ttt/articles/garnham.htm

Gaubatz, N. (2003). Course scheduling formats and their impact on student learning. *National Teaching and Learning Forum, 12*(1).

Hafner, W., & Ellis, T. J. (2004, January). Project-based, asynchronous collaborative learning. In *Proceedings of the IEEE Hawaii International Conference on Systems Science,* Waikoloa, HI.

Hamilton, K. C. (2002). *Teaching adult learners: A supplemental manual for faculty teaching in the GBM program at FDU*. Madison, NJ: Fairleigh Dickinson University. Retrieved from http://www.fdu.edu/webresources/sitewidesearch.html

Hiltz, S. R. (1994). *The virtual classroom: Learning without limits*. Norwood, NJ: Ablex.

Horn, L. (1996). *Nontraditional Undergraduates*. Washington, DC: U.S. Department of Education. (ERIC Document Reproduction Service No. ED402857).

Hottenstein, D., & Malatesta, C. (1993). Putting a school in gear with intensive scheduling. *The High School Magazine, 2*, 28–29.

Hsu, J. (2008). Innovative technologies for education and learning: Education and knowledge-oriented applications of blogs, wikis, podcasts, and more. *International Journal of Web-Based Learning and Teaching Technologies, 3*(3), 62–81. doi:10.4018/jwltt.2008070106

Hsu, J., & Hamilton, K. (2010). Facilitating adult learner persistence through innovative scheduling and teaching methods. *International Journal of Management in Education, 4*(4), 407–424. doi:10.1504/IJMIE.2010.035608

Huang, H. M. (2002). Toward constructivism for adult learners in online learning environments. *British Journal of Educational Technology, 33*(1), 27–37. doi:10.1111/1467-8535.00236

Hughes, M. A. (1998). Active learning for software products. *Technical Communication, 45*(3), 343–352.

Hurt, A. (2007, February 28-March 4). *Exploring the process of adult computer software training using andragogy, situated cognition, and a minimalist approach*. Paper presented at the International Research Conference in the Americas of the Academy of Human Resource Development, Indianapolis, IN.

Jinoyiannis, A., & Gravani, M. (2010). Digital literacy in a lifelong learning programme for adults: Educators' experiences and perceptions on teaching practices. *International Journal of Digital Literacy and Digital Competence*, *1*(1), 40–60. doi:10.4018/jdldc.2010101903

Johnson, M. (2009). *Adult Learners and Technology: How to deliver effective instruction and overcome barriers to learning*. San Jose, CA: San Jose State University. Retrieved from http://ic.sjsu.edu/mjportfolio/found/AdultLearnersAndTechnology

Judge, S., Puckett, K., & Cabuk, B. (2004). Digital equity. *International Journal of Research on Technology in Education*, *36*(4), 383–397.

Kember, D. (1989). A longitudinal process model of drop out from distance education. *The Journal of Higher Education*, *60*(3), 278–301. doi:10.2307/1982251

Knowles, M. (1984). *Andragogy in action: Applying modern principles of adult education*. San Francisco, CA: Jossey-Bass.

Knowles, M., Holton, E., & Swanson, R. (1998). *The adult learner* (5th ed.). Houston, TX: Gulf Publishing.

Lawson, K. G. (2005). Using eclectic digital resources to enhance instructional methods for adult learners. *OCLC Systems & Services*, *21*(1), 49–60. doi:10.1108/10650750510578154

Li, Q., & Edmonds, K. A. (2005). Mathematics and At-Risk Adult Learners. *International Journal of Research on Technology in Education*, *38*(2), 143–166.

Lieb, S. (1999). *Principles of adult learning*. Retrieved from http://www.hcc.hawaii.edu/intrnet/committees/facdevcom/guidebk/teachtip/adults-2.htm

Livingstone, D. (2001). *Adults' Informal Learning*. Toronto, ON, Canada: University of Toronto. Retrieved from http://www.oise.utoronto.ca/oise/Home/index.html

Maddux, C. D., Johnson, D. L., & Willis, J. W. (1997). *Educational computing, learning with tomorrow's technologies 2/E*. Needham Heights, MA: Allyn and Bacon.

Martinez, M. (2003). High attrition rates in e-learning: Challenges, predictors, and solutions. *The eLearning Developer's Journal*.

Martyn, M., & Bash, L. (2002, October 9-12). Creating new meanings in leading education. In *Proceedings of the Twenty-Second National Conference on Alternative and External Degree Programs for Adults*, Pittsburgh, PA.

McKinney, V. R., Wilson, D. D., Brooks, N., O'Leary-Kelly, A., & Hargrave, B. (2008). Women and men in the IT profession. *Communications of the ACM*, *51*(2), 81–84. doi:10.1145/1314215.1340919

Merriam, S., & Caffarella, R. (1999). *Learning in adulthood 2/E*. San Francisco, CA: Jossey-Bass.

Milheim, K. (2007). Influence of technology on informal learning. *Adult Basic Education and Literacy Journal*, *1*(1).

Morris, M. G., & Venkatesh, V. (2000). Age differences in technology adoption decisions. *Personnel Psychology*, *53*(2), 375–403. doi:10.1111/j.1744-6570.2000.tb00206.x

National Center for Research in Vocational Education (1987). *Report on education*. Berkley, CA: National Center for Research in Vocational Education. Retrieved from http://vocserve.berkeley.edu/

Ornstein, A. C., & Hunkins, F. P. (1998). *Curriculum: Foundations, principles, and issues* (3rd ed.). Needham Heights, MA: Allyn and Bacon.

Paas, F. G., Renkl, A., & Sweller, J. (2004). Cognitive load theory: instructional implications of the interaction between information structures and cognitive architecture. *Instructional Science, 32,* 1–8. doi:10.1023/B:TRUC.0000021806.17516.d0

Perry, W. G. (1970). *Forms of intellectual and ethical development in the college years: A scheme.* New York, NY: Holt, Rinehart, and Winston.

Piaget, J. (1973). *To understand is to invent: The future of education.* New York, NY: Grossman.

Rao, R. (2009). Digital divide: Issues facing adult learners. *Canadian Center of Science and Education Journal, 2*(1), 132–136.

Saade, R. G., & Kira, D. (2007). Mediating the impact of technology use on perceived ease of use by anxiety. *Computers & Education, 49,* 1189–1204. doi:10.1016/j.compedu.2006.01.009

Scott, P. A. (1993, November). A comparative study of students' learning experiences in intensive and semester-length courses. In *Proceedings of the North American Association of Summer Sessions*, Portland, OR.

Scott, P. A. (1995). Learning experiences in intensive and semester-length classes: Student voices and. experiences. *College Student Journal, 29,* 207–213.

Scott, P. A. (1996). Attributes of high-quality intensive course learning experiences: Student voices and experiences. *College Student Journal, 30*(1), 69–77.

Scott, P. A., & Conrad, C. F. (1991). *A critique of intensive courses and an agenda for research.* Madison, WI: University of Wisconsin. (ERIC Document Reproduction Service No. ED337087).

Scott, P. A., & Conrad, C. F. (1992). A critique of intensive courses and an agenda for research. In Smart, J. C. (Ed.), *Higher education: Handbook of theory and research.* New York, NY: Agathon Press.

Seng, J., & Lin, S. (2004). A mobility and knowledge-centric e-learning application design method. *International Journal of Innovation and Learning, 1*(3), 293–311. doi:10.1504/IJIL.2004.004885

Serdyukov, P., Subbotin, I., & Serdyukova, N. (2003). Short-term intensive college instruction: What are the benefits for adult learners? *Technology and Teacher Education Annual, 2,* 1550–1552.

Singh, P., & Martin, L. R. (2004). Accelerated degree programs: Assessing student attitudes and opinions. *Journal of Education for Business, 79*(5), 299. doi:10.3200/JOEB.79.5.299-305

Sloffer, S. J., Dueber, B., & Duffy, T. M. (1999). Using asynchronous conferencing to promote critical thinking: two implementations in higher education. In *Proceedings of the 32ⁿᵈ Hawaiian International Conference on Systems Science,* Maui, HI.

Sponder, B. (2004). Technology and adult education: New tools for new experiences. In *Proceedings of the Adult Learning Colloquium: Current Issues in Adult Learning and Motivation,* Ljubljana, Slovenia (pp. 150-160).

Stein, D. S. (2009). How a novice online learner experiences transactional distance. *Quarterly Review of Distance Education, 10*(3), 305–311.

Sweller, J., & Chandler, P. (1994). Why some material is difficult to learn. *Cognition and Instruction, 12*(3), 185–233. doi:10.1207/s1532690xci1203_1

Taylor, M. C. (2006). Information adult learning and everyday literacy practices. *Journal of Adolescent & Adult Literacy, 49*(6), 500–509. doi:10.1598/JAAL.49.6.5

Turban, E., King, D., Liang, T., & Turban, D. (2010). *Electronic Commerce 2010* (6th ed.). Upper Saddle River, NJ: Prentice-Hall.

Tyler-Smith, K. (2006). Early attrition of first time e-learners. *MERLOT Journal of Technology and Learning, 2*(2), 73–85.

U.S. Department of Education. (2002). *The Condition of Education (Tech. Rep. No. NCES 2002-025)*. Washington, DC: NPO.

Usun, U. (2003). Advantages of computer based educational technologies for adult learners. *The Turkish Online Journal of Educational Technology, 2*, 4.

Vygotsky, L. S. (1978). *Mind in Society*. Cambridge, MA: Harvard University Press.

Whipp, J. L., & Chiarelli, S. (2004). Self-Regulation in a web-based course: A case study. *Educational Technology Research and Development, 52*(4), 5–22. doi:10.1007/BF02504714

Wlodkowski, R. J. (2003). Accelerated learning in colleges and universities. *New Directions for Adult and Continuing Education, 97*, 5–15. doi:10.1002/ace.84

Yang, F., Shu, Y., Lin, M., & Hsu, C. (2007). Study of basic computer competence among public health nurses in Taiwan. *The Journal of Nursing Research, 12*(1), 1–9.

Young, G. (2002). Hybrid teaching seeks to end the divide between traditional and online instruction. *The Chronicle of Higher Education*, 33–34.

*This work was previously published in the International Journal of Digital Literacy and Digital Competence, Volume 2, Issue 1, edited by Antonio Cartelli, pp. 52-70, copyright 2011 by IGI Publishing (an imprint of IGI Global).*

# Section 3
# Digital Technologies, Blended Learning, and Reflecting Competences

# Chapter 9
# Good Teaching Practice and Quality Indicators for Virtual and Blended Learning:
## Project M.A.T.R.I.X

**M. Esther del Moral Pérez**
*University of Oviedo, Spain*

**Lourdes Villalustre Martínez**
*University of Oviedo, Spain*

## ABSTRACT

*The M.A.T.R.I.X (Modalities of Telematic Learning and Inter-university Results that can be Extrapolated to Blended Learning)[1] project identified and described the diverse teaching methods and practices applied in a representative sample of virtual and blended learning degree courses taught at different Spanish Universities using the G9[2] Shared Virtual Campus. The purpose was to extrapolate the experiences considered as "good practice" in the new blended learning contexts and methodologies proposed by the EHEA, using as indicators the quality of the learning design as assessed by experts, the satisfaction level of the students taking the courses, their effective contribution to attaining specific and generic competence in different subjects.*

## INTRODUCTION

Innovation involves deliberate and systematic changes to achieve objectives more effectively (Hannan & Silver, 2000). The use of technological tools can facilitate this process of innovation, since they offer new possibilities when planning and effectuating the teaching-learning processes.

The "hybrid" concept of organising learning (Marsh, 2003) in which virtual and traditional learning are combined, with virtual elements complementing the face-to-face part of the process, can facilitate this process.

DOI: 10.4018/978-1-4666-2943-1.ch009

So, following on from the experiences and studies on blended learning in different courses or subjects (Koohang, 2009; Allen, Seaman, & Garrett, 2007; Clark & Mayer, 2007; Bliuc, Goodyear, & Ellis 2007; Graham, 2006; Oliver & Trigwell, 2005; Cox, Carr, & Hall, 2004), the SWOT technique was used to study the efficacy of technological resources in the attainment of learning objectives, within the courses included in the M.A.T.R.I.X project, with the final aim of ensuring that students' cognitive activity enabled them to transform information into knowledge.

Similarly, there have been many studies focusing on the effectiveness of teaching and its relationship to learners' satisfaction, such as the work done by Durkin, Simkin, Knox, and Conti-Ramsden (2009), Lin (2008), So and Brush (2008), Burnett, Bonnici, Miksa, and Kim (2007), Lin and Overbaugh (2007), Pascual (2007), Love and Scoble (2006), Molero and Ruiz (2005), Chang (2005), Beran and Violota (2005), Apodaka and Grad (2002), and Tejedor (2002).

Students' opinions on their learning experience provides us with a wealth of information that allows us to learn more not only about the success of learning and teaching changes themselves but also about learners' own demands, as inferred from their ratings and assessment.

## DESCRIPTION AND METHODS

### Context

The M.A.T.R.I.X. project was financed by the Ministry of Education (Spain) under the Research and Analysis Programme and it was carried out during the 2007/2008 academic year, with the involvement of some twenty researchers. A sample of fourteen different degree courses were assessed, all taught totally or partially on the G9 Shared Virtual Campus (SVC), by the five Spanish Universities of Oviedo, Navarra (Public), Basque Country, Extremadura and Zaragoza.

## Aims and Stages of the M.A.T.R.I.X Project

To identify technical and instructional quality indicators to be taken into account in the design of virtual and blended courses (see Table 1), based on:

**Aim and stage 1:** The creation of a map showing the diversity of teaching and learning practices in the M.A.T.R.I.X courses, according to the descriptive reports given by teachers, clarifying their technical and methodological criteria.

**Aim and stage 2:** Qualitative analysis of the sample of fourteen courses (virtual and blended learning) by experts in e-learning project design and implementation, in order to extrapolate those experiences considered as "good practices", - both for the quality of their technical and pedagogical design, and for their effective contribution to the development of generic and specific skills in each degree course -, in the new learning contexts proposed by the European Higher Education Area (EHEA), characterised by the use of blended learning methodology and/or blended learning supported by the use of virtual environments.

**Aim and stage 3:** The appraisement of a sample of 290 university students who attended courses in the G9 SVC, and their level of satisfaction with their virtual learning environments (VLE), gathered via an opinion questionnaire. Proposals for improvement being inferred from users' own demands.

Given the above, different activities were undertaken in the M.A.T.R.I.X project, revolving around three basic action lines:

*Table 1. Action areas of the M.A.T.R.I.X. project*

| THREE BASIC ACTION LINES: | | |
|---|---|---|
| 1) Map showing diversity of teaching practices. "Good practices" (Personal reports) | 2) SWOT Analysis (sample of 14 subjects) by external assessors. | 3) Appraisement by G9 SVC students (sample of 290 students) |
| OUTCOME: Formulation of quality indicator that extrapolate to virtual and blended learning. | | |

## Research Methods Converging in M.A.T.R.I.X

Firstly, a descriptive methodology was adopted somewhat similar to an ethnographic study (Goetz & Lecompte, 1988), as the teachers, either individually or collectively, had to draw up a descriptive report on the instructional aim guiding their teaching activity totally or partially supported by the use of virtual environments. This report had to conform to some common norms taking into account, amongst other things, the objectives of the course for which they were responsible, the topics developed, activities proposed, assessments made, tutorial action taken etc., all suitably illustrated by screen shots of the environment, the presentation of contents and of representative resources.

So by way of careful self-examination and analysis of their own practices, all teachers made their course methodology known to the others through a transparent process, as these reports were made available to all members of the M.A.T.R.I.X community to serve as reference and later, to guide the external assessors in their identification of weak and strong points in each subject (SWOT analysis).

The descriptive methodology, similar to an ethnographic study, therefore afforded a highly valuable series of qualitative data, requiring researchers to immerse themselves in their own virtual or blended learning courses, by drawing up an exhaustive report with fixed criteria, showing the methodological principles guiding the instructional process in each course. These reports were an interesting source of information when drawing up the map on different instructional practice, including individual and group work, in the course sample under study.

In addition to the data obtained from the personal contributions of teachers by means of the aforesaid descriptive reports of their own subjects, it was established that each subject had to be examined externally by at least three assessors taking part in the M.A.T.R.I.X project. It was thought appropriate to opt for the SWOT analysis method to identify weaknesses, threats, strengths and opportunities in each of the fourteen project courses. This meant the creation of a common assessment and observation tool that would encompass the three blocks to be analysed: the technical design of materials, instructional design and tutorial action.

So it was the detailed case study, according to Bogdan & Biklen (1982), in the form of an interactive, deep, intense, detailed and systematic examination of each course carried out individually by the assessors, with the aim of finding their strengths and weaknesses, that led to the final, joint formulation of the improvements key to ensure success in instructional processes supported by VLE.

On the other hand, interesting quantitative data were obtained from a questionnaire appraising the university students' satisfaction level with learning contents, proposed activities, the assessment system, tutorial action and the communicative skills of the teacher... among other aspects.

In order to present the results obtained from the different phases throughout the M.A.T.R.I.X project in an organised and systematic fashion, we sum them up below, divided into their relevant sections.

## PRESENTATION OF THE RESULTS

### Qualitative Data

### Map Showing the Diversity of Teaching Practices Within M.A.T.R.I.X

As explained above, a total of 14 different G9 SVC degree courses were analysed. Each teacher drew up a brief report explaining the methodological principles guiding their virtual or blended learning course, in relation to course objectives, generic skills they wished to develop or strengthen (instrumental, interpersonal and systemic), course contents, individual and group activities, assessments and tutorial action planned etc. As a result of these reports, a map was drawn up identifying the diversity of instructional practice within the M.A.T.R.I.X sample of courses.

Moreover, after being submitted to a SWOT analysis, "good teaching practices" were identified for dissemination as models. From a pedagogical viewpoint we understand, as Epper and Bates (2004), that "good practices" can be considered as those which contribute to the improvement of a learning process, using an innovative approach in the quest for excellence, and thus able to be extrapolated to other contexts.

In the M.A.T.R.I.X project many courses were considered "good practices", where instructional innovations supported by VLE contributed to a qualitative improvement in the teaching learning processes. Below is a graphic presentation of the map (see Table 2 and 3), showing eight individual practices and in each case the kind of skills to be developed or consolidated.

Both group and individual practices proposed foster the acquisition and development of generic skills as reflected in Tables 2 and 3. Nonetheless, it must be pointed out that the planning of different activities leading to holistic learning through the acquisition and strengthening of diverse skills, is a fresh challenge to teachers' pedagogical practice in a blended learning meth-

odology, what it means to be amended teaching models that have been used so far. So the practices analysed in the M.A.T.R.I.X project underwent a progressive evolution towards more participative, learner-centred methods, supported by the use of technological tools, constituting a broad compendium of "good teaching practices".

*Table 2. Map showing the diversity of individual practices and generic transversal skills developed*

| Individual Practices | Generic Transversal Skills Developed |
|---|---|
| Questions with short answers | - Ability to analyse and synthesize<br>- Basic subject knowledge<br>- Written communication<br>- Ability to criticise others and self<br>- Ability to work on one's own. |
| Self assessment, Questionnaires | - Basic subject knowledge<br>- Skill to manage information<br>- Skill to develop connections<br>- Working independently |
| Practical exercises | - Written communication<br>- Information management skills<br>- Ability to analyse and synthesize<br>- Ability to criticise others and self<br>- Applying theory to practice |
| Learning contracts | - Basic subject knowledge<br>- Information management skills<br>- Developing connections<br>- Applying theory<br>- Working independently |
| Document synthesis | - Basic subject knowledge<br>- Ability to analyse and synthesize<br>- Written communication<br>- Developing connections<br>- Working independently |
| Web search and analysis | - Ability to analyse and synthesize<br>- ICT skills<br>- Information management<br>- Ability to criticise others and self<br>- Research ability<br>- Working independently |
| Autobiographical memories | - Capacity to analyse and synthesize<br>- Basic subject knowledge<br>- Written communication<br>- Ability to criticise others and self<br>- Search for excellence and quality |
| Questions with short answers | - Ability to analyse and synthesize<br>- Basic subject knowledge<br>- Written communication<br>- Ability to criticise others and self<br>- Ability to work on one's own |

Incorporating individual and collaborative activities develops and strengthens a whole range of instrumental, interpersonal and systemic skills in the students, thus fulfilling the new requirements promoted by the European convergence process. This process involves certain changes affecting the structural organisation of study plans, as well as teaching methodology, assessment practices, the student tutorial system etc., and has caused many teachers to make alterations to their courses, adopting a new learner-centred methodology, which entails reassigning the roles to be played by the different actors involved in the educational process.

Students, for instance, must develop new skills, involving a more active and committed attitude toward their own learning, constantly ready to adapt to social change, encouraging intellectual growth and broadening of skills. This switch in understanding teaching-learning processes gives rise to a learner-centred pedagogical design, facilitating independent and collaborative work and the acquisition of skills specific to one's professional profile as well as generic, transversal skills, categorized as instrumental, interpersonal and systemic (Del Moral & Villalustre, 2008).

It should be emphasized that the use of e-learning platforms and the technological resources offered by the Internet and the ever more sophisticated tools of Web 2.0 (social software) etc. (Del Moral, Cernea, & Villalustre, 2007) makes it possible for students to acquire not only all the professional skills they require, but also others related to the efficient use of ICT.

## SWOT Analysis of M.A.T.R.I.X Courses

The SWOT method was chosen to assess each of the 14 courses, and it was established that each subject should be analysed by at least three

*Table 3. Map showing the variety of group practices and the generic transversal skills developed*

| Group Practices | Generic Transversal Skills Developed |
|---|---|
| Final work on content | - Information management<br>- Planning and organizing<br>- Team work<br>- Interpersonal skills<br>- Leadership skills<br>- Research abilities |
| Working with Wiki and Blogs | - Information management<br>- Planning and organizing<br>- Skill in handling ICT<br>- Team work<br>- Leadership skills<br>- Project design and management |
| Manual creation by Wiki | - Skill in handling ICT<br>- Written communication<br>- Information management<br>- Team work<br>- Leadership qualities<br>- Application of theory to practice |
| Project using Webquest & Wiki | - Skill in handling ICT<br>- Information management<br>- Team work<br>- Leadership qualities<br>- Researcch skills<br>- Project design and management |
| Discussion on works read | - Oral communication<br>- Basic subject knowledge<br>- Interpersonal skills<br>- Critical ability of others and self<br>- Leadership qualities<br>- Application of theory to practice |
| Case solving | - Planning and organising.<br>- Information management<br>- Decision making<br>- Team work<br>- Generalizing learning to other contexts |
| Creation of a Round table | - Oral communication<br>- Basic subject knowledge<br>- Interpersonal skills<br>- Critical ability of others and self<br>- Leadership skills<br>- Application of theory |
| Practical work | - Basic subject knowledge<br>- Problem solving.<br>- Team work<br>- Interpersonal skills<br>- Applying theory to practice<br>- Leadership skills |

external evaluators, experts in e-learning. To this effect, given that the members of the research team were professionals with considerable experience in distance learning, they were asked to assess three of the courses studied in the project, from different analysis standpoints.

An assessment template was created, identifying the main elements to be evaluated, which were: 1) the presentation of the environment and materials, 2) the instructional design and 3) the tutorial action. In each of these areas various factors were analysed:

1.  **Technical and learning material design aspects rated:**
    a.  Design of home page or entry portal (quality and quantity of icons, organisation and accessibility of different elements and tools in each course...)
    b.  Organisation of content and navigation map
    c.  Presentation, readability, accessibility, usability ... of learning materials
2.  **Instructional Design aspects covered:**
    a.  Presentation of the instructional objectives (study guides, course summary sheet etc.).
    b.  Flexibility and structure of learning content.
    c.  Types of individual and collaborative activities proposed.
    d.  Appropriateness of activities to achieving objectives.
    e.  Consistency between objectives, content, suggested activities and assessment.
    f.  Assessment formulas adopted (assessment tests, assessment calendar ...)
3.  **The analysis of the tutorial action assessed the following elements:**
    a.  Adaptation to learners' prior knowledge and cognitive diversity.
    b.  Fostering communication and student participation.

c.  Development of a course virtual community.
d.  Personalised counselling and guidance.
e.  Teaching roles (as organiser, motivator, communicator, assessor, supplier of educational resources, technical support, etc.)

Below the evaluations carried out by the assessors on each of the fourteen courses in our sample is reported. They are grouped in the areas of knowledge to which they belong, so observations are made generically. In Table 4 their strengths are identified and in Table 5, their weaknesses.

As for the *strengths* identified, external evaluators are:

*   **In relation to technical design:** Clarity in the presentation of content, appropriate use of various multimedia resources, interactivity and the use of an intuitive navigation system.
*   **In instructional design:** The presence of a study guide, activities to encourage participation, the use of different tools of study, the consistency between activities, objectives and content.
*   **With regard to the tutorial:** The existence of individual and group tutoring aimed at creating communities of learning using tools such as forums, chat, wikis, etc.

Moreover, the *deficiencies* identified include:

*   **In relation to technical design:** Lack of appropriate technical design of learning materials, with no interactive elements and limited navigation.
*   **In instructional design:** Inconsistency between the instructional design and assessment objectives chosen.
*   **Tutorial action:** The weakness of the tutorial to enhance student participation and communication.

## Presentation of the Most Notable Quantitative Results Obtained from G9 SVC Student Opinion Questionnaire

In accordance with the objectives of the M.A.T.R.I.X project it was thought appropriate to seek university students' opinions about the contexts in which their learning was taking place. A questionnaire was therefore distributed to G9 SVC course students, during the second term of the academic year 2008/9, to obtain their views.

Some of the most representative data obtained show 70% of the students' general satisfaction level with regard to course presentation and tutoring to be "high" or "very high". The majority of students reveal that among the factors influencing their positive assessment was the fact that, in the main, teachers responsible for each subject made it easy to access learning materials and activities by means of an appropriate structural organization, as 67% of them point out. Likewise, 58% think the teachers "always" or "almost always" proposed activities

*Table 4. Strengths of M.A.T.R.I.X courses detected by SWOT analysis*

| STRENGTHS DETECTED IN THE M.A.T.R.I.X SUBJECTS BY AREAS OF KNOWLEDGE | | | |
|---|---|---|---|
| **Area of Knowledge** | **Aspects being analysed** | | |
| | **Technical design of Materials** | **Instructional design** | **Tutorial Action** |
| Sciences | - Clear and orderly presentation of the main page of the course<br>-Good presentation of the teaching materials.<br>- Suitable use of different multimedia resources | - The teaching guide describes accurately all the curricular elements.<br>- Student participation is fostered by planned activities<br>- Suitable timing of activities. | - Fluent communication. Group practices using discussion forums on different topics.<br>-Personal counselling by internal mail specific to course |
| Engineering and Technology | - Interactive presentation of learning contents<br>- Use of different multimedia resources<br>- Incorporation of an intuitive navigation system<br>-Learning contents presented in various formats. | - Presentation of a clear, detailed teaching guide.<br>- Incorporation of complementary materials.<br>- Use of "learning contracts" to encourage motivation.<br>-Continuous assessment used.<br>- Use of tools to facilitate study (Calendar, notice board, etc.)<br>- Coherence between aims contents, activities and assessment. | - Participation encouraged<br>- Creation of an active, virtual learning community.<br>- Use of a friendly but assertive tone in teachers' participations.<br>- Individual and group tutorial practices. |
| Social sciences and Law | - Use of a multimedia presentation as a study guide.<br>-Use of conceptual maps for a schematic presentation of the contents.<br>- Use of different multimedia resources<br>-Clear and orderly presentation of the main page of the course.<br>-Interactive presentation of learning contents. | - Continuous assessment through monitoring interviews.<br>- Coherence between aims, contents, activities and assessment.<br>- Use of tools that facilitate study (Calendar, notice board, etc.)<br>- Incorporation of self-assessment exercises.<br>- Presentation of a clear, detailed teaching guide .<br>- Complementary materials included. | - Individual and group tutoring.<br>- Creation of a virtual learning community.<br>- Participation encouraged and assessed.<br>- Friendly teacher participation.<br>- Creation of different topic forums.<br>- Participation fostered by leaving co-ordination of forums/wikis to students. |
| Biological and Health Sciences | - Very thorough and high quality teaching materials.<br>- Clear and orderly presentation of the course main page. | - Incorporation of a detailed teaching guide<br>-Coherence between teaching elements<br>- Complementary materials included.<br>- Use of self-assessment exercises. | - Participation promoted by way of different course communication tools. |

*Table 5. Weaknesses of M.A.T.R.I.X courses, detected by SWOT analysis*

| WEAKNESSES DETECTED IN THE M.A.T.R.I.X SUBJECTS BY AREAS OF KNOWLEDGE | | | |
|---|---|---|---|
| **Area of Knowledge** | **Aspects under analysis** | | |
| | **Technical design of materials** | **Instructional design** | **Tutorial Action** |
| Sciences | - Lack of any kind of messages to guide the student on the main page of the course | - An inaccurate study guide | - Group work is not fostered. It is therefore suggested that work groups should be formed to carry out group activities. |
| Engineering and Technology | -An overloaded presentation of resources on the main course page<br>- A confusing lack of homogeneous style for icons, graphics etc.<br>- Learning material contents are duplicated<br>- Contents only presented in *pdf* format for printing.<br>- Icons giving access to contents and resources placed chaotically | - Study guide is too extensive and lacks accuracy<br>-Lack of continuous assessment formulas.<br>- The virtual course is conceived, exclusively, as a material and resource bank. | - Lack of coordination on the part of the teacher in topic forums<br>- The instructional aspect of the forums is not exploited.<br>- Makeshift participation in the forums. |
| Social Sciences and Law | - Contents only presented in *pdf* format for printing.<br>- Learning contents lack interactivity.<br>- Pages used are overlong, entailing use of the "scroll", making them harder to consult and navigate. | -Assessment criteria are not clearly established.<br>- There are no clear explanations as to what the activities to be undertaken by the students consist of.<br>- In certain courses there is a lack of planning in group activities. | -Chat sessions are not envisaged in course programming .<br>- Lack of learner communication, interaction and participation.<br>-Individual tutoring is not fostered.<br>- No virtual learning communities created. |
| Biological and Health Sciences | - Design used lacks contrast between text and background.<br>-Contents only presented in *pdf* format for printing. | The carrying out of group activities not envisaged. | - No virtual tutorial action making use of the tools on the platform (only face-to-face tutorials) |

that made it possible to assimilate contents thus facilitating their learning process.

Somewhat more than 65% of the students make it clear that most course teachers used continuous assessment tests or exercises, which they valued as highly positive, since it has a direct bearing on learners staying in the virtual learning environment (VLE), encouraging regular study of the subject and successful achievement of the learning objectives. Moreover, it influences students' intrinsic motivation level by giving them ongoing feed-back on their learning progress in the course.

It should also be pointed out that 40% of the learners say that most teachers of the subjects they took encouraged collaborative work by proposing different learning activities. More than 43% of them consider that the teacher "almost always"

promotes participation and communication among learners, something we consider essential to ensuring the satisfactory outcome of collaborative activities.

Despite the high level of satisfaction and good results obtained in most of the learners' assessments, both as regards content presentation and learning activities in the virtual courses taken and tutorial action offered by the teachers, we must point out that 11% of learners reveal a satisfaction level of "low" or "very low". This fact is directly related, and in similar ratios, to their opinion on some key, intrinsic aspects of the teaching method adopted, since a little more than 17% of the students do not think the teachers responsible for the virtual courses apply suitable and effective assessment formulas to ascertain the level of content assimilation and achievement of objectives. Similarly, 14% consider contents not to be adequately suited to achieving learning objectives, since their structure did not facilitate study of the course subject matter. These students also declare that course teachers did not present learning objectives clearly and explicitly - basic, indispensable factors to be borne in mind in every instructional action undertaken, in order to steer the teaching-learning process.

Furthermore, on aspects such as those linked to the tutorial function carried out by teachers, it has to be stressed that a quarter of learners think that tutors failed to adapt to their level of prior knowledge, or to their individual learning and cognitive styles. Another 35%, a not inconsiderable percentage, would like tutors to give personalised comments of support and encouragement on their learning progress. Both demands can be considered as closely related to their motivation level for participating in course dynamics.

On asking learners to assess teachers' skills in managing communication and participation in these virtual environments, more than 34% said that at the start of the course there were no ice-breaking activities suggested, such as introduction forums, meant to foster a first contact among all participants, with the aim of establishing links favouring future interaction and group work, and helping to consolidate the course learning community. It is worth pointing out also that 18% of the students thought the feed-back given by the tutor was not dynamic enough for them, factors of vital importance in preventing learner drop-out.

## FORMULATION OF QUALITY INDICATORS

Taking as a reference framework both education quality factors and indicators in general, stated by various authors Sarramona (2004), Villar Angulo and Alegre de la Rosa (2004), Ramsden (1991), Kwan and Ng (1999) etc., and those for virtual learning processes in particular, Del Moral

and Villalustre (2005), Marcelo (2008), we've developed a precise list of quality indicators that help to define good teaching practices in virtual or blended learning environments. Arising from the analysis processes undertaken throughout the M.A.T.R.I.X project, we have defined a set of quality indicators for use in designing a proposal for improving the success of teaching practices opting for a virtual or blended learning modality, based on three core areas:

- Technical design of teaching materials
- Instructional design
- Tutorial action

## A. Quality Indicators Relative to Technical Design of Learning Materials

When designing learning materials for virtual and blended learning, attention must be paid to a set of factors that ensure the quality of the learning scenario and more specifically of the graphic user interface (GUI). The following elements must be taken into account: 1) Interface design; 2) Icons and navigation maps; 3) Environmental metaphors; 4) Presentation of information.

When designing a graphic interface, various criteria of usability, accessibility, interactivity and adaptability must be borne in mind (Del Moral, 1999, 2004; Krug, 2000; Nielsen, 2000; Cabero, 2002; Chaney, 2009; Menon, Rama, Lakshmim & Bhatm, 2007; Del Moral & Villalustre, 2005). These authors look at aspects as diverse as content organisation, the design of interactive hypermedia elements, the setting up of different levels of interactivity and accessibility etc., with the structure and presentation of the information being as important as its quality. The visual presentation and organisation format will be what influences interaction with the materials in the VLE, and the more visually attractive information will be to a great extent what the learner picks up and then assimilates.

As in face-to-face teaching, many on-line pupils see their learning process conditioned by the virtual environment they are immersed in. On occasion this causes the students to drop out as they feel uncomfortable with the visual format. It is, therefore, a priority to be exigent from a technical and aesthetic standpoint and to comply with the basic norms of usability, legibility, accessibility etc. (Krug, 2000).

Structured teaching contents also enable exploration of the information, which should be organised in such a way that learners can access it and navigate through it efficiently, facilitating their journey through the virtual environment.

In addition, the use of metaphors in the VLE that learners can easily identify will facilitate their understanding of the structure and their assimilation of the different interactive mechanisms used (Barker & Manji, 1991). So when the chosen metaphor is familiar to the learner, it guarantees their comprehension of the environment and simplifies their cognitive activity, ensuring that the learning environment does not itself become an obstacle.

## B. Quality Indicators Relating to Instructional Design

From a pedagogical viewpoint, we need to assess those factors directly related to the satisfactory cognitive development of the students and that contribute to the optimisation of the teaching-learning process in virtual or blended learning contexts. Among these it is worth mentioning the *a priori* definition of the learning objectives to be attained by the students; the proper formulation of activities that allow students' learning progress to be assessed and the transparency of the assessment system, ensuring that learners know what criteria will be used.

It is essential to start from the premise that instructional design must offer students contextualized learning experiences and environments, which support knowledge acquisition and the development of various kinds of skills. Hence we try to generate an area that fosters meaningful learning, through the activities planned, the definition of objectives, the availability of contents etc., thus favouring extrapolation of the learning to similar experiences.

## C. Quality Indicators Relating to Tutorial Action

The tutor's role in the new virtual or blended learning scenarios is of necessity substantially different from the one they played in conventional teaching, since they now have to use new skills, vital to the success of the learning project. Constant support and guidance largely determine the success of both keeping the VLE student drop-out rate down and of ensuring high learner participation in VLE assignments and activities.

Tutorial action must always foster the maximum development of student potential, offering learners the resources needed to achieve this and guiding them into overcoming on their own any difficulties that arise during their learning process, while never forgetting the contextual framework and attending to their individual needs, motivations and interests. This is a task that needs systematic and careful planning, as the tutor needs to be capable of inducing everyone to participate actively and effectively, to inspire trust, but also to be assertive, in order to optimise learning activities and self-learning. Consequently, the teacher who works professionally with virtual environments, not only needs to know how to transmit the contents of a subject but also to have the skills needed to guide and facilitate learning (Del Moral, 2004).

## CONCLUSION

The M.A.T.R.I.X project's aim was to promote reflection on the best methodological criteria, strategies and activities to be adopted in blended learning. The conclusions of the project are as follows.

## Stemming from the Community of Experts

The learning experiences in virtual environments analysed represent innovative teaching practices, which, according to the external evaluators, have many strengths:

- Those relating to the technical design of learning materials incorporating multimedia, interactive presentation of learning contents etc., facilitating study and learning.
- The diversity of individual and group activities incorporated in the virtual courses, leading to the development of skills of various kinds.
- Tutorial practices ensuring the guidance and participation of students.

Among the weaknesses identified should be mentioned:

- Technical design presentation of learning materials using pdf files.
- Proposed activities with little motivational value, and presentation of an incomplete or confusing study-guide.
- Not promoting participation and communication among learners.

## Stemming from Learners' Opinions

70% of learners said their overall satisfaction level was "high or very high", and for 19% it was "average"; nonetheless, a not inconsiderable 11% said they were dissatisfied (low level) with the methodology and learning attained in the virtual courses they took, a fact linked directly with their consideration of some key and intrinsic aspects

of the teaching and tutorial methodology adopted by teachers, such as:

- Unclear and inexplicit learning objectives.
- Content design unsuitable to achieving learning objectives.
- The use of ineffective and inappropriate assessment methods to evaluate the level of assimilation of contents and achievement of learning objectives.
- The lack of personalised feedback and encouragement with regard to their learning progress, etc.

Similarly, according to the results, students establish positive aspects of the training received with the use of technologies:

- The quick tutorial to answer your questions via email.
- The presentation of interactive content, motivating and attractive.
- Show content supported concept maps
- Innovative activities: projects by webquets realistic and implementable.
- Collaborative work practices through wikis.
- Ongoing evaluation and processing.

However, among the negative aspects that stand out from the virtual training received, noting:

- The excessive production of documents in pdf format (e-learning is Not e-reading).
- The lack of logical structure in the presentation of content.
- A calendar of activities inflexible.
- The completion of final exams.

## Proposed Indicators

Thus, both the improvements formulated by the experts from the SWOT analysis carried out as well as the student assessments on the virtual environments in which they learn, stress the need to:

- Clarify *a priori* the learning objectives that will constitute the instructional goals to be reached by the students.
- Develop and present the contents in a coherently structured, contextualized and hierarchical form.
- Present a diversity of individual and group activities by which student progress can be assessed.
- Make the assessment system transparent, showing evaluation criteria to be used in accordance with objectives to be achieved.
- Foster spaces for individual tutoring that contribute to the guidance, support and motivation of learners.

All this can serve as a reference for university teachers, enabling them to create and design their virtual or blended learning courses in the sure knowledge that they will enhance the efficiency of the instructional task at hand.

# REFERENCES

Allen, I. E., Seaman, J., & Garrett, R. (2007). *Blending in: The extent and promise of blended education in the United States*. Needham, MA: Sloan-C. Retrieved from http://www.blendedteaching.org

Apodaka, P. (2001). Calidad y evaluación de la educación superior: Situación actual y prospectiva. *Revista de Investigación Educativa, 19*(2), 367–382.

Area de Tecnologias, P. L. D. Grupo G9 (2010). Qué es el Campus Virtual del Compartido del G9. Retrieved from http://www.uni-g9.net

Barker, P., & Manji, K. (1991). Designing electronic books. *Educational and Learning Technology International, 28*(4).

Beran, T., & Violato, C. (2005). Ratings of university teacher instruction: How much do student and course characteristics really matter? *Assessment & Evaluation in Higher Education, 30*(6), 593–601. doi:10.1080/02602930500260688

Bliuc, A., Goodyear, P., & Ellis, R. (2007). Research focus and methodological choices in studies into students' experiences of blended learning in higher education. *The Internet and Higher Education, 10*, 231–244. doi:10.1016/j.iheduc.2007.08.001

Bogdan, R., & Biklen, S. (1982). *Qualitative research for education: An introduction to theory and methods*. Boston, MA: Allyn and Bacon.

Burnett, K., Bonnici, L., Miksa, S., & Kim, J. (2007). The development of a facet analysis system to identify and measure the dimensions of interaction in online learning. *Journal of the American Society for Information Science and Technology, 58*(11), 1569–1577. doi:10.1002/asi.20641

Cabero, J. (2002). *Diseño y Evaluación de un Material Multimedia y Telemático Para La Formación y Perfeccionamiento del Profesorado Universitario para la utilización de las Nuevas Tecnologías Aplicadas a la Docencia*. Sevilla, Spain: Universidad de Sevilla. Retrieved from http://tecnologiaedu.us.es/nweb/htm/pdf/EA2002_0177

Chaney, B. (2009). A primer on quality indicators of distance education. *Health Promotion Practice, 10*(2), 222–231. doi:10.1177/1524839906298498

Chang, W. (2005). The rewards and challenges of teaching innovation in university physics: 4 Years' Reflection. *International Journal of Science Education, 27*(4), 407–425. doi:10.1080/0950069042000323728

Clark, R. C., & Mayer, R. E. (2007). *E-learning and the science of instruction* (2nd ed.). San Francisco, CA: Jossey-Bass.

Cox, G., Carr, T., & Hall, M. (2004). Evaluating the use of synchronous communication in two blended learning courses. *International Journal of Computer Assisted Learning*, *20*, 183–193. doi:10.1111/j.1365-2729.2004.00084.x

Del Moral, M. E. (1999, July 5-7). *Metáforas, recursos interactivos y ambientes hipermedia para el aprendizaje.* Paper presented at the 1st Educational Multimedia Conference, Barcelona, Spain.

Del Moral, M. E. (2004). Redes como soporte a la docencia: Tutoría online y aplicaciones telemáticas. In Rodríguez, R. (Ed.), *Docencia Universitaria- Orientaciones para la formación del profesorado* (pp. 193–212). Oviedo, Spain: Universidad de Oviedo.

Del Moral, M. E. (2004). Sistemas interactivos hipermedia educativos. In Del Moral, M. E. (Ed.), *Sociedad del conocimiento, ocio y cultura: Un enfoque interdisciplinar* (pp. 33–64). Oviedo, Spain: Ediciones KRK.

Del Moral, M. E., Cernea, D. A., & Villalustre, L. (2007, September 12-14). Contributions of the Web 2.0 to collaborative work around learning objects. In *Proceedings of the International Conference on Technology, Training and Communication*, Salamanca, Spain. Retrieved from http://ftp.informatik.rwth-aachen.de/Publications/CEUR-WS/Vol-361/paper13.pdf

Del Moral, M. E., & Villalustre, L. (2005, February, 7-27). *Indicadores de calidad para un interfaz gráfico centrado en el aprendiz.* Paper presented at the V Congreso Internacional Virtual de Educación (CIVE), Seville, Spain.

Del Moral, M. E., & Villalustre, L. (2008). Desarrollo de competencias y estilos de aprendizaje en contextos virtuales: Prácticas colaborativas y trabajo autónomo en Ruralnet. In Del Moral, M. E., & Rodríguez, R. (Eds.), *Docencia Universitaria- Experiencias docentes y TIC* (pp. 97–129). Barcelona, Spain: Editorial Octaedro.

Del Moral, M. E., & Villalustre, L. (2009). *Modalidades de aprendizaje telemático y resultados interuniversitarios extrapolables al nuevo EEES (Proyecto MATRIX).* Barcelona, Spain: Editorial Octaedro.

Dodge, B. (1995). *Some thoughts about WebQuest.* Retrieved from http://webquest.sdsu.edu/about_webquests.html

Durkin, K., Simkin, Z., Knox, E., & Contiramsden, G. (2009). Specific language impairment and school outcomes II: Educational context, student satisfaction, and post-compulsory progress. *International Journal of Language & Communication Disorders*, *44*(1), 36–55. doi:10.1080/13682820801921510

Epper, R., & Bates, A. W. (2004). *Enseñar al profesorado cómo utilizar la tecnología. Buenas prácticas de instituciones líderes.* Barcelona, Spain: Editorial UOC.

Goetz, J. P., & Lecompte, M. D. (1988). *Etnografía y diseño cualitativo en investigación educativa.* Madrid, Spain: Morata.

Graham, C. R. (2006). Blended learning systems: Definition, current trends, and future directions. In Bonk, C. J., & Graham, C. R. (Eds.), *Handbook of blended learning: Global perspectives, local designs.* San Francisco, CA: Pfeiffer Publishing.

Hannan, A., & Silver, H. (2000). *Innovating in higher education: Teaching, lerning and institucional cultures.* Buckingham, UK: Open University Press.

Koohang, A. (2009). Learner-centred model for blended learning design. *International Journal of Innovation and Learning, 6*(1), 76–91. doi:10.1504/IJIL.2009.021685

Krug, S. (2000). *Don't make me think: A common sense approach to web usability.* New York, NY: ACM Press.

Kwan, P., & Ng, P. (1999). Quality indicators in higher education - comparing Hong Kong and China's students. *Managerial Auditing Journal, 14*(1-2), 20–27. doi:10.1108/02686909910245964

Lin, S., & Overbaugh, R. C. (2007). The effect of student choice of online discussion format on tiered achievement and student satisfaction. *Journal of Research on Technology in Education, 39*(4), 399–415.

Lin, Q. (2008). Student satisfactions in four mixed courses in elementary teacher education program. *The Internet and Higher Education, 11*(1), 53–59. doi:10.1016/j.iheduc.2007.12.005

Love, S., & Scoble, R. (2006). Developing a quality assurance metric: A panoptic view. *Active Learning in Higher Education, 7*(2), 129–141. doi:10.1177/1469787406064749

Marcelo, C. (2008). Evaluación de la calidad para programas completos de formación docente a través de estrategias de aprendizaje abierto y a distancia. *Revista de Educación a Distancia, 8*(7), 2–6.

Marsh, G. E. (2003). Blended instruction: Adapting conventional instruction for large classes. *Online Journal of Distance Learning Administration, 6*(4). Retrieved from http://www.westga.edu/~distance/ojdla/.

Menon, M., Rama, K., Lakshmi, K., & Bhat, D. (2007). *Quality indicators for teacher education.* Vancouver, BC, Canada: Commonwealth of Learning. Retrieved from http://www.col.org/resources/publications/Pages/detail.aspx?PID=244#

Molero, D., & Ruiz, J. (2005). La evaluación de la docencia universitaria: Dimensiones y variables más relevantes. *Revista de Investigación Educativa, 23*(1), 57-84.

Nilsen, J. (2000). *Designing web usability: The practice of simplicity.* Indianapolis, IN: New Riders Publishing.

Oliver, M., & Trigwell, K. (2005). Can 'blended learning' be redeemed? *E-learning, 2*(1), 17–26.

Pascual, I. (2007). Análisis de la Satisfacción del Alumno con la Docencia Recibida: Un Estudio con Modelos Jerárquicos Lineales. *RELIEVE, 13*(1), 127–138.

Ramsden, P. (1991). A performance indicator of teaching quality in higher education: The Course Experience Questionnaire. *Studies in Higher Education, 16*(2), 129–150. doi:10.1080/03075079112331382944

Sarramona, J. (2004). *Factores e indicadores de calidad en la educación.* Barcelona, Spain: Editorial Octaedro.

So, H. J., & Brush, T. A. (2008). Student perceptions of collaborative learning, social presence and satisfaction in a blended learning environment: Relationships and critical factors. *Computers & Education, 51*(1), 318–336. doi:10.1016/j.compedu.2007.05.009

Tejedor, F. J. (2002). La Complejidad Universitaria del Rendimiento y la Satisfacción. In Villar, L. M. (Ed.), *La Universidad: Evaluación Educativa e Innovación Curricular* (pp. 3–40). Seville, Spain: Kronos.

Villar, L. M., & Alegre, O. M. (2004). *Manual para la excelencia en la Enseñanza Superior.* Madrid, Spain: McGraw-Hill.

## ENDNOTES

1.  Del Moral Pérez, M.E.(dir.) M.A.T.R.I.X Project (Modalities of Telematic Learning and University Results Extrapolatable to Blended Learning). Financed by the Ministery of Science and Education (MEC) EA2007, in which 20 teachers f rom the S G9 hared Virtual Campus .participated.

2.  The Shared Virtual Campus consists of nine Spanish universities (University of Navarra, Oviedo, País Vasco, Islas Baleares, Castilla-La Mancha, Extremadura, La Rioja, Cantabria and Zaragoza) that offer virtual subjects within the same campus (https://www.uni-g9.net/portal/quienesSomos.html)

*This work was previously published in the International Journal of Digital Literacy and Digital Competence, Volume 2, Issue 1, edited by Antonio Cartelli, pp. 37-51, copyright 2011 by IGI Publishing (an imprint of IGI Global).*

# Chapter 10
# Blended Collaborative Learning through a Wiki-Based Project:
## A Case Study on Students' Perceptions

**Dimitrios Roussinos**
*University of Peloponnese, Greece*

**Athanassios Jimoyiannis**
*University of Peloponnese, Greece*

## ABSTRACT

*Wikis are currently gaining in popularity in schools and higher education institutions and they are widely promoted as collaborative tools supporting students' active learning. This paper reports on the investigation of university students' beliefs and perceptions of a wiki authoring activity, designed to support blended and collaborative learning. The study was administered in the context of an authentic coursework project activity in a first semester university course on Information and Communication Technologies (ICT), attended by 47 first year students. Research findings indicated that the students in the sample were generally positive about the collaborative experience offered through the wiki and the consequent learning outcomes. Students' perceptions of the functionality and usability of the wiki environment were also positive. They considered the wiki as an effective and easy to use technology. In overall, they evaluated positively the wiki assignment, as well as the technical and learning support they received on-line, through the wiki pages, and by their instructors during the class sessions.*

## 1. INTRODUCTION

During the last decade, Web 2.0 applications, including but not limited to, blogs, wikis, social networking, media sharing, social bookmarking, RSS, podcasting, etc., have received intense and

growing educational interest. At the core of the Web 2.0 tools are a) user control, b) architecture of openness and participation, c) the remixability and transformation of data, d) communication and sociability, and e) the harnessing of collective intelligence (O'Reilly, 2007). The emerging tools of Web 2.0 have the potential to promote important innovations in the way people conceptualize the

DOI: 10.4018/978-1-4666-2943-1.ch010

relationships between learning and thinking and, especially, how those relationships are conceptualized and developed in educational settings.

The use of Web 2.0 for learning purposes is expected to exert a significant impact on education and to change the boundaries between school and home; formal, non formal and informal learning; teachers and learners; education and entertainment. Undoubtedly, social media have the potential to transform the learning context by providing multiple opportunities for shared content and resources, self-directed learning, collaborative learning, ubiquitous and lifelong learning (Glassman & Kang, 2011; Jimoyiannis, 2010). Among Web 2.0 applications, blogs and wikis have received particular educational interest, with uses expanding to include diverse learning groups, ranging from primary (Tse et al., 2010; Woo et al., 2011) and secondary education (Angelaina & Jimoyiannis, in press; Forte & Bruckman, 2007) to higher education (Tan et al., 2010; Wheeler et al., 2008; Zorko, 2009; Yang et al., 2009) and teachers' professional development as well (Luehmann & Tinelli, 2008; Wheeler & Wheeler, 2009).

Because of their organizational features (hypertext format, easy to use environment, open access with no time and place restrictions) and the pedagogical affordances, wikis can offer enhanced opportunities to the students, not only to improve their authoring and communications skills, but to construct new knowledge through expressing and exchanging ideas, sharing of resources, critical and reflective thinking, collaborative and group work. Previous research findings show that wikis support collaboration, facilitate peer review, encourage reflective writing and support students' movement from surface learning to deeper understanding and knowledge construction (Bradley et al., 2010; Forte & Bruckman, 2006; Wheeler et al., 2008; Hemmi et al., 2009). In a recent study on the use of a wiki in a class of primary-five students, where English is taught as a second language, Woo et al. (2011) found that the students enjoyed using

the wiki, and the overall perception was that it helped foster teamwork and improved writing. In addition, Trentin (2009) presented a methodological approach for using wikis in the assessment of collaborative learning activities. Despite that there is growing interest in the use of wikis to promote collaboration in higher education, there is little consensus on how best to integrate wikis with other student activities and existing technologies (Naismith et al., 2010).

An evaluation of a wiki, compared with a forum for online tutorials, has shown that students and tutors felt that the wiki is more difficult to use than a forum, and highlighted the importance of good usability in collaborative software (Kear et al., 2010). In her study on sociology students who used a wiki in a blended learning environment, Zorko (2009) found that most peer communication and content creation took place face-to-face while students preferred to use familiar tools such as email and MSN Messenger for their communication. Similar findings were noted by Thomas et al. (2009), who found that business students preferred email and MS Word to compose content by copying into the wiki. Existing research indicates that students believe that wikis enhance collaboration, even though their using patterns may not provide evidence that collaborative knowledge construction took place through the wiki (Hughes & Narayan, 2009) and there is no measurable performance improvement (Neumann & Hood, 2009). Likewise, Lin and Kelsey (2009) found that collaborative writing and learning were the exception rather than the norm among participants in the early stages of wiki work.

This investigation has the ambition to contribute to a deeper improved understanding of how university students perceive the educational affordances of wikis, and how they use wikis as collaborative learning tools. The paper begins with a literature review concerning current research on educational wikis. The design of the wiki-based project is presented, and the implementation in a university course at the Department of Social and

Educational Policy, University of Peloponnese, in Greece. Following, the empirical study and the research findings regarding students' perceptions and ideas about the usability and the functionality of the wiki, and the consequent collaborative learning experience are presented.

## 2. THE EDUCATIONAL AFFORDANCES OF WIKIS

A wiki can be thought of as a combination of a Web site and a text editor, which provides its users with both the reader and the author privileges. But, the major advantage of wikis is that any participant can collaboratively contribute to the content by authoring, revising, reviewing, modifying and sharing content, which is automatically published online. Because of its friendly interface wikis constitute an easily to use authoring space where students' barriers to modifying wiki pages are minimal. Moreover, the results of their actions on the content of the wiki are instantly visible to their fellows and the instructor as well. Wikis can incorporate content in multimedia format (pictures, graphics, movies, and sounds) while they may be used as a simple tool to create multimedia presentations and simple digital content products. Wiki capabilities are currently being added to many Learning Management Systems (e.g., Moodle, Sakai, Claroline).

It is their format and organization, and the great range of affordances, offered for both students and educators, which have largely dominated the discussion about the potential of wikis to support instruction and improve learning (Larusson & Alterman, 2009; Parker & Chao, 2007; Wheeler & Wheeler, 2009). Typically, wikis are not the most appropriate tool to apply where quick answers are required. On the other hand, they are efficient tools for long term project or group activities, where a community space is required for virtual meetings, discussions, content sharing, and general course management.

Beyond this ease of editing, another powerful feature of a wiki is its ability to keep tracks of the history of every wiki-page, as it is revised (revision history). Each time a student makes changes to a wiki-page, that content revision becomes the current version, and the older version is stored. Versions of the page can be compared and presented in a backward format. The characteristics above justify why wikis are gaining educational and pedagogical interest, as a powerful tool offering to the students increasing opportunities for

- Engagement, participation and reflection, and community building.
- Learning to work together (group working) and to learn from each other.
- Reflective and collaborative creation of content and, consequently, for collaborative knowledge construction.
- Extending learning beyond the classroom boundaries by allowing students' access to resources and their participation from any location.
- Blended learning activities and collaborative activities that might not be possible in the classroom.

As a result of their non-hierarchical and collaborative attributes, wikis have been used in educational settings in many different ways, aiming at various educational objectives. There is growing evidence that wikis can be deployed successfully in a variety of educational contexts as easily accessible content composition systems, online discussion spaces, information repositories, and collaboration tools. Under well-designed situations, wikis could be transformed into student-owned and student-centred learning spaces. Literature review on the educational uses of wikis suggested the following categories: a) course management tool, b) group authoring tool, c) project development environment, d) e-portfolio, e) research and data collection tool, and f) a presentation tool. However, most applications of wikis in educational practice make worthy more that one of the aspects discussed.

## 2.1. Wiki as On-Line Course Management Tool

A course wiki acts as a place where students can collaboratively write reviews of the courses taken and articulate their impressions and perspectives by extending the boundaries of the classroom. In a study exploring the potential for wikis to promote collaborative learning, teacher students used wikis regularly during their classroom sessions as a space to store and edit collaboratively the work from their research exercises, and as a forum for discussion (Wheeler et al., 2008). Following, a blended and problem-based learning approach, Zorko (2009) used a wiki environment in an English for Specific Purposes course to promote collaboration among sociology students at university level. Within the context of an English language course, a recent study recorded three types of engineering students' activity in a wiki showing different ways of collaboration and sharing content online (Bradley et al., 2010): contributing and writing together, evaluating and peer reviewing, arguing and discussing.

## 2.2. Wiki as a Group Authoring Tool

Group authoring is a learning activity where the wiki acts more as a collective or collaborative space than as an individual one. In this activity class students are divided into groups. All students in each group are expected to contribute consistently to their own group wiki space. Collaborative writing of assignments is a relatively new approach in educational settings (primary, secondary and higher education). A group wiki is an excellent and efficient tool for the students to express themselves, to discuss and debate on their ideas, to define key ideas, to reach a consensus, and write and build new content in a collaborative and constructive way etc. This strengthens the

sense of community within the group by allowing students with overlapping or similar ideas to see and collaboratively build on each other's work (Sheehy, 2008).

Forte and Bruckman (2007) launched a wiki to support learning in high school science classrooms through the collaborative production of an online science resource. Similarly, Wheeler and Wheeler (2009) explored how wikis were used by undergraduate teacher trainees to communicate ideas and generate course-specific content. Their results showed that students, through wiki activities, were able to improve their academic writing skills and get involved in collaborative learning.

## 2.3. Wiki as a Project Development Environment

A wiki can act as a private intranet to support project development or project-based learning activities. All participants can communicate, share resources (including texts, videos, hyperlinks, etc.), and construct collaboratively a report, a term paper or any other assignment product (presentation, web site etc.). Molyneaux and Brumley (2007) reported on the implementation of a group wiki used to facilitate the project management and design process of an environmental design exercise in an engineering university course.

Besides improving student engagement in the projects, the wiki was found to enhance the instructor's ability to observe (and guide) group dynamics and to facilitate timely feedback. The students can take advantage of accessing project wiki from anywhere and, therefore, they save time by seeing what sources others have already checked, they can receive support from tracking their own and fellows' research, ideas and posts on the wiki etc. In his research exploring the potential of wikis in a project-based software engineering course, Chao (2007) found that students soon discovered a number of innovative ways in which wikis can augment collaborative software development activities.

## 2.4. Wiki as an E-Portfolio

An e-portfolio is an assigned website, were individuals post and reflect on their work. In opposition with a blog which is organized chronologically, a wiki has the advantage of being organized by content subjects. In a specific learning context, both technologies can be used effectively as an e-portfolio supporting students' personal digital collection and presentation of information while illustrating each student's learning and development processes (Schaffert et al., 2006). These processes can support both self-directed learning and community learning. Even if some educators are cautious about the value of wikis as e-portfolios, the main idea behind wiki-portfolios is to give access to a simple web publishing system so that any student can easily post his work.

## 2.5. Wiki as a Research Tool

Properly designed wikis can be used as powerful tools for supporting academic research. Because of its ease of editing, a wiki can constitute a platform for ongoing literature review for academic purposes, a data collection and compilation tool, or a space to share the results of students' research according to the course assignments. A wiki is a great way to organize various types of content (e.g., a glossary of terms used in a specific field, a list of suggested content sources etc.). Hoffmann (2008) reported on WikiGenes, a dynamic, collaborative publishing wiki system for life sciences. It combines the collaborative affordances of wikis with explicit authorship and provides a knowledge base that can evolve via continual revision and traditional peer review into a rigorous scientific tool. Wikis can also be used for social bookmarking as well. They give to all participants the possibility to post, comment, group, and classify links in a specific field. In the same way, wikis can also be used to build an online repository of relevant documents or FAQs for the participants.

## 3. RESEARCH FRAMEWORK

### 3.1. The Course Context

The wiki reported in this paper implemented during the fall semester of 2010, in the context of a course under the title "Introduction to Information and Communication Technologies", at the Department of Social and Educational Policy, University of Peloponnese, in Greece. The course was a graduate obligatory offered to the first semester students and was designed as an introduction to both technical and social aspects of Information and Communication Technologies (ICT). As a result the students had the opportunity to develop a wide range of knowledge and skills on ICT and online communication. The course was supported by a Course Management System (Claroline) and structured in week units. Students utilized a variety of software and materials over a 13-week period, including course content, textbooks, information resources through the CMS and the Web, etc.

The non-project component of the course was carried out during the first six weeks of the semester. Students developed technical knowledge and software skills by completing a series of individual competency tasks and submitting complete artefacts into the CMS, which accounted for 25% of their course grade. After practicing the technical skills needed for the wiki development, students moved on to the project-based component of the course, which took place during weeks 7-12. They worked on a group authoring wiki-project administered by the authors and hosted in Wikispaces (http://www.wikispaces.com). The content for the wiki pages was outlined in an assignment description available through the main wiki page. Help and guidelines, a wiki example page, FAQ, and a tutorial were also provided to the students on-line, through the wiki.

## 3.2. The Wiki Environment

Of the many wiki environments available, Wikispaces (http://www.wikispaces.com) was chosen because

- It is a particularly simple to use environment, free for academic purposes.
- It incorporates features allowing comparison of previous versions (history), discussion pages, and user authentication.
- It allows instructor to track back edits and discussion comments, and thus to identify the contribution of each student.
- It is easy to manage settings in order that only invited members (students) are able to edit the content.

The features above were expected to allow the students to take ownership of their wikis without public interference, and thus that they will be encouraged to participate in and collaboratively contribute into their group work.

## 3.3. Design and Workflow of the Wiki

Using a *project-based learning* approach, the wiki was designed to engage students in a collaborative large-scale group authoring activity aiming

- To integrate content knowledge from different ICT subject areas, e.g., information systems, multimedia, network technology, ICT in society, ICT in education, ICT and labour sector etc;
- To develop ICT literacy skills, e.g., information access, managing, integration, evaluation and communication;
- To support collaborative work and reflection between students.

Rooted on the ideas of authentic learning (Herrington & Kervin, 2007), this wiki was designed and evolved for a period of six weeks, as an obliga-

tory project activity. It followed a *blended learning* philosophy by including classroom sessions and face-to-face discussions between the tutors and the students, individual work in the computer lab, and on-line collaborative wiki work (information seeking through suggested resources from the Internet, peer communication, exchanging ideas, content sharing, etc.) from both computer lab and outside classroom (mostly from home).

The instructor (second author) assigned randomly (e.g., in alphabetic surname order) the students to 11 groups of between four and five. The students in every group worked on their own separate wiki page topic. All students were required to participate in the group wiki and to collaboratively create a completed wiki site by the end of the semester. Accordingly, students were also encouraged to debate in the discussion pages in order to decide about the content submitted to the wiki and to help each other resolve technical or cognitive problems. They also had access rights to view the other group wiki pages. The first author was an assistant instructor for the course; he provided help and feedback on students' wiki coursework, facilitating discourse in the wiki pages and encouraging students to share knowledge as a community.

The students in each group were individually responsible for planning, designing, authoring, discussing, modifying, conceptualizing, and criticizing their group wiki pages. They were informed that their active participation and collaboration in their group wiki would be graded for the course with a contribution coefficient of 20%.

The wiki development process (workflow) was structured into four project phases, as following:

**Week 1:** At the starting of the project, the instructor introduced students to the wiki assignment and specified the learning goals, dates, time frames, and modes of work. He presented various types of wikis to help students to understand what a wiki is, how one can use it and participate in, the functionality of the

Wikispaces environment, the usability differences between editing and discussing etc. The students discussed in their group, both Face to Face (FtF) and on-line in the wiki space, about key concepts, the structure of the wiki, roles and responsibilities etc. These predefined activities had a clear goal; to support students' interaction, collaboration and also their presence in the wiki.

**Weeks 2-4:** During this phase, the students developed the structure of their wiki topics; they uploaded content into the pages, reported resources and references used, discussed in the wiki space and decided about the collaborative activities, etc. Moreover, the students worked individually, from both the computer lab and home, seeking for information and resources related to their topic. Guidelines given from the instructors aimed to convince students to avoid plagiarism and focus their work on debating, ideas interchange and synthesis, and collaborative authoring. The students were asked to reflect upon and edit regularly (at least once a week), and also to interact with peer contributions through discussing, modifying and expanding content.

**Weeks 5-6:** The students work focused on improving the quality of their pages by adding, modifying and transforming content, grammatical and syntactical editing, making technical-format changes, introducing hyperlinks to other group pages with common terms, etc. in order to produce a complete and reliable wiki site on the topic assigned.

**Closing day:** FtF meeting in the classroom devoted to the presentation of the wikis by each group, discussion about wiki and students collaboration, learning outcomes and evaluation issues, conclusions and project closing.

# 4. METHODOLOGY

## 4.1. Objectives and Research Questions

There are two main purposes justifying this study. To replicate and extend previous research concerning students' attitudes and beliefs about wikis as collaborative and learning tools (Bradley et al., 2010; Wheeler et al., 2008; Hemmi et al., 2009; Kear et al., 2010; Zorko, 2009; Thomas et al., 2009). We hypothesized that, in particular, it could offer information useful a) to evaluate the impact of the wiki project, b) to design and implement future learning activities using wikis as collaborative tools, and c) to suggest efficient ways for supporting students' engagement and cognitive development though wiki-based projects.

This study was designed to provide information to better understand students'

- Difficulties when using the wiki as a technological and collaboration space.
- Needs for on-line and face to face (ftf) support to effectively participate in a wiki.
- Perceptions and beliefs about the impact and learning outcomes of the wiki-project.

## 4.2. The Instrument

The instrument was an on-line anonymous questionnaire containing 44 items presenting statements of perceptions and beliefs toward the wiki, its functionality and collaborative aspects, and the learning outcomes of the wiki assignment. The design of the questionnaire was based upon the theoretical knowledge already known from the literature, and the practical knowledge and the research experience of the researchers. A 5-point Likert-type scale ranged from 1 (strongly disagree) to 5 (strongly agree) was used. There were four dimensions represented in the scale, aiming at students' perceptions and beliefs about

- The functionality and usability of the wiki as a technological space.
- The wiki as a collaboration and community space.
- The on-line and ftf support and guidelines they received by their instructors.
- The design and learning outcomes of the wiki-project.

Remaining items included the instrument were seven open-ended questions concerning design, organization and management issues of the wiki. Demographic information such as gender, age, previous ICT experience and competence, was also requested.

## 4.3. Sample and Procedure

The survey presented has been administered three weeks after the course was completed. The sample included all the 47 students (7 male and 40 female) enrolled in this graduate course, conducted at the Department of Social and Educational Policy. Most of them were between 18-20 years old while 10 were older than 20. They were familiar with computers and the Web; 46 students reported that they had PC at home and 41 an Internet connection. Only 4 of them had a previous wiki authoring experience.

The students were informed of the questionnaire guidelines and details of the study were given, e.g., that individual student identities would not be used or presented in the analysis, and that the results of the analysis would have no impact on their grades. The students were asked to respond to the on-line questionnaire from the university computer laboratory. They also asked to respond as honestly as they could and they were assured that there was no right or wrong answer. The researchers' role was restricted to answering students' questions in order to clarify the items under research.

## 5. RESULTS

### 5.1. Students' Participation and Wiki Content Created

The students were engaged into the wiki not only during the ICT sessions, from the computer lab area, but also in time and place outside the university, as observed from the posts details (date and time). The students in the sample reported that they usually were engaged in wiki coursework (activities) from their home (38 of them), from the computer lab (6) and from other places (3). They also reported visiting into the wiki everyday (10 students), 3-4 times a week (30) and once a month (7 students). They also reported engagement into the wiki coursework, through information uploading and editing the wiki pages, as following: a) everyday: 3 students; b) 3-4 times a week (26); and c) once a week (18 students).

Complete text edit information was extracted from the wiki. The data under analysis concern a time period of 6 weeks, from December 2010 to January 2011. Students' contributions were divided into

- *Page edits*, which included content information (e.g., text, photo, visual, audio, video).
- *Discussion posts*, which typically were publications in text format and incorporated questions, replies and guidelines, new ideas or comments to edited pages, etc.

The analysis included both content edits and discussion posts. Subject and group identity is protected, as all posts were analyzed anonymously, and results were reported in aggregate (see Table 1). A total of 423 wiki pages were created in the class wiki, during the investigation period. In addition to text and hyperlink edits, multimedia content was also embedded into the wiki pages as following: 208 in photo and graphic format, and 7 in video (most of them were embedded

*Table 1. Analysis of wiki activities per group*

| Wiki group | Total group pages | Page edits | Discussion student posts | Discussion instructor posts |
|---|---|---|---|---|
| G1 | 11 | 102 | 12 | 3 |
| G2 | 41 | 190 | 64 | 7 |
| G3 | 22 | 104 | 19 | 3 |
| G4 | 45 | 249 | 44 | 2 |
| G5 | 15 | 129 | 53 | 1 |
| G6 | 34 | 269 | 52 | 1 |
| G7 | 17 | 73 | 85 | 2 |
| G8 | 40 | 405 | 162 | 5 |
| G9 | 94 | 492 | 166 | 6 |
| G10 | 71 | 363 | 140 | 3 |
| G11 | 33 | 166 | 57 | 2 |
| **Total** | **423** | **2542** | **854** | **35** |

YouTube videos). There were 2542 edits recorded and 854 student discussion posts. Students' edit actions were related to a) begging a new page, b) adding or expanding content in an existed page, c) reorganizing content, d) enriching pages with multimedia elements (photo, video etc.), and e) editing (e.g., grammatical, syntactical and technical-format changes). In addition, 42 posts were uploaded in the Help page and 13 messages were sent to the instructors via e-mail.

Figure 1 shows a screenshot of the central wiki page regarding the topic "ICT in everyday social life". *Home*, *Help*, *Students* (personal information details), *Resources* and the *Wiki news* were the common pages of the whole project, while *Group topics* were the authoring space for each individual group.

Figure 2 presents the Discussion on "Multimedia" wiki page which had 127 contributing messages.

## 5.2. Students' Pre-Existing Beliefs of the Wiki Activity

The first research axis aimed to reveal students' pre-existing views and beliefs about the wiki activity before their engagement and wiki work. Table 2 shows the mean values of the student beliefs across the items of this research dimension. In general, the students in the sample were initially cautious or negative towards the wiki assignment. The underlined values represent the items in the questionnaire worded negatively. This means that, in the analysis presented in Table 2, those values were reversed to be consistent with the negative-positive (1-5) attitude scale.

## 5.3. Students' Perceptions of the Functionality and Usability of the Wiki

The first research axis aimed at studying students' views and perceptions of the functionality and usability of the wiki space used to support this project. The students in the sample, in their majority, were in general positive about the Wikispaces environment and reported their satisfaction of

*Table 2. Students' pre-existing beliefs of the wiki activity*

| | Item | Mean* | SD |
|---|---|---|---|
| Q1 | At the beginning of the wiki assignment I did not felt confident that I would be able to use Wikispaces | 2.38 | 1.19 |
| Q14 | At the beginning of the wiki assignment I did not felt confident that I would be able to collaborate with my group peers | 2.87 | 1.42 |
| Q34 | I was cautious about the learning outcomes of my participation into this wiki assignment | 2.06 | 1.12 |
| Q35 | I understood from the beginning my individual responsibilities for this assignment | 2.60 | 1.27 |

* The values underlined were reversed to represent the negative (1) – positive (5) scale

*Figure 1. Topic wiki page (ICT in social life: education)*

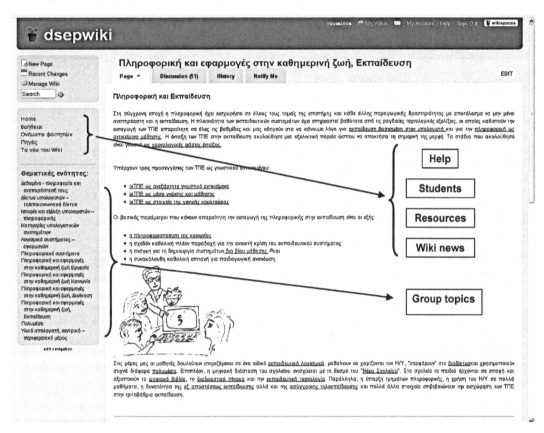

the usability and the functionality of the system (editor, discussion space) in relation to the wiki assignment. Table 3 shows the mean values of the students' responses across the items of this research dimension.

## 5.4. Students' Perceptions of the Received Support Through the Wiki

The second research axis consisted of six items regarding students' perceptions of the support they received, during the wiki coursework, from both their instructors and the wiki pages. As one can see in Table 4, the great majority of the students were satisfied of (and considered necessary) the instructors' guidelines uploaded in the wiki (e.g., News and Help pages), the wiki example embedded, as well as the guidelines given during the face

to face class sessions. Mean values of the students' responses were ranging from 3.34 up to 4.30.

## 5.5. Students' Perceptions of Collaborative Learning and Sense of Community Through the Wiki

The third research axis concerned the investigation of students' beliefs and perceptions of collaborative learning and sense of community through the wiki. There were nine items in the questionnaire representing collaborative learning in this axis (see Table 5). The majority of the students stated positively, with mean values ranging from 3.04 to 3.72, while they stated that their attitudes were progressively hanged to more positive.

The next ten items represent students' beliefs regarding the development of sense of commu-

*Figure 2. Wiki discussion page (topic: Multimedia)*

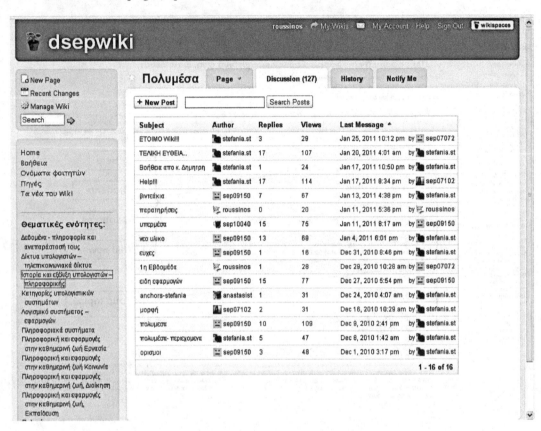

nity through the wiki (see Table 6). The majority of the students stated positively, with mean values ranging from 3.09 to 4.66 (regarding their respect of peers' ideas in the wiki discussion area).

## 5.6. Students' Beliefs About the Impact and the Learning Outcomes of the Wiki

The forth research axis consisted of twelve items regarding students' overall impression of the wiki assignment and their beliefs on the learning outcomes they achieved through the wiki. Table 7 shows that the great majority of the students stated positively toward this dimension, with mean values ranging from 3.09 up to 4.36 (regarding their perception of the wiki project as a positive learning experience).

## 6. CONCLUSION

Wikis have been widely promoted as collaborative tools through which students are not passive recipients of information; rather they are actively involved and work with peers to research, share content and ideas, review, construct and edit new knowledge in a collaborative way. The present study reported on an investigation of a wiki project designed to support students' engagement and collaborative learning using a blended approach in the context of a university course on ICT. The research results, based on students' responses to the wiki scale, contributed to our understanding of the different characteristics, benefits and difficulties of wikis for collaborative learning.

The findings of this research clearly have shown that integration of ideas and collaborative construction of meaning are directly inferred from

*Table 3. Students' beliefs about the functionality and usability of the wiki environment*

| | Item | Mean* | SD |
|---|---|---|---|
| Q2 | Using Wikispaces was an easy task for me | 3.62 | 1.18 |
| Q3 | I needed help to overcome technical difficulties in using the Wikispaces environment | 2.87 | 1.48 |
| Q4 | In general, I am satisfied of the usability of the Wikispaces environment | 3.77 | 1.04 |
| Q5 | I am satisfied of the functionality of the Wikispaces discussion area | 3.85 | 1.13 |
| Q6 | I am satisfied of the functionality of the Wikispaces editor | 3.91 | 1.11 |
| Q7 | During my wiki work, I encountered difficulties requiring specific technical knowledge | 3.61 | 1.30 |

\* The values underlined were reversed to represent the negative (1) – positive (5) scale

*Table 4. Students' perceptions of the received support through the wiki*

| | Item | Mean | SD |
|---|---|---|---|
| Q8 | The instructors' guidelines uploaded in the wiki were adequate | 4.17 | 0.88 |
| Q9 | The page 'Wiki News' was very helpful to my wiki coursework | 3.78 | 1.03 |
| Q10 | I received timely help from the instructors when I was referring any problem in the wiki 'Help' page | 4.30 | 1.07 |
| Q11 | The wiki example given helped me to understand what I had to do in this wiki assignment | 4.09 | 1.09 |
| Q12 | I believe that the assignment guidelines given during the class sessions were necessary | 4.22 | 0.92 |
| Q13 | I believe that the assignment guidelines given during the class sessions were more effective than the general guidelines uploaded in the wiki | 3.34 | 1.29 |

*Table 5. Students' perceptions of collaborative learning through the wiki*

| | Item | Mean* | SD |
|---|---|---|---|
| Q16 | I feel that peer collaboration in my group was improving during the evolvement of the wiki coursework | 3.72 | 1.20 |
| Q17 | I believe that the contribution of the other members in my group helped me to be more active in the wiki | 3.45 | 1.35 |
| Q20 | I believe that peer ideas in the wiki discussion area were influential to my content edits in the wiki pages | 3.47 | 1.07 |
| Q21 | I believe that my ideas were influential to my peer contribution to the wiki | 3.36 | 1.02 |
| Q26 | I believe that the wiki coursework reinforced group cohesion and collaboration between the members in my group | 3.62 | 1.10 |
| Q30 | I feel that I helped peers in my group to find information recourses related to our wiki assignment | 3.30 | 1.17 |
| Q31 | I think that the other members in my group helped me to find information recourses related to our wiki assignment | 3.60 | 1.10 |
| Q32 | I fell that I would learn more working individually for the same wiki assignment | 3.04 | 1.41 |

\* The values underlined were reversed to represent the negative (1) – positive (5) scale

students' participation in the wiki community. The analysis presented hereby, confirming previously existing literature (Bradley et al., 2010; Hemmi et al., 2009; Wheeler et al., 2008; Woo et al., 2011), has shown that the students were generally posi- tive about the collaborative experience they had, through the wiki project, and the received learning outcomes. Contrary to their initial perceptions of the wiki assignment, since most of the students in the sample were initially cautious or nega-

*Table 6. Students' perceptions of community sense through the wiki*

| | Item | Mean* | SD |
|---|---|---|---|
| **Q15** | I feel that the attitudes of my group members, regarding the wiki-project, became more positive during the evolvement of the wiki coursework | 3.70 | 1.20 |
| **Q18** | I believe that my contribution to the wiki motivated the other members in my group to be more active | 3.09 | 1.23 |
| **Q19** | I believe that the other members in my group were responsible to the wiki work. | 3.11 | 1.10 |
| **Q22** | I believe that the members in my group respected my ideas in the wiki discussion area | 4.15 | 1.03 |
| **Q23** | I believe that I respected the ideas in the wiki discussion area, coming from the other members in my group | 4.66 | 0.59 |
| **Q24** | I believe that I worked more than the other members in my group to create the topic pages for the wiki assigned | <u>3.34</u> | 1.28 |
| **Q25** | I did not felt confident that the other groups could see the wiki pages created by my group | <u>4.15</u> | 1.24 |
| **Q27** | I visited the wiki pages of the other groups frequently | 3.45 | 1.37 |
| **Q28** | The possibility to see the wiki coursework of the other groups motivated my group to be more efficient | 3.55 | 1.20 |
| **Q29** | The possibility to see the wiki coursework of the other members in my group motivated me to be more efficient | 3.87 | 1.16 |

* The values underlined were reversed to represent the negative (1) – positive (5) scale

tive, the majority of the students considered the wiki as an effective and easy to use technology. Moreover, they reported their a) satisfaction of the usability and the functionality of the wiki environment, b) positive beliefs that their wiki facilitated interaction, collaboration and sense of community among peers in the group, and c) positive perceptions about the learning outcomes in relation to ICT subjects.

Despite that most of the students had no previous experience in using wikis, their presence in the wiki pages demonstrated enhanced interest for the project and willingness-motivation to participate in this assignment (content and resources

*Table 7. Students' beliefs about the impact and the learning outcomes of the wiki*

| | Item | Mean* | SD |
|---|---|---|---|
| **Q33** | If this wiki was an elective assignment I would not choice to contribute | 2.91 | 1.30 |
| **Q36** | I felt confident of the evaluation of my contribution to this assignment because of the page history | 4.02 | 1.16 |
| **Q37** | I feel that the time offered to complete this assignment was adequate | 4.32 | 1.05 |
| **Q38** | In overall, I believe that this wiki assignment was a positive experience for me | 4.36 | 0.98 |
| **Q39** | I believe that I comprehensively learned more about the theoretical concepts covered in this course. | 4.06 | 1.19 |
| **Q40** | I believe that the completed wiki pages provided by my group constitute a reliable information recourse on this topic | 4.28 | 0.71 |
| **Q41** | I would prefer an alternative group-collaborative assignment instead of wiki | 2.79 | 1.35 |
| **Q42** | I would prefer an individual assignment instead of wiki | 3.40 | 1.48 |
| **Q43** | I believe that wikis could be used also in other courses offered in my Department | 3.32 | 1.31 |
| **Q44** | This wiki experience offered to me convincing evidence that I can effectively participate in similar social media spaces (e.g., Wikipedia) | 4.50 | 0.99 |

* The values underlined were reversed to represent the negative (1) – positive (5) scale

sharing, ideas interchanging, discussion topics etc.). In overall, they evaluated positively the wiki assignment, as well as the technical and learning support they received on-line through the wiki pages. Not all students in the sample found the wiki an easy technology to use. However, most of their difficulties seemed to be successfully addressed by providing students with extensive training on using the wiki software, continuous on-line support (e.g., FAQ, Help page, discussions with instructors and group peers in the wiki), and general-technical guidelines provided through both classroom sessions and the wiki pages. This is contradicting to the results of Zorko (2009), who found that most peer communication and content creation in the wiki took place face-to-face while students preferred to use other familiar tools for their communication (email and MSN).

A unique feature of wikis is that they enable individual reflection, peer interaction and authoring. This investigation showed evidence that students are motivated to participate in a wiki-based project, to share content and ideas and construct knowledge within a supportive community of inquiry. Using a blended learning philosophy to design and implement wiki learning activities seems to be a promising alternative for higher education settings and an efficient way to integrate wikis in educational practice (Naismith et al., 2010). Our results confirmed a recent study, using asynchronous online discussions (Koh et al., 2010), which argues that online project-based learning has the potential to provide students with opportunities for knowledge construction at advanced levels. It seems that, under well-designed wiki-based projects, learners are becoming empowered, motivated, more reflective and interactive practitioners in new learning experiences.

In conclusion, this investigation suggested that a wiki can be implemented effectively within a blended approach to support students' collaborative learning. Further research is required to determine whether and how wiki design issues, student characteristics, instructors' scaffolding

and supportive actions, students' evaluation, the discipline area, the wider educational context, etc., influence the effectiveness of wikis in educational practice. Our current research is directed to the investigation of students' wiki activity patterns within their groups and the interaction levels between student-student, student-content and student-instructor as well. The ultimate objective of the investigation presented here is to contribute to the development of an integrated framework conceptualizing the pedagogical value and the affordances of wikis and guiding the instructional design of effective wiki activities, applicable in practice. Undoubtedly, constructive critiques and debates are welcome and extremely beneficial to identify potential problems and weaknesses in this blended learning approach.

# REFERENCES

Angelaina, S., & Jimoyiannis, A. (in press). Educational blogging: Developing and investigating a students' community of inquiry. In Jimoyiannis, A. (Ed.), *Research on e-learning and ICT in education*. New York, NY: Springer.

Bradley, L., Lindstrom, Rystedt, H., & Vigmo, S. (2010). Language learning in a wiki: Student contributions in a web based learning environment. *Themes in Science and Technology Education*, *3*(1-2), 63–80.

Chao, J. (2007). Student project collaboration using wikis. In *Proceedings of the 20th Conference on Software Engineering Education & Training* (pp. 255-261).

Forte, A., & Bruckman, A. (2007). Constructing text: Wiki as a toolkit for (collaborative?) learning. In *Proceedings of the International Symposium on Wikis*, Montréal, QC, Canada (pp. 31-41).

Glassman, M., & Kang, M. J. (2011). The logic of wikis: The possibilities of the Web 2.0 classroom. *Computer-Supported Collaborative Learning, 6*, 93–112. doi:10.1007/s11412-011-9107-y

Hemmi, A., Bayne, S., & Land, R. (2009). The appropriation and repurposing of social technologies in higher education. *Journal of Computer Assisted Learning, 25*, 19–30. doi:10.1111/j.1365-2729.2008.00306.x

Herrington, J., & Kervin, L. (2007). Authentic learning supported by technology: Ten suggestions and cases of integration in classrooms. *Educational Media International, 44*(3), 219–236. doi:10.1080/09523980701491666

Hoffmann, R. (2008). A wiki for the life sciences where authorship matters. *Nature Genetics, 40*(9), 1047–1051. doi:10.1038/ng.f.217

Hughes, J. E., & Narayan, R. (2009). Collaboration and learning with wikis in post-secondary classrooms. *Journal of Interactive Online Learning, 8*, 63–82.

Jimoyiannis, A. (2010, April 8-9). Integrating Web 2.0 in education: Towards a framework for Pedagogy 2.0. In *Proceedings of the Web 2.0 Conference Abstracts*, London, UK (p. 5).

Kear, K., Woodthorpe, J., Robertson, S., & Hutchison, M. (2010). From forums to wikis: Perspectives on tools for collaboration. *The Internet and Higher Education, 13*, 218–225. doi:10.1016/j.iheduc.2010.05.004

Koh, J. H. L., Herring, S. C., & Hew, K. F. (2010). Project-based learning and student knowledge construction during asynchronous online discussion. *The Internet and Higher Education, 13*, 284–291. doi:10.1016/j.iheduc.2010.09.003

Larusson, J. A., & Alterman, R. (2009). Wikis to support the "collaborative" part of collaborative learning. *Computer-Supported Collaborative Learning, 4*, 371–402. doi:10.1007/s11412-009-9076-6

Lin, H., & Kelsey, K. D. (2009). Building a networked environment in wikis: The evolving phases of a collaborative learning in a wikibook project. *Journal of Educational Computing Research, 40*, 145–169. doi:10.2190/EC.40.2.a

Luehmann, A. L., & Tinelli, L. (2008). Teacher professional identity development with social networking technologies: Learning reform through blogging. *Educational Media International, 45*(4), 323–333. doi:10.1080/09523980802573263

Molyneaux, T., & Brumley, J. (2007). The use of wikis as a management tool to facilitate group project work. In *Proceedings of the AAEE Conference*, Melbourne, Australia.

Naismith, L., Lee, B.-H., & Pilkington, R. M. (2010). Collaborative learning with a wiki: Differences in perceived usefulness in two contexts of use. *Journal of Computer Assisted Learning, 26*, 1–15.

Neumann, D. L., & Hood, M. (2009). The effects of using a wiki on student engagement and learning of report writing skills in a university statistics course. *Australasian Journal of Educational Technology, 25*, 382–398.

O'Reilly, T. (2007). What is Web 2.0: Design patterns and business models for the next generation of software. *Communications & Strategies, 65*(1), 17–37.

Parker, K. R., & Chao, J. T. (2007). Wiki as a teaching tool. *Interdisciplinary Journal of Knowledge and Learning Objects, 3*, 57–72.

Schaffert, S., Bischof, D., Bürger, T., Gruber, A., Hilzensauer, W., & Schaffert, S. (2006, June 11-14). Learning with semantic wikis. In *Proceedings of the First SemWiki Workshop - From Wiki to Semantics, co-located with the 3rd Annual European Semantic Web Conference*, Budva, Montenegro.

Sheehy, G. (2008). The wiki as knowledge repository: Using a wiki in a community of practice to strengthen K-12 education. *TechTrends, 52*(6), 55–60. doi:10.1007/s11528-008-0219-9

Tan, S. M., Ladyshewsky, R. K., & Gardner, P. (2010). Using blogging to promote clinical reasoning and metacognition in undergraduate physiotherapy fieldwork programs. *Australasian Journal of Educational Technology, 26*(3), 355–368.

Thomas, P., King, D., & Minocha, S. (2009). The effective use of a simple wiki to support collaborative learning activities. *Computer Science Education, 19*, 293–313. doi:10.1080/08993400903384943

Trentin, G. (2009). Using a wiki to evaluate individual contribution to a collaborative learning project. *Journal of Computer Assisted Learning, 25*, 43–55. doi:10.1111/j.1365-2729.2008.00276.x

Tse, S. K., Yuen, A. H. K., Loh, E. K. Y., Lam, J. W. I., & Ng, R. H. W. (2010). The impact of blogging on Hong Kong primary schoolstudents' bilingual reading literacy. *Australasian Journal of Educational Technology, 26*(2), 164–179.

Vratulis, V., & Dobson, T. M. (2008). Social negotiations in a wiki environment: A case study with pre-service teachers. *Educational Media International, 45*, 285–294. doi:10.1080/09523980802571531

Wheeler, S. (2009). Learning space mashups: Combining Web 2.0 tools to create collaborative and reflective learning spaces. *Future Internet, 1*, 5–13. doi:10.3390/fi1010003

Wheeler, S., & Wheeler, D. (2009). Using wikis to promote quality learning in teacher training. *Learning, Media and Technology, 34*(1), 1–10. doi:10.1080/17439880902759851

Wheeler, S., Yeomans, P., & Wheeler, D. (2008). The good, the bad and the wiki: Evaluating student-generated content for collaborative learning. *British Journal of Educational Technology, 39*(6), 987–995. doi:10.1111/j.1467-8535.2007.00799.x

Woo, M., Chu, S., Ho, A., & Li, X. (2011). Using a wiki to scaffold primary-school students' collaborative writing. *Journal of Educational Technology & Society, 14*(1), 43–54.

Xiao, Y., & Lucking, R. (2008). The impact of two types of peer assessment on students' performance and satisfaction within a Wiki environment. *The Internet and Higher Education, 11*, 186–193. doi:10.1016/j.iheduc.2008.06.005

Yang, S.-H. (2009). Using blogs to enhance critical reflection and community of practice. *Journal of Educational Technology & Society, 12*(2), 11–21.

Zorko, V. (2009). Factors affecting the way students collaborate in a wiki for English language learning. *Australasian Journal of Educational Technology, 25*(5), 645–665.

*This work was previously published in the International Journal of Digital Literacy and Digital Competence, Volume 2, Issue 1, edited by Antonio Cartelli, pp. 37-51, copyright 2011 by IGI Publishing (an imprint of IGI Global).*

# Chapter 11
# Developing a Reflective Competence for a Master's Level Programme on E-Learning:
## The Leonardo Project REFLECT

**Antonella Nuzzaci**
*Université de la Vallée d'Aoste, Italy*

## ABSTRACT

*This study examines the effects of an activity of reflection on a group of students enrolled in the Master for Intercultural Education and European dimension of distance education, who participated in the construction of the model for a "reflection participant" and a self-evaluation tool to be used for training teachers. The activity is part of the research carried out within the Leonardo da Vinci "REFLECT" - "reflective practice for training the trainers" - Reflective Practice and VET (Vocational Education and Training), aimed at the creation of a specific methodology for the implementation of reflective practices in VET contexts, so that new processes of updating and re-professionalization required by the challenges of today's society can be started. It envisaged the creation of a testing laboratory, organized within the Faculty of Education at the University of Valle d'Aosta, which brings together teaching and research functions, contemplating an experiment involving the direct training of educators and teachers and demonstrating how to make a significant change in the actors who take part in the process. The study results show that it is possible to develop, enhance and strengthen skills through reflective mode online. The study indicates in post-treatment that the impact of such differences is based on the contextual features of the training.*

DOI: 10.4018/978-1-4666-2943-1.ch011

# 1. REFLEXIVITY AND REFLECTION: SOME IMPLICATIONS

In recent years, terms like "reflection", "reflexivity", "critical reflection" and "critical incident" have appeared in much of the literature, to indicate above all a way of intervening in the training of teachers. The same terms have, over time taken on different meanings, migrating from one area to another, thus requiring different types of action, t o such a point that it is not always possible to specify either the nature of these processes or to understand exactly what these words mean to those who use them. In addition, a substantial part of the vocabulary that revolves around reflexivity has become part of the teaching, and via translations from international literature, has found new concepts in terms which in Italian already had a precise meaning. And we know that the use of linguistic terms makes no sense unless it is placed in a rigorous context of analysis. Hence the need to bring some of these words to their respective interpretative models and forms of reflexivity employed in education, avoiding reductionism and attempting to assert their specific meanings.

The study aims at presenting a research activity adopting a precise model of reflection, developed with the help of ICT and on the possibility of its extension in the domain of management of educational processes, keeping in mind a literature aimed at developing reflective approaches both participant and on-line (Valli, 1992). This starting from the re-centering of the concepts of "experience" and "practice" as well as the re-conceptualization of the notion of "routine" (Nuzzaci, 2011a).

It is useful here to recall how reflexivity is placed in between theories of action, on the one hand, and devices from distance teacher training, on the other, proposing a different approach to professional education as a whole, at a time when the path of professionalism, while providing "structural conditions", and presenting itself as a socially defined construct, is undergoing a serious "stagnation" which makes the country's increasingly mobile professional education in need of new skills. Within this framework, the reflective paradigm and the new ICT can both be considered emblems of this professionalization, conceived as the power of teachers to intervene on their work from the analysis of practices openly and consciously assumed. They should therefore be correlated with the teacher training (at all stages), without being thought of as the only carrier capable of professionalization but certainly raising the level of competence, autonomy and responsibilities. It follows that there cannot be professionalism without the ability to reflect on the action or without the introduction of technological devices which facilitate the task.

The combination of technologies-reflexivity becomes an opportunity to question the nature of professionalism, the way to exercise it and learn the skills; aimed at reaching a deeper dimensions of professional culture (structure, values, thoughts, beliefs), it expresses a certain way of being "professional educators" and promotes an equal relationship between humans, a relationship which, rejecting the economic imbalances, political, social, re-defines the problem of attitudes (related to the self, the evaluation of others, etc.), knowledge (of self and other, individual and social interaction) and skills (interpret, discover, interact) and requires a mutual recognition of cultural and professional teachers, an assumption of the perspective of others, and a knowledge of how to look at their professional tradition through the eyes of a stranger, the ability to act on their routines and learn from each other elements of the new professionalism.

The experience is translated, through online discussion, into a "changed conceptual perspective" (Mezirow, 2003), which sees the process of acquiring knowledge capable of promoting the change and growth of the educator (and his community), causing him continuous "identity crises" and the loss of dogmatic temptations.

The "reflective practicing educator", described in the literature, is constantly reviewing his objectives, his practices, his skills and his knowledge (common, formal, theoretical, tacit, praxeological, practical etc.) thus becoming part of a virtuous cycle of improvement inside of which he theorizes his practices on his own or in a team. A self-regulatory capacity and an awareness of his professional learning should be noted in the subject, starting from the analysis of the experience and dialogue with others, and the idea that reflection is crucial for the "learning experience" (Mezirow, 2003) and the co-elaboration of the knowledge of the latter (Vinatier, 2006). But how then to query professional experience? How to understand the relationship built by professionals with experience of education? What is the role of technologies in this route?

Isabelle Vinatier (2006) says that working with someone on his own experience has a deep ontological dimension to the extent that it is reviewing the phenomena experienced by individuals and involved in their understanding and interpretation with the perspective to reconsider the habits, the usual, "ways of doing things "that can help to discern the characteristics of an event. It is clear that the conceptualization of a problem here transforms the praxis (often confined to the realm of evidence), which becomes a carrier of meanings for the actor. This allows us to account for different aspects of presenting the "reflective way" of teachers (and students) towards the conceptualization of the teaching-learning processes and at the same time, includes the construction of the amount of time required for professional experience and construction of social knowledge. In this sense we speaks precisely of "social self-construction" of the habitus, the know-how, the representations, the professional skills and attitudes that become more specific in relation to the practice, the self, self-observation, to self-analysis and experimentation guided by reflection on action. However, when the individual moves away from the reflection of a single action to reflect on

the structures of his actions and on the system in which he is inserted, we speak of reflecting on the "action system".

The foregoing raises (already at a first level of analysis), the question of the foundations of rational action (information, treatment, methods etc.) and the different models of interpretation of experience to which it refers, in addition to routine operations which are carried out without the guidance of reflection. Notice for example, that in education the greater the difficulties in learning to manage time, the more frequent the opportunities to act automatically, without thinking, without questioning the validity of the routines which lead to certain practical conclusions.

Starting then from a rereading of the conscious and rational part of the professional action, to which the reflexivity activity was added to attempt to highlight the unconscious part of the action, which includes not only acts, but also intellectual operations, which are in no way surprising since they can be considered activities, concrete or abstract, gradually internalized, which apply to representations and symbols rather than to objects (Perrenoud, 2001, p. 37). The constituent elements of the action patterns allow us to act quickly, automatically, in an almost improvised way, until it comes across, in the experience, an unusual obstacle. On this subject, Jean Piaget speaks of "practical unconscious" (Piaget, 1974a, 1974b) to emphasize the fact that certain patterns are implicitly built in the space of experience, without the subject being aware of it and that the internalized procedures then unconsciously become routine.

The reflection on the patterns of action is rooted in the literature on the "prise de coscience", the repetitive nature of certain reactions, sequences that tend to reproduce themselves in similar situations, creating recurring patterns, attitudes, and often resulting in a high level of professional dissatisfaction. The "prise de coscience" is the passage from practical knowledge to, reflexive knowledge, it is the conceptualization of "knowledge in action"

(Vergnaud, 1996), or moreover the transformation of patterns of action into operations. Awareness is the action of the subject and the representation that he has built, it is related to abstraction in its double dimension, "empirical" and "mirroring" (Piaget, 1977): the first has effect on objects and on the material aspects of the action, leading to an experiential knowledge, while the second has an effect on the child's cognitive (or co-ordination of action plans, operations, etc.), the object and the subject's ability to transpose an action which has become reflexive. The reflecting abstraction includes two dimensions: its "reflection" which is the projection at a higher level of what has been transferred from the lower level and the reflection, which is the structural reorganization, at a higher level. In an action of support for learning, for example, these dimensions are visible when the teacher's role becomes crucial in enabling pupils to become aware of their difficulties by the use of precise mechanisms.

This approach shows how the "reflexivity" arises questions also regarding stable dispositions that are conducted from time to time in the educational practice and how the reflection should result in the acquisition of an awareness of the existence of a durable "habit" of acting and thinking and, which when examined, allows us to infer the properties constitutive of "practice teaching". At the same time, remarks by many as the reflection is made more complex by the very components that make up the habit, something that brings scholars Vermersch (1994) to emphasize the limits of free discussion. When asked what is important to reflect, then, becomes spontaneously say, "first action", but this introduces the idea that the actor is embedded within a social system of relationships (the system of collective action) that enriched, differentiated and relates with his habit, explaining why it is often difficult to implement change. The reflection on the action embodies the idea of reflection on relationships, on how to create and maintain ties with others, the dynamics of groups and organizations, but especially on the articles of teaching-learning process that sees the teacher "co-elaborate" with the students.

This is the direction that our study took.

## 2. THE LEONARDO DA VINCI "REFLECT" PROJECT

The objectives of the Leonardo da Vinci "REFLECT" Programme - "Reflective Practices for the training of trainers" - Reflective Practice and VET (Vocational Education and Training) should first be clarified. The promoter and coordinator of the project was the Foundation Institute "William Tagliacarne" in Rome, with the following European partners: the Katholieke Hogeschool Leuven, the Bulgarian Institute of Human Relations, New Bulgarian University, the Italian Association of Trainers (AIF), the Department of National Accounting and Analysis of Social Processes of "La Sapienza" University (CNAPS), Faculty of Education, University of Aosta, Fundatia Romana-Germana, Centru de Calificare Perfectionare Profesionala, Vladimirescu (Romania), the University of Worcester Institute of Education and the ECAP Zurich.

The aim of the project was:

- To promote skills and competencies in initial vocational training, taking advantage not only of students' knowledge but also experience, with the help of specific methodologies;
- To improve the quality of learning, acting on key competences for interconnection between training sessions, both experiential and applicative;
- To strengthen the contribution of professional training in the innovation process, to foster cooperation between educational institutions, vocational training, universities and businesses to promote the activation of a community with a shared common reflective approach to industry training.

In terms of priority (Priority 4 –To promote the continuous training of teachers and trainers –), the project, primarily attempted to outline and to have a positive impact on the expertise necessary for trainers and other staff in different learning contexts throughout the course of their lives, seeking to strengthen their role as "facilitators of the learning process" designed as an integrated route in which the phase of acquisition of knowledge is closely linked to the ability to apply and use the same. Secondly, to transfer methodologies that allow the interpretation of the educational action and training in the broadest social and economic horizon in which the effects of learning could unfold; to facilitate the sharing of methodologies that sustain the effectiveness of the actions of professional orientation, by using informal and non-formal agents, of methods that support the effectiveness of vocational guidance. More generally, one of the strategic goals outlined in the Copenhagen Declaration was drawn on, or more exactly the one which acts on VET systems in order to transform them into learner-centered systems based on an approach to learning focused on the activation and enhancement of students' experience.

The change, unanimously considered more important with regard to the national systems and practices in vocational training, is that which concerns the transition from training based on predetermined, long- term paths of learning, to training designed in close relation to employability, the outlook for lifelong learning and the emerging innovations in production environments. This led to a radical rethink on the part of institutions on how to make school education or culture viewed in relation to the complexity of learning processes that must be promoted supported, valued and recognized.

To this end, the project employed highly functional tools which are conceptually advanced compared to the traditional training model, and consistent with a number of innovations under way at national level in initial training. In fact, the reorganization of training that has characterized the various reforms in recent years and the methodological assumptions that have inspired these reforms, constantly recall these changes (think of law on compulsory education and on the education on the right-duty to education and training, new apprenticeships, etc.) embodying principles such as equal dignity of contexts, the variety of learning opportunities (alternation etc.) and the central value of individual experience through the individualization of flexible pathways, learning skills for the recognition of credits. To meet the pressing need to develop, equip and qualify the system of continuous training, which still suffers from lack of attention and regulation in Italy, the project sought to support the sharing of methodological approaches alternative to the traditional view of education based on the simple transfer of know-how. That is why the instruments proposed were intended to enhance the learning experience as "productive" for the employee and the organization. Both in the case of training policy aimed at strengthening the skills of local production systems through integrated training pathways and intervention and the creation of communities of practice among local professionals), and in European strategies for vocational training, a high degree of consistency is shown with policies aimed at enhancing the practices of informal and non-formal learning, alongside moments of formal education, thus developing practical tools to be used by the main protagonists of training systems and implementing the provisions of the EU Commission Memorandum on Lifelong Learning released in 2000[1] and the strategy of European cooperation started with the Copenhagen Declaration of 2002, which commits the VET systems of all countries to work on quality and innovation of systems and to re-center on the individual dimension, non-formal and informal learning.

The highly innovative project proposed, attempted to create and disseminate tools to evolve the way of training in different contexts, moving away from the traditional training model, which though it foresees the use of workshops, is often characterized by a marked separation from practice and has a poor reflective structure. The effects of training-in-action are considered only on the basis of the observable results of the training itself. The decisive step in the development of a new kind of training is the development of instruments for the observation and analysis of the unforeseen effects, which should not be considered as "irrelevant accidents" or *defaillances* of the training process, but as bearers of information from which to move forward in an "expansive" learning process. It is for this reason that the proposed methodology makes extensive use of the technique of "critical incidents" and different kinds of learning practice based on empowerment, on *active learning* and enhance and social within the three categories mentioned. The three above-mentioned categories, as learning-agents had different needs and aspirations and were directly interested in the methodology as they were involved in a wide range of training and development variables (technical, cultural, educational and social etc.), often underestimated or taken for granted. They should have been considered from a European point of view in which there were significant developments and differences. The needs in this case regarded above all, the opening of a more formative complex model, based on reflective skills which would complement the technical-rational ones.

Reflective practice has received increasing attention in the educational environment in recent years, as witnessed by the vast literature which has accumulated in the field, and supported not only by theoretical interest but also by extensive research experiences. Several scientific journals devoted to reflective practice were established, such was the interest in the field, and the proliferation of publications in adjacent fields such as Action Research are also testimony to the richness of the debate. It is true that reflexivity is positioned between the theories of action on the one hand, and arrangements for teacher education on the other, proposing a different approach to professional education as a whole, at a time when the path to professionalism, although providing "structural conditions" and defining itself as a social construct, is in a phase of severe "stagnation" that makes the area of education increasingly mobile and in need of new skills. Within this framework, the reflective paradigm can be considered an emblem of professionalism, understood as the power of trainers to intervene in their work starting from the analysis of openly and consciously assumed practices, which are correlated with initial and continuous training of educators and teachers, without being perceived as the only professionals, though certainly capable of raising the level of competence, autonomy and responsibilities of each (Nuzzaci, 2001, 2009).

The scope of reflective practice is currently the subject of intense debate in which the most important trends are compared: from the Anglo-Saxon one (Calderhead & Gates, 1993) which has in its interior important experiences of professional development in education, to the Northern European situation which considers complex experiences at a system level, to the French system characterized by sophisticated calculations (Altet, 2001; Pasquay, Altet, Charlier, & Perrenoud, 1996).

The common feature is that practices have been established that have strong similarities at the level of target groups, identifying these as the corner stone of a new culture and new levels of professional dialogue between institutions, applicative realities and research system. In Italy, where the debate is proportionally less robust, the REFLECT project has provided a base for this important link with the different realities in the partnership to develop new responses to the problem, which is very much alive in the vocational training context.

## 3. THE OBJECTIVES OF THE AOSTA LABORATORY OF EXPERIMENTAL REFLECTIVE PRACTICES

The REFLECT project was therefore aimed at creating a specific methodology for implementing reflective practice in VET environments and, more generally, in the acquisition of learning, capable of initiating new processes for updating and re-professionalization required by the challenges of modern society. This instrument is closely related to the development of evaluation and self-evaluation processes in training, such as the tacit and non-formal use of feedback which the training action produces. The main effect is to help create a culture of evaluation which expounds and brings the relevant skills to the awareness of the trainers and agents implicit in learning, and which are not merely technical conceptions of assessment. The main purpose is directly connected to at least three other very important objectives:

1.  The systematization of knowledge in the reflective tools in education-training, particularly regarding the valuation of the unexpected effects of the training;
2.  Verification of operation of these instruments through the analysis of cases of skills development in operators at different levels;
3.  Promotion of community of practice among those involved in the processes of research and experimentation on new reflective methodologies.

The objective was to develop a reflective methodology which, starting from a broad overview of concepts and models of "reflective practice" ("state of the art"), permitted the production of a multifocal approach to the problem of reflexivity, aimed at identifying and implementing the conditions designed to encourage change, innovation and individual and organizational improvement in a specific training sphere.

The project involved the activation of experimental laboratories in all the institutions involved, with the aim of establishing within a common framework, a tool capable of synthesizing the work carried out by the partners. In this paper, particular attention is focused on the contribution which the University of Aosta, Faculty of Education team, partners in the project, made to the research. Assessment assumed the role of "guide" and "aim" of the activity, allowing the creation of a portfolio, initially individual and then collective, from which some useful indicators of reflexivity for the definition of a self-assessment tool for use in education derive.

The workshop includes:

*   Testing of reflective practice by teachers and educators with different levels of experience (experienced and young professionals);
*   Testing of reflective practice by teachers and educators working in different educational contexts.

The goals of the Aosta Laboratory can be summarized as follows:

*   Identification of some descriptors to characterize reflexivity at different levels of teaching experience/expertise (experts and young professionals);
*   Definition of the central nuclei of the conceptual and technical apparatus of a self-assessment tool (for reflection) to be used in the context of teacher/educator training.

The Laboratory started from two complementary theoretical paradigms: reflexivity, defined as a set of elements that are part of a process by which we understand the reasons why we act in a certain way and that implies a deliberate cognitive process based on a complex network of relationships designed to give meaning to actions and to stimulate new ones (Atkins & Murphy, 1995;

Boud, Keogh, & Walker, 1985; Boyd & Fales, 1983; Chambers, Clarke, Colombo, & Askland, 2003; Fitzgerald, 1994; Reid, 1993; Daudelin, 1996; Mezirow, 1991; Schön, 1983); evaluation, designed as a strategic tool, which becomes a reflective practice when it manages to make us understand how and why we act in this way and that allows us to critically analyze and interpret the work (Fitzgerald, 1994), namely to consider some activities in order to give rise to "reflection for action" (reflection for action), in the course of action (reflection in action) or the action (reflection on action).

The search started from the central idea that reflectivity could have a decisive influence on the growth of skills in the subjects, as it was mutually conceived as:

- An important means of learning;
- The ability to recognize, manage and exploit the learning that comes from experience;
- One possibility to bridge the gap between theory and practice, allowing subjects to confront ambiguity and change and to develop critical awareness.

The proposed intervention then tried to go to the "heart" of the issue of "professionalism" to ascertain that the promotion of reflection in the training of those involved in education and training is something that feeds the pool of knowledge, although too often, the literature shows that it is not always clear "what" trainers/teachers/educators should supposedly reflect on. This was the problem from which the Aosta research group set out to define "experimental activity". As a first step, internationally recognized reflective practices (state of the art) were shared with all the partners in the REFLECT project and the first conductors of the Laboratory tried to figure out how to profitably help the players/participants to reflect on specific aspects of their professionalism and on significant experiences in their profes-

sionalization process, as well as the implications that follow on from this action. It was made clear, above all how, according to common guidelines specified by the project team, that the workshop activities could lead to an increase in a different understanding of the phenomenon investigated.

It was necessary, therefore, to first identify the central dimensions on which to concentrate reflection and action, and that is why, in the so-called "preparation" phase, which was mainly aimed at distinguishing different levels of reflectivity as a function of the object on which reflection was directed, specifying the importance of:

- Being reflective about their skills;
- Being reflective about their experience;
- Being reflective about the kind of professionalism and business profile;
- Being reflective about their own professional convictions;
- Being reflective about the specifics of their own sector.

And the analysis focused on three main areas:

- The nature of professional education;
- How it is performed;
- How to learn skills.

The workshop was divided into two phases corresponding to different periods of implementation of the reflective process and was used as a testing ground for the Distance Masters Degree in Intercultural Education and European dimensions of Education, jointly run by the University of Valle d'Aosta and the University of Salento, the objectives of which, were the acquisition and reinforcement of teaching skills useful to those working in multicultural contexts and to those who wish to give an intercultural perspective to their professionalism. The Masters foresees training based on distant learning techniques (ODL) and includes three residential workshops. Recipients of the Masters were experts in the design and management of intercultural educational intervention in schools and in training, consultants and practitioners in public administrations, institutions and companies, NGOs, professionals in research, documentation and training facilities and experts in the field of socio-cultural integration of minority cultures.

As the course provided mostly for distance learning, it was decided to organize the structure of the Laboratory operating in two modes, each of which proposed a different approach to reflective practice: "distance" (mode A) and "presence" (mode B). For the character of this contribution and the implications that have derived, we will refer in particular to the group with mode A. which focused on the experimental work.

The membership of the subjects in the project, since it was done deliberately, for reasons of residence, as for mode B, the entire Laboratory performance was required to be in presence. The group with mode A, "remote", had been thought of, to study the effects of reflective practices in the network, but also so as not to exclude those who wanted to participate in the project but who were unable to do so for logistical reasons. However, it appears necessary to recall, that it was the first time that an attempt to enter a Master Course, which already included in its formative structure moments assigned to Laboratory activities, was recorded. An initiative to which students can contribute in innovative and effective ways in the training of individuals, with a proposal that could be considered truly alternative.

The two groups (A and B) would consist of 10 and 7 subjects and were quite heterogeneous in terms of experience, age, profession etc., which allowed to better fulfill the main objective of the workshop, namely to be able to track some indicators of reflexivity that could be used in education to decline any skills or meta-reflexive skills. It is obvious that if it is true that reflexivity is an important element of professionalism we must be able to clarify the different components and different level.

The Laboratory had a duration of 30 hours, including 4 of preparation, 21 and 5 of course completion, in addition to 4 hours of final assessment, with the inclusion of a summer phase called "latency" (and production) in which subjects were asked to document, through a series of written reflections, the work done in the first phase (see Figure 1).

## 4. METHODOLOGY AND RESEARCH STAGES

From the methodological point of view, the general structure of the workshop contained an "overall assessment plan" which covered both the construction of the evaluation report-reflexivity (in action and inside the action) and the processes and outcomes of the project. The focus of the trial was to study the relationship between the narrative structure and the performance of application (action). The work included the development of an experimental technique based on a multi-methodological approach and multifocal critical incident, considered also in terms of event/obstacle, and the link between the narratives and narratives of critical materials, oral and written, to establish connections between the qualitative and quantitative structures. In fact, two analysis techniques were used: the critical incident and reflection structured along the lines of Christopher Johns, combined with a dynamic semi-structured reflective cycle (Gibbs, 1981, 1988) punctuated by a series of activities (description, analysis, evaluation, conclusion and plan action).

The term, critical incident is used here to indicate a critical problem in an experienced event, rather than a typical one, the analysis may become a useful tool to identify significant personal experiences, to develop reflective skills in individuals and to create a means to bridge the gap between theory and practice. The incident is defined as "critical" when the action has helped to produce an effective result, to solve a problem

*Figure 1. Summary table meetings*

| No Dating | Time | Activities | Meaning | Analysis |
|---|---|---|---|---|
| A meeting | 2 hours | Preparation | | |
| B Meeting | 2 hours | Preparation | | |
| I Meeting | 3 hours | Presentation of the project | Presentation of participants | Description |
| II Meeting | 3 hours | Treatment of critical incident | Analysis multifocal | Description |
| III Meeting | 3 hours | Feed analysis and questioning of the micro-portfolio | Sharing in the presence of path analysis | Perception |
| IV Meeting | 2 hours | | Educational size analysis | Interpretation |
| STATE OF LATENCY | Summer break | | | |
| V Meeting | 2 hours | Definition of the macro-portfolio | Analysis of the roles in the interaction and interpersonal communication (pragmatic) Sharing the collective network | Interpretation |
| VI Meeting | 2 hours | Construction of a virtual path on critical incidents experience of relationship | Individual experience becomes a collective experience | Relationship |
| VII Meeting | 2 hours | Interpretation of the nuclei of meaning that bind incidents | The macro-portfolio as a mirror of the collective experiences | Relationship |
| VIII Meeting | 2 hours | Distancing and self-assessment | Competence goal: the dimension of reflexivity | Restitution |
| IX Meeting | 2 hours | The narrative of the experience | Critical dimension of the experience Meta-narrative | Restitution |
| C Meeting | 2,30 hours | Conclusion | | |
| D Meeting | 2,30 hours | Conclusion | | |
| E Meeting | 2 hours | Final evaluation | | |

or a particular situation, but even when the action does not lead to a concrete result, meaning that it partially solves a problem while at the same time creating new obstacles or future needs. It describes a situation or action which was important, significant, "critical" in determining the effectiveness of results, and which imprinted on the individual contains a unique, special meaning, creating awareness through knowledge of the event and providing a way to remember points of view, biases and errors (Chambers, Clarke, Colombo, & Askland, 2003, pp. 101-122; Flanagan, 1954, pp. 327-358; Tripp, 1993, p. 43; Scanlan, Care, & Udod, 2002, pp. 136-143; Soini, 2000).

The reflective cycle (Liston & Zeichner, 1996; Parker, 1999; Perrenoud, 1994; Pollard, 2002; Reagan, Case, & Brubacher, 2000[2]; Ritchie & Wilson, 2000; Schön, 1983, 1987; Zeichner & Liston, 1996; Norlander-Case, Reagan, & Case, 1999; Usher, Bryant, & Johnston, 1997) was considered key to the experimental design as it was conceived as an interface between international "leaders" reflexivity and the research design, as a process and capable of developing, directing or blocking barriers between "science" and "practice" that is useful to address the assumption of the existence of a non-linear relationship between teaching scientific and technical knowledge and school and educational practices. This approach, coming into contact with in-depth experience, lived in an attempt to ask questions, find solutions, and create links with past experiences, tried to reach a better relationship between situations and meanings and to make a useful integration between the different components of knowledge and experience, drawing a red line between learning experience and reflexivity closely related to action and involvement of professionals, in addition to specific contexts. The reflective cycle was used to decline as meta-reflexivity expertise capable of managing the learning experience of teaching.

The choice of incidents was made by bargaining among the participants, within a range of incidents presented by each one, so that they would be able, on reflection, to express their choices, following

which, they could define a strategy of interpretation. This has involved the following steps

- Collection of critical incidents and choice of the two most important (process identification to reflect on experiences);
- Handling of accidents (diary of reflection and learning log);
- Use of structured and semi-structured reflection;
- Reflective reading cycle and its repayment.

The incidents chosen by the participants contained some "common denominators" that had an important significance for the people concerned and involved substantial changes in employment (such as the passage of two members of the group, one of whom, was a trade unionist and became a teacher. And one who was a teacher and who became responsible for overseeing regional educational facilities) were based on the difficulties in relating to students / learners with colleagues and superiors and were characterized by the presence of great emotional tensions linked in their complexity, to a number of events that were significant episodes in professional learning and were presented accompanied by a decrease in the degree of responsibility that the subjects had previously shown, a decrease in opportunities for choice, an increasing job security and increased uncertainty of their personal ambitions.

The exploration of "reflective conversation" (see Figure 2) took place at two levels:

- *Narrative*, which consisted of transcriptions of meetings, professional autobiographies, narratives of incidents and personal perceptions of the participants, as well as assessments of the incident;
- *Meta-narrative*, which consisted of records and self-evaluations of the facilitators and participants of the reflective experience, immediately after it had occurred and again after a period of time.

*Figure 2. Diagram of reflective activity*

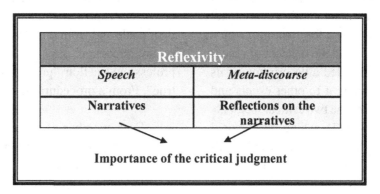

Critical reflection was needed to reverse (Freire, 1971) the concept and the "conventional explanation of reality" and to understand how beliefs, rules and habits even if incorrect, are strengthened in professional contexts. One of the nuclei involved reflexive awareness of the subjects' capacity to influence and change the professional situations in which they were involved, in order to take concrete steps aimed at eliminating the obstacles that were hindering communication and action. Their task was to adopt a constructive self-criticism on their actions in order to reach an improvement (Calderhead, 1989; McNamara, 1990; Zeichner & Liston, 1990; Gore, 1987; Wildman & Niles, 1987) or to determine whether what was learned was justified in the current dimension (Mezirow, 1990). It can be assumed, however, that this concept implied the acceptance of a particular ideology, defined assumptions and a specific epistemology (McNamara, 1990, pp. 147-160; Zeichner & Liston, 1990; Gore, 1987, pp. 33-39; Wildman & Niles, 1987, pp. 25-31) and that it rested on precise conditions leading to the transformation of both the "learning" and the "perspective", defining the latter as "the process that allows us to become critically aware of how and why our assumptions have shaped the way we perceive, understand and feel the world, to reformulate these assumptions allowing a more inclusive, discriminating, permeable and integrated perspective, and to make decisions or otherwise act on the basis of these new acquisitions" (Mezirow, 1990, p. 14). Critical reflection has been used, as a systematic form of evaluating experience, which considers an event, situation etc. from different points of view, to identify key assumptions, influences and personal meanings to use experience as an element which facilitates learning. The theoretical assertions made by Jürgen Habermas (1990), were used as an example, he tried to show that the power of reason based on the reflection process, explained how critical reflection is able to produce the emancipation of individuals making them free, independent and responsible. He distinguishes between criticism that seeks to expose self-deception and ideology and reflexive articulation of formal structures of knowledge, giving critical reflection the ability to reveal "the traces of violence that deform repeated attempts at dialogue and regularly block the road that leads to communication without constraints". In our model, the critical reflection (Gore, 1987) went back to the hierarchy outlined by Van Manen (1977, pp. 205-228), who proposed, inspired by Habermas (1990) three different reflective levels: that of "techniques of reflection", which concerned the efficiency and effectiveness of the means by which to achieve certain ends; that of the practice of reflection, which allows us to examine, not only the means but also the objectives and assumptions on which they are based and the actual results.

On this basis, the analysis process focused on the unexpected in action and in professional relationships with an area for treating critical incident (see Figure 3) and the concept of objective / obstacle that included a description of its interpretation and linking it to other events and to the parallel incident. The two critical incidents were used similarly to build teaching and personal stories, by means of which, according to a multifocal perspective, highlighting errors and unexpected effects of teaching professionalism, which showed characteristics of complexity, uncertainty, instability, uniqueness and conflict of values.

In order not to succumb to the effects of stereotyping, different kinds of narrative explanation have been used for the same incident (version independent, oral and written, to be submitted to the group for discussion and analysis) and its collective rewriting in order to identify connections and types of errors to be shared at the relational level. Obviously, this route was necessary to take into account individual perception and representation of the "incident" by the parties, which required reading with the use of a "stepping back" from the events strategy, which threw light on the role of suggestion. In this sense, the governance of the treatment contemplated the relationship between purpose, evidence and reflection. In this direction, events and expectations of the subjects have been investigated, together with the interpretation of the 'incident' as a factor triggering the unexpected, interpreted as an interruption of what is expected. An analysis of content was then made and from this it was possible to clarify an important passage which involved the professional action "prophecies may not come true". From a procedural standpoint:

- Each member of the group reported both orally and in writing a critical incident, after the facilitators had clarified what is meant by critical incident;
- The group, after an appropriate intervention and accurate interpretive discussion, chose to treat the two incidents in the Laboratory.

In this direction the following points were touched on:

- Various components and dimensions were brought into play by the incident;
- The criteria for its specification were found;
- Thoughts and feelings about relations with the events of the accident were specified;
- The influence of the accident on other events and situations was considered;
- Various forms of analysis were applied;
- Reasons, values, relationships and skills brought into play by the incident were examined;

*Figure 3. Summary of critical incident analysis process*

| Activity | Operations |
| --- | --- |
| Professional biography written | Presentation |
| Oral narration of the incident | Description |
| Written narration of incident | Distancing |
| Individual micro-portfolio Collective portfolio | Restitution |

- The fallout of the incident on the entire professional domain (learning/education) was considered
- Obstacles, problems or *defaillances*, defective connections were identified;
- Incidents in terms of relationships were shared;
- Incidents were rewritten in the light of new interpretations;
- Prospects for future professional activities were considered.

In this kind of study activity, variations in the responses obtained from individuals and groups were taken into account, as were the different actors and strategies that the team used to manage the different positions of interpretation of the external influence which school culture has on individuals and groups. The process structurally initiated could be considered fruitful in terms of cognitive (skills that teachers need), critic (in the sense of ethics) and narrative (the subjects talk about their experience coming in contact with the group that shares and rewrites the critical incident and traces the reflexive path) for the participants, enabling them to live in retrospect the contexts in which they are professionally inserted and rethink educational problems they addressed/resolved/failed to resolve.

## 5. THE ROLE OF EXTERNAL AND INTERNAL EVALUATION AND IDENTIFICATION OF THE INDICATORS OF REFLEXIVITY

### The Work of Internal Evaluation

The workshop was based on the reading of the internal and external evaluation. All members of the workshop were present at the internal reading sessions, whereas at the external ones there were all the conductors, plus two independent evaluators

(external) who were there to verify the internal coherence of the material produced.

The Laboratory has assumed an intensive evaluation process focusing on different points:

- Clarification of the purposes for which the assessment was conducted;
- Definition and involvement of the working group in the evaluation process;
- Use of assessment in determining the final instrument;
- Establishment of the various steps in the laboratory and discussion of the quality of the instrument to be defined;
- Discussion of the evaluation of data found on the progress of the laboratory and their restitution;
- Evaluation of the experience.

Although at the start, the evaluation process was a work of negotiation between different stakeholders (experts and participants) who were not immediately convinced of its utility, as the students proceeded along the reflexive path, they changed their minds and had a clearer idea of its aims. The inter-subjective nature, which aimed at improving the negotiating environment meant that the descriptors became the "stakes" of the Laboratory. However the latter, characterized by an assessment that we called "open spiral" because of the special objectives that arose and the kind of activity, in the last stage, i.e., in the two final meeting, tried to:

- Identify the best possible practices;
- Consider the problem of replication of such practices;
- Obtain information regarding structured descriptors.

This phase has been termed "circumstantial evidence" in relation to the descriptors on which it worked. As we are unable to display all the steps of the work, we simply propose below a summary of the categorization, obtained by close examination of the different levels of analysis, relating to the development of self-assessment tools and its descriptors. The continuous internal assessment was carried out by using detailed reports prepared both by participants and facilitators, during and immediately after the activity and after a certain period of time, which were recorded at each step of the process and the criteria summarized in grills. The descriptive parts were followed by pigeonholed data grids used to make comparisons and repeated quantifications. Interviews and a propositional analysis of the contents produced by participants and facilitators were carried out. With the internal evaluation process it was possible investigate the following aspects:

- Adaptation process, i.e., a positive effect of the evaluation process put in place, which, after an initial period of difficulty, has led to greater internal cohesion of the group with the positive consequence of making all participants feel at ease, united by a common idea of arriving at a "reflexive" assessment that could be construed as a product;

- Identification of "anomalies", i.e., the continuous assessment work has identified situations and difficulties related to what one might call "ordinary level" of the Laboratory and represented by functional deviations and changes of behavior made by different actors. Based on observations, anomalies are emphasized as an event that is not always easy to understand;

- Learning of reflexivity, that is how the verification process of reflexivity has permitted individuals to expand and adapt favorably with regards to the variability of working conditions and professionalism of the participants. It was possible to consider the capability that reflexive action has to determine what is useful and eliminate what is not needed, including the conduct

of the activity, verifying what was said through the meta-evaluation process.

- Attitudes, i.e., the study of those conditions related to the ways in which an individual reacts in relation to certain elements or aspects of their professionalism (people, situations and problems), indicating the assumption of positive and negative behaviors and attitudes with reference to activities conducted in the Laboratory.

## The External Evaluation Activity

With regards to the external evaluation it was necessary to measure the Laboratory's capacity to guarantee a reflexive and adequate reflexive activity:

1. Coherence with respect to the objectives.
2. Adequacy of the path with respect to its users.
3. Effectiveness of the communication and relations.
4. Relations between the participants' expectations and the results.

To achieve this, all the material produced in the laboratory was given to external evaluators who had never participated in the activities, so as to measure the degree of reflexivity and gender used with respect to the objectives proposed. On the basis of this evaluation, the distance between "the degree of success for the internal and the external degree of success" of the activity, i.e., the gap between external and internal evaluation was then measured. This showed a statistical significance of 0.72 (i.e., very high).

## 6. THE ROLE OF ICT IN THE LABORATORY

The role of ICT workshop in the activity did not substantially change the way that the reflective cycle was structured, since the same approach was used in both modes in the presence and distance. The study used a design that provided explanatory mixed methods to examine the effects of the two ways since it was not always possible for all the variables to make a direct comparison between the two groups. The analysis showed how the online environment has particularly affected the reflective writing component of the portfolios individually and collectively, as indicated by the results of quantitative research, greatly improving the length, the characters and details of written assignments. In addition, correlational analysis revealed that there was a positive relationship (0.76 with p. 0.001) between the highest level of reflection and articulation of the documentation, probably due to the variable "individual time" for the performance of deliveries from subjects who participated. The collection of qualitative data will also contribute to explain how and why the "reflective discourse participant" on-line is more constrained than in presence, and this is due to the use of "critical situations" as elements that serve to anchor the reflective writing seeing the text online as more integrated.

If the use of technology to "reflect" does not necessarily change the way participants understand and learn the skills, it can sometimes encourage a clearer focus on some aspects that concern them. Reflection on-line, integrated with that in the presence, does not reflect on the changing perceptions of the "teacher role" but changes the ratio depending on the reflective physical relationship in favour of the virtual, allowing an even greater structuring of the "reflective discourse" that is more precise especially in terms of internal evaluation. Using ICT does not change the acquisition process of "reflective competence", but it certainly changes the way of understanding the significance of this acquisition, which probably affects the meaning of professionalism and a deep understanding of the subject in different ways. This is confirmed by the studies reporting that the addition of elements of reflection in professional development

programs for teachers can go towards new conditions of learning beyond skill development and move towards the adoption of truly educational technologies (Collis, 1996; Ertmer, 2003; Geyer, 1997), which addresses the integration of technology into the reflective dimension to stimulate a more effective professional development and help educators to identify concrete possibilities and limitations for producing knowledge.

The physical space of reflection is not conceived by the participants as relevant, and an on-line course is considered to be a minor problem (or even an element that leads to a definite improvement of the activity), as the conduct of meetings in chat would speed responses, help the comprehension and avoid overlapping in the discussion or any possible distractions. The reading of the research protocols, in the external evaluation showed that participants in the chat "consume" the available time better than in person. It helps to confirm this figure the problem of "registrability", which allowed students to finish the session with clear notes, useful and well structured, with the advantage that the contents could be partially or fully downloaded by all, reproduced in print or simply on the screen, exactly when and as required.

In the "virtual laboratory" the value of interest of the content and reflective delivery has presented a statistically significant correlation (0.85 and P <0.01) with the ability of "facilitators" to motivate the participants, even if this dimension also involved the laboratory "in presence", because, as already mentioned, the same principles were used in a physical space that is reflective of the virtual world. This suggests that the on-line reflection does not give an automatic guarantee of a successful discussion, but the nature of the Laboratory has contributed to developing the relationship with other dimensions, with obvious extensions of the reflection to other situations of network usage, including that of e-mail and forums. Significant additions have emerged in the process of acquisition of other kinds of learning, especially in the final phase of training, which included the drafting of a "project" at the end of the Master Course. This result would still need to be further investigated and supported by subsequent studies.

The most obvious result is related to what we might call "facilitated interaction", given by the discussion list, which has increased the degree of intervention and exchange among participants, allowing them to bring the discussion out of the "virtual classroom". The communication that supported critical reflection, allowing participants to focus on other conversations not covered by the Laboratory, not lastly the internship situation, reveals the interest and sense of shared reflection, as a model which is more suitable for a learning situation on-line.

The flexibility of the learning environment has obviously made it possible in the various "virtual spaces" involved, the spontaneous discussion in unexpected "meetings", encouraging students to reason, express their thoughts and views on teaching and on reflective learning even at times of non-didactical on-line use. On the other hand, critical thinking and reflection in the interval of time, called "latency" coincides with the summer break, then allowing electronic means to extend the interaction with others and enable the readers activation of other functions attached to weblog comments.

However, it clearly emerges that ICT-Reflection, compared to the immediacy of the environment class, requires a translation, interpretation and a critical approach to reflexivity which considers some skills to be essential and central to this activity, which is particularly interpersonal and social.

In addition, the importance of an on-line environment that maximizes the reflection is given by the forms of communication adopted by the "on-line facilitator", who can use a greater control of the "reflective discourse" and encourage the sharing of messages and faculty concerns, and can employ strategies to encourage the use of other forms besides the chat, such as the forums or e-mail for example, to launch a discussion

on an issue, including the use of visual material relevant to the discussion.

However, it clearly emerges in the evaluation, that the reflection on-line needs the creation of a welcoming and friendly environment, which not only predisposes the participant to engage in a serene communication, but above all one destined to last. This happens if there is a constant and regular exchange between the participants, as well as a continuous monitoring that controls the flow of information and communication, as technology does not impair the dialectical relationship between teachers and students but it feeds it following different procedures. However, an element that seems to have decisively influenced the success of the experience was especially the low number of participants (No 10) that definitely made the job easier, more effective and has ensured a more detailed discussion in the group, precise and shared, even with respect to the material sent by e-mail at precise times (in the words of the participants, it has always been clear and helpful, the answers were always detailed and well annotated). This confirms the full "visibility of the on-line facilitator" confirming the impact of the intervention on the mechanisms of group cohesion, thus leading to greater student participation, and the opportunity to explore issues in depth.

## 7. THE ONLINE ENVIRONMENT: HOW SKILLS SUCH AS THE REFLECTIVE ACT AFFECT THE USE OF ICT AND VICE VERSA

The ICT environment has certainly affected the organization of reflexivity and how it should be structured in order to achieve a greater and more specific use of the technological tools (e.g., e-portfolio and chat) and improving at the same time, understanding, management and the use of online materials and the information platform. But some comments can be made on the digital skills by analyzing the data instruments used to understand the role of ICT in the reflexive survey, although one must be very cautious before coming to conclusions that can be considered exhaustive. We report below on some exploratory activity results that appear most significant in establishing a relationship between reflexivity and increased digital skills. These results need to be better investigated, in order to collect more reliable empirical evidence.

According to the participants, the reflection had had an impact on an improved use of ICT. This was detected by using a questionnaire containing 35-crafted ad hoc questions administered on-line and a focus group study that took place later, during the final - face to face - stages, which urged the parties to explore in depth, those aspects that we considered the most problematic of the relation between-reflective skills and-digital skills, which had already emerged in the questionnaire.

There reflection recorded an improved use of ICT in terms of:

- Planning and rationalization of time and activities available in both the workshop activities and those pertaining to the Master's curriculum;
- Performance and duties provided in the Master's Course, in particular in the management of activities such as questions, answers, group work, and discussions;
- Concentration on learning tasks (in particular that of writing fiction), minimizing external interruptions and placing greater emphasis on the activities to be performed and how they are learning, why they are doing it and what they want to achieve;
- Awareness in the selection and deployment of digital resources available for their use as appropriate in all the activities planned in the Master's Course, recognizing the factors involved in the organization of a particular structure of e-learning, which act as barriers to communication and hinder our action;

- Greater control of all activities of self-evaluation and self-testing in the Master's Course in contemplation, allowing individuals to gain better control and regulation of the flow of information that was used for subsequent access to the training sessions;
- Interaction between the participants through the creation of discussion groups, which increased the cohesion within the virtual group and fuelled a favorable disposition to collaborative learning;
- Self-evaluation processes and methods of use of ICT and the operation of their facilities;
- Flexibility in the use of ICT within the same context and in different contexts (inside and outside the reflective activity) and at various times both during training and not;
- Speed of use and application of advanced analysis techniques, such as the use of visual aids for the examination of critical incidents that led to a more complete reading;
- Extensive technology approach which led to a different use of resources and teaching aids to address ICT issues, case studies etc. and to carry out the analysis of critical incidents;
- Deeper understanding of how ICT can be used in a logic of continuity in and out of the teaching-learning processes formalized;
- Harmonization of digital skills of a different order (elementary skills, intermediate skills and advanced skills), families of different skills (basic, transversal etc.) And of different areas (belonging to different areas, cognitive, social, etc.) (Nuzzaci, 2004, 2011).

The online activities, because of their multimodal, nature increased, from the point of view of reflexivity:

- Observation, collection, identification, analysis of phenomena, situations, cases and documents according to different perspectives and approaches;
- The comparison and the control points of view and different perspectives;
- The conscious state of decision-making, examining the condition and the formulation of the expression;
- The organization of the writing of the elements, required by the individual and collective portfolio and its structure on the whole incident adequately treated and examined;
- The proper study of the problems and discussions initiated;
- The presentation of the contexts, situations, phenomena and case studies and their syntheses;
- Planning of the relationship between the speeches (audio, video, text,) the semiotic codes and symbolic systems, with an obvious influence on the cohesion between different skills.

In conclusion, although the ICT and reflection are closely related to the nature of the learning task, reflective activity and skills, they would be mutually reinforced by improving the overall profile of the subjects mainly because the workshop activities focused on the recovery of skills and prior knowledge of the subjects and the review of experience "relevant to professional learning" producing a visible improvement:

- Planning, organization and management of learning by individuals;
- Appropriateness of the use of ICT resources to acquire information efficiently and effectively;
- Awareness of the ability to influence and modify learning situations by the use of specific technological tools;

- Cohesion between knowledge and skills of a different nature;
- Explicit and effective communication of feelings, insights and critical thinking.

The use of an online discussion, compared to those conducted face-to-face permitted the subjects to:

- Select the ideas more precisely, making them focus on key ideas and critical points of the learning tasks;
- Think about all the components of the instruments of self-testing in the course;
- Increase the skills at a meta-cognitive level;
- Use the various components and functions of ICT, mainly those relating to the administration and processing of information more appropriately;
- More effectively control and management of the different learning sequences.

This requires more research in order to develop:

- Methodological skills for technological-reflexive;
- Ability to communicate technical information and technology;
- Procedures, techniques, tools and management methods of reflective skills in order to improve and maintain technological *habitus*;
- Skill in use of formal drawings as a means of communicating technical information;
- Reflection on specific procedural knowledge-technology;
- Meta and transversal skills related to self-evaluation and meta-evaluation for a more productive point of contact, particularly in terms of research, including reflexivity and technology.

*Table 1. Reflexivity versus technology*

| Technology vs. Reflexivity | Reflexivity vs. Technology |
|---|---|
| Meta-competence | Questions |
| Show own knowledge and help peers | What are my habits when using ICT? |
| Interact in the group by making suggestions and proposals | What ICT resources could I use to improve my learning? |
| Reflect on their own progress and on the learning process both in the use of reflexivity and of technology in terms of skills, knowledge and objectives | Do I have any bad habits when using ICT? |
| Bring out, identify and analyze their difficulties and problems with respect to both reflection and technology | How can I change them? |
| Self-questioning, explicitly describing their learning obstacles with regard to both the languages of reflexivity and those of Information Technology | What barriers prevent me from improving my habits when using ICT? |
| | What could I do to overcome them? |

## 8. RESULTS AND RESEARCH PRODUCTS

The path analysis was made in relation to some elements of the reconstruction of professional history highlighting passages common to both incidents/stories:

- The need to contain and support the subjectivity;
- Control of stereotypes;
- The problem of routine work;
- Presence of "occasions" in the need to plan their own future;
- The relationship between critical incident and desired professional growth;
- Reinforcement of subjective identity, which is evident in the transition from the expression of general need to the expression of self-referenced desires;
- Raising awareness of the relationship between history and career development;
- Recognition of the contribution of the relationships lived among the group attending the laboratory, with regards to their personal and professional growth.

In particular, it has highlighted:

- Operational decisions involved in particular situations (e.g., dealing with interpersonal issues, such as an argument with a colleague or manager).
- The management decisions of the process, which allows them to cope with the unexpected (e.g., a delay in carrying out a task has produced communication problems with a colleague, but similarly a delay in concluding the didactic curricula has slowed and hampered a path defined in advance while planning them, etc.).
- Decisions concerning the management of work, which modify the orientation of the activities (for example, a careful re-analysis of particular difficulties when working within a group – the case of the trade unionist who became a teacher– lead him to choose new professional paths but not always the ones desired, so in the strictest sense, a re-examination of the characteristics of the students brings the teacher to reconsider his/her positions or to take particular decisions).

The reflective process also questioned deeper aspects of culture and professionalism (structures, values, thoughts, beliefs) of the subjects and expressed a certain way to be "professionals" of culture, education, etc. but above all, it revealed how reflexivity helps to reject the asymmetric aspects (educational, economic, social etc.) encouraging an equal relationship between subjects.

The problem of "asymmetry" becomes visible on different levels:

1. Attitudes (regarding self- assessment and the other etc.);
2. Knowledge (of self and other, individual and social interaction);
3. Skills (play, discover and interact).

This reflexivity has proved to be, with regards to the professional experience, a valid tool, capable of identifying the "feelings and actions of inconsistency" and to classify, not only by actively participating in a conscious way, to their treatment, but also to their re-definition, identifying the link with everyday situations and perceive the progressive enrichment it brings. On the other hand, this aspect had already been underlined by literature which had defined professionalism in terms of a symmetry which requires continuous redefinition of the relation between the level of awareness and training process. The Laboratory has indicated as one of the dangers that threatens today the analysis of educational actions, the growth of the gap between two "visibilities", that of the level of awareness and that of the specificity of training, involving mainly the ability to choose and make decisions, to design, plan and implement training activities, the ability to assess building tools (which are always cultural), and the propensity to (self) learning. These are the procedural aspects of the teaching-learning courses that have proven difficult to incorporate in the routines of teachers, indicating the problem of incorporating the "science of education" in the educative *habitus* and in practical teaching, even though trainers/teachers/educators at the theoretical level, tend to evaluate positively all training which increases motivation to produce higher learning outcomes in the students (Steffensky & Wilms, 2006, pp. 14-20). The concept of "asymmetry" has revealed that those who are aware of some professional aspects are not necessarily able to translate this awareness into behaviors and that the reflective process, acting at this level of "impasse" presupposes the re-definition of fundamentals (theory), of development (history), of needs, contents, processes (teaching), and the modes and forms of learning (methodology) of individual learning (subject learning with their biographies, socio- psychological and socio-cultural background) and their models of acquisition and interpretation. This also includes addressing and defining the purposes of the professional groups (target environment/participants), legal status and institutional structure of the general conditions and trends of development of national and international policies. In the background certain elements related to the broader issues of professional education have emerged, such as feelings of isolation, stress, communication problems (with superiors, with colleagues), the need or desire for change (the meta-reflection however revealed a disagreement in the group regarding the static nature of the issue of professional education), an obstacle determined by someone (or a difficult situation caused by someone) professional growth, continuous relation between personal and professional dimension and the relation between experience / skill and perception of their skills, time and place of education and teaching which allows greater autonomy of action (what constitutes the restriction of the action?), substantial differences between working in private / public structures, professional relationships which affect the quality of work. These are all elements that should be brought back and subjected to further, deep examination (as is happening to the problem of routines). Some of these elements have found their place within the self-assessment tool developed by the research group of which we give a small example in Figure 4.

*Figure 4. Examples of descriptors*

| Areas | | |
|---|---|---|
| **Work experiences** | | |
| **A. The professional relationship experiences** | - entry-inclusion/initial impact | |
| | - climate | |
| | - responsibilities | |
| | - teamwork | |
| | - organization | |
| | - integration | |
| | - interpersonal - relationships | - relationships with colleagues |
| | | - relationships with superiors ecc. |
| | - socialization of work performed | |
| | - management/conflict resolution | |
| | - cooperation | |
| | - competition | |
| **B. Professional activities** | | |
| **B1 – Professional profile** | - defining the role and mode | Defining the role and mode |
| | - tasks of the function | |
| | - type of tasks or activities | - Tasks of the function |
| **B2   Work organization** | - routine items | - Type of tasks or activities |
| | - personnel involved | - Routine items |
| | - other figures | - Personnel involved |
| | - responsibilities | - Other figures |
| | - planning | - Responsibilities |
| | - clarity of the task | - Planning |
| | - management autonomy | - Clarity of the task |
| | - substitutability | - Management autonomy |
| | - time organisation | - Substitutability |
| | - space organisation | - Organization of time |
| **B3 – Works progress** | - career profile | - Organization of space |
| | - career planning | - Career Profile |
| | - professional growth | - Career planning |
| | - in- service training/updating | - Professional growth |
| | - formal recognition | - In-service training / refresher |
| | - opportunities | - Formal recognition |
| **C. Area self** | - perception of the experience | - Opportunities |
| | - recognition  of  their activities | - Perception of the experience |
| | - knowledge of their skills | - Recognition of their activities |
| | - commitment | |
| | - recognition of the work style | Recognition of the elements of |
| | - motivation for self-realization | reflective time of reflection |
| | - acceptance of its role | techniques collective reflection |
| | - perception of change | detached observation |
| | - involvement | |
| | - recognition and acceptance of risks | |
| | - satisfaction | |
| | - overcoming the obstacle | |
| | - awareness of the work dynamics | |
| | - acceptance of work | |
| | - recognition of work transitions | |
| | - identification of uncertainties | |
| | - expectations | |
| | - recognition of the learning | |
| | - degree of awareness of decision-making | |
| | - reference work values | |
| | - ability to identify the level of stress | |
| | - recognizing elements of the reflective capacity | time of reflection |
| | | techniques |
| | | collective reflection |

All the end products of the research were presented in the Fieldbook available on the website www.reflect-project.net, which is the official electronic version of the research materials and theoretical analysis produced during the project, accompanied by their printed manual (in English and Italian) which represents the methodological work translated into several languages (Stroobants, Chambers, & Clarke, 2007). The main product of this research consists of the methodology used to support the project target group in the process of training on reflective practice which has produced an interpretation and evaluation of survey routes for the self-understanding of the processes themselves.

To sum up, the Laboratory of Aosta, in spite of all its procedural limits, has shown, in accordance with international research (Doyle, 1986, pp. 435-481), according to which, the evaluation and evolution of analysis on the interactive styles of teaching, determines the differences between different forms of training and educational professionals and the logics which guide them in action. That the introduction of reflexive paradigms in the field of vocational training, would represent a real opportunity for teachers and educators to ease the complexity of their task and learn to manage (individual and collaborative) teaching-learning processes, as well as to clarify the mechanisms of stereotyping teaching behavior. And this because in education "Consciously, we teach what we learn, unconsciously, we teach what we are" (Hamachek, 1999, p. 209).

## REFERENCES

Adler, S. (1991). The reflective practitioner and the curriculum of teacher education. *Journal of Education for Teaching, 17*(2), 139–150. doi:10.1080/0260747910170203

Alrichter, H., & Posch, P. (1989). Does the 'grounded theory' approach offer a guiding paradigm for teacher research? *Cambridge Journal of Education, 19*(1), 21–31. doi:10.1080/0305764890190104

Altet, M. (1994). *La formation professionnelle des enseignants*. Paris, France: PUF.

Altet, M. (2001). L'analyse de pratiques. Une démarche de formation professionnalisante? *Recherche et Formation, 35*, 25–41.

Altet, M. (2002). Une démarche de recherche sur la pratique enseignante: l'analyse plurielle. *Revue Française de Pédagogie, 138*, 85–93. doi:10.3406/rfp.2002.2866

Atkins, S., & Murphy, K. (1995). Reflective practice. *Nursing Standard, 9*(45), 31–35.

Beillerot, J. (1998). *Formes et formations du rapport au savoir*. Paris, France: L'Harmattan.

Blanchet, A., & Gotman, A. (2000). *L'indagine e i suoi metodi: l'intervista, trad. e cura di F. G. Merlina, A. Nuzzaci*. Roma, Italy: Kappa.

Boud, D., Keogh, R., & Walker, D. (Eds.). (1985). *Reflection: turning experience into learning*. London, UK: Kogan Page.

Bourdieu, P. (1972). *Esquisse d'une théorie de la pratique*. Genève, Switzerland: Droz.

Boyd, E., & Fales, A. (1983). Reflective learning: the key to learning from experience. *Journal of Humanistic Psychology, 23*(2), 99–117. doi:10.1177/0022167883232011

Brookfield, S. (1995). *Becoming a critically reflective teacher*. San Francisco, CA: Jossey-Bass.

Calderhead, J. (1989). Reflective teaching and teacher education. *Teaching and Teacher Education, 5*(1), 43–51. doi:10.1016/0742-051X(89)90018-8

Calderhead, J., & Gates, P. (Eds.). (1993). *Conceptualizing reflection in teacher development*. London, UK: Falmer.

Chambers, P., Clarke, B., Colombo, M., & Askland, L. (2003). Significant learning incidents and critical conversations in an international context: promoting reflexivity with in-service students. *Journal of In-service Education, 29*(1), 101–122. doi:10.1080/13674580300200239

Clark, C. M. (1995). *Thoughtful teaching*. New York, NY: Teachers College.

Clarke, B. L., & Chambers, P. A. (1999). The promotion of reflective practice in European teacher education: conceptions, purposes and actions. *Pedagogy, Culture & Society, 7*(2), 291–303.

Collis, B. (1996). The internet as an educational innovation: lesson from experience with computer implementation. *Educational Technology, 36*(6), 21–30.

Cooper, J. M. (1999). The teacher as a decision-maker. In Cooper, J. M. (Ed.), *Classroom teaching skills* (pp. 1–19). Boston, MA: Houghton-Mifflin.

Cruickshank, D. (1985). Uses and benefits of reflective teaching. *Phi Delta Kappan, 66*(10), 704–706.

Daudelin, M. W. (1996). Learning from experience through reflection. *Organizational Dynamics, 24*(3), 36–48. doi:10.1016/S0090-2616(96)90004-2

Dewey, J. (1916). *Democracy and education. An introduction to the philosophy of education*. New York, NY: Free Press.

Dewey, J. (1933). *How we think: a restatement of the relation of reflective thinking to the educative process*. Boston, MA: Heath.

Doyle, W. (1986). Paradigm in research of teachers' effectiveness. In Crahay, M., & Lafontaine, D. (Eds.), *L'art et la science de l'enseignement* (pp. 435–481). Bruxelles, Belgium: Labor.

Eraut, M. (1994). *Developing professional knowledge and competence*. London, UK: Falmer.

Eraut, M. (1995). Schön shock; a case for reframing reflection-in-action? *Teachers and Teaching, 1*(1), 9–22. doi:10.1080/1354060950010102

Eraut, M. (2004). The practice of reflection. *Learning in Health and Social Care, 3*(2), 47–52. doi:10.1111/j.1473-6861.2004.00066.x

Ertmer, P. (2003). Transforming teacher education: visions and strategies. *Educational Technology Research and Development, 51*(1), 124–128. doi:10.1007/BF02504522

Farrah, H. (1988). The reflective thought process: John Dewey re-visited. *The Journal of Creative Behavior, 22*(1), 1–8.

Feiman-Nemser, S. (1990). Teacher preparation: structural and conceptual alternatives. In Houston, W. T. (Ed.), *Handbook of research on teacher education*. New York, NY: Macmillan.

Fitzgerald, M. (1994). Theories of reflection for learning. In Palmer, A., & Burns, S. (Eds.), *Reflective practice in nursing*. Oxford, UK: Blackwell Scientific.

Flanagan, J. C. (1954). The critical incident technique. *Psychological Bulletin, 5*(4), 327–358. doi:10.1037/h0061470

Francis, S. (1997). A time for reflection: learning about organizational learning. *The Learning Organization, 4*(4), 168–179. doi:10.1108/09696479710170860

Freire, P. (1971). *La pedagogia degli oppressi*. Milano, Italy: Mondadori.

Geyer, R. W. (1997). Approaching ground zero with today's technology tools. *T.H.E. Journal, 25*(1), 56–59.

Ghaye, T., & Lillyman, S. (2000). *Reflection: principles and practice for healthcare professionals*. Wiltshire, UK: Mark Allen.

Gibbs, G. (1981). *Teaching students to learn: a student centred approach.* Oxford, UK: Oxford University Press.

Gibbs, G. (1988). *Learning by doing: a guide to teaching and learning method.* Oxford, UK: Further Education Unit, Oxford Polytechnic.

Ginsburg, M. B. (1988). *Contradictions in teacher education and society: a critical analysis.* New York, NY: Falmer.

Gore, J. (1987). Reflecting on reflective teaching. *Journal of Teacher Education, 55*(2), 33–39. doi:10.1177/002248718703800208

Gore, J., & Zeichner, K. (1991). Action research and reflective teaching in preservice teacher education: a case study from the United States. *Teaching and Teacher Education, 7*(2), 119–136. doi:10.1016/0742-051X(91)90022-H

Grant, C., & Zeichner, K. (1984). On becoming a reflective teacher. In Grant, C. (Ed.), *Preparing for reflective teaching* (pp. 1–18). Boston, MA: Allyn & Bacon.

Habermas, J. (1990a). *Conoscenza e umano interesse.* Bari, Italy: Laterza.

Habermas, J. (1990b). *Moral consciousness and communicative action.* Cambridge, MA: MIT Press.

Hamachek, D. (1999). Effective teachers: what they do, how they do it, and the importance of self-knowledge. In Lipka, R., & Brinthaupt, T. (Eds.), *The role of self in teacher development* (pp. 189–224). Albany, NY: State University of New York Press.

Hatton, N., & Smith, D. (1995). Reflection in teacher education: towards definition and implementation. *Teaching and Teacher Education, 11*(1), 33–49. doi:10.1016/0742-051X(94)00012-U

Holborn, P., Wideen, M., & Andrews, I. (Eds.). (1992). *Devenir enseignant, à la conquête de l'identité professionnelle.* Montréal, QC, Canada: Èditions Logiques.

Hole, S., & McEntee, G. (1999). Reflection is at the heart of practice. *Educational Leadership, 56*(8), 34–37.

Johns, C. (1991). The Burford nursing development unit holistic model of nursing practice. *Journal of Advanced Nursing, 16*(9), 1090–1098. doi:10.1111/j.1365-2648.1991.tb03370.x

Killen, L. (1989). Reflecting on reflective teaching. *Journal of Teacher Education, 40*(2), 49–52. doi:10.1177/002248718904000209

Kolb, D. (1984). *Experiential learning: experience as the source of learning and development.* Upper Saddle River, NJ: Prentice Hall.

Kottamp, R. (1990). Means of facilitating reflection. *Education and Urban Society, 22*(2), 182–203. doi:10.1177/0013124590022002005

LaBoskey, V. K. (1994). *Development of reflective practice: a study of preservice teachers.* New York, NY: Teachers College.

Lasley, T. (1990). Editorial. *Journal of Teacher Education, 40*(2), 2–8.

Lewin, K. (1951). *Teoria e sperimentazione in psicologia sociale.* Bologna, Italy: Il Mulino.

Liston, D., & Zeichner, K. (1996). *Culture and teaching.* Mahwah, NJ: Lawrence Erlbaum.

McNamara, D. (1990). Research on teachers' thinking: its contribution to educating student teachers to think critically. *Journal of Education for Teaching, 16*(2), 147–160. doi:10.1080/0260747900160203

Mezirow, J. (1990). *Fostering critical reflection in adulthood.* San Francisco, CA: Jossey-Bass.

Mezirow, J. (1991). *Transformative dimensions of adult learning*. San Francisco, CA: Jossey-Bass.

Mezirow, J. (2003). *Apprendimento e trasformazione*. Milano, Italy: Cortina Editore.

Munby, H., & Russell, T. (1989). Educating the reflective teacher: an essay review of two books by Donald Schon. *Journal of Curriculum Studies*, *21*(1), 71–80. doi:10.1080/0022027890210106

Noffke, S., & Brennan, M. (1988, April). *The dimensions of reflection: a conceptual and contextual analysis*. Paper presented at the Annual Meeting of the AERA, New Orleans, LA.

Noordhoff, K., & Kleinfeld, J. (1988). Rethinking the rhetoric of 'reflective inquiry' in teacher education programs. In Waxman, H., Freiberg, H., Vaughan, J., & Weil, M. (Eds.), *Images of reflection in teacher education* (pp. 27–29). Reston, VA: Association of Teacher Educators.

Norlander-Case, K., Reagan, T., & Case, C. (1999). *The professional teacher: preparation and nurturance of the reflective practitioner*. San Francisco, CA: Jossey-Bass.

Nuzzaci, A. (Ed.). (2004). *Profili di competenza e trasformazioni sociali. Insegnare e apprendere*. Cosenza, Italy: Lionello Giordano.

Nuzzaci, A. (2006, May 24-26). Per la costruzione di una banca dati italiana dei progetti di ricerca internazionali. In C. Laneve & C. Gemma (Eds.), *La ricerca pedagogica in Europa. Modelli e temi a confronto* (pp. 375-387). Atti del XXII Convegno Nazionale della Società Italiana di Pedagogia (SIPED), Cassino, Italy. Lecce: Pensa MultiMedia.

Nuzzaci, A. (2007). For a community of the European educational research. *Revista Complutense de Educación*, *18*(1), 217–232.

Nuzzaci, A. (2009a). La riflessività nella progettazione educativa: verso una riconcettualizzazione delle routine. *Giornale Italiano della Ricerca Educativa*, *1*(2-3), 59–76.

Nuzzaci, A. (2009b). La riflessività nella pedagogia della progettazione: il ruolo delle routine. In Paparella, N. (Ed.), *Il progetto educativo* (*Vol. 3*, pp. 71–81). Roma, Italy: Armando.

Nuzzaci, A. (2009c, December 11-13). Il Progetto LEONARDO REFLECT. Competenze riflessive e processi valutativi: per un'analisi dell'azione dentro l'azione. In G. Domenici & R. Semeraro (Eds.), *Le nuove sfide della ricerca didattica tra saperi, comunità sociali e culture* (pp. 35-51). Atti del Convegno SIRD (Società Italiana di Ricerca Didattica), Roma, Italy. Roma, Italy: Monolite.

Nuzzaci, A. (2011). Pratiche riflessive, riflessività e insegnamento. *Studium Educationis*, *12*(3), 9–27.

Osterman, K. F. (1990). Reflective practice: a new agenda for education. *Education and Urban Society*, *22*(2), 133–152. doi:10.1177/0013124590022002002

Paquay, L., Altet, M., Charlier, E., & Perrenoud, P. (Eds.). (1996). *Former des enseignants professionnels. Quelles stratégies? Quelles compétences?* Bruxelles, Belgium: De Boeck.

Parker, S. (1999). *Reflective teaching in the postmodern world*. Buckingham, UK: Open University Press.

Perrenoud, P. (1994). *La formation des enseignants entre théorie et pratique*. Paris, France: L'Harmattan.

Perrenoud, P. (2001). *Développer la pratique réflexive dans le métier d'enseignant*. Paris, France: ESF.

Pescheux, M. (2007). *Analyse des pratiques enseignantes en FLE/S. Mémento pour une ergonomie didactique du FLE*. Paris, France: L'Harmattan.

Piaget, J. (1974a). *La prise de conscience*. Paris, France: PUF.

Piaget, J. (1974b). *Réussir et comprendre*. Paris, France: PUF.

Piaget, J. (1977). *Recherche sur l'abstraction réfléchissante*. Paris, France: PUF.

Pollard, A. (2002). *Reflective teaching: effective and evidence-informed professional practice*. London, UK: Continuum.

Posner, G. J. (1996). *Field experience: a guide to reflective teaching*. White Plains, NY: Longman.

Rabardel, P. (2005). Instrument subjectif et développement di pouvoir d'agir. In Rabardel, P., & Patré, P. (Eds.), *Modéles du sujet pour la conception; dialectique activités développement* (pp. 11–29). Toulose, France: Octarés.

Reagan, T., Case, C., & Brubacher, J. (2000). *Becoming a reflective educator: how to build a culture of inquiry in the schools*. Thousand Oaks, CA: Corwin Press.

Reid, B. (1993). But we're doing it already! Exploring a response to the concept of reflective practice in order to improve its facilitation. *Nurse Education Today, 13*, 305–309. doi:10.1016/0260-6917(93)90058-A

Ritchie, J., & Wilson, D. (2000). *Teacher narrative as critical inquiry*. New York, NY: Teachers College.

Saint-Arnaud, Y. (1992). *Connaître par l'action*. Montréal, QC, Canada: Presses de l'Université de Montréal.

Scanlan, J. M., Care, W. D., & Udod, S. (2002). Unravelling the unknowns of reflection in classroom teaching. *Journal of Advanced Nursing, 38*(2), 136–143. doi:10.1046/j.1365-2648.2002.02157.x

Schön, D. (1983). *The reflective practitioner: how professionals think in action*. New York, NY: Basic Books.

Schön, D. (1987). *Educating the reflective practitioner: toward a new design for teaching and learning in the professions*. San Francisco, CA: Jossey Bass.

Smith, D., & Lovat, T. (1991). *Curriculum: action on reflection*. Wentworth Falls, Australia: Social Science Press.

Smyth, J. (1989). Developing and sustaining critical reflection in teacher education. *Journal of Teacher Education, 40*(2), 2–9. doi:10.1177/002248718904000202

Soini, H. (2000, October 20-22). *Critical learning incident technique as a research method for studying student learning*. Paper presented at the Workshop on Qualitative Research in Psychology, Blaubeuren, Germany.

Sparks-Langer, G., Simmons, J., Pasch, M., Colton, A., & Starko, A. (1990). Reflective pedagogical thinking: how can we promote it and measure it? *Journal of Teacher Education, 41*(4), 23–32. doi:10.1177/002248719004100504

Steffensky, M., & Wilms, M. (2006). Chemisches Experimentieren im Sachunterricht – welche Impulse geben Schülerlabore und Lehrerfortbildungen? *Chemie konkret, 13*(1), 14-20.

Stones, E. (1994). Reform in teacher education: the power and the pedagogy. *Journal of Teacher Education, 45*(4), 310–318. doi:10.1177/0022487194045004012

Stroobants, H., Chambers, Ph., & Clarke, B. (Eds.). (2007). *Reflective journeys*. Leuven, Belgium: Belgium by Acco.

Tripp, D. (1993). Critical incidents in teaching. In Fish, D., & Coles, C. (Eds.), *Developing professional judgement*. London, UK: Routledge.

Usher, R., Bryant, I., & Johnston, R. (1997). *Adult education and the postmodern challenge*. London, UK: Routledge.

Valli, L. (1992). *Reflective teacher education: cases and critiques*. Albany, NY: State University of New York Press.

Valverde, L. (1982). The self-evolving supervisor. In Sergiovanni, T. (Ed.), *Supervision of teaching* (pp. 81–89). Alexandria, VA: Association for Supervision and Curriculum Development.

Van Manen, M. (1977). Linking ways of knowing with ways of being practical. *Curriculum Inquiry*, *6*(3), 205–228. doi:10.2307/1179579

Vergnaud, G. (1996). Au fond de l'action, la conceptualisation. In Barbier, J.-M. (Ed.), *Savoirs théoriques, savoirs d'action* (pp. 275–292). Paris, France: PUF.

Vermersch, P. (1994). *L'entretien d'explicitation*. Paris, France: ESF.

Vinatier, I. (2006, May 18-20). Des dispositifs de co-explicitation: un travail de conceptualisation de son activité par l'enseignant, le formateur. In *Proceedings of Faciliter les apprentissages autonomies 7ème Colloque européen sur l'autoformation*, ENFA Toulouse-Auzeville, France.

Waxman, H., Freiberg, H., Vaughan, J., & Weil, M. (1988). *Images of reflection in teacher education*. Reston, VA: Association of Teacher Educators.

Wenger, E. (1998). *Communities of practice: learning, meaning, and identity*. Cambridge, UK: Cambridge University Press.

Wildman, T., & Niles, J. (1987). Reflective teachers: tensions between abstractions and realities. *Journal of Teacher Education*, *38*(1), 25–31. doi:10.1177/002248718703800405

Zeichner, K. M. (1994). Research on teacher thinking and different views of reflective practice in teaching and teacher education. In Carlgren, I., Handal, G., & Vaage, S. (Eds.), *Teachers' minds and actions - Research on teachers' thinking and practice* (pp. 9–27). London, UK: Falmer Press.

Zeichner, K. M., & Liston, D. (1990). *Traditions of reform and reflective teaching in US teacher education*. East Lansing, MI: National Centre for Research in Teacher Education, Michigan State University.

Zeichner, K. M., & Liston, D. (1996). *Reflective teaching: an introduction*. Mahwah, NJ: Lawrence Erlbaum.

## ENDNOTES

[1] The innovation principle in teaching and learning that it was necessary to provide for the sustained activation of training and education systems based on user requirements and transform teachers and trainers, mentors and mediators.

*This work was previously published in the International Journal of Digital Literacy and Digital Competence, Volume 2, Issue 4, edited by Antonio Cartelli, pp. 24-49, copyright 2011 by IGI Publishing (an imprint of IGI Global).*

# Section 4
# Digital Technologies and Competences for Education and Communication

# Chapter 12
# Educators' Expectations on Technology Enhanced Education (TEE):
## Should and Could they be Modified?

**Carlo Giovannella**
*University of Rome Tor Vergata, Italy*

**Claudia Di Lorenzo**
*University of Rome Tor Vergata, Italy*

**Simona Scarsella**
*University of Rome Tor Vergata, Italy*

**Corrado Amedeo Presti**
*University of Rome Tor Vergata, Italy*

## ABSTRACT

*This paper reports and discusses the result of a survey focused on the perceptions and expectations on TEE applications, conducted among 500 Italian educators (university, high/middle/elementary schools and professionals) involved in on-line or blended learning practices. The expectations are quite basic ones, although may depend on the educational level: support to content sharing and production, communication, assessment and team working are at the top of rank; much less relevant appear to be items like: support to socialization, process design and personalization. Very similar results have been obtained also from a survey among schools' teachers, novices for TEE, attending a Master in "e-learning: methods, techniques and applications". The survey was conducted after the conclusion of the first part of the master carried on according to a very traditional distance learning process: content download, self-evaluation tests, tutor assistance upon request. However, after the participation to the second part of the Master, organized as a collaborative, design inspired P³BL (problem, project and process based learning) experience, their opinions on TEE changed in a considerable manner. This indicates how necessary a dissemination action on a large scale among educators with regard to both TEE potentialities and design literacy would be.*

DOI: 10.4018/978-1-4666-2943-1.ch012

## INTRODUCTION

There is a general agreement that innovation is fostered only upon social acceptance and there are also few doubts that investments on methodological and technological researches carried out in recent years in the domain of the Technology Enhanced Education (TEE) have not been able to transform themselves into veritable innovation or, in other words, into a socially accepted phenomenon able to produce a significant and tangible impact on educational processes. On the other hand the rapid development of Web 2.0, of mobile networks and appliances (phone, pad, etc.) and, as well, of other relevant technological related domains, like games, in which technologies are diffused and used at mass level, demonstrate that the problem does not lies in the penetration of technologies but, rather, in the matching among expectations/motivations and the ability of technologies to meet them, and sometime, as well, on "time to market" and business strategies.

In education the achievement of such matching is certainly complicated by the fact that technologies are part of processes that are informed by pedagogical strategies or, in other words, by "points of views" on strategies that are expected to shape the society through education: for example, during a discussion on TEE it would be not very difficult to be traced back to ancestral and inevitable conflicts such as that between "nature" and "culture" (Cambi, 2003). In such context it is not surprising that technologies, in the absence of any certainty about their neutrality, may generate distrust and misunderstanding, or incomplete understanding of their potentialities. This is especially true when we consider people more aged than the digital natives (Prensky, 2001), for example teachers who were trained by mean of traditional educational processes.

With the aim to get a detailed description of the current situation, we decided, at the beginning of 2010, to conduct among educators (elementary, middle, high school, university teachers and pro-

fessionals, including free lances) a survey on the penetration and motivation to adopt open source software and/or web services - with particular regard to the TEE domain. About 500 educators accepted our invitation and participated in the survey.

At the same time we asked ourselves the following question: could and should an educational process modify perceptions and expectations of educators with regards to technology, and its potentialities to support and enhance educational processes?

In the attempt to give a preliminary answer to this question, we studied the effect of attending a honored Master in E-learning on a group of high school teachers, novices for TEE [it is worth to stress that the Master adopted a designed inspired P³BL (Giovannella, 2009; Giovannella & Graf, 2010) process]. Their beliefs and expectations about educational technologies were investigated before and after the process through appropriate questionnaires. The results will be presented in the third paragraph, just before to come to the conclusions and to a brief discussion on future perspectives.

## A PANORAMIC VIEW ON PERCEPTION AND EXPECTATIONS OF ITALIAN EDUCATORS WITH REGARD TO TEE

The survey were conducted among educators who have been already involved at least few times in on-line or blended learning practices or, at least, very well informed about them. Almost all educators were sufficiently confident in using the computer, as shown in Figure 1. In fact, on average the penetration of open source software was found to be 88%, the use of web services 92%, while the use of applications specialized for TEE (including open service) stood at 79%.

As regards more specifically the use of TEE applications: 79% experienced on-line learning

*Figure 1. Use of open source (blue bars), open services (green bars) and application for TEE (yellow bars) by Italian educators*

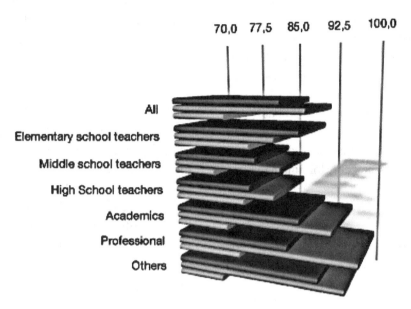

environments, 51% used self-training applications (with the larger diffusion among primary and high school teachers and professionals), 31% edutainment applications (primary school teachers and professionals) and 25% simulation software (high school teachers and academics). Those that in average seem to be less involved with TEE, including online environments, are the middle school teachers.

The number of people that used web services (see Table 1) to produce content (any sort of) comes out to be, on average, almost equal to those

that used online environments, and becomes even higher in the case of high school teachers, academics and professionals. This indicates, unequivocally, that the content is still the king: the sharing and production of content (63%) is what most teachers and professionals are interested in, much more than in socialization (49%) and communication (46%). Disaggregating further the results one finds that socialization matters most to elementary school teachers and professionals, the latter, probably, because of the importance that communities have taken in professional activities;

*Table 1. TEE's applications: Percentage of use*

|  | TEE | environments | self-training | edutainment | simulations |
|---|---|---|---|---|---|
| All (average) | 79 | 62 | 39 | 25 | 21 |
| Elementary school docents | 83 | 60 | 48 | 33 | 15 |
| Middle school docent | 77 | 52 | 37 | 25 | 20 |
| High School docent | 82 | 64 | 46 | 24 | 28 |
| University docent | 79 | 70 | 29 | 25 | 25 |
| Professional | 81 | 68 | 57 | 39 | 18 |
| Others | 78 | 71 | 40 | 20 | 18 |

immediately after we find the academics probably because involved in scientific communities. Also the communication activities matter at most for professionals, followed by academics. It is worth noting that only 30% of those involved in TEE are showing interest in using web services to create personal space. This latter is an activity that involves especially professionals, probably because they use such spaces as a showcase to publicize their own activities; immediately after we find the academics, probably for similar reasons (see Table 2).

## EXPECTATIONS ON TECHNOLOGIES FOR TEE

After having outlined the habits of categories who participated in the survey, we investigated how such habits could affect expectations and desires about the role of technology in supporting and enhancing educational processes. Faced with the request to indicate which features were deemed necessary to deliver a successful TEE process, a very high percentage of respondents indicated - in line with the acquired habits - tools for content sharing (76%) and production (63%). Immediately after we find tools for evaluation and assessment (61%). Communication facilities were indicated by 56% of the participants. Interestingly, the team

working tools are considered much more relevant (58%) with respect to tools for socialization (40%) which suggests that team working is seen more as a practice aimed at achieving cooperatively a goal rather than as a collaborative practices that can foster the establishment of a veritable community.

Much less relevant and, probably, also less practiced appears the process design (33%); it matters at most for academics and elementary school teachers. There could be many reasons that may account for this result, that certainly would deserves further investigation: it may depend on a scarce diffusion of a design culture that is substituted by an "extemporaneous design practice"; it may also due to the fact that technology enhanced activities are not considered very relevant, for example in blended processes; or, trivially, to the fact that most educators are satisfied with old-fashion on-line processes based on content-delivery, self-evaluation tests, technical support via email or forum and face-to-face final examination.

In the last position we find tools for personalization and self promotion (32%), that although fostered by some transnational projects (European Commission, 2010), currently are not considered among the major priorities among educators (see Table 3); it matters at most for academics, but we do not know if it is because of their theoretical beliefs or because of their daily practice.

*Table 2. Purposes for which educators use open/web services (percentages)*

|  | content sharing/prod | socialization | communication | personal space |
|---|---|---|---|---|
| All (average) | 63 | 49 | 46 | 24 |
| Elementary school docents | 62 | 54 | 49 | 16 |
| Middle school docent | 58 | 37 | 44 | 17 |
| High School docent | 70 | 47 | 40 | 26 |
| University docent | 67 | 49 | 49 | 36 |
| Professional | 64 | 57 | 57 | 39 |
| Others | 58 | 55 | 46 | 26 |

*Table 3. Educators' expectations about the role of technology: Features deemed necessary to deliver a successful TEE process (percentages)*

| | content sharing | content production | coll. team working | evaluation/assess. |
|---|---|---|---|---|
| All (average) | 76 | 63 | 58 | 61 |
| Elementary school docents | 76 | 70 | 65 | 63 |
| Middle school docent | 78 | 64 | 49 | 63 |
| High School docent | 80 | 74 | 53 | 55 |
| University docent | 81 | 67 | 62 | 64 |
| Professional | 68 | 54 | 64 | 68 |
| Others | 83 | 66 | 68 | 61 |
| | communication | socialization | process design | personalization |
| All (average) | 56 | 40 | 33 | 32 |
| Elementary school docents | 59 | 40 | 42 | 38 |
| Middle school docent | 54 | 34 | 30 | 29 |
| High School docent | 56 | 37 | 28 | 27 |
| University docent | 72 | 44 | 47 | 46 |
| Professional | 46 | 39 | 36 | 28 |
| Others | 66 | 45 | 32 | 38 |

## TEE: EXPECTATIONS FOR IMPROVEMENTS

As next step we focused on expectations for improvements that may result from the use of technologies.

On top of the list we find the effectiveness of the educational process, indicated by 63% of participants in the survey. The second position in the ranking is occupied by the quality of the educational experience (see Table 4), 60% (we will come back on this aspect in more detail below). Descending in the ranking it comes out that technologies are considered by 51% of the educators (mainly academics and professionals) as potential amplifiers of interaction. The efficiency of the educational process can be improved for 45% of the subjects (far ahead in this belief are the professionals). It is also interesting to note that despite the lack of interest in the design process, a larger proportion of the participants, 48%, believes that the use of technology can improve the management of the process. The support to the development of a sense of belonging to the community is desired by 44% of the participants. In the last position of the ranking, only 24%, once again the support to the promotion of the individual that can be considered the first step toward a personalization of the educational process.

## QUALITY OF EDUCATIONAL EXPERIENCE

Finally we tried to bring out what may make the educational experience more appealing and, at same time, improving its quality (see Table 5). Once more at the top of rank a better content and cognitive interaction (61%). Professionals, however, are an exception since they attach much less relevance to this item than to social interaction which, on average, lies in the second position of the rank (55%). Next, in line with the first choice, we find learning/training (50%). After a relevant

*Table 4. Educators' expectations about the role of technology in supporting and enhancing various aspects of the educational processes (percentages)*

| | effectiveness | experience quality | interaction | process manag. |
|---|---|---|---|---|
| All (average) | 63 | 60 | 51 | 48 |
| Elementary school docents | 66 | 72 | 49 | 52 |
| Middle school docent | 71 | 58 | 47 | 46 |
| High School docent | 69 | 69 | 50 | 52 |
| University docent | 58 | 64 | 60 | 53 |
| Professional | 57 | 61 | 61 | 46 |
| Others | 66 | 60 | 48 | 49 |

| | efficiency | community belonging | digital self |
|---|---|---|---|
| All (average) | 45 | 44 | 24 |
| Elementary school docents | 44 | 46 | 26 |
| Middle school docent | 37 | 34 | 15 |
| High School docent | 47 | 43 | 25 |
| University docent | 37 | 53 | 29 |
| Professional | 57 | 57 | 21 |
| Others | 51 | 45 | 26 |

*Table 5. Educators' expectations about the role of technology in enhancing quality of the educational processes to make them more appealing (percentages)*

| | contents/cogn int | social interaction | learning | individual promot |
|---|---|---|---|---|
| All (average) | 61 | 55 | 50 | 36 |
| Elementary school docents | 63 | 61 | 59 | 39 |
| Middle school docent | 64 | 41 | 56 | 36 |
| High School docent | 67 | 54 | 53 | 43 |
| University docent | 62 | 65 | 51 | 40 |
| Professional | 50 | 68 | 39 | 36 |
| Others | 66 | 46 | 50 | 26 |

| | emotional interact | playful interaction | process design |
|---|---|---|---|
| All (average) | 33 | 28 | 24 |
| Elementary school docents | 34 | 43 | 24 |
| Middle school docent | 39 | 37 | 15 |
| High School docent | 32 | 26 | 24 |
| University docent | 30 | 22 | 35 |
| Professional | 29 | 21 | 32 |
| Others | 35 | 23 | 25 |

jump, that is consistent with what has been shown in previous sections, we find in succession: the promotion of the individual (36%), the emotional interaction (33%), the playful interaction (28%) and at the bottom the process design (24%).

## SUMMARIZING 1

Overall, the results described define a framework that can be defined quite conservative and focused on the content. This latter, in fact, is the central element around which turns and is carried on the learning process; content is considered shareable and its production is expected to be supported by technology, but, in general, it is not expected to be the outcome of a collaborative processes.

The emerging framework is altogether surprising given that the participants in the survey represent a technologically advanced meaningful sample of Italian educators operating at all levels of both public educational institutions and professional world.

Surprisingly, despite the current diffusion of social networks, the development of community and socialization practices within educational processes matter only to about 60% of educators who highlighted the relevance of content. Only one third of the participants, then, matter about the personalization of the process or the promotion of the individual.

Another incontrovertible fact is the lack of design culture, while a little bit more diffused seems to be the culture of the process management.

In our opinion the framework described above provides a clear explanation for the poor penetration of advanced methodological practices, processes and technologies. Regardless of the evolution of technologies and social behaviors, the expectations of educators (including those that maybe considered technologically advanced) seem to be satisfied by the basic functionalities offered by traditional environments, like Moodle (http://moodle.org), that have been built around

the content delivery and that, sometimes, unfortunately, is identified with the main task of the educational process.

I addition we have to consider also the potential barriers represented by: a) the lack of an adequate media and design literacy; b) the belief that the adoption of technologically mediated processes would lead to an excessive waste of energy and time.

In conclusion the message that emerges is very clear: the first and greatest barrier to the massive penetration of TEE has a cultural origin.

This is the reason why we asked ourselves what actions can be promoted to bridge the gap between advanced research on TEE and the everyday educational practices.

## BRIDGING THE GAP: THE MASTER IN E-LEARNING

Among the actions that we put in place to bridge the gap, one of the most significant was, without doubt, the on-line Master in "E-learning: Ergonomics, Methods, Techniques and Application" at the Iad School of the Rome Tor Vergata University (Giovannella, 2010). The master is aimed to diffuse among at school's teachers (primarily middle and high schools' ones) TEE advanced technologies and practices, through a design inspired $P^3BL$ process, that will be briefly summarized below.

The achievement of the Master's objective, however, is in general not easy. In fact we found that the initial beliefs of Master's students - in average younger than 35 years - always match, and even tend in many aspect to be more extreme of, the cultural framework emerged in the previous paragraph.

## THE INITIAL SITUATION

The initial attitude towards technologies is usually marked by an apparent openness and interest in TEE, considered as a quick way to carry out training processes (possibly simplified ones) for those who have already work- an/or family-commitments.

Considering as example the last cohort, consisting of a dozen of elements, that ended the master in March 2011, the starting point was represented by a set of individuals that resulted to be accustomed to the passive use of the content provided by the web. This latter was used mainly for information search (89%), content sharing/production (54%/44%) and social networking (44%). Less than a third had previous TEE experiences of any sort.

Faced with the request to list the features deemed necessary to manage a TEE process, fully in line with the results of the second paragraph, they indicated in order of relevance: content production (78%), content sharing (67%) and tools for 'the evaluation and assessment' (67%). Only 33% indicated the support to collaboration/team-working and process design; even less, 11% the support to socialization. Differences with respect to the results of the previous paragraph are observed for the support to personalization, increased to 44%, and for that to communication that, on the other hand, went down to 22%.

As far as expectations for improvements that may result from the use of technologies at the top of rank we found the effectiveness of learning (100%), followed by the quality of the educational experience (90%), the efficiency of learning (67%), the management of the educational process (56%), the support to the development of a sense of belonging to the community (44%) and of the interaction (44%), at the bottom, again, the support to the development of the individual (22%).

Quite in line with the results shown in the previous paragraph are also the opinion on the elements that can make the experience more challenging and improve the quality of the process. Once again in pool position content and cognitive interaction (100%), followed by motivation (67% - element not evaluated previously), learning/training and social interaction, both at 55%, same percentage as for creativity. Emotional interaction and the

support to the individual were indicated by 44% of the participants; at the bottom of the list, with 33%, the support to process design and the ludic dimension.

Apart from some fluctuations in the percentages, probably attributable to the numerically limited sample, and an increase of interest in personalization, the initial situation that emerges from the survey carried on the participants in the last cohort of the Master seems to confirm the more general findings of the previous paragraph. This fact leads us to conclude that the greater familiarity with TEE possessed by the sample of 500 educators who took part in the survey is not sufficient, actually, to determine significant cultural differences with respect to the much smaller group of Master's students having a quite limited experience on TEE.

## AN OVERVIEW OF THE EDUCATIONAL EXPERIENCE

The honored Master in "E-learning: Ergonomics, Methods, Techniques and Application" is organized in two parts. The first one is based on a very old-fashion e-learning scheme (content-delivery, self-evaluation tests, technical support via email or forum) and is used to realign the students' prior knowledge, while the second part adopts the Organic Process, OP (Giovannella, 2007) interpreted as a design inspired "problem", "project" and "process-based" learning (P³BL) process. The OP has been inspired by "living organisms" and, at any level, fulfills three basic functionalities:

- **Investigate:** The environment to collect information & learn;
- **Elaborate:** The information to design/produce;
- **Communicate:** The "products" by means of "actions" that, in the case of very complex organisms, make use of highly structured and conventional languages.

The vital functions can be carried on as collective activities, always in osmotic interaction with the context, and should be kept always active during the whole development of the educational process. We refer the reader who wants more information on the functional layers of OP, and on associated guidelines, to previous publications (Giovannella, 2007). Here we limit ourselves to list the macro-phases of the educational processes (Master) we are considering here and that has been carried on fully online: 1) opening phase of acclimatization; 2) preliminary exploration activities; 3) critical analysis of her/his own working place; 4) collaborative data processing and problem setting + thematic lab on communication; 5) preliminary discussion on project works; 6) collaborative project work development; 7) preparation for the final examination; 8) debriefing, "take leave" and future plans.

Accordingly to the change in the educational process that occurred between the first and the second part of the Master, the activities have been transmigrated in a more suitable on-line learning environment: from Moodle to LIFE (http://life.mifav.uniroma2.it). The first one, as well known is built around the object course, while LIFE is organized around the object community and, coherently offers (Giovannella et al., 2010) more suitable monitoring tools like SNA (Bolasco, 1999) and Automatic Text Analysis (Wasserman & Faust, 1994).

## THE FINAL OUTCOMES

Two of the questions included in the initial survey were reiterated also in the survey proposed to the students at the end of the course.

In the final survey (see Table 6), as regards to the improvements that can be induced by the use of technology, we found at the top of rank the quality of the educational experience, albeit with only 67%, immediately followed by the support to communication (58%) that recovered 36 percent-

age points, which is positioned at the same level of content sharing and evaluation & assessment. Only in the fifth position the effectiveness of the learning and the process management (with 50%). Paired in seventh position content production, collaboration and team working (42%) paired, surprisingly, to the support for personalization of the educational process. Only at 33% the efficiency of learning, the same percentage found for the support to the sense of belonging to a community. In the last positions remain the process design and the support to development of the digital self dimension.

In this final survey we asked also questions intended to gather in a more direct way opinions on the educational process put in place and the

*Table 6. Educators' expectations about the role of technology in supporting and enhancing various aspects and qualities of the educational processes (percentages). First column: after the end of the first part of the Master; second column: at the end of the Master*

|  | After I part survey | Final survey |
|---|---|---|
| Content production | 78 | 42 |
| Content sharing | 67 | 58 |
| Evaluation&assessment | 67 | 58 |
| Process Personalization | 44 | 42 |
| Collaboration/team work. | 33 | 42 |
| Process design | 33 | 17 |
|  |  |  |
| Communication/ Interation | 22 | 58 |
| Socialization/Comm. Belonging | 11 | 33 |
|  |  |  |
| Effectiveness | 100 | 50 |
| Quality educat. exper. | 90 | 67 |
| Efficiency | 67 | 33 |
| Process management | 56 | 50 |
| Personal development | 22 | 8 |

changes that this may have caused in the students (see Table 7).

With regard to the educational process adopted in the second half of the master, 83% have appreciated the originality of the design and teaching methods. For 58% was noticeable the stimulus to creative design, while 50% have found very valuable the peer interaction and, as well, the interaction with the tutors.

As regards the changes to the point of view onto the educational process induced by the Master, here are some of the answers we collected:

1. "Certainly from now on, I'll be even more motivated to stimulate the students' creativity with the aid of technology."
2. "I've been transported to new horizons where, actually I hoped to be brought."
3. "The distance between learner and teacher shortened substantially. I very much valued collaborative and active learning with respect to bookish and individual learning."
4. "I put more attention in a careful analysis of the situation and the instructional design, leaving the 'improvisation.'"

*Table 7. Expectations of the master's students about the role of technology in enhancing quality of the educational processes to make them more appealing (percentages)*

| | After I part survey | Final survey |
|---|---|---|
| Content/cognitive interaction | 100 | 75 |
| Motivation | 67 | 58 |
| Learning quality | 55 | 42 |
| Social interaction | 55 | 92 |
| Creativity | 55 | 50 |
| Emotional interaction | 44 | 33 |
| Personal development | 44 | 33 |
| Process design | 33 | 25 |
| Ludic dimension | 33 | 17 |

5. "The educational process has appeared to me in all its complexity, versatility, peculiarity and social value."
6. "My background has been enriched by new and important strategies to achieve the same objective, i.e., the education/training of students."
7. "I feel I have abandoned the usual patterns and to be more capable and more in charge for my results and therefore more motivated to learn more."

In the comments we did not find any criticism but some concerns such as:

1. "I hope that is not only a utopian, considering the conditions faced by the public schools' teachers."
2. "I hope to have the possibility to obtain soon the necessary means and cutting-edge tools that can give value to my work."
3. "The master has stimulated a reflection on the potentialities of the technologies that can be considered still *white flies* in the endowment of Italian schools."
4. "Awareness of looking at things with fresh eyes and, unfortunately, at the same time, the ability to perceive the blindness of so many colleagues."

## SUMMARIZING 2

The results are certainly quite satisfactory but not without some shadows. One may feel satisfied because the above results demonstrate the relevance of an adequate education for a conscious use of TEE, i.e., a use adequately informed about the educational potentiality of the technological enhancement. We may consider without doubt a major achievement to have been able, solely on the basis on the teaching practice, to undermine the centrality of the content that has been replaced by the relevance of the social interaction/collaborative practice. It is also significant that the master provoked a fall of the perceived relevance of effectiveness and efficiency while maintaining in a relevant position the attention to evaluation. These are facts that maybe interpreted as the emergence of a growing awareness about the need of more appropriate evaluation and assessment strategies, not strictly related, or at least not only related, to the product and to the efficiency of the process, but rather to its quality.

It would seem that the educational process has contributed also to foster, or to keep alive, a greater attention toward personalization of the educational process.

Among the shadows we could include the limited attention that has been given to items as sense of belonging to the community, emotional interaction, and creativity. A shadow maybe considered, as well, the decrease of interest in the playful interaction. We believe that these shadows are the result of the limited duration of the second part of the Master (4 months). With more time and a greater number of P$^3$BL cycles, probably we could have succeeded in inducing at least a reflection and maybe a rethinking of the students' beliefs on other additional aspects of the educational experience.

## DISCUSSION AND PERSPECTIVES

It seems to us that the results described - although referred to a well-defined context like the Italian one (it would be interesting to compare our results with others obtained in other European or industrialized countries) - proves the existence of a considerable gap between what is produced by the technological and and methodological research on TEE and what is actually absorbed by the society. The technological education of society, even considering its more advanced components, proceed basically along two lines: a) through the models imposed by major producers of operating systems (and/or hardware); b) through the

diffusion of open source applications and, even more, the use of open services made available from the web (thanks also to the communities of developers/users and to the social networks that they produce).

The results discussed in the previous paragraphs, however, seem to suggest that such processes are much closer to a transfer of technological skills than to an informed absorption of expertise that can be critically reused and adapted, in the most appropriate, way to contexts and individuals. A demonstration of this assertion is the rather conservative picture that emerges from the survey with 500 educators accustomed to TEE. They seem to consider technologies only as a useful support to reproduce on-line a transmissive process of content delivery. A further confirmation is given to us by the lack of qualitative differences between the results of the survey conducted with the 500 educators and that conducted with the master's students at the beginning of the educational process.

The emergence of such "landscape" is not fully surprising because there is a diffuse convincement that transmissive processes of content delivery are also those that allow for larger incomes because of the need for fewer resources and of the possibility to operate a standardization at several levels.

The fact that in four months, thanks to the adoption of appropriate process, teaching methods and technological environments, it was possible to induce in the participants a fairly substantial reflection and reconsideration on TEE, makes us realize that there is a urgent need to operate to prevent the emergence of a new form of digital divide: among those who are able to critically use technology and those that make a conformist/standardized use of technologies based on the fashions of the moment.

The problem, in fact, does not lies, or at least not exclusively, in the dissemination of an adequate media literacy. In our opinion the main problem is represented by the lack of competences that allow to use such literacy to design for adequate technologically enhanced educational experiences (also self-directed) and, overall, meaningful to the learners. It is not by chance that several authors and institutions, in the recent past tried to work out lists of new Digital competence for learning (ETS, 2002; European Schoolnet, 2005; UNESCO, 2008; ISTE, 2008) and, as well, assessment models (Calvani et al., 2008; Cartelli et al, 2010; Gulikers et al., 2004; Ivanova & Chatti, 2011) and tools.

On the point of view of the Digital competence & literacy (European Union), this paper shows that the gap in the technological competencies can be relatively easily recovered and is strongly supported by the technological innovation that pervades the society. The ability to use the media (text, photographs, sounds, movies and. in some cases, graphic sketches) and the knowledge of some applications (navigation and use of basic web services, preparation of slides, use of the email and, in some cases, spreadsheets) are basic prerequisites that can be achieved (at least at a minimum level) in a reasonably short time, even on-the fly, especially if one is driven by needs. Most of these skills, as well known, are the basis of the European Computer Driving Licence (ECDL, http://www.ecdl.org/) and, as well, of the recommendations by ETS (Educational Testing Service), but these are also skills that have their focus on the content and it is quite clear that if their acquisition will not be accompanied by that of other, more significant competencies, the final effect would be that to reinforce, and not to change, the framework emerged from the survey described in the first paragraph of this article.

The definition of other relevant competences is certainly not trivial and may depend on the particular cultural pedagogical context (Calvani et al., 2008). Nevertheless we believe that there are some cross-cutting and universal competencies that should be part of the toolbox of each individual like: the critical thinking (Horkheimer & Adorno, 1976), an adequate design literacy (Giovannella, 2010) and the meta-design ability

needed to tame the complexity (Giovannella, in press), competencies that are not limited to the ability to execute specific tasks or use a given approach and to accomplish a given phase of a process, nor are specific to IT, although the continuous IT development has the effect to enhance their relevance.

Certainly there is much to be done to deepen and better understand many details of the research conducted so far and described above, but it is very clear that the more urgent need, and perhaps the "greatest challenge", is to bridge the gap between research and society to operationalize within the latter the results produced by the former. However, this is a grand challenge that cannot be addressed without the help of political guidelines that could make the ecosystem "research-society" globally competitive. Perhaps for the TEE is not yet too late because have not yet appeared players as dominant as Google, Facebook, etc. and because the educational domain is permeated by quite resistant antibodies against conformism ... however the time available is not infinite. Will governments and institutions be able to take on this need?

## REFERENCES

Bolasco, S. (1999). *Analisi multidimensionale dei dati*. Rome, Italy: Carocci.

Calvani, A., Cartelli, A., Fini, A., & Ranieri, M. (2008). Models and instruments for assessing digital competence at school. *Journal of E-learning and Knowledge Society, 4*(3), 183–193.

Cambi, F. (2003). *Manuale di storia della pedagogia*. Roma-Bari, Italy: Editori Laterza.

Cartelli, A., Dagiene, V., & Futschek, G. (2010). Bebras contest and digital competence assessment. *International Journal of Digital Literacy and Digital Competence, 1*(1), 24–39. doi:10.4018/jdldc.2010101902

ETS. (2002). *Digital transformation: A framework for ICT literacy.* Princeton, NJ: Educational Testing Service.

European Commission. (2010). *FP7 projects in technology-enhanced learning.* Retrieved from http://cordis.europa.eu/fp7/ict/telearn-digicult/telearn-projects-fp7_en.html

European Schoolnet. (2005). *Assessment schemes for teachers' ICT competence.* Retrieved from http://www-old.eun.org/insight-pdf/special_reports/PIC_Report_Assessment%20schemes_insightn.pdf

European Union. (2008). Recommendation the European Parliament and the Council of 18 December 2006 on key competences for lifelong learning. *Official Journal of the European Union. L&C, L394,* 10–18.

Giovannella, C. (2007). An organic process for the organic era of the interaction. In Silva, P. A., Dix, A., & Jorge, J. (Eds.), *HCI educators 2007: Creativity3: Experiencing to educate and design* (pp. 129–133). Rome, Italy: University of Rome Tor Vergata.

Giovannella, C. (2009). DULP: Complexity, organicity, liquidity. *IxD&A, 2009*(7-8), 11-15.

Giovannella, C. (2010). Beyond the media literacy. Complex scenarios and new literacies for the future education: The centrality of design. *International Journal of Digital Literacy and Digital Competence, 3*(1), 18–28. doi:10.4018/jdldc.2010070102

Giovannella, C. (in press). Is complexity tameble? Toward a design for the experience in a complex world. In *Proceedings of the Conference on Human Factors in Computing.*

Giovannella, C., & Graf, S. (2010). Challenging technologies, rethinking pedagogy, being design-inspired. The grand challenge of this century. *eLearn Magazine, 2010*(2), 8.

Giovannella, C., Spadavecchia, C., & Camusi, A. (2010). Educational complexity: Centrality of design and monitoring of the experience. In G. Leitner, M. Hitz, & A. Holzinger (Eds.), *Proceedings of the 6th Symposium of the Workgroup Human-Computer Interaction and Usability on HCI in Work and Learning, Life and Leisure* (LNCS 6389, pp. 353-372).

Gulikers, J. T. M., Bastiaens, T. J., & Kirschner, P. A. (2004). A five-dimensional framework for authentic assessment. *Educational Technology Research and Development, 52,* 67–86. doi:10.1007/BF02504676

Horkheimer, M., & Adorno, T. W. (1976). *The culture industry: Enlightenment as mass deception.* London, UK: Continuum International Publishing.

Ivanova, M., & Chatti, M. A. (2011). Competences mapping for personal learning environment management. In *Proceedings of the PLE Conference,* Southampton, UK (pp. 1-13).

Prensky, M. (2001). *Digital natives, digital immigrants on the horizon.* Bradford, UK: MCB University Press.

UNESCO. (2008). *ICT competency standards for teachers: Implementation guidelines.* Retrieved from http://unesdoc.unesco.org/images/0015/001562/156209e.pdf

Wasserman, S., & Faust, K. (1994). *Social network analysis: Methods and applications.* Cambridge, UK: Cambridge University Press.

*This work was previously published in the International Journal of Digital Literacy and Digital Competence, Volume 2, Issue 3, edited by Antonio Cartelli, pp. 41-55, copyright 2011 by IGI Publishing (an imprint of IGI Global).*

# Chapter 13

# Benefits and Risks of Social Networking Sites:
## Should they also be Used to Harness Communication in a College or University Setting?

**Angelina I. T. Kiser**
*University of the Incarnate Word, USA*

## ABSTRACT

*One of the challenges facing university and college professors is the use of effective and efficient communication with their students. One solution could be the use of social networking sites to engage students and the U.S. 2010 Digital Year in Review (2011), social networking continues to grow as one of the web's top activities with 9 out of every 10 U.S. Internet users accessing break down communication barriers, according to a social networking site every month. The study includes an in-depth review of the uses, benefits and risks of social networking sites as well as how they might be utilized in a college or university setting. The researcher in this study surveyed university business students at a private, four-year, Hispanic-serving institution in Texas about their use of social networking sites and how professors might integrate these sites into the curriculum.*

## INTRODUCTION

Being electronically connected to most everything – friends, family, news, entertainment, and music, just to name a few -- is the norm for the college and university student of today. Students face a barrage of new technologies on a regular basis, and they are becoming quite adept at adapting to these technologies. Technology has become an integral part of our lives, and one way that many students stay connected is through the use of social networking sites such as Facebook, MySpace, Twitter, LinkedIn, etc. And now, not only are

DOI: 10.4018/978-1-4666-2943-1.ch013

students staying connected with the computers, they are using iPads and smartphones as well.

Research indicates that the use of social networking sites has been increasing for all age groups over the last five years. According to the Pew Internet and American Life Project Surveys (2006, 2010), the amount of time Americans spent on social networking sites in 2006 was 9% compared to 38% in 2010. For the 18-29 age group, time spent on social networking sites increased from 31% in 2006 to 60% in 2010. The use for 30 to 49 year-old Americans increased from 4% in 2006 to 39% in 2010. From June 2009 to June 2010, time spent on social networking sites increased from 16% to 23% respectively (Womack, 2010). It is evident that social networking is changing how people communicate.

The use of social networking sites has expanded to include not simply social aspects of our lives, but now these sites are being utilized by job seekers, employers, hiring managers, and educational personnel. However, issues such as privacy and security have become major concerns for social networking site users. Controversies over what is acceptable and appropriate have caused law suits and employment issues. New policies are being implemented by employers to protect themselves against negative information on their employees' social networking sites. Scam artists have moved from emails to social networking sites to try to cheat people. Controversy also abounds as to whether or not the use of social networking sites for educational purposes serves a legitimate purpose or if it simply disengages the learners from the educators. Should these sites remain "social" sites or can a gap be bridged to make them useful when implementing university and college curricula? The capability to make them educationally useful is already present, but capability, in and of itself, does not make it valuable, and it may not benefit the students.

The purpose of this research was to investigate different types of social networking sites, how they are currently being used, their benefits, their risks,

and how university and college professors might utilize them to bridge the communication gap with their students. The research concludes with a study that was conducted to determine how students at a four-year Hispanic serving institution in Texas utilize social networking sites and how they felt these sites could be utilized by their professors in the students' coursework. Students provided demographic data regarding age, ethnicity, gender, and classification (freshman, sophomore, junior, or senior). Statistical analyses were then performed to determine if there were any statistical relationships between variables.

## Types of Social Networking Services

The term "social network site" can be defined as a web-based service that allows users to construct a profile, create a list of users with whom they share a connection, and view the information of their connections (Boyd & Ellison, 2007). Once a member of a site, users can specify their "friends", "contacts", or "fans." Once the connections are established, those within the group can view each other's information that has been provided in the profiles.

For the purpose of this research, four types of social networking services will be reviewed: 1) profile-based, 2) content-based, 3) mobile, and 4) work-based. Profile-based social networking services are largely centered around members' profile pages that contain information about the member such as likes, dislikes, and interests (Childnet International, 2008). Some of the most common profile-based services include Facebook, MySpace, and Bebo. All three of these sites are on the top ten list of the most popular social networking sites (Strickland, 2011; Geeks Desk, 2011). Facebook is the number one site with over 750 million users; Bebo has over 117 million users, and MySpace boasts more than 100 million users (Bennett, 2011).

With content-based social networking services the focus is on the posting of content as opposed to the user's profile, which is secondary (Childnet International, 2008). Examples of content-based services include YouTube, Flickr, and Shelfari. Flickr is an image and video sharing site where users share their images and videos with friends, family or the world, whichever they choose. In 2010, there were 5 billion photos hosted by Flickr. More than 3000 photos are upload to site every minute, which equates to 130 million uploads per month (Pingdom, 2011). YouTube is a video hosting site and has 35 hours of video uploaded every minute, and each day, 2 billion videos are watched (Pingdom, 2011). Shelfari is the largest social media site dedicated to book, and it allows users to create a profile and add friends, but the primary purpose is to allow book searches, make book recommendations, provide author profiles, and conduct discussion forums (Tibbs, 2010).

Mobile social networking services allow members to interact with their friends via their phones (Childnet International, 2008). In-Stat, a market research firm, estimates that nearly 30 million millennials in the United States will subscribe to mobile social networking services by 2012 (Ankeny, 2008). The shift of social networking to mobile devices is evident as Color, a mobile social networking platform acquired $41 million in venture capital allows people in close proximity to share photos, videos and text automatically with multiple phones as it creates a social network around the user,, combining the real-time element of Twitter with the multimedia of Facebook. Essentially it creates a social network around the user, dynamically and with no privacy; everything is shared with everyone (Hanluain, 2011). Zannel allows user to send out short group messages along with pictures and videos in realtime. Like Twitter, Zannel allows users to follow others so that they can keep up with what you are doing (Biggs, 2007).

Professional/business based social networking services include sites such as LinkedIn and XING. Both of these sites are used for professional networking. Users can post their resumes and other job related information in order to showcase their professional background and capabilities. LinkedIn is the world's largest professional network with over 120 million members in over 200 countries and territories. In 2010, there were almost 2 billion searches on LinkedIn (LinkedIn, 2011). XING has more than 10.8 million members who promote their businesses, search for jobs, colleagues, new assignments, and experts. Members can also meet and exchange ideas with over 45,000 special groups and get together at networking events (XING AG, 2011)

## Privacy and Security Issues with Social Networking Sites

How we interact and communicate with friends, family, and even strangers has drastically changed with the evolution of new technologies via smartphones and the Internet. Social networking sites now allow us to keep others fully updated about our daily lives. However, while it may seem advantageous to use these social networking sites as a convenient and simple medium for communication, their use brings challenging issues to light. People instinctively make trust judgments with face-to-face communication by analyzing facial expressions, gestures, and verbal inflections. However, the use of social networking eliminates those cues (Juels, 2010).

The Internet was initially set up as a mechanism where users could gather information. It then became interactive as users began to make purchases online (Clarke, 2010). These online purchases brought the first wave of unease as the protection of personal information such as credit card details became a concern. Now the Internet is a social space where people can share personal and private information with others (Clarke, 2010). Therefore, privacy and security are now even greater issues.

A privacy issue does not necessarily indicate a security breach; it may simply mean that someone has gained unwanted access to private or personal information. Although in 2009 Facebook introduced a new method for its members to set and adjust their privacy settings (Hof, 2009), in 2010, Facebook was highly criticized when the private details from its millions of users were exposed and searchable on search engines such as Google, Bing, and Yahoo (Sangani, 2010). Furthermore, Facebook has been accused of having confusing privacy settings that made it easy for Internet stalkers, cyber criminals, and nosy people to access private information without the users being aware. Although the company agreed to step up its privacy options (Sangani, 2010), Facebook was back in the news when it was discovered that nearly 100,000 apps were leaking private user information to third parties. Once the third party has what they call a "spare key", it can access profiles, photographs, chat logs, and personal information as well as pose as the user (Liebowitz, 2011). Despite the fact that privacy cannot be guaranteed on social networking sites, users continue to post very personal and private information on their pages, making it accessible to unwanted eyes.

According to the most recent What Keeps Network Administrators Up at Night survey from Amplitude Research, 41% of the network administrators are concerned about security breaches to their networks. Furthermore, when asked about their greatest concerns with regards to social media, the named viruses, potential data leaks, and intrusion risk at the top of their lists (Rashid, 2011). When a social networking site is compromised, it might lead to the spread of malicious code, the compromise of users' computers, or access to information about a user's identity, location, and contact information (McDowell & Morda, 2011). An attacker might be able to pose as a friend or contact in order to try to get money from you. For example, while email is still the most commonly used method for Internet scams, the scam artists are now moving to social networking sites as more users create profiles according to the Federal Bureau of Investigation and the National White Collar Crime Center (MacMillan, 2008). Table 1 provides some common threats to social networking services (McDowell & Morda, 2011).

Security breaches are not always intended to be malicious, but they can be very inconvenient in other ways. In 2005, a worm called "Samy" infected MySpace and shut the site down for several days. The intent was not to gain unauthorized access to users' accounts; instead, the worm added the words "Samy Is My Hero" to the top of every MySpace profile page (Collins, 2008). Although not all privacy and security breaches are malicious, privacy and security issues with social networking services should still be a concern for both administrators and users. People should exercise common sense and take a careful approach

*Table 1. Threats to social networking services*

| Threat | Description |
| --- | --- |
| Viruses | An attacker could potentially infect millions of computers by relying on users to share the malicious links with their contacts. |
| Tools | An attacker could take control of a user's account, giving them access to the account. Once the attackers gain access they can pose as the user and post malicious content. |
| Social Engineering Attacks | Attackers may send an email or post a comment that appears to originate from a trusted service or user leading to a link to a malicious URL, disclosure of sensitive information, or a security compromise. |
| Identity Theft | Attackers may be able to obtain enough information about a user or the user's contacts to be able to steal identity or be able to guess passwords for email, credit card accounts, or bank accounts. |
| Third-party Applications | Third-party applications such as games and quizzes that you download onto your site may provide access to your profile without your knowledge. The information could then be used for personalized marketing, research, sending spam email, or accessing your contacts. |

to what they share and with whom, and administrators should make every attempt to make their sites as safe and secure as possible.

## Employers and Social Networking Sites

Social networking sites have become both a resource and a concern for employers, and more employers are now using them to research potential employees and to monitor their actions after they have been hired (Kiser, Porter, & Vequist, 2010). During the hiring process employers are interested in references, experiences, and work history (Fechenda, 2011); therefore, it is important that what they see on your social networking site is appropriate and informative. Professional networking sites such as LinkedIn are good resources for employers, but they may also check your other social networking sites such as Facebook or MySpace.

According to a CareerBuilder.com survey, 45% of employers are now using social networking sites such as Facebook, MySpace, and Twitter to research potential employees, and 35% of the employers have stated that they have opted not to hire people based on the content of their social networking sites (Lechner, 2010). However, as employers use social networking sites in the hiring process, they should be careful to avoid areas that may pose legal pitfalls: 1) accessing information related to protected-class status, 2) evaluating or verifying qualifications, 3) using leisure activities as a basis for decision making, and 4) asking friends or contacts to provide references (Harpe, 2009).

Once job candidates have been hired, employers may continue to monitor their social networking sites. Some employers now have specific policies in place to address the content their employees are permitted to post on their sites, and complaints about these policies as well as consequences such as firing or discipline have led to cases before the National Labor Relations Board (Eastman, 2011). Smith and Kanalley (2010) discuss several cases

in which people have been fired from their jobs because of postings on their Facebook pages:

1. An 18-year-old New England Patriot's cheerleader was fired for inappropriate photos.
2. A former waitress complained about her job and the customers after she had to stay late for a table of two that she felt did not leave a good tip.
3. A Canadian grocery store, "Farm Boy", fired seven employees for creating a Facebook group that mocked customers. According to the store, the group made "verbal attacks against customers and staff."
4. A Georgia high school teacher was called in by the principal and fired for photos she had posted of her holding wine and beer along with having an expletive on the page.

Employers are regularly searching the Internet for information about potential job candidates. It is the responsibility of people who post information about themselves to be aware of the possible consequences of posting what might be considered inappropriate content on their pages. While you may think that it is unethical for an employer to judge you by what is on your social networking site, the reality is that employers are doing just that, and you need to make sure that what they see on your site will help, not hinder, you in getting a job.

## University and College Students' Uses for Social Networking Sites

A meta-analysis was conducted by Coyle and Vaughn (2008) in order to ascertain how college students used social networking sites. Their findings indicated that 41% use them for keeping in touch with friends, 17% find them fun and entertaining, and 12% use them to look at and or post photos. Of the 35,000 subjects, no respondents indicated educational uses for social networking sites. However, the educational landscape on college and university campuses may change how these sites can be utilized by professors.

Some educators feel that social networking is innately disruptive to the education process. Students may access the sites on their laptops or cell phones during class. Some educators respond by banning these electronic devices (Pence, 2009) On the other hand, there are educators who see learning potential and benefits to social networking being used in the teaching process (Walling, 2009). Social networking can be used for communication and sharing of ideas as well as more advanced uses such as creating a Facebook page or other social media. It is important to recognize that students, educational tools, and skills necessary for student success are all changing, and the evolution of social networks can have many applications in the classroom (Pence, 2009).

Some researchers suggest that social networking can actually serve to re-engage students and motivate them so that they are not simply passive observers in the learning process (Ziegler, 2007). Others suggest that using social networking in education will promote "critical thinking in learners, which is definitely one of the more traditional objectives of education (Bugeja, 2006). However, some educators continue to believe that social networking serves only as a distraction to learning. Therefore, the debate continues as to whether or not social networking can be an effective educational tool.

## Research Study

The purpose of this research was to ascertain how university and college students utilize social networking sites and how students felt these sites could be utilized by their professors in the students' coursework. Students provided demographic data regarding age, ethnicity, gender, and classification (freshman, sophomore, junior, or senior). Statistical analyses were then performed to determine if there were any statistical relationships between variables.

The sample for this study consisted of undergraduate students taking one or more business classes at a four-year, Hispanic-serving institution. Of the 254 students who were asked to complete the survey, a total of 227 of them completed it, giving an 89% response rate. The survey was available during a four week period in the Spring 2011 semester. Each participant volunteered to take the survey; none were compelled to do so. Students provided survey data via Survey Monkey. Results were then formulated using SPSS software, and aggregate data was collected. The following information was gathered in the questionnaire:

1. Demographic: Age, gender, ethnicity, student classification (see Figure 1).
2. Use of social networking sites (SNS): Hours per week spent on a SNS, activities conducted on a SNS, possible SNSs for college coursework, professors' use of SNSs.

Table 2 provides information regarding the number of respondents as well as the percent of respondents with respect to age, gender, ethnicity, and classification.

Using SPSS, crosstabs were run and the chi-square test for independence was calculated to determine if there were any significant relationships between variables. Two categorical variables are considered independent if there is no consistent, predictable relationship between them. Relationships were considered significant at the $p < .05$ level.

## RESULTS

Respondents were asked how many hours per week they typically spent on the following social networking sites: 1) Facebook, 2) MySpace, 3) Twitter, and 4) LinkedIn. Facebook, by far, had the greatest percentage of students spending the most time on their site. Table 3 illustrates how many hours per week students spent on Facebook, MySpace, Twitter, and LinkedIn. Table 4 lists the

*Table 2. Frequency distribution of sample*

| Age | No. of Respondents | % of Respondents |
|---|---|---|
| 20 or younger | 92 | 40.5 |
| 21-25 | 108 | 47.6 |
| 26-30 | 14 | 6.2 |
| 31-35 | 5 | 2.2 |
| 36-40 | 3 | 1.3 |
| 41 or older | 5 | 2.2 |
| Gender | | |
| Female | 101 | 44.5 |
| Male | 126 | 55.5 |
| Ethnicity | | |
| Hispanic | 120 | 53.1 |
| White, non-Hispanic | 74 | 32.7 |
| Black, non-Hispanic | 12 | 5.3 |
| Asian/Pacific Islander | 7 | 3.1 |
| American Indian/ Alaskan | 1 | .4 |
| Other | 12 | 5.3 |
| Classification | | |
| Freshman | 15 | 6.6 |
| Sophomore | 46 | 20.3 |
| Junior | 108 | 47.6 |
| Senior | 58 | 25.6 |

percentage of students in the study who conduct the listed activities (also see Figure 2).

Results of the calculated statistics indicated no relationship between student classification and the dependent variables. There was also no relationship between ethnicity and the dependent variables. The following table displays those variables that had a statistically significant relationship at the $p < .05$ level. Table 5 provides a list of the variables that had a statistically significant relationship at the $p < .05$ level using the chi-square test of independence.

With respect to age, respondents in the 20 or younger and 21 to 25 age groups updated their profiles more often than the respondents in the other age groups. The respondents in the same aforementioned age groups were less likely, however, to use social networking sites to seek employment information. The gender crosstabs and chi-square results indicated the greatest number of significant relationships with the dependent variables. Females spent more time than males on Facebook, posted photographs more often, updated their profiles more often, and were more likely to seek employment information on a social networking site.

Participants were also asked to respond to an open ended question about how they felt university and college professors could use social networking sites as part of their curriculum. Although there were a number of students who felt that these sites should remain for social activities only, several themes emerged from the responses that indicated opportunities for professors. Students wanted immediate access to information and felt that Twitter would be a great opportunity for communication that provided immediate feedback. They further stated that using Twitter would be much better than using the standard email communication. Another theme was using Facebook for posting messages, answering questions, and discussion boards. They responded that since they regularly check their Facebook accounts, it would be much easier than having to access their school communication tool, in this case, Blackboard. Finally, students felt that the university should use social networking to market their programs to students. Their responses indicated that perspective and current students are much more likely to look at a Facebook page than a school website.

## Limitations

There are some noteworthy limitations to this study. All participants were undergraduates attending a private, four year, Hispanic-serving institution. Therefore, 88.1% of the respondents were between the ages of 18 and 25. A sample

*Figure 1. A graphical representation of the demographic information for the sample*

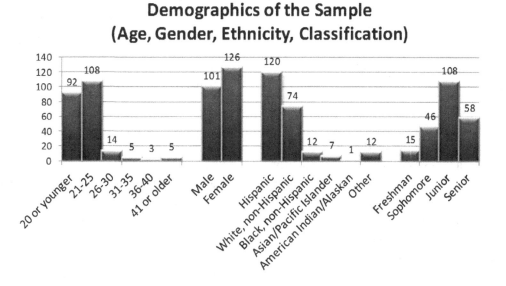

*Figure 2. A graphical representation that illustrates the percent of students who spend time on social networking sites performing the listed activities*

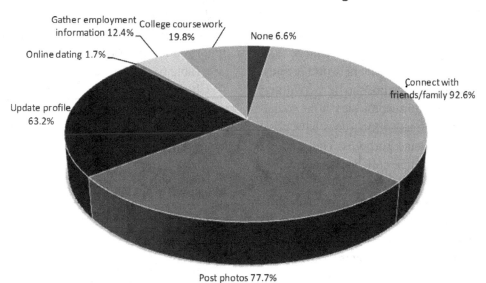

with students over the age of 25 may have yielded more significant results for those students over age 25. Additionally, 53% of the respondents were Hispanic and 32.7% were White, leaving few respondents in the Black, Asian/Pacific Islander, American Indian/Alaskan, and Other ethnicity groups. Finally, only 6.6% of the students were freshmen, while sophomores, juniors, and seniors comprised 20.3%, 47.6%, and 26.6% of the population respectively. A greater number

*Table 3. Number of hours per week students spend on social networking sites*

| Site | None | 1-5 | 6-10 | 11-15 | 16-20 | >20 |
|---|---|---|---|---|---|---|
| Facebook | 6.7% | 43.6% | 24.9% | 15.1% | 5.8% | 4.0% |
| MySpace | 89.3% | 10.1% | 0.6% | 0.0% | 0.0% | 0.0% |
| Twitter | 81.1% | 12.6% | 5.7% | 0.6% | 0.0% | 0.0% |
| LinkedIn | 96.4% | 3.0% | 0.6% | 0.0% | 0.0% | 0.0% |

of participants from some of the ethnic groups as well as freshmen students may have made for richer results.

The results of this study highlight the need for further research in the use of social networking sites in the learning environment. Future studies should be conducted with students from larger, public universities in various geographic regions in order to obtain deeper results. Another interesting aspect for future research would be to sample students from universities outside the United States.

## CONCLUSION

As the number of students on our college and university campus using social networking sites continues to grow, educators should be willing to engage students and become part of the social environment. Social networking does have possibilities for educational purposes. They can be used for communication, collaboration, creativity, just to name a few. Using social networking creates a student-centered approach to teaching and learning. To keep students engaged, it is imperative that educators are up-to-date with the latest technologies that the students are using and for them to understand the educational potential behind the technology. Educators cannot be lulled into a classroom taught only by methods designed for students without access to or knowledge of our digital world.

This study was conducted with students who will ultimately become part of our workforce, and regardless of the students' majors, they will most likely work for a company or business that has not only a website, but also a Facebook page. Hence, it stands to reason that students be aware not only the social aspect of social networking but also the business aspect of social networking. Educators can be creative in how they use social networking in their classrooms and make it relevant to the students and the learning environment.

Using social networking sites within a learning environment provides further opportunities for professors to further students' understanding of how they should be maintaining their sites and what is appropriate content. Students should be made aware of the types of information on social networking services and the risks to professional opportunities, personal relationships, and safety (see Table 6) (McDowell & Morda, 2011).

Ultimately, users of social networking sites need to take precautions in the amount and type of content they post. University and college professors have opportunities to teach students about

*Table 4. Student activities on social networking sites*

| Activity | % of Students |
|---|---|
| None | 6.6% |
| Connect with friends and family | 92.6% |
| Post photos | 77.7% |
| Update profile | 63.2% |
| Online dating | 1.7% |
| Gather employment information | 12.4% |
| College coursework | 19.8% |

the appropriateness of their social networking sites and how they can be used to the students' advantage while also using them in their courses for better communication with their students. The learning environment can be enhanced while students also reap benefits from using their sites in a way that benefits them in the job market.

Using the digital landscape should enhance, and not replace, face-to-face communication. Social sites can serve as supplements to the course curriculum in order to facilitate a better learning environment. Since college and university students of today and digitally connected, social sites offer a way for professors to teach in a way that allows students to utilize their digital skills. However, care should be taken not to use their social sites in a "social" matter; rather, the sites should be used in educational ways such as program marketing, communication, and providing information. If using social networking in an educational setting is successful, students graduate with a better understanding of how to effectively and efficiently use social networking sites, which makes them better prepared to enter the workforce.

Ultimately, digital literacy should reach far beyond simply being able to use an application; it should include an understanding of the implications and impacts on our lives and others' lives. Students today can interact with the entire world, instantaneously, at any time. There is no longer the distance and time limitation that was present decades ago. Students also no longer just

*Table 5. Statistically significant relationships between variables*

| Independent Variable | Dependent Variable | p-value |
|---|---|---|
| Age | Update profile | .004 |
| Age | Employment information | .007 |
| Gender | Hours spent on Facebook | .009 |
| Gender | Posting photographs | .000 |
| Gender | Update profile | .033 |
| Gender | Employment information | .039 |

read information. They create and publish their own information, whether on a social networking site, webpage, blog, etc. This access has created many issues such as cyber bullying, inappropriate content leading to job loss, as well as an array of other problems. It is time to make changes, and those changes can be initiated in our classrooms. We do not want to continue to create digital illiterates who only understand how to push buttons and make digital media work. Instead, we want to also educate students about the effects of what they create, post, and publish. Curricula that includes both the how's and why's of social media create people who are digital literates who have a much greater understanding of the impact of this technology.

*Table 6. Professional and personal implications*

| Business Data | Posting sensitive company data that is only intended for internal use such as customer information, intellectual property, human resource issues, etc., could result in liability to both you and the organization. |
|---|---|
| Professional Reputation | Inappropriate content could have negative consequences for educational and career prospects. Companies and schools that check social networking sites may not hire or accept you, and if currently employed, you might even lose your job. |
| Personal Relationships | Once content is posted and it is online, there is no way to control who sees it, and even if it is removed, it is too late for those who have already seen the content, and the damage is done. |
| Personal Safety | You could risk the safety of yourself and others if you post too much information on your site. Sharing personal information such as your address and when you will be away leaves the door open for someone with malicious intent. |

# REFERENCES

Ankeny, J. (2008). Five mobile social networking services you should get to know. *Fierce Mobile Content*. Retrieved July 20, 2011, from http://www.fiercemobilecontent.com/special-reports/five-mobile-social-networking-services-you-should-get-know

Bennett, S. (2011). Social media showdown: Top 10 social networking sites of 2011. *Infographic*. Retrieved August 2, 2011, from http://www.mediabistro.com/alltwitter/social-networking-2011_b12969

Biggs, J. (2007). Zannel: Twitter with pictures and video. *Aol Tech*. Retrieved August 2, 2011, from http://techcrunch.com/2007/10/01/zannel-twitter-with-pictures-and-video/

Boyd, D. M., & Ellison, N. B. (2007). Social network sites: Definition, history, and scholarship. *Journal of Computer-Mediated Communication, 13*(1), 11. Retrieved August 11, 2011, from http://jcmc.indiana.edu/vol13/issue1/boyd.ellison.html

Bugga, M. (2006). Facing the Facebook. *The Chronicle of Higher Education, 52*(21), C1–C4.

Childnet International. (2008). *Types of social networking service*. Retrieved August 5, 2011, from http://www.digizen.org/socialnetworking/downloads/Young_People_and_Social_Networking_Services_full_report.pdf

Clark, M. C. (2010). Controlling privacy on social networking services. *UX Matters*. Retrieved August 4, 2011, from http://www.uxmatters.com/mt/archives/2010/04/controlling-privacy-on-social-networking-services.php

Collins, B. (2008). Privacy and security issues in social networking. *Fast Company*. Retrieved August 2, 2011, from http://www.fastcompany.com/articles/2008/10/social-networking-security.html

ComScore. (2011). *2010 digital year in review*. Retrieved July 15, 2011, from http://www.comscore.com/Press_Events/Presentations_Whitepapers/2011/2010_US_Digital_Year_in_Review

Coyle, C. L., & Vaughn, H. (2008). Social networking: Communication revolution or evolution? *Bell Labs Technical Journal, 13*(2), 13–18. doi:10.1002/bltj.20298

Eastman, M. J. (2011). A survey of social media issues before the NLRB. *U.S. Chamber of Commerce*. Retrieved August 18, 2011, from http://www.uschamber.com/sites/default/files/reports/NLRB%20Social%20Media%20Survey.pdf

Fechenda, E. J. (2011). Social vs. professional networking sites. *Healthcare IT News*. Retrieved August 2, 2011, from http://healthcareitnews.com/blog/social-vs-professional-networking-sites

Geeks Desk. (2011). *Top ten social networking sites*. Retrieved August 9, 2011, from http://www.geeksdesk.com/top-10-social-networking-websites/

Hanluain, D. (2011). Money rushes into social networking. *Mobiledia Network*. Retrieved August 2, 2011 from, http://www.mobiledia.com/news/85010.html

Harpe, L. D. (2009). Social networks and employment law. *Peopleclick Research Institute*. Retrieved August 1, 2011, from http://www.iowaabi.org/documents/filelibrary/events/social_media/Social_Networks_Employment_Law_eBoo_C3A386C1048E1.pdf

Hof, R. (2009). Facebook to introduce new, simpler privacy settings. *Bloomberg Businessweek*. Retrieved August 6, 2011, from http://www.businessweek.com/the_thread/techbeat/archives/2009/07/facebook_introd.html

Juels, A. (2010). The primal cue. *Communications of the ACM, 53*(3), 120–119. doi:10.1145/1666420.1666448

Kiser, A. I. T., Porter, T., & Vequist, D. (2010). Employee monitoring and ethics: Can they co-exist? *International Journal of Digital Literacy and Digital Competence, 1*(4), 30–45. doi:10.4018/jdldc.2010100104

Lechner, J. P. (2010). Employers: Be careful when checking employees' social networking sites. *Greenberg Traurig, LLP*. Retrieved August 3, 2011, from http://www.gtleblog.com/ 2010/04/articles/privacy/employers-be-careful-when-checking-employees-social-networking-sites/

Liebowitz, M. (2011). Facebook apps leak private info again. *Security News Daily*. Retrieved August 9, 2011, from http://www.securitynewsdaily.com/facebook-apps-leak-private-info-again-0780/

LinkedIn. (2011). *About us*. Retrieved August 2, 2011, from http://press.linkedin.com/about

MacMillan, D. (2008). Cyberscams befriend social networks. *Bloomberg Businessweek*. Retrieved August 1, 2011, from http://www.businessweek.com/print/technology/Content/nov2008/tc20081119_974324.htm

McDowell, M., & Morda, D. (2011). Socializing securely: Using social networking services. *United States Computer Emergency Readiness Team*. Retrieved August 8, 2011, from http://www.us-cert.gov/reading_room/safe_social_networking.pdf

Pence, H. E. (2009). Teaching in the 21st century. *Journal of Educational Technology Systems, 38*(2), 103–110. doi:10.2190/ET.38.2.c

Pew Internet & American Life Project Surveys. (2006). *Typical daily Internet activities of adult Internet users* (U.S. Census Bureau Publication No. 1130). Retrieved August 3, 2011, from http://www.census.gov/compendia/statab/2008/tables/08s1130.pdf

Pew Internet & American Life Project Surveys. (2010). *Typical daily Internet activities of adult Internet users* (U.S. Census Bureau Publication No. 1159). Retrieved August 3, 2011, from http://www.census.gov/compendia/statab/2011/tables/11s1159.pdf

Pingdom. (2011). *Internet 2010 in numbers*. Retrieved August 2, 2011, from http://royal.pingdom.com/2011/01/12/internet-2010-in-numbers/

Rashid, F. Y. (2011). *Network breaches, social media, smartphones worry administrators: Survey*. Retrieved August 4, 2011, from http://www.eweek.com/c/a/Security/Network-Breaches-Social-Media-Smartphones-Worry-Administrators-Survey-430279/

Sangani, K. (2010). Who owns your personal data? *Engineering & Technology, 5*(11), 28–29. doi:10.1049/et.2010.1103

Smith, C., & Kanalley, C. (2010). Fired over Facebook: 13 posts that got people CANNED. *Huffington Post*. Retrieved August 1, 2011, from http://www.huffingtonpost.com/2010/07/26/fired-over-facebook-posts_n_659170.html#s115707&title=Swiss_Woman_Caught

Strickland, J. (2011). Top ten social networking sites. *Discovery News*. Retrieved August 2, 2011 from http://news.discovery.com/tech/top-ten-social-networking-sites.html

Tibbs, E. R. (2010). *History of Shelfari*. Retrieved August 5, 2011, from https://wiki.itap.purdue.edu/display/INSITE/Shelfari#Shelfari-History

Walling, D. R. (2009). Idea networking and creative sharing. *TechTrends, 53*(6), 22–24. doi:10.1007/s11528-009-0339-x

Womack, B. (2010, August 2). Social networking and games leap in web use. *Bloomberg Businessweek*. Retrieved August 5, 2011, from http://www.businessweek.com/technology/content/aug2010/tc2010081_994774.htm?link_position=link6

XING AG. (2011). *What is XING?* Retrieved August 2, 2011, from http://www.xing.com/help/help-and- faqs-2/my-xing-and-my-network-55/about-us-155/what-is-xing-159

Ziegler, S. (2007). The miseducation of Generation M. *Learning, Media and Technology*, *32*(1), 69–81. doi:10.1080/17439880601141302

# Chapter 14
# Using Precision Teaching Method to Improve Foreign Language and Cognitive Skills in University Students

**Francesca Cuzzocrea**
*University of Messina, Italy*

**Anna Maria Murdaca**
*University of Messina, Italy*

**Patrizia Oliva**
*University of Messina, Italy*

## ABSTRACT

*Learning a foreign language takes time and effort. In the last few years, too much emphasis has been placed on oral communication skills and English teachers make their students speak English without paying enough attention to grammatical accuracy. As a result, while students' ability in terms of fluency has improved, they often cannot communicate appropriately in English due to a lack of grammatical knowledge. The aim of the study was to explore the potential of Precision Teaching software developed for the improvement of English grammar rules. Two groups were compared, one having used the software and the other following a traditional textbook-based approach. The students who used the software showed significantly higher learning scores than students who did not. In addition, after using the software students show increased scores in some cognitive abilities that are related to foreign language learning.*

Acquiring a linguistic competence, such as a foreign language, involves complex learning. Neural commitment to the native language interferes with foreign-language processing, causing difficulty in foreign-language speech perception in infancy and adulthood (Iverson et al., 2003). In recent years, many studies have indicated that the use of multimedia technology for foreign

DOI: 10.4018/978-1-4666-2943-1.ch014

language instruction can increase learning' levels (Brandl, 2002; Chikamatsu, 2003; Meskill & Anthony, 2005).

Several advantages can be gained by incorporating computers into language learning instruction. They can facilitate oral communication, reduce anxiety, enhance student motivation, and improve writing skills (Arnold, 2002; Conti-Ramsden, Durkin, & Walker, 2010; Davis & Kim, 2001; Tsou, Wang, & Li, 2007). For these reasons, multimedia technology in learning contexts has expanded rapidly during the last few decades. Researchers have reported that innovative use of computers in language learning is characterized by greater participation and interactions, and students enrolled in computer-mediated projects demonstrated more fluent conversation and improved their communication skills (Beauvois, 1998; Lee, 2002). Moreover, the use of Internet technology (electronic mail, electronic journals, search engines, chat and video conferencing) increases confidence in speaking and writing English, and listening and reading comprehension are also helped (Ware, 2004; Xiaoqiong & Xianxing, 2008).

Several studies have demonstrated the effectiveness of multimedia instruction (Mayer, 2001; Moreno & Mayer, 2000), although it has also revealed that multimedia materials can produce negative effects on learning outcomes (Kalyuga, Chandler, & Sweller, 2000) and on spatial and verbal ability (Jonassen & Grabowski, 1993). This damaging effect could be explained by cognitive overload occurred in multimedia-based learning and by individual differences on working memory capacity (Plass, Chun, Mayer, & Leutner, 1998).

Nevertheless, using computer and educational software provides many positive effects, especially for English language learners, to improve their skills and to check their language proficiency (Wang, 2005). Unfortunately, too much emphasis has been placed on oral communication skills and English teachers make their students speak English without paying enough attention to gram-

matical accuracy. Consequently, while students' fluency has been improved, they often cannot communicate appropriately in English due to a lack of grammatical knowledge (Padilla, 2006).

For these reasons, various methods for teaching a foreign language have evolved in the last few years. Numerous researchers have tried to identify the most effective educational technique in different contexts. Among the different learning procedures, behavioral technology has been shown to help students in the acquisition of basic skills, as it is more effective on behavior modification which allows learning and memorization (Lindsley, 1991; West, Young, & Spooner, 1990). The learning paradigm, such as Precision Teaching method (PT), based largely on Skinner's operant conditioning (Skinner, 1938, 1968), uses continuous and precise measurement and charting of behavior frequencies to assess student progress. Moreover, the psychologist and the teacher can see immediately whether an educational or treatment program is working or not.

Precision Teaching is a type of programmed instruction that focuses heavily on the acquisition of fluent behavior - that is both accurate and fast (Binder, 1996; Pennypacker, Heckler, & Pennypacker, 1977). *Fluency* is the ability to complete a task accurately and quickly. To measure fluency, Precision Teaching utilizes a semi-logarithmic chart called Standard Celeration Chart (Pennypacker, Gutierrez, & Lindsley, 2003). This chart allows for demonstration of changes in the rate of acquisition and allows the teacher to quickly assess student's performance. By utilizing this chart, teachers are able to quickly adjust the curriculum to maximize the student's learning, stimulating the student's ability of self-monitoring and guaranteeing an adequate fluency assessment (Cavallini, 2005; Truzoli, 2004). In other words, through a direct measure of the performance, teachers and students have a graphic feedback of the course and, at the same time, fluent acquisition is promoted by a repeated exercise that requires speed in execution.

Precision Teaching uses specially-designed decks of teaching cards and practice sheets, error drill, home instruction, SAFMEDS (say all facts one-minute each day shuffled) (Eshleman, 1985) and daily charting. Moreover, Precision Teaching arranges curricula step-by-step and in an individual way, applying behavior modification procedures (reinforcement) to improve students' learning. The learner can monitor frequency daily, use self-recording, and use standard charts to display major changes; so he/she learns more, much more quickly and, above all, with a higher level of mastery and resistance to distractions.

Precision Teaching is a useful tool for improving a wide variety of foreign language skills. In a few minutes per day, students can systematically practice specific skills in need of improvement. Precision Teaching records daily student performance gains, and provides visual motivation for students, information for instructional decisions, and understandable communication with students and teachers. The use of Precision Teaching builds fluency in the target language and has been shown to have positive effects on student achievement. Precision Teaching is adaptable to many skills and levels found specifically in a classroom. The cost of the technique in terms of time and expense is small compared to the potential benefits for students and teachers. In particular, the teacher can easily adapt the program to any didactic content ("content-free") (West & Young, 1992); furthermore students' correct responses are positively reinforced and they don't experience frustration. Through Precision Teaching method, students can learn quickly, answering to a default sequence of items (stimuli picture or questions). They are also able to self-monitor their progress, recording the number of correct answers.

In the present study, educational software, based on Precision Teaching method (Caravita, 2003), was developed to highlight English grammar rules. So, the aim of this investigation was to verify the efficacy of the software to improve the knowledge and use of English grammar rules among Italian university students, focusing on cognitive abilities (memory, attention and concentration). The following questions were asked: (1) Does the Precision Teaching software training produce higher learning scores in students than a traditional learning approach? (2) Does the Precision Teaching software training positively affect the student's cognitive abilities?

## METHOD

### Participants

28 Italian university students were recruited as volunteers from a beginners' psychology class. All students had a basic level of English proficiency. After agreeing to take part in the study, all participants completed a preliminary task to assessing their level of English knowledge and cognitive abilities, to ensure comparable groups. Two groups were selected: one used Precision Teaching software (n=14), the other used a traditional learning method, based on textbook teaching materials (n=14). None of the participants in this study had used the Precision Teaching software and the textbook materials prior to the experiment.

### Materials

### PT Software

Precision Teaching software (Caravita, 2003) consists of three areas: 1) *Insegno* (to set didactic contents of learning training), 2) *Imparo* (to perform assigned tasks) and 3) *Performance Analyzer* (to assess student performance). Use by the trainee requires no specific knowledge, either for the execution of the test, or for the training phase.

Through *Insegno*, the didactic contents to learn during the training (English grammar rules and their applications) were arranged. Students simply had to answer a default sequence of items (choosing between pictures or writing the answer by keyboard). Items are presented from easier to more difficult ones. 14 lessons of training on principal grammar rules and correct use of verbs in English language were selected for this study.

## Traditional Textbook Materials

*English Grammar in Use* (Murphy, 2003) is a grammar text known for its simple, clear explanations and innovative format. This book is aimed at elementary students and is designed as a first grammar book, covering all the major grammatical problems with numerous examples and illustrations. It can be used as a classroom text or for self-study. Each lesson-unit is a two-page spread that teaches a specific grammar point on the left hand side and provides practice exercises on the right.

## Cognitive Abilities

*Attenzione e Concentrazione test* (Di Nuovo, 2000) was used to assess attention, concentration and memory abilities. This uses computer technology to give a greater understanding of these valuable capabilities; it's based around a simple, accessible item-format which looks at the ability to pay attention and memorize instructions and applies these quickly and accurately.

Concentration and sustained attention (vigilance) were assessed by using digit span (forward and backward), already computerized by Jarvis and Jarvis (1991). It consists of the number of digits a person can absorb and recall in correct serial order after hearing them. The test begins with 2 to 3 numbers, increasing as the test progresses. At the end of a sequence, the subject is asked to recall and write using a keyboard the items in the same order presented.

Also divided attention was measured, using a dual-task methodology. In particular, the subject had to press a button when a stimuli target appeared on the screen; at the same time, a list of words was read and the participant had to click

another button every time word target was heard. So, attention ability must be distributed in two parallel tasks, one for the visual search and the other for auditory recognition.

Reaction time is the elapsed time between the presentation of a stimulus and the subsequent behavioral response and, in particular, in a recognition reaction time task some stimuli should be responded to and others should get no response (distracter set). The user had to press a button when one stimulus type appeared and withhold a response when other stimulus types appeared. Assessing this kind of reaction time is important to define the time required for an observer to detect the presence of a stimulus and to measure the duration of mental operations.

## Procedure

The study applied a pre-test/post-test/follow-up design with use of the Precision Teaching software as the treatment variable. Testing sessions occurred in university classrooms, during the laboratory activities of the psychology course. Data concerning each participant's skill level in the areas of precise mouse clicking and basic keyboard-use was collected. Based on preliminary test scores, students were assigned to either a PT group or a control group with 14 in each group. The participants followed the training contemporaneously, in separate classrooms.

All students who enrolled in PT group were given a laptop computer on which the didactic software was installed. Each worked individually at his/her own computer and used a headset to avoid distraction. Students were requested to complete a pre-test on English grammar rules and cognitive abilities; then, they attempted the Precision Teaching training at their own pace. After the training session, students were asked to complete a post-test.

In the control group, after students completed the pre-test on English grammar rules and cognitive abilities, they were provided with a textbook

(Murphy, 2003) and teaching materials from the text to study English grammar rules. Students had to read and understand grammar rules introduced in the didactic units and then provide practice exercises. After this, students were asked to complete the post-test.

## Pre-Test

The pre-test had the same type and number of questions as the post-test. All questions were related to the English and grammar rules introduced in the unit lesson proposed during the training. The pre-test was carried out to check students' initial knowledge of English language and cognitive skill levels. In addition, the anticipated differential performance of the pre-test and post-test would shed light on the relative learning efficiency of the two instruction methods.

The assessment measures of learning process included the number of correct answers and the amount of completed units focused on English grammar rules. Data on concentration and attention levels, and memory span was also recorded.

## Precision Teaching Training

During training session, just as any student in the traditional learning process has his/her own textbook, in the conducted experimental work all subjects had their own computer. Computers with standard keyboard, mouse and 15'' color monitors were used. The conditions of layout were the same for all participants; in fact, the textbook material was scanned and displayed on the computer screen in the same way it appears in the textbook. To answer, the subject had only to look at the video and use the mouse to indicate the correct choice or to write the correct answer. A picture-item: on the video a question appears, such as "Choose the correct picture/sentence?"…. with 4 options. The student had to click or write the correct answer. Naturally, the correct answers did not always appear in the same position; the

software automatically randomized the position of the answers. After each item, an appropriate feedback followed: a green circle (plus a pleasant sound) for the correct answers, while a red circle appeared when the answer was wrong.

When exercise finished, the students assigned to PT group continued the session, reviewing the items that were answered incorrectly. The task was valid when, twice consecutively, errors were not committed. Then, a new Precision Teaching unit was introduced.

For all participants, at the end of every session, the software counted the number of correct answers. The subjects had the possibility to see a particular graphic form, *Standard Celeration Chart*, which highlighted the level of accuracy achieved.

## Traditional Textbook Method

The teaching material came from the textbook by Murphy (2003). The learning units involve the use of pictures with an attached text in which people introduce themselves, greet and ask questions by using simple words or specific grammar rules. Some tables explain the grammar rules and there are a number of exercises to test levels of ability using the content of the lesson. For this study, 14 lessons of training on principal grammar rules and correct use of verbs in English language were selected, as reported in Table 1. The control group had to read and understand grammar rules introduced in the units (for not more than five minutes) and then provides practice exercises. The task was valid only when, on two consecutive trials, no errors were committed. Then, the subsequent lesson-unit was introduced.

## Post-Test and Follow-Up

Finally, data was collected during post-test and follow-up (a month later) sessions, on each of the dependent measures: learning scores (number of correct answers) and cognitive abilities (memory,

*Table 1. Content of the lessons training and number of items*

| Unit | Training contents | Items |
|------|-------------------|-------|
| 1 | am/is/are | 41 |
| 2 | am/is/are (questions) | 35 |
| 3 | Present continuous | 34 |
| 4 | Present continuous (questions) | 26 |
| 5 | Present simple | 30 |
| 6 | Present simple (negative) | 36 |
| 7 | Present simple (questions) | 33 |
| 8 | Present continuous and present simple | 24 |
| 9 | I have…/I've got | 28 |
| 10 | Was/were | 21 |
| 11 | Past simple | 41 |
| 12 | Past simple (negative and questions) | 29 |
| 13 | Past continuous | 11 |
| 14 | Past continuous and past simple | 20 |

concentration and attention). It was necessary to verify learning efficiency of the two instruction methods and its maintenance over the time.

## Results

Table 2 presents the means and standard deviations for the pre-test, post-test and follow-up on learning scores. Data revealed that both groups improved their performance from pre-test to post-test, and also to follow up; but the PT group showed a greater and more significant improvement than the traditional approach group in correct answers [$t(26)=2.43$; $p=.02$] and in the number of completed didactic units [$t(26)=2.86$; $p=.008$].

Comparisons indicated that students in the PT group learned more efficiently than the control group. In particular, significant differences between pre-training and post-training phases were recorded [PT group: $t(13)=6.47$; $p<.001$; control group: $t(13)=4.87$; $p<.001$]; the number of correct answers increased significantly in all students. But comparing pre-training and follow-up, it seems

that the learning of the control group is not sustained over the time, instead PT group performances improve, in a significant way, during follow-up phase [$t(13)=4.08$; $p=.001$].

Data also showed significant differences between groups during the follow-up phase ($t(13)=$; $p=.001$); students that used PT method, that ensures the opportunity to review errors, seem to maintain competences they have learned better than those who did not use it.

With regard to didactic units, comparing data of pre-training and post-training, all subjects had significantly improved their performances in terms of completed units [PT group: $t(13)=7.61$; $p<.001$; control group: $t(13)=3.73$ $p=.002$]; but comparing results of pre-training and follow-up, only the computer-assisted group had increased the number of completed units [$t(13)=4.77$; $p<.001$]. In particular, participants who used the computer-assisted method seem to complete didactic units better and faster than the control group, and this ability seems to be maintained over the time.

## Cognitive Abilities

Concentration and sustained attention (vigilance) were assessed by using digit span (forward and backward). Also divided attention and reaction time were measured.

Results have shown no significant differences in reaction time and in the attention ability, both between groups and between phases. Instead, significant improvement was found in memory abilities in subjects who learned using Precision Teaching method, especially comparing follow-up phases [$t(26)=3.580$; $p=.001$]. The educational software seems not affect the cognitive mechanisms that require individual's ability to maintain high concentration over time. While the effect on the development of attention skills related to memory abilities is clear.

Table 3 shows the means and standard deviations for the pre-test, post-test and follow-up on both digit spans.

*Table 2. Means (M) and standard deviation (SD) related to the number of correct answers and completed didactic units*

| | Correct answers | | | Completed units | | |
|---|---|---|---|---|---|---|
| | pre | post | follow-up | pre | post | follow-up |
| **PT group** | 27.07 (9.595) | 43.07 (12.149) | 47.93 (10.90) | 3.14 (1.610) | 5.93 (1.328) | 6.14 (2.82) |
| **Control group** | 21.64 (6.523) | 32.29 (11.432) | 32.64 (9.06) | 2.57 (1.158) | 4.21 (1.805) | 3.5 (1.29) |

When comparing data of forward digit span, although students improve their scores, there are no significant differences between training phases in PT group. While, for backward digit span, significant differences are revealed comparing pre-training and follow up [t(13)=-3.226; p=.007], and post training and follow up [t(13)=3.822; p=.002].

With regard to the control group, no significant differences between training phases were recorded.

## Discussion

The aim of the present study was to investigate the potential of the Precision Teaching method to improve foreign language learning, with particular attention on cognitive abilities (memory, attention, and concentration). Precision Teaching can be a helpful method since it enhances speed of production, endurance and generalizing behavior; it has been used successfully with university graduates, as well as students with autism, learning difficulties, attention deficit or severe intellectual disabilities (Fabrizio & Moors, 2003; Leach, Coyle, & Cole, 2003).

Results indicate that Precision Teaching software is a useful educational tool that enables educators to draw on their classroom expertise to facilitate the learning process. Moreover, data highlighted an improvement in the degree of knowledge in all groups, but the results obtained by the PT group are significantly better. PT students showed more accuracy and fluency in learning compared to students involved in the traditional teaching method. Besides, the methodology of Precision Teaching is more effective and efficient in comparison to traditional methodology. In particular, when compared with a traditional learning method group, the PT group learned more and more quickly, and the learned responses became automatic and lasted over time.

Likewise, it seems that computer learning influences the development of cognitive skills, encouraging an increase of memory abilities. The follow-up data showed maintenance of these affects in the short and long term, probably because working without the support of theory increases student motivation and, consequently, activates mnemonic capacities. This suggests that it is opportune to address future research in this direction.

Finally, the Precision Teaching method, based on behavior analysis principles, underlines the importance of feedback and the standard celeration chart helps students to monitor their own

*Table 3. Means (M) and standard deviation (SD) related to the forward and backward digit spans*

| | Forward digit span | | | Backward digit span | | |
|---|---|---|---|---|---|---|
| | pre | post | follow-up | pre | post | follow-up |
| **PT group** | 6.07 (2.16) | 7.07 (1.59) | 7.71 (1.59) | 5.21 (1.72) | 6.86 (1.83) | 7.57 (1.34) |
| **Control group** | 6.00 (2.22) | 6.79 (1.58) | 6.43 (2.14) | 5.07 (2.20) | 6.29 (1.98) | 5.50 (1.70) |

learning trend, without teacher mediation. This indicates that students are able to work independently, enhancing their performances in computer based learning, and monitoring their own learning experience. Literature has widely showed that feedback has the potential to promote learning, and computer-based feedback seems to offer advantages over traditional didactic approach, it urges students to reflect about their own errors and self-correction (Nagata, 1996, 1997). So the efficacy of Precision Teaching method on learning may depend more on its particular content configuration and application method rather than its computer mediation.

While using a computer in learning set is more pleasant than reading a book, it might be not enough to explain the improved and lasting performances of participants. Technology tools make the lesson more efficient and catch the students' attention and interest. Precision Teaching software may be a valuable learning and teaching resource, and students are happy when working with it. Students' perception and motivation of the relevance to their course is a necessary factor in facilitating learning.

It's clear that the conditions offered for the control group are less attractive than the experimental condition. Having a laptop with frequent feedback and support will probably lead to a self-fulfilling prophecy, whereby students with laptops are more stimulated than students who only had the textbook. Also, as the cognitive assessment conducted in pre, post and follow-up was done through computerized questionnaires; it might be that the experimental group is more experienced with computer usage than those who used only the traditional textbook. Future studies will need to determine the effect of this specific assessment on student's abilities.

However, more studies need to be conducted to generalize the results of the study. Future studies should include a higher number of subjects with different competence levels to see whether the same conclusions stand. Studies could also be done with students of different age levels and in different language learning environments to see whether similar results are yielded.

A final remark is that the overall sample size of each condition is rather small, thereby extending the problems due to random occurrences. It is also possible that since this study was limited to students at university level, studies exploring learning process and achievement at fewer advanced levels might yield more significant results. Researchers may also want to try to replicate the findings of the present study to determine whether these findings are extended to other samples and educational contexts. Future research should continue to investigate whether any learning variables interact with cognitive, affective, and other personality variables to predict success in foreign language learning by using Precision teaching technology. So, gaining more specific information on the influence of gender, study motivation, cognitive abilities, social background, and prior knowledge of English should be a goal for future research aimed to enhance our understanding of Precision Teaching effectiveness in learning process.

## CONCLUSION

This paper contributes to highlighting the need to rethink the role and use of technology in school context, especially in what concerns didactic tools for achieving specific skills, and, in this case, for improving English language proficiency. A didactic paradigm that uses digital competences to innovate traditional learning methods reaching a "dynamic learning" aimed to capture the real process in which the information is received, elaborated and re-elaborated. This cognitive process is meaningful because it is not a passive reception of content but places itself in a perspective of constructive knowledge (from the simple use of didactic content to its cooperative construction), and in which the learner builds his own conceptual networks, depending on his cognitive, affective and motivational involvement (Digital native).

The perspective moves from technological tools (more or less sophisticated) *tout court* to their use in order to reach individualized learning paths through a symbolic negotiation of meanings. From this new point of view, it follows that rethinking their importance is necessary to create a discovery-based learning for improving problem-solving and self-monitoring skills. On the other hand, promoting digital literacy in the institutional learning environment, as hoped by European Commission, does not automatically follow from the ability to use technological tools, but involves the confident and critical use of technology education for promoting discovery and experiential learning, problem-solving skills, and self-development (Ardizzone & Rivoltella, 2008; Maconato, 2008).

In conclusion, it is necessary to focus on new media culture and technologies in the educational context, in order to support European Recommendations that aim "to acquire more linguistic, mathematical and advanced digital competence, etc, for all learners", as indicated also by the OCSE surveys. Practically, as Ardizzone and Rivoltella (2008) claim, a more mature way of thinking about media education and technology education should be encouraged, within the widest paradigm of digital skills and digital literacy.

Finally, future pedagogical and didactic findings should start building significant pedagogical patterns that "are consistent with the aims of the school and can be easily integrated into the didactic curriculum" (Calvani, Fini, & Ranieri, 2010). For this reason, it is necessary for teachers, in their practice and planning activity, to work towards building an integrated approach to *media education*, in order to create individualized learning environments, in which technological tools are used to facilitate skills achievement (Calvani, 2011).

Innovation, therefore, should be towards teaching practices and discipline transformation, especially in educational environments, integrating the technological tools with the didactic activity, in order to place learners at the center and engage them actively in the learning process.

This is what we hoped to achieve with this study, that is, combining the improvement of language skills in foreign language acquisition and the promotion of digital skills (in this regard, the Italian ministerial project- E-English for digital didactic - Miur 4.7. 2011).

## REFERENCES

Ardizzone, P., & Rivoltella, P. C. (2008). *Media e tecnologie per la didattica*. Milano, Italy: Vita e pensiero.

Arnold, N. (2007). Reducing foreign language communication apprehension with computer-mediated communication: A preliminary study. *System, 35,* 469–486. doi:10.1016/j.system.2007.07.002

Beauvois, M. H. (1998). Conversations in slow motion: computer-mediated communication in the foreign language classroom. *Canadian Modern Language Review, 54*(2), 198–217. doi:10.3138/cmlr.54.2.198

Binder, C. (1996). Behavioral fluency: Evolution of a new paradigm. *The Behavior Analyst, 19,* 163–197.

Brandl, K. (2002). Integrating Internet-based reading materials into the foreign language curriculum: from teacher-to-student-centered approaches. *Language Learning & Technology, 6*(3), 87–107.

Calvani, A. (2011). *Principi dell'istruzione e strategie per insegnare*. Italy: Carocci.

Calvani, A., Fini, A., & Ranieri, M. (2010). La competenza digitale nella scuola. Modelli, strumenti, ricerche. *Giornale Italiano della ricerca educativa, 3,* 5.

Caravita, L. (2003). *Insegno/Imparo. PT software*. Milano, Italy: ORSEC.

Cavallini, F. (2005). Finalmente fluenza tra i banchi! *Journal of Applied Radical Behavior Analysis*, *1*, 49–69.

Chikamatsu, N. (2003). The effects of computer use on L2 Japanese writing. *Foreign Language Annals*, *36*(1), 114–127. doi:10.1111/j.1944-9720.2003.tb01937.x

Conti-Ramsden, G., Durkin, K., & Walker, A. J. (2010). Computer anxiety: A comparison of adolescents with and without a history of specific language impairment (SLI). *Computers & Education*, *54*, 136–145. doi:10.1016/j.compedu.2009.07.015

Davis, C., & Kim, J. (2001). Repeating and remembering foreign language words: Implications for language teaching systems. *Artificial Intelligence Review*, *16*, 37–47. doi:10.1023/A:1011086120667

Di Nuovo, S. (2000). *Attenzione e concentrazione* [CD-ROM]. *7 test e 12 training di potenziamento*. Trento, Italy: Edizioni Erickson.

Eshleman, J. W. (1985). Improvement pictures with low celerations: An early foray into the use of SAFMEDS. *Journal of Precision Teaching*, *6*, 54–63.

Fabrizio, M. A., & Moors, A. L. (2003). Evaluating mastery: Measuring instructional outcomes for children with autism. *European Journal of Behavior Analysis*, *4*, 23–36.

Iverson, P., Kuhl, P. K., Akahane-Yamada, R., Diesch, E., Tohkura, Y., Kettermann, A., & Siebert, C. (2003). A perceptual interference account of acquisition difficulties for non-native phonemes. *Cognition*, *87*, B47–B57. doi:10.1016/S0010-0277(02)00198-1

Jarvis, P. E., & Jarvis, C. P. (1991). A tool to assist in the serial testing of attention as a means of monitoring the effectiveness of rehabilitation. *Cognitive Rehabilitation*, *9*, 20–23.

Jonassen, D. H., & Grabowski, B. L. (1993). *Handbook of individual differences, learning, and instruction*. Mahwah, NJ: Lawrence Erlbaum.

Kalyuga, S., Chandler, P., & Sweller, J. (2000). Incorporating learner experience into the design of multimedia instruction. *Journal of Educational Psychology*, *92*, 126–136. doi:10.1037/0022-0663.92.1.126

Leach, D., Coyle, C. A., & Cole, P. G. (2003). Fluency in the classroom. In Waugh, R. F. (Ed.), *On the forefront of educational psychology*. New York, NY: Nova Science.

Lee, L. (2002). Enhancing learners' communication skills through synchronous electronic interaction and task-based instruction. *Foreign Language Annals*, *35*(1), 16–24. doi:10.1111/j.1944-9720.2002.tb01829.x

Lindsley, O. R. (1991). Precision teaching's unique legacy from B. F. Skinner. *Journal of Behavioral Education*, *1*, 253–266. doi:10.1007/BF00957007

Maconato, G. (2008). *Usi didattici delle tecnologie: quale stato dell'arte*. Trento, Italy: Erikson.

Mayer, R. E. (2001). *Multimedia learning*. Cambridge, UK: Cambridge University Press.

Mayer, R. E., & Moreno, R. (1998). A split-attention effect in multimedia learning: evidence for dual processing systems in working memory. *Journal of Educational Psychology*, *90*, 312–320. doi:10.1037/0022-0663.90.2.312

Meskill, C., & Anthony, N. (2005). Foreign language learning with CMC: forms of on-line instructional discourse in a hybrid Russian class. *System*, *33*(1), 89–105. doi:10.1016/j.system.2005.01.001

Moreno, R., & Mayer, R. E. (2000). A coherence effect in multimedia learning: the case for minimizing irrelevant sounds in the design of multimedia messages. *Journal of Educational Psychology, 92,* 117–125. doi:10.1037/0022-0663.92.1.117

Murphy, R. (2003). *English grammar in use.* Cambridge, UK: Cambridge University Press.

Nagata, N. (1996). Computer vs. workbook instruction in second language acquisition. *CALICO Journal, 14*(1), 53–75.

Nagata, N. (1997). An experimental comparison of deductive and inductive feedback generated by a simple parser. *System, 25*(4), 515–534. doi:10.1016/S0346-251X(97)00052-3

Padilla, A. M. (2006). Second language learning: Issues in research and teaching. In Alexander, P. A., & Wine, P. H. (Eds.), *Handbook of educational psychology* (2nd ed.). Mahwah, NJ: Lawrence Erlbaum.

Pennypacker, H. S., Gutierrez, A., & Lindsley, O. R. (2003). *Handbook of the standard celeration chart.* Cambridge, UK: Cambridge Center for Behavioral Studies.

Pennypacker, H. S., Heckler, J. B., & Pennypacker, S. F. (1977). The personalized learning center: A university wide system of personalized instruction. In Brigham, T. A., & Catania, A. C. (Eds.), *Handbook of applied behavioral research* (pp. 591–617). New York, NY: Irvington.

Plass, J. L., Chun, D. M., Mayer, R. E., & Leutner, D. (1998). Supporting visual and verbal learning preferences in a second language multimedia learning environment. *Journal of Educational Psychology, 90,* 25–36. doi:10.1037/0022-0663.90.1.25

Skinner, B. F. (1938). *The behavior of organisms.* Upper Saddle River, NJ: Prentice Hall.

Skinner, B. F. (1968). *The technology of teaching.* New York, NY: Appleton-Century-Crofts.

Truzoli, R. (2004). Il Precision Teaching nei trattamenti comportamentali finalizzati all'acquisizione di comportamenti fluenti. *Psicoterapia Cognitiva e Comportamentale, 10,* 37–49.

Tsou, W., Wang, W., & Li, H. (2002). How computers facilitate English foreign language learners acquire English abstract words. *Computers & Education, 39,* 415–428. doi:10.1016/S0360-1315(02)00078-7

Wang, L. (2005). The advantages of using technology in second language education. *T.H.E. Journal, 32*(10), 1–6.

Ware, P. D. (2004). Confidence and competition online: ESL student perspectives on web-based discussions in the classroom. *Computers and Composition, 21,* 451–468. doi:10.1016/S8755-4615(04)00041-6

West, R. P., & Young, K. R. (1992). Precision teaching. In West, R. P., & Hamerlynck, L. A. (Eds.), *Designs for excellence in education: The legacy of B. F. Skinner* (pp. 113–146). Longmont, CO: Sopris West.

West, R. P., Young, K. R., & Spooner, F. (1990). Precision teaching: An introduction. *Teaching Exceptional Children, 22*(3), 4–8.

Xiaoqiong, H., & Xianxing, J. (2008). Using film to teach EFL students English language skills. *Changing English, 15*(2), 235–240. doi:10.1080/13586840802052468

*This work was previously published in the International Journal of Digital Literacy and Digital Competence, Volume 2, Issue 4, edited by Antonio Cartelli, pp. 50-60, copyright 2011 by IGI Publishing (an imprint of IGI Global).*

# Section 5
# Digital Technologies and Literacy

# Chapter 15
# Use of the Internet by Medical Practitioners in Private Hospitals in Warri, Delta State, Nigeria

**Esharenana E. Adomi**
*Delta State University, Nigeria*

**Ericson Egbaivwie**
*Petroleum Training Institute, Owerri, Nigeria*

**Jonathan C. Ogugua**
*Federal University of Technology, Owerri, Nigeria*

## ABSTRACT

*This study explores the use of the Internet by medical practitioners in private hospitals in Warri Delta State, Nigeria. Descriptive survey design was adopted and questionnaire was the instrument used to collect data. The total population and sample for the study were 137 medical practitioners from 30 private hospitals in Warri. Findings revealed that most medical practitioners used the Internet on a regular basis; a majority of the medical practitioners started using the Internet between 1 – 5 years ago; most of the medical practitioners spend 2 – 5 hours using the Internet per visit; a majority of medical practitioners used the Internet without assistance. Medline, journals and PubMed were the Internet resources used by most of the medical practitioners. Internet use enables the respondents to improve patient care, keep up-to-date; high cost of Internet access and lack of access to the Internet were some of the problems facing most of medical practitioners. The study recommends that hospital management should provide their medical practitioners with Internet facilities to enable them access to the most recent and accurate information for effective service delivery. The findings will help health care authorities especially in developing countries to improve on Internet access facilities to medical practitioners.*

DOI: 10.4018/978-1-4666-2943-1.ch015

# INTRODUCTION

The Internet is currently transforming many aspects of life, especially in the ways people are accessing health information. Networked computers now allow health professionals to connect among themselves as well as patients around the world, providing access to medical information that until recently was reserved for academicians and professionals only, and making it possible for lay people to gain extensive insights into their own health. The Internet and the World Wide Web allow anyone with access to a computer the opportunity to be a researcher, to scan and look through literally millions of sources of information (Bass, 2003).

Health care is a complex and information-intensive process in which data that concern the health and medical conditions of individual patients are stored and used for clinical care and management. Also, data are aggregated for secondary purposes, such as the management of local health services, the monitoring and surveillance of diseases, and for planning the delivery of health services at local, regional, national and international levels. Within health care organizations, services and systems, large volumes of data are collected, stored, analysed, transferred, and accessed on a daily basis. Data on individual patients, up-to-date information on how to prevent, diagnose, treat and manage diseases from research is being published and is required by medical practitioners to provide effective and safe care for patients and the public (Bath, 2008). This medical data and information are increasingly being made available on the Internet for the use of medical practitioners, patients and the public.

Information is essential for health and development, but the world's scientific knowledge remains largely out of reach for many countries. This is due, in no small part, to financial, technological, and infrastructure challenges. In recent years the role of information and communication technologies, particularly the Internet, has been central to efforts to remedy the situation. The effective use of these new technologies can enhance the flow of scientific knowledge and contribute to the improvement of the conduct and sharing of health research, the formulation of sound health policy, and the advancement of health services (Dzenowagis, Kuruvilla, & Aronson, 2002).The effective use of the Internet can enable medical practitioners to receive health information and advance the health of patients.

A medical practitioner also known as physician, doctor of medicine, or medical doctor is a person who practices medicine, and is concerned with maintaining or restoring human health through the study, diagnosis, and treatment of disease and injury; which he/she accomplishes through a detailed knowledge of anatomy, physiology, diseases and treatment — the science of medicine — and its applied practice — the art or craft of medicine. Many medical practitioners specialise in one or other of the branches of medicine such as gynecology (women's health), psychiatry (mental health), pediatrics (children's health) etc. Training in these specialised areas takes about four years, after which an examination is written to qualify as a specialist (SA Study, 2011)

Several studies have been conducted on the use of Internet by medical practitioners. It has been observed in a study that medical practitioners use the Internet to look for diagnostic and treatment information online (Bazzoli, 2000). Koller, Grütter, Peltenburg, Fischer, and Steurer (2001) found in a study of use of Internet by medical doctors in Switzerland that Internet was available to a majority of the respondents, that the main reasons for using the Internet during consultations were retrieval of information on drugs, patient-specific information, vaccination recommendations and advice to persons travelling to foreign countries, and computation of the risk of atherosclerotic disease, while the reasons for not using the Net among some of them were inappropriate time demands, possible interference with the physician-patient relationship, lack of

Internet use experience, confusing information content and lack of access in the consulting room

It has been observed by Ahmed and Yousif (2007) that factors such as lack of Internet use skills, time and financial constrains, negative attitude and resistance to change, poor working and information-seeking behavior militate against the use of Internet by medical doctors in Sudanese.

Oduwole and Oyewumi (2010) investigated the use of web-based resources by physicians in a psychiatric institution in Nigeria and found that the physicians have aceess to and use Health Inter-Network Access to Research Initiative (HINARI) database and that they used the database in Internet cafes in and around the institution; PubMed is the most widely used database in the HINARI portal; information retrieved is used mostly for clinical decision making, but that respondents are faced with inadequate time for research because of their busy schedule, poor internet access and inadequate information retrieval skills.

Dolan (2010) reported that 86% of United States physicians use the Internet to locate health, medical or prescription drug information; of physicians who use the Internet for health information, 92% indicated that they accessed it from their office, while 21% did so with a patient in the examination room; 88% looked for health information online from home, while 59% reported doing so from a mobile device.

Several studies have explored the use of the Internet medical practitioners in different parts of the world but a review of the literature has not revealed any on the use of the Internet by medical practitioners in privately owned hospital in Warri, hence this study.

Warri, which is the study setting, is the headquarters of Warri South Local Government Area of Delta State Nigeria with a population of approximately 400,000 inhabitants. There is a sea port located in the town and a petroleum refinery situated in an adjourning town known as Ekpan. Warri hosts regional offices of multinational petroleum companies such as Shell Petroleum Development Company as well as Chevron. As at 2003, there were 2 cybercafes in the town which provided public Internet services to the inhabitants (Adomi, Okiy, & Ruteyan, 2003) but at present there are over 30 of such in addition to existence of the presence of major telecommunications operators like Mobile Telecommunication Network (MTN), Airtel, Glo, Etisalat, Visafone, and Starcom which are currently providing Internet in addition to voice services, enabling subscribers to have personal Internet access on mobile telephone handsets and laptops. The telecom operators have now made it possible for individuals to have easy access to the Internet at home, offices and other locations, not only in Warri but different parts of Nigeria.

## Methodology

The research design adopted for this study was the descriptive survey design. This design was used in order to enable the researchers to find out the current status of Internet use among the medical practitioners in private hospitals in Warri metropolis of Delta State, Nigeria. The population of this study consisted of all medical practitioners in private hospitals in Warri metropolis. These were 137 medical practitioners in number in 30 private hospitals. The detail of the population is shown in Table 1.

The questionnaire was the only instrument used to collect data for the study. The questionnaire was made up of two parts. The first part consisted of items intended to obtain biodata of respondents, such as name of the hospital, gender and age. The second part consisted of items meant to elicit data on the use of Internet by medical practitioners in private hospitals in Warri. In order to ensure high response rate, the copies of questionnaire were personally administered with the aid of some research assistants to the respondents and the completed copies were retrieved immediately from them administered to the frequency counts and percentages were used to analyse the data generated.

## Findings and Discussion

Table 2 reveals that a total of one hundred and thirty seven (137) copies of questionnaire were

*Table 1. Private hospitals and medical practitioners in Warri Metropolis*

| Hospital | No. | % |
|---|---|---|
| Cyracus Hospital | 2 | 1.5 |
| New Era Hospital | 3 | 2 |
| Saint Louis | 3 | 2 |
| MacDonald Hospital | 4 | 3 |
| Lily Hospital | 4 | 3 |
| Capitohill Hospital | 4 | 3 |
| Veenell Hospital | 5 | 4 |
| Larry Hospital | 3 | 2 |
| High land Hospital | 2 | 1.5 |
| Estate Hospital | 2 | 1.5 |
| Somane Hospital | 6 | 4 |
| Regal Hospital | 5 | 4 |
| Avenue Hospital | 5 | 4 |
| Modern Hospital | 7 | 5 |
| Abieyuwa Hospital | 6 | 4 |
| Rapha Hospital | 5 | 4 |
| Mayoma Hospital | 6 | 4 |
| Raphal Children Hospital | 5 | 4 |
| Phoenix Hospital | 6 | 4 |
| Moss children Hospital | 4 | 3 |
| Ilare Hospital | 3 | 2 |
| Joescas Hospital | 2 | 1.5 |
| Divine Grace Hospital | 3 | 2 |
| Loyola Hospital | 4 | 3 |
| Humanity Hospital | 5 | 4 |
| Castle Hospital | 3 | 2 |
| Saint Mary Hospital | 5 | 4 |
| Chevron Hospital | 10 | 7 |
| Shell Hospital | 12 | 9 |
| Lizmat Hospital | 3 | 2 |
| TOTAL | 137 | 100 |

Source: Delta Stae Ministry of Health, Asaba (2011).

administered and retrieved from the respondents.

Table 3 shows the gender distribution of the respondents with 92(67%) males and 45 (33%) females. The male dominance in this study is a reflection of the general medical profession (Adams, 2010).

The age ranges of the respondents is depicted in Table 4. The medical practitioners between 31 – 36 years of age rank highest with 42 (31%) followed by respondents between 37 – 42 years of age with 36 (26%), respondents between 43 and above years of age with 33(24%), and respondents between 25 – 30 years of age with 26 (19%). The data imply that a majority of the medical practitioners in private hospitals in Warri are quite young.

Table 5 indicates that the medical practitioners that use the Net daily are in highest majority - 52 (38%) – followed by those who use it 2 – 3 times

*Table 2. Response rate*

| No of questionnaire administered | No of questionnaire received | % |
|---|---|---|
| 137 | 137 | 100 |

*Table 3. Gender of respondents*

| Gender | No. | % |
|---|---|---|
| Male | 92 | 67 |
| Female | 45 | 33 |
| Total | 137 | 100 |

*Table 4. Age of the respondents*

| Age ranges | No. | % |
|---|---|---|
| 25 – 30 | 26 | 10 |
| 31 – 36 | 42 | 31 |
| 37 – 42 | 36 | 26 |
| 42 and above | 33 | 24 |
| Total | 137 | 100 |

a week - 46 (34%). Thus a majority of the respondents use the Internet regularly. This finding corroborates that reported by Tapp (n. d.) that medical practitioners in New Zealand use the Internet regularly. The reason for this could be due to the fact that most of the respondents use the Internet to keep current on medical practice and to help them improve on patient treatment.

Table 6 shows when the medical practitioners started using the Internet. The data imply that most of the respondents have been using the Internet for quite a long time now.

Table 7 presents the length of time spent by medical practitioners on the Internet. A majority of the respondents 56 (41%) spend 2 – 5 hours on the Internet. This is followed by respondents with 36 (26%) who spent 1 hour on the Internet.

Table 8 shows the various places the medical practitioners use the Internet. A total of 59 (43%) respondents use the Internet in their offices, while 43 (31%) respondents use the Internet at home.

This finding corroborates Dolan (2010) reported that of physicians who use the Internet for health information in the United States, indicated that they accessed it from their office, but does not agree with finding of Oduwole and Oyewumi whose respondents use cybercafes as Internet access points. It has been earlier observed by Adomi (2008) that private telephone and mobile network operators are currently providing Internet services as part of their network operations in Nigeria, which has increasingly made it possible for private individuals to have personal Internet connectivity. This is possibly the reason that most of the medical practitioners access the Internet in their offices and homes.

Table 9 shows the mode of Internet usage by medical practitioners. It is clear from the study that 99(72%) use the internet without assistance, 31(23%) were assisted and 7(5%) No response. This is an indication that many of the medical practitioners are computer literate and can surf Internet independently. This finding corroborates

*Table 5. Frequency of internet use by the medical practitioners*

| Frequency | No. | % |
|---|---|---|
| Daily | 52 | 38 |
| 2-3 times a week | 46 | 34 |
| Once a week | 18 | 13 |
| Once in two weeks | 10 | 7 |
| Once a month | 7 | 5 |
| Occasionally | 4 | 3 |
| Total | 137 | 100 |

*Table 6. When medical practitioners started using the internet*

| Year | No. | % |
|---|---|---|
| 1 – 5 years | 59 | 43 |
| 6 – 10 years | 50 | 37 |
| More than 10 years | 28 | 20 |
| Total | 137 | 100 |

*Table 7. Length of time spent (per visit) by medical practitioners on the internet*

| Time | No. | % |
|---|---|---|
| 1 hour | 36 | 26 |
| 2 – 5 hours | 56 | 41 |
| 6 hours and above | 27 | 20 |
| Overnight | 18 | 13 |
| Total | 137 | 100 |

*Table 8. The places medical practitioners use the Internet*

| Place | No. | % |
|---|---|---|
| Office | 59 | 43 |
| Home | 43 | 31 |
| Library | 9 | 7 |
| Cybercafé | 15 | 11 |
| All of the above | 11 | 8 |

*Table 9. The mode of internet usage by medical practitioners*

| Mode | No. | % |
|---|---|---|
| Assisted | 31 | 23 |
| Not Assisted | 99 | 72 |
| No response | 7 | 5 |
| Total | 137 | 100 |

the study of Ajuwon (2004) who reported that majority of his respondents used the Internet without assistance from anybody.

Table 10 shows the reasons the medical practitioners used the Internet. A majority of the respondents 90 (66%) strongly agree that to keep current on medical practice is a reason for using the Internet. Research attracted 81(59%) and e-mail 75(55%) respondents as the reasons for using the Internet.

Table 11 shows the Internet resources medical practitioners use. Medline ranks highest as Internet resource used by respondents followed by Pub Med and journals. This finding does not corroborate that by Oduwole and Oyewumi (2010) in which Pub Med ranked highest as resource used by physicians.

Table 12 presents the benefits medical practitioners derived from the use of Internet. Thus,

98 (71%) of the respondents strongly agreed that improved patient care is one of the major benefits medical practitioners derived from their use of the Internet. It has been observed in a study that medical practitioners use the Internet to look for diagnostic and treatment information online (Bazzoli, 2000). Also Koller, Grütter, Peltenburg, Fischer, and Steurer (2001) found in a study of use of Internet by medical doctors in Switzerland that that the main reasons for using the Internet during consultations were retrieval of information on drugs, patient-specific information, vaccination. This is with a view to improving patient care.

Table 13 shows the problems medical practitioners encounter in their use of the Internet. Thus, 101 (74%) strongly agree that lack of access to the Internet by most patients is a problem militating against Medical practitioners' use of Internet. This problem would make it difficult for the practitioners to communicate with the patients via e-mail. Also, high cost of Internet access attracted 99 (72%) and slow Internet connection 91(66%), inadequate/lack of Internet search skills 72 (53%) are some of the major problems militating against the medical practitioners' use of the Internet. These findings agree with those of Ahmed and Yousif (2007) and Oduwole and Oyewumi (2010). Electricity interruption is another problem indicated by some of the respondents. Some cities

*Table 10. Reasons the medical practitioners use the internet*

| Reasons | Strongly Agree | | Agree | | Disagree | | Strongly Disagree | | Total | |
|---|---|---|---|---|---|---|---|---|---|---|
| | No | % | No | % | No | % | No | % | No | % |
| E-mail | 75 | 55 | 23 | 17 | 11 | 8 | 28 | 20 | | |
| Research | 81 | 59 | 34 | 25 | 15 | 11 | 7 | 5 | 137 | 100 |
| Claims Submission | 33 | 24 | 49 | 36 | 38 | 28 | 17 | 12 | 137 | 100 |
| Ordering Supplies | 52 | 38 | 49 | 36 | 27 | 20 | 9 | 7 | 137 | 100 |
| Patience Medical practitioners communication/ patient care | 29 | 21 | 14 | 10 | 53 | 39 | 41 | 30 | 137 | 100 |
| To be kept current on medical practice | 91 | 66 | 42 | 31 | 4 | 3 | - | - | 137 | 100 |

*Table 11. Internet resources used by medical practitioners*

| Resources | Strongly Agree | | Agree | | Disagree | | Strongly Disagree | | Total | |
|---|---|---|---|---|---|---|---|---|---|---|
| | No | % | No | % | No | % | No | % | No | % |
| Medline | 99 | 72 | 22 | 16 | 9 | 7 | 7 | 5 | 137 | 100 |
| Pub Med | 68 | 50 | 41 | 30 | 11 | 8 | 17 | 12 | 137 | 100 |
| Journals | 87 | 64 | 38 | 28 | 5 | 4 | 7 | 5 | 137 | 100 |
| Medical practitioners' Websites | 17 | 12 | 26 | 19 | 48 | 35 | 46 | 34 | 137 | 100 |
| Patient Informant Site | 27 | 20 | 11 | 8 | 47 | 34 | 52 | 38 | 137 | 100 |
| Continuing Medical Education Site | 58 | 42 | 25 | 18 | 16 | 12 | 38 | 28 | 137 | 100 |
| Clinical Guidelines | 53 | 39 | 40 | 29 | 28 | 20 | 16 | 12 | 137 | 100 |
| Travel Medicine Sites | 15 | 11 | 7 | 5 | 54 | 39 | 61 | 45 | 137 | 100 |
| Cochrane Library | 55 | 40 | 38 | 28 | 15 | 11 | 29 | 21 | 137 | 100 |
| Other Professional Practitioners Association Sites | 49 | 36 | 44 | 32 | 38 | 28 | 6 | 4 | 137 | 100 |
| Medical School Sites | 53 | 39 | 32 | 23 | 19 | 14 | 33 | 24 | 137 | 100 |

*Table 12. Benefits medical practitioners derived from the use of internet*

| Benefits | Strongly Agree | | Agree | | Disagree | | Strongly Disagree | | Total | |
|---|---|---|---|---|---|---|---|---|---|---|
| | No | % | No | % | No | % | No | % | No | % |
| Improved patient care | 98 | 71 | 35 | 26 | 4 | 3 | - | - | 137 | 100 |
| Ease of getting medical information | 89 | 65 | 22 | 16 | 20 | 15 | 6 | 4 | 137 | 100 |
| Keeping Medical practitioners up-to-date | 96 | 70 | 18 | 13 | 16 | 12 | 7 | 5 | 137 | 100 |
| Assisted me to keep current with medical practice | 92 | 67 | 26 | 19 | 19 | 14 | - | - | 137 | 100 |

*Table 13. Problems militating against medical practitioners' use of the internet*

| Problems | Strongly Agree | | Agree | | Disagree | | Strongly Disagree | | Total | |
|---|---|---|---|---|---|---|---|---|---|---|
| | No | % | No | % | No | % | No | % | No | % |
| Slow internet connection | 91 | 66 | 26 | 19 | 12 | 9 | 8 | 6 | 137 | 100 |
| Too much information | 43 | 31 | 16 | 12 | 22 | 16 | 56 | 41 | 137 | 100 |
| High cost of Internet access | 99 | 72 | 23 | 17 | 9 | 7 | 6 | 4 | 137 | 100 |
| Inadequate/lack of Internet search skills | 72 | 53 | 17 | 12 | 48 | 35 | - | - | 137 | 100 |
| Electricity Interruption | 89 | 65 | 32 | 23 | 16 | 12 | - | - | 137 | 100 |
| Lack of access to the Internet by most patients for interaction with their doctors | 101 | 74 | 36 | 26 | - | - | - | - | 137 | 100 |
| Lack of internet search skills by patients | 12 | 9 | 17 | 12 | 64 | 47 | 44 | 32 | 137 | 100 |

in Africa and most rural areas may only have power for limited periods (Adomi, 2005; Adomi, Okiy, & Ruteyan, 2003; Rosenberg, 2005). This is the reason that these medical practitioners are indicated power interruption as problem they face with use of Internet.

## CONCLUSION

It can be concluded that a majority of the medical practitioners are digitally competent as they can use the Internet on regularly; most of them spent more than one on the Internet. Also, a majority of the medical practitioners use the Internet independently and use the Internet to keep current with medical practice. Medline, journals, Royal New Zealand College site and Pub Med are the major Internet resources they use. Some of the respondents encounter problems such as lack of access to the Internet, high cost of Internet access, slow Internet connection and frequent power outage with use of the Internet.

Based on the findings of study, the following recommendations are made:

1.	Private hospital managements should provide their medical practitioners with Internet facilities to enable them have access to the most recent and accurate information for effective service delivery and make every medical practical practitioner digitally competent.
2.	Government should do everything at its disposal to improve the power situation of the country while the Hospital managements should make provision for standby electric plants to serve as alternative source of power supply to enable medical practitioners make use of the Internet in their various offices regularly.

3.	The Government and Internet service providers should work in one accord to ensure that the cost of Internet accessibility is reduced to enable medical practitioners and their patients enjoy smooth access to the Internet.

## REFERENCES

Adams, T. L. (2010). Gender and feminization in health care professions. *Social Compass*, *4*(7), 454–465. doi:10.1111/j.1751-9020.2010.00294.x

Adomi, E. E. (2005). Internet development and connectivity in Nigeria. *Program*, *39*(3), 257–268.

Adomi, E. E. (2008). Africa and the challenges of bridging the digital divide. In Garson, G. D., & Khosrow-Pour, M. (Eds.), *Handbook of research on public information technology* (*Vol. 1*, pp. 303–313). Hershey, PA: Information Science Reference. doi:10.4018/978-1-59904-857-4.ch029

Adomi, E. E., Okiy, R. B., & Ruteyan, J. O. (2003). A survey of cybercafes in Delta State, Nigeria. *The Electronic Library*, *21*(5), 487–495. doi:10.1108/02640470310499876

Ahmed, A. M., & Yousif, E. (2007). *Problems and factors that influence use of internet by the Sudanese doctors*. Retrieved August 20, 2011, from http://www.sjph.net.sd/files/vol2i3p177-182.pdf

Ajuwon, G. A. (2004). Use of computer and the Internet in a Nigerian teaching hospital. *Journal of Hospital Librarianship*, *4*, 73–78. doi:10.1300/J186v04n04_06

Bass, S. B. (2003). How will internet use affect the patient? A review of computer network and closed internet-based system studies and the implications in understanding how the use of the internet affects patient populations. *Journal of Health Psychology*, *8*(1), 25–38. doi:10.1177/1359105303008001427

Bath, P. A. (2008). Health informatics: Current issues and challenges. *Journal of Information Science, 34*(4), 501–518. doi:10.1177/0165551508092267

Bazzoli, F. (2000). Gateways to the Internet. *Internet Health Care Magazine, 1*, 70–77.

Dolan, P. L. (2010). *86% of physicians use Internet to access health information.* Retrieved August 20, 2011, from http://www.ama-assn.org/amednews/2010/01/04/bisc0104.htm

Dzenowagis, J., Kuruvilla, S., & Aronson, B. (2002). Access to information for health and development: the health internetwork *Information Development, 18*(3), 177-180.

Koller, M., Grütter, R., Peltenburg, M., Fischer, J. E., & Steurer, J. (2001). *Use of the Internet by medical doctors in Switzerland.* Retrieved August 20, 2011, from http://www.smw.ch/docs/pdf200x/2001/17/smw-09719.pdf

Oduwole, A. A., & Oyewumi, O. (2010). Accessibility and use of web-based electronic resources by physicians in a psychiatric institution in Nigeria. *Program, 44*(2), 109–121.

Rosenberg, D. (2005). *Towards the digital library: Findings of and investigation to establish the current status of university libraries in Africa.* Retrieved June 6, 2005, from http://www.inasp.info/pubs/INASP/digilalhb.pdf

Study, S. A. (2011). *Medical practitioner.* Retrieved August 23, 2011, from http://www.sastudy.co.za/index.php?option=com_content&view=article&id=2109&Itemid=428

Tapp, D. (n. d.). *Doctors and their continuing medical education: Interactions with the Internet.* Retrieved August 23, 2011, from http://www.mcnz.org.nz/portals/0/publications/summerstudentships/Dylan%20Tapp%20-%20Doctors%20and%20their%20Continuing%20Medical%20Education.pdf

*This work was previously published in the International Journal of Digital Literacy and Digital Competence, Volume 2, Issue 4, edited by Antonio Cartelli, pp. 14-23, copyright 2011 by IGI Publishing (an imprint of IGI Global).*

# Chapter 16
# Literacy and Space Technology In Nigeria

**Christopher Babatunde Ogunyemi**
*Joseph Ayo Babalola University, Nigeria*

## ABSTRACT

*This paper examines literacy as it affects Space Technology in Nigeria. The place of digital technology enables a proper understanding of literacy in Nigeria. The paper is divided into four parts. The first section redefines literacy in order to understand the possibilities of meanings based on the perceptions of James (1984), Onukaogu (2008), Arua (2009) and Ajayi (2009) that conceptualize the complex nature of literacy and its indispensability. The second part visualizes the role played by literacy in educating technological advancement in Nigeria, bearing in mind that in 1999, the Federal Government of Nigeria approved the Nigerian Space Policy and the implementation of the space program. The third section underscores the socio-economic relevance of literacy in enhancing global space technology for Nigeria while the fourth section relates Ajayi's (2009) projection in a meta-critical manner, so that Nigeria can become a world power. The theoretical framework for this paper is the "Transformational Theory". The theory opines that "learning occurs as a result of transformation of participation in culturally valued activities" such as space technology. The paper emphasizes practical findings to stimulate excellence and literacy relevance in science and technology.*

## INTRODUCTION

From the traditional perspective, literacy has been projected as the ability to read and write at considerable adequate level of proficiency that facilitates communication. As a result of global literacy arising from globalization, we could mention technological literacy, visual literacy and literary literacy which underscore the essence of adult and adolescence literature (Ajayi, 2009). Literacy is a complex phenomenon that has affected virtually all aspects of human endeavours. The complexities have addressed all aspects in a way that it lends axiomatic credence to the understanding of man's activities in stimulating excellence. However:

DOI: 10.4018/978-1-4666-2943-1.ch016

*This complex situation is further exacerbated by the growing influences of multimedia technologies and space technology which have produced a shift in what counts as texts and what it means to be literate. It is no longer just the ability to read and write; it is now viewed as the ability to construct and understand the different possibilities of meanings made available by differing textual forms associated with diverse domains such as the internet, video-games, visual images, graphics and layouts (p. 585).*

In broad terms, literacy is the ability to make and communicate meaning from and by the use of a variety of socially contextual symbols. Within various levels of developmental ability, a literate person can derive and convey meaning, and use his knowledge to achieve a desired purpose or goal that requires the use of language skills, be they spoken or written. A literate person can mediate his world by deliberately and flexibly orchestrating meaning from one linguistic knowledge base and apply or connect it to another knowledge base. For example, knowing that letters symbolize sounds, and that those sounds form words to which the reader can attach meaning, is an example of the cognitive orchestration of knowledge a literate person conducts. Literacy is "not in isolated bits of knowledge but in students' growing ability to use language and literacy in more and broader activities". The definition of literacy is dynamic, evolving, and reflects the continual changes in our society. Literacy has, for instance, expanded to include literacy in information and communication technologies and critical literacy (http://www.bridgew.edu/library/cags_projects/ldubin/Definition%20of%20Literacy.htm).

Technology has taken different shapes in facilitating literacy in different ways. These ways are either individualistic or collective. Space technology, however, is a new invention in Nigeria that has showcased reading and writing in a more globalized phenomenon. To understand the

space and literary framework, we shall visualize the relationship between technology and literacy. According to the UNESCO's space research, many changes are now taking place throughout the world and they are of enormous concern and relevance to adult learning. Adults are under pressure to develop and utilize new knowledge frameworks, skills and value systems. It is time for literacy providers to have the courage to experiment, to try out new alternatives and renew the assault on illiteracy. Innovations in technology can improve literacy programs and accelerate the spread of literacy. This forges an inevitable link between the use of technology and literacy. With reference to the results of a panel discussion on "Literacy and Technology", held during the CONFINTEA V (Hamburg, 14–18 July 1997) as quoted by UNESCO, The term technology here embraces educational *technologies such* as the Internet, TV, interactive video and radio. The aim of the panel discussion was to explore the relationship between literacy and technology, and the potential role of technology as a tool in literacy provision.

The important question was not whether, but how technology can adapt to changing demands. The panel was chaired by Jan Visser, UNESCO LWF, Learning Without Frontiers (LWF), UNESCO, France. Mohamed Maamouri, International Literacy Institute (ILI), Tunisia, served as discussant. The remaining panel members were: Alan Tuckett, the National Institute of Adult Continuing Education, England and Wales, (NIACE), UK, Minda Sutaria (INNOTECH, Philippines), Shigeru Aoyagi, Asia Pacific Cultural Centre (ACCU) UNESCO, Japan, Sibiri Tapsoba (IDRC, Senegal), and Christopher Hopey, National Centre on Adult Literacy, USA. An important observation is that technological innovation with costs of technology facilitates the introduction of technology into literacy. The real concern is how to ensure that literacy providers have the capacity and total will to apply the technology appropriately (http://www.unesco.org).

## LITERACY AND TECHNOLOGICAL ADVANCEMENT IN THE WORLD

With reference to the UNESCO findings, technology is viewed as a tool for improving literacy programs. Today's world is moving towards a more open and global society. In order to deal with its changing demands, people need to learn how to cope with change and at the same time to interact constructively with it and retain control of the processes involved. Alternative strategies need to be identified to ensure greater learning effectiveness and meet the literacy needs of masses of people in a timely and economical manner. Technology is a useful tool to improve the quality and the efficiency of literacy provision (James, 1984). It helps create learning environments ideally suited to the needs and interests of previously unreached populations and offers new learning opportunities as vistas. 'It stimulates learners to be more creative and innovative' (Onukaogu, 2008). In fact, it 'revolutionizes the way we handle information - with the focus moving from teaching to self-directed learning, from learning as a one-time event to a lifelong learning process' (Ikpeze, 2009) and 'it conveys meanings' (Arua, 2009).

Technology is introducing radical changes, with non-formal and informal education assuming an important place in addition to formal education. Non-formal education is already improving because of the advantages of technology. It has proved to be effective in reaching out to vast unreached school-age populations. In fact, the distinction between those categories is becoming increasingly irrelevant. Technology is not an end in itself or an answer to all educational problems. It is a tool to improve literacy programs, raise awareness about the literacy problems and reach a vast number of unreached illiterates. Technology deals not only with textual literacy, but also with visual literacy. Adopting technology demands also a process of selection and decision making regarding which technology is appropriate, by and for whom it is to be used and for what kind of communication and content. This process is

itself useful because it helps to crystallize ideas, create visions, and motivate greater numbers to pursue literacy through technology. It encourages participation (http://www.unesco.org).

Technology does not operate in a vacuum It is important to view technology in the wider political, social and economic context, rather than merely defining it in terms of hardware and software packages. By considering all of the interrelated components, technology can create learning environments suited to the needs of the learners and be made highly relevant to literacy programs. Technology offers the possibility of quality education for all in less time than required by traditional strategies, provided that its deployment is well thought out, planned and subject to continuing evaluation and renewal. The following are some of the principles in planning the integration of technology into literacy programs: Depart from existing strategies and structures. This might require using a combination of old and new technologies. Focus on affordability of initial investment in setting up the system. Include a training program in the use of technology. This often requires the largest investment, yet it is most crucial to successful implementation of technology. It includes issues such as: – commitment to a long-term plan for maintenance and support; – commitment to periodically upgrading the system; be flexible about time schedules. There should be no definite deadline for introducing technology. It is more important to seek the best solution. In this context, it is important to think about the possible marginalization of people, and the creation of new zones of power depending on the advantages being created for some through technology. For technology to play its full role, it should be accessible to those who have been deprived of it in the past. If all societies in all their diversity are to be motivated and persuaded that reading and communication matters really, then their voices must all be heard. Technology should be for people's empowerment (http://www.unesco.org).

## THEORETICAL FRAMEWORK: TRANSFORMATIONAL THEORY

The theoretical framework that is best suitable for the understanding of literacy and space technology is transformational theory; this is because transformational theory deals with the creation and change of a whole new form, function or structure. To transform is to create something new that has never existed before and could not be predicted from the past. Transformation is a "change" in mindset. It is based on learning a system of profound knowledge and taking actions based on leading with knowledge and courage. Transformation occurs when leaders create a vision for a system to continually question and challenge beliefs, assumptions, patterns, habits and paradigms with an aim of continually developing and applying management theory, through the lens of the system of profound knowledge. Transformation happens when people managing a *system* focus on creating a new future that has never existed before, and based on continual learning and a new mindset, take different actions than they would have taken in the past.

A theory of transformation means there will be a profound change in structure that creates something new. The system of profound knowledge provides the *method for transformation*. Transformation occurs through a system of continual questioning, challenging, exploration, discovery, evaluation, testing, and creation of an organization's management theory and application; beginning with the realization or revelation that the organization's current thinking (i.e., management theory) is incomplete, limiting, flawed, or even worse – destructive. In transformation, there is no known destination, and the journey has never been travelled before. It is uncertain and unpredictable. It embraces new learning and taking actions based on the new discoveries for leading transformation, Dr. W. Edwards Deming offers the system of profound knowledge as our new lens. It includes appreciation for a system,

knowledge about variation, theory of knowledge, and theory of psychology (Daszko & Sheinberg, 2005).

Literacy and space technology give room for new innovation that incorporates new changes. New changes are the framework of transformation. Transformation, therefore, helps in the development of space technology because it is a new direction for Nigerian economy and literacy. Domesticating Nigerian innovation in this area of literacy development could make Nigeria to strive as future world power! Friere (1972), Rogoff (1994), and Stolle (2007) in Ikpeze (2009) conceptualize transformational theory within techno-education perspective. Their notion is good for a proper placement of literacy and space educational perspective. According to these scholars:

*Learning occurs as a result of transformation of participation in culturally valued activities and how people develop is a function of their transforming roles and understanding in the activities in which they participate "Through participation in culturally relevant activities, individuals appropriate new ideas, attitudes, skills and practices or transform and re-conceptualize the old". Everyday human activity "consist of actions and reflection: it is praxis; it is transformation of the world". As we use tools and language to shape action, tool use changes us, even as we change the tools Through integrating technology in one graduate literacy course, observing novice teachers and reflecting on my actions, I worked to transform my knowledge, skills and pedagogy as well as my students' competencies in using technology for instruction. Transformations involve, among other things, interrogating one's beliefs and actions. Prior studies indicate that teachers' pedagogical beliefs and knowledge are important factors in their quest for technology integration. In addition, teacher educators trying to integrate technology need to develop a critical disposition toward technology. This implies that teacher educators should be able to develop an understanding of why, when and how to use technology for learning and the ability to model and deliver technology-infused curricula, pedagogy and assessment. They need to help teacher candidates develop technological pedagogical content knowledge (TPCK). TPCK involves "development of subject matter with the development of technology and of the knowledge of teaching and learning". This framework posits that stand alone technology courses and workshops are not enough to improve teachers' technology integration knowledge and skills. Instead, educators should utilize an integrated approach that fuses technology, pedagogy and content. TPCK recognizes that the integration of technology should not be done in a generic sense but should be situated within authentic contexts to enable prospective teachers learn content specific ways to use technology (Ikpezi, 2009, pp. 8-9).*

## TECHNOLOGY: LITERACY AND SPACE TECHNOLOGY IN ANALYSIS

UNESCO research reports of different types of technology which can be used to promote literacy, either independently or in combination. The main selection criteria is the appropriateness and affordability of the space technology which is an important source for lifelong and life wide learning. The Nigerian government wants to borrow a live from this resource when she launched NigeriaSat1 in 2003. The effect of this scientific innovation enables us to understand the new transformation which Nigeria experienced in learning and industry. This leads to economic transfiguration and educational elevation. Huge numbers of non-literate or marginally literate individuals, for whom formal education has little practical applicability, with little or no reading material in their homes, have regular access to radio and often TV as well. The educational use of television and radio include: generating awareness of the literacy problem developing consumer demand for learning retaining learners in a program

reaching a large number of individuals. The Space Technology facilitates literacy through awareness because national broadcasters are also involved in educational broadcasting as well as specific educational initiatives. Positive feedback on high quality educational broadcasting has shown that people for whom the education system has failed do not trust educators as much as they trust broadcasters. Educational broadcasting often has a motivational function, rather than an instructional function. Experience with the use of computers and other technologies, such as interactive video, suggest that they can contribute to the development of thinking skills and make instruction more individual. They also provide ways to collect and evaluate information efficiently as well as help learners to communicate what they think and feel. Space Technology in Nigeria has developed literacy by inculcating the internet awareness on the people.

*Space Technology comes with* the internet *which* is another tool that can be used in improving literacy programs. Though, the adults can be provided with higher quality materials and access to information in homes, workplaces and public libraries. It also provides adults with greater choices which are the key to motivation, retention and enriched learning experience. Using the Internet in literacy promotion means learning faster what is happening around the world and having access to almost unlimited resources for the sharing of professional ideas and problem-solving Technologies based on Internet do not need to be expensive. Many people in developing countries, as in industrialized countries, already have the technology, but they lack extra phone lines or faster modems to allow effective and extended networks. In fact, the problem of introducing *space* technology in literacy programs lays not so much in its cost or the rate of innovation, but rather in the human factors of reinforcing human competence and political will. Does technology increase inequity? Technology often raises the fear of inequity. There are also fears that technology may be a new form of colonization, resulting in reducing diversity. The use of technology can widen the gap between those who have access and those who do not. The dilemma is that introducing new technologies requires an initial level of technological competence in Nigeria (http://www.unesco.org). Figure 1 shows an image of the satellite set to launch next year.

The crucial question is: who will be the user? Will it be an experienced user, or a learner who was deprived of technology in the past? Or Government and non-governmental agencies should be aware of this problem and must address the issues of who will be the users and who will be controlling, constructing and policing the technology. To address the issue of inequity, there is a need for trust, political will and devotion to the people, if the gap is not to widen; respect for diversity of language and culture; promotion of technology for two-way communication. Information should flow from top to bottom and vice-versa, as well as horizontally; reliable information on beneficiaries in order to identify clearly how to disseminate information and to whom, while developing different strategies for different contexts. This information may include literacy

materials, statistics, relevant organizations, curricula, literacy publications, and a literacy glossary. In the short term, it may be true that technology can widen the gap between those with access and those without it, but in the long term, it is worth remembering that radio and television were once instruments of the rich people. It may perhaps be wise to take a time horizon into account when talking about these fears. Summary of existing experiences Below are some of the conclusions from the panel discussion on "Literacy and Technology" during CONFINTEA V, Technology has transformed many literacy programs, by providing access to information especially in areas of public policy, and by advocating rights of adults and learners. It has made a big difference to the level of funding and resources that flow into literacy.

Space Technology encourages adult learners to be much more creative and imaginative. It offers new learning opportunities for adults, such as instruction online, video, audio and other tools.

Technology provides adults with greater choice which is the key to motivation, retention and enriching learning experience. New technologies also provide new places to learn. Through the Internet and other new technologies adults can

*Figure 1. New satellite to launch next year (image credit: photo © 2010 NNSANews)*

have access to higher quality material and more learning opportunities from homes, workplaces and public libraries. This in turn extends resources from local literacy programs into those places. Technology does not need to be expensive. The crucial point is to make the optimal use of time, energy and staff. Through technology such as the Internet, teachers themselves become adult learners. They learn how to use the computer, how to integrate it into the curriculum, how to organize the resources, how to be creative and imaginative. Teacher training in technology use is absolutely essential for the successful integration of technology into literacy programs (http://www.unesco.org). It is expedient to note that:

*The role that technology plays in advancing multiple literacies in the information age is extensive, and this applies as much literacy as it does to higher education. For younger students, technology provides vital opportunities to capitalize on real-life activities, problem-solving skills, and authentic literacy conversations with other learners. Consequently,these learners can both consume and create content in preparation for their future in a connected society (Brown, Bryan, & Brown, 2005).*

Interlinking technology and literacy make sense when it deals with technology not only as a vehicle, but also as an important content area for the promotion of adult education.

The real issue behind literacy and technology is about educators taking a lead in the field of education and providing new ways of learning, rather than waiting for others to tell them what to do and how to do it. New technologies are not necessarily the whole answer to the problem of delivering literacy programs. There is room for both old and new technologies. Technology must be appropriate and should help people to learn as quickly, as economically and as effectively as possible. Technology properly used, i.e., in a way appropriate to the communities that learn through

them, can facilitate the learning of new higher level skills needed for a world which is becoming increasingly global and which is therefore more and more in need of local empowerment. Technology should be well thought out and planned for that context.

There should be a continuing evaluation and revision process to promote the best mix of technologies. It is no longer cost-effective to ignore technology. In particular, adult education, the least funded area of education, just cannot afford to avoid the use of technological opportunities (http://www.unesco.org).

## THE SPACE TECHNOLOGICAL MOVEMENT IN NIGERIA

According to GLOBAL SECURITY, in 1999, the Federal Government of Nigeria approved the Nigerian Space Policy and the implementation of the space program, as outlined in the policy, commenced with the establishment of a National Space Research and Development Agency (NASRDA), under the Federal Ministry of Science and Technology. The mission of NASRDA is to vigorously pursue the attainment of space capabilities and the enhancement of the quality of life of its people. The space policy has a 25-year program tailored towards the development of Space Science and Technology in Nigeria through research and development (R&D), as well as capacity-building in the fields of science, engineering, space law and administration for sustainable national development. The policy has both short- and long-term space mission programs. The implementation of the programs focuses on the achievement of the United Nation's Millennium Development Goals (MDG's) and other regional and national socio-economic development objectives as highlighted by the New Partnership for Africa's Development (NEPAD) and National Economic Empowerment & Development Strategies (NEEDS).

Nigeria intends to vigorously pursue the attainment of space capabilities as an essential tool for its socio-economic development and the enhancement of the quality of life of its people. The Nation shall achieve this through research, rigorous education, engineering development, design and manufacture of appropriate hardware and software in space technology, including transport and payloads, such as satellite, telescopes and antennas for scientific research and applications. The Government shall also foster Bi-lateral and international cooperation in all aspects of Space Science and Technology to ensure that Nigerian Scientists and Engineers benefit from global developments in the space enterprise. The vision of Nigeria and Africa is to attain competence and capabilities in relevant areas of space science and technology that would impact on sustainable socio-economic development and improve the quality of life of Nigerians and Africans, and to make Africa pro-active and also compete in space exploration.

For the attainment of space capabilities, Nigeria's space efforts focus on research and rigorous education, engineering development, design and manufacture, particularly in the areas of instrumentation, rocketry and small satellites as well as in satellite data acquisition, processing, analysis and management of related software. The establishment of a national earth observation station for remote sensing and satellite meteorology data acquisition enhanced the indigenous ability to adopt, modify and create new techniques for national resources inventories, monitoring, evaluation and management. Nigerian Space Agency – the National Space Research and Development Agency [NASRDA] was established with a mission to pursue the development and application of space science and technology for the socio-economic benefits of the nation and the Nigerian space programme constitutes an important component of the national strategy for socio-economic development through space application and participation in the global industry. The overall agenda of the Nigeria's space agenda

is geared towards sustainable national development and security including the development of new resources, understanding of our environment and the maintenance of national security. The National Geospatial Data Infrastructure [NGDI] coordinated by [NASRDA], will facilitate efficient production, management, dissemination and use of geospatial information for the attainment of the Millennium Development Goals (MDGs).

Nigeria launched its first satellite, NigeriaSat 1, into orbit in September 2003, after Nigerian experts underwent training in London. The National Space Research and Development Agency (NASRDA) also embarked on the next generations of satellites: a communication satellite to be called NigcomSat-1 and a high resolution African Resources Management Constellation (ARMC) satellite, NigeriaSat-2. Further plans to develop a communication satellite were in progress; it was recognized that ineffective communications represented one of the greatest barriers to socio-economic development and NigComSAT would be designed to contribute to providing an adequate telecommunications system throughout Nigeria and regional coverage to ECOWAS countries. Nigeria realized the importance of this technology, did not hesitate in leapfrogging to the technology. Satellite can perform several different operations depending on the type of payload. Most notable are Remote Sensing Satellite, Communication Satellite, Astronomical Satellite, Meteorology Satellite, and Space Station. Nigeria is presently pursuing the development of the first two types of satellite. Short Term Program Objectives are access to real-time and affordable Earth Observation data, (meteorology and remote sensing), for weather forecast, resources inventory and environmental and disaster management, through either direct purchase of images from existing satellites or the development of (a) Earth observation satellite and (b) low cost ground receiving station. Access to affordable satellite communication back-bone, such as the on-going NigcomSat-1 project and Rascom, and infrastructure to meet the need for

ICT-based investment/business opportunities and socio-economic development (http://www.globalsecurity.org/space/world/nigeria/index.html)

## LITERACY AND SPACE DEVELOPMENT IN NIGERIA

Part of the implications of space technology in Nigeria is literacy awareness that comes with it. Economic and social factors are also considered valuable. With the transformation of Nigeria into the space technology, the country is gradually graduating into the type of strategic scientific technology that is found in the USA, Britain, Germany, China and Japan. Reading and writing are now taking advanced methodology. 'In response to the new demands of the information age, *space science in Nigeria* now integrates technology across the curriculum. Traditional literacy instruction involve the use of textbooks, skills lessons, ability groups, numerous worksheets and workbook pages, as well as writing that only the teacher reads. In contrast, literacy in the 21st century *that comes with space technology requires* that children not only communicate with classroom peers, but also read e-books, receive and send e-mail, locate and evaluate online information, prepare reports with presentation software establish dialogue with learned individuals in other regions, and write for both a local and global community' (Brown, Bryan, & Brown, 2005).

Space technology is developing the digital, analytical and theoretical interpretation of literacy in Nigerian reading and writing culture; it is a systematic process in the facilitation of mental and physical development. 'It is indispensable, it is a process in progress, it helps the critical thinking, it evaluates information' (Arua, 2009; Onukaogu, 2008; Okereke, 1993). In Nigeria, 'academic literacy has a great impact over how a person expresses and presents himself in a scholastic environment- *an environment that presents hypothetical space technology* (emphasis added).

The tools to effectively read, write and critically think are skills that not only help a person in the scholastic environment, but also in personal discovery. Through positive experiences with academic literacy, people do not only learn to improve their writing and other critical skills, but they also apply this toward learning about themselves and becoming a more confident person in everything they do. Setting a positive environment for students to engage in and become comfortable with their surroundings is an effective way to aid students. Teachers have a great impact on how learners learn to apply their academic literacy *to space technology in Nigeria*. When the support is there, *learners* know, and feel free to *align with space science'* (http://www.megaessays.com/viewpaper/81892.html).

The concept of literacy clearly has become more differentiated and more expansive in the wake of the technological revolution and the space evolution in Nigeria. As a result, Leu (2000, as cited in Brown et al., 2005) states that literacy is "no longer an end point to be achieved but rather a process of continuously learning how to be literate". He claims that literacy is constantly changing, not static, and that teachers also must change in order to prepare children for increased technology demands In the midst of this new environment, many teachers are adopting newer literacy models for classroom instruction. Space technology in Nigeria offers exciting latitude for dialogue in cyberspace and literacy education, which in many respects reinforces the classical notion of literacy introduced by the Greeks—sharing knowledge with others. But instead of interacting with classmates in real time, children can now establish "communities of literates" with anyone, anytime, anywhere. This community-based model of education, along with the multiple forms of literacy that sustain it, provides a foundation for preparing students to succeed in an increasingly interdependent, global landscape. The development of space technology in Nigeria explores 21st-century literacy and offers some illustrations of how technology may help educators and students meet the challenges of the future while also expanding the classical ideal of literacy inherited from the past (Brown, Bryan, & Brown, 2005).

In the new connected paradigm, Nigerian teachers harness the power of computers as communication tools for students to access information and share findings with others. Thus computers are no longer merely vehicles for drill and practice, but vehicles for problem-solving and active learning. This modification requires new understandings of the various ways learners interact with digital media, as well as increased opportunities for learners to participate within a growing community of literates. When teachers interact differently with technology, students' interactions change also. As Selfe and Hilligoss (1994) presciently argued more than 10 years ago, "It is not simply that the tools of literacy have changed; the nature of texts, of language, of literacy itself is undergoing crucial transformations" (p. 18). It is this transformation that informs the appraisal and development of literacy and space technology in Nigeria. Space technology is developing personal human initiative in Africa and in Nigeria to be specific. Emejulu (2006) makes a survey of African contributions to world learning when he opines that we should

*Take short census of African contributions to world learning, science and technology The Igbo-ukwu bronze technology, the Benin moats and brass works, the Kano city walls, the Nok culture, the Ife bronze works, the Cross River monoliths, the Egyptian pyramids, the great Zimbabwe walls, the Sankore University of Timbuktu, the medical sciences, especially orthopaedics, and Nsibidi writings, to mention but a few. What knowledge base informed these achievements? What became of all these and why? Like my mother's people and their space science and technology, all of these African contributions to knowledge and the sciences (Emejulu, 2006).*

## CONCLUSION

The paper uses transformational theory to delineate literacy and space technology in Nigeria. It begins with a capsule presentation of literacy and its educational implications in bringing concrete reading and writing revolution to the people. The paper makes a survey of technology and how it affects literacy. Literacy is *indispensable* in the words of Onukaogu and that is why various technologies have addressed literacy. From the traditional medium in reading and writing to the cyberspace technology, literacy has addressed complex human predicaments. The paper shows various areas and problems associated with the space technology and it showcases the need for this technology to be embraced by all in order to facilitate the efforts of Nigerian government in making literacy an affordable phenomenon.

## REFERENCES

Ajayi, L. (2009). English as a second language learners: Exploration of multimordal texts in a junior high school. *Journal of Adolescent & Adult Literacy*, *52*(7), 585–595. doi:10.1598/ JAAL.52.7.4

Arua, E. A. (2009). *Reading comprehension skills for college and university students*. Ibadan, Nigeria: CELL.

Brown, J., Bryan, J., & Brown, T. (2005). *Past issues*. Retrieved from http://www.innovateon-line.info/

Daszko, M., & Sheinberg, S. (2005). *Survival is optional: Only leaders with new knowledge can lead the transformation*. Retrieved from http://www.mdaszko.com/theoryoftransformation_final_to_short_article_apr05.pdf

Emejulu, O. (2006, January 23-24). *Literacy as a backbone of African development.* Paper presented at the Workshop on Literacy Training With Focus on Nomadic Fulani, Kaduna, Nigeria.

Freire, P. (1972). *Pedagogy of the oppressed.* London, UK: Shedd and Ward.

Global Security. (2011). *Nigeria space programs.* Retrieved from http:www.globalsecurity.org/space/world/nigeria/index.html

Ikpeze, H. C. (2009). Integrating technology in one literacy course: Lessons learned. *Journal of Literacy and Technology, 10*(1).

James, S. (1984). *Reading for academic purposes.* New York, NY: Holt, Rinehart and Winston.

Ogoegbulem, S. (2010). *Nigeria's SAT-1 replacement next year.* Retrieved from http://www.itnewsafrica.com/2010/11/nigeria%E2%80%99s-sat-1-replacement-next-year/

Okereke, G. E. (1993). Literacy as a redemptive factor in Nigerian politics in Chinua Achebe's "A Man of The People" and "Anthills of the Savannah". In Aboderin, A. O., (Eds.), *Literacy and reading in Nigeria* (*Vol. 6*). Calabar, Nigeria: Reading Association of Nigeria.

Onukaogu, C. E. (2008). *Biliteracy and the attainment of sustainable development in multilingual Nigeria.* Ibadan, Nigeria: CELL.

Rogoff, B. (2003). *The cultural nature of human development.* Oxford, UK: Oxford University Press.

Selfe, C. L., & Hilligoss, S. (1994). *Literacy and computers: The complications of teaching and learning with technology.* New York, NY: Modern Language Association.

Stolle, E. (2008). Teachers, literacy & technology: Tensions, complexities. *National Reading Conference Yearbook, 57,* 56-69.

*This work was previously published in the International Journal of Digital Literacy and Digital Competence, Volume 2, Issue 3, edited by Antonio Cartelli, pp. 31-40, copyright 2011 by IGI Publishing (an imprint of IGI Global).*

# Chapter 17
# Hybrid Wireless Networks for E-Learning and Digital Literacy:
## Testing and Evaluation

**Munir Abbasi**
*Brunel University, UK*

**Lampros K. Stergioulas**
*Brunel University, UK*

## ABSTRACT

*Today, satellite communication networks are being integrated into the infrastructure of modern Terrestrial communication networks and becoming popular for the delivery of educational content and data, as well as education-centric services, including information, tele-conferencing, entertainment, or "edutainment" services. With fresh demand for new services and applications, it is becoming essential that wireless network architecture seamlessly interoperate with new and existing technologies, protocols and standards. This paper presents recent work on the use of hybrid wireless network infrastructures for delivering tele-education and e-learning applications to remote communities by combining a variety of satellite, terrestrial and wireless technologies, and provides the results from live scenarios carried out employing various methods of interoperability testing. The analysis of the results examines a number of different issues such as delay, jitter, packet loss, latency, throughput measurement, and bandwidth. By combining satellite and terrestrial (wireless) technologies, full coverage and high capacity can be achieved for true broadband services for delivering educational content. The interoperability among such diverse networks imposes a number of challenges regarding service provision and management.*

DOI: 10.4018/978-1-4666-2943-1.ch017

## 1. INTRODUCTION

Satellite communications systems have a prominent role in the global information infrastructure (Chitre & Henderson, 1995). Based on today's challenging requirements, satellite network communications should be viewed as an integrated part of the global telecommunications infrastructure rather than as an individual entity (Evans et al., 2005). In a related context, Sugarbroad (1990) shows roaming possibilities between satellite and terrestrial networks. The study explains in detail the technical framework requirements to realize satellite and terrestrial roaming and its advantages to the end user. Accordingly, it highlights that fully proven network components that can make global satellite roaming practical and valuable feature are available within the 2.5G and 3G operator's service portfolio. Having this in mind, the author Shave (2002) predicts that the trend will continue into the 3G networks and multi-standard handsets where data services and especially Internet-based services become increasingly important.

From a more theoretical perspective, another study (Abuelma'atti, Merabti, & Askwith, 2006) aims to design wireless networked appliances interoperability architecture. In their approach, the interoperability is associated with many operational phases including: Coexistence, Internetworking, System Interoperability and End-to-end Interoperability. An OSI-based interoperability architecture for managing hybrid networks confirms that interoperability could be investigated at various levels of the OSI network model (Evans et al., 2005) e.g. coexistence problem caused by the interference of devices that use same frequency and/or end-to-end interoperability issues due to application communication protocol mismatch.

The aim of our investigation in this paper is to investigate this interoperability problem in hybrid wireless networks at application level, within the context of delivering tele-education and e-learning services across a wide area network (WAN) which is targeted towards meeting the needs of communities situated in geographically remote areas, and thus towards bridging the related geographical and digital gaps.

In our interoperability evaluations, we assume that there is no coexistence problem at the physical level. Therefore, a series of testing has been carried out in order to establish the interoperability requirements for hybrid wireless network technology with the objective to take live measurements from various scenarios by using appropriate measurement and analysis tools. The aims of this testing are firstly to identify any interoperability issues and secondly to ensure that the performance requirements from the perspective of the end user are met. Thus the needed capabilities and challenges for the seamless operation of the heterogeneous satellite-terrestrial wireless networks are identified. Various traffic data, files, packets and traces were captured and filtered.

The paper is organised as follows: Section 2 describes the various services deployed on the developed hybrid communications platform, including virtual classroom service, Learning content management service, Tele-conference Service, Webinar/Webcast Service Clix, and Isabel applications; Section 3 shows the test set up for interoperability testing with different scenarios; Section 4 analyses the test data and evaluated the findings and results; finally Section 5 provides the conclusions from this research.

## 2. TELE-EDUCATION NETWORK SERVICES

There are a number of different software tools with various protocols that are available to use in applications related to tele-education, including audio, video, web conferencing, white board, VOIP, application sharing, application remote control and instant messaging. In the following subsections, different services such as virtual class room, learning content management service, tele-conference services and webinar/webcast services are discussed. In this study, we have used mainly two tele-education applications for hybrid network evaluation: Clix and Isabel—both are described in later subsections.

## 2.1. Virtual Classroom Service

A virtual classroom provides a distributed learning environment at *any time, any place with anyone* (Stergioulas et al., 2008). A variety of applications and tools are typically used, which may include:

1. Teleconferencing or collaborative environment systems (for tele-education use), such as Isabel or NetMeeting
2. Broadcast/multicast e-learning service
3. Learning content management service
4. Real-time Audio Video
5. Chat and Conference
6. Collaboration tools

In the context of this service, a tutor based in a studio or in a lecture theatre provides the material and lecture to the learners. In case of tele-education classrooms, each room is equipped with TV, VCRs, video projectors and PCs (installed with the necessary receiver cards), receiving satellite antennas and hubs or wireless access points, microphones and speakers. Also, there are few latest 3D virtual learning interactive boards available, which can provide multi-user platforms.

## 2.2. Learning Content Management System (LCMS) Service

An LCMS service facilitates the authoring, publication and management of learning content, including multimedia content adaptation aspects, from the view point of system administrator and author but at the same time it provides personalised access to combined Learning Objects in a Learning Path that is most suitable to learners of the participating communities.

The access to such a web-based LCMS Service is facilitated using wireless-enabled PCs over a broadband wireless network interlinked with a core satellite-based transmission network. Communication is accomplished using IP protocols (IPv4, IPv6).

## 2.3. Tele-Conference Service

This service can be delivered using any type of satellite network infrastructure to tele-education halls/classrooms, which can be further transmitted to learners' PCs over a broadband wireless network interlinked with a core satellite network.

Each one of the classroom can be equipped with presentation boards (flipcharts, white/blackboards etc.), video cameras, microphones, speaker systems, DVD/VCR player, a TV set/projector, a satellite set-top box and one or two PCs (equipped with the necessary receiver cards, for remote video display purpose as well as for local presenting/sharing or running shared applications). This service can be used for unicast, multicast or broadcast distribution. For teleconferencing, the following tools and applications can be used:

1. Chat
2. File Transfer
3. Program/Application Sharing
4. Shared Notepad
5. Remote Desktop Sharing

## 2.4. Webinar/Webcast Service

Many research companies are using these services to enable them carry out live or pre-recorded transmission of content from one site to the rest of remote sites. The content could be sent by unicast if it is a point-to-point communication, otherwise by multicasting. Since this is a unidirectional transmission, the high propagation delays of satellite networks do not affect performance. However, a low packet inter-arrival delay (jitter) is desired. The service can be delivered using any type of satellite network that can transmit to learners' PCs over a broadband wireless network interlinked with a core satellite network. For Webinar/Webcast, the following applications can be used:

1. Real Player
2. Windows Media Player
3. Apple QuickTime
4. VLC

## 2.5. The Clix Application

CLIX (Corporate Learning and Information exchange) is a software application with which the users control all information, learning and knowledge processes via their browser in the intranet or internet, in real-time.

CLIX (see Figure 1) is based on a scalable, multi-layer client server architecture, which not only allows distributed data management and a distributed application operation, but also allows the graphical user interface to be customised to integrate corporate design.

At the heart of CLIX is an eLearning framework consisting of Java components on the server side. The key advantage of the eLearning framework

depends in its platform impartiality and interoperability flexibilities. CLIX is based exclusively on the existing hard and software components (browser, Web server, application server, and database and media server) of the e-learning provider infrastructure. CLIX has adopted and employed the LOM and SCORM standards on learning resources.

The IEEE Learning Object Metadata (LOM) family of standards specifies a conceptual data schema that defines the structure of a metadata instance for a learning object. A learning object is defined as any entity (digital or not) that can be used for learning. It is not necessary that each application will suitable for every program and platform (Kraan, 2007).

The Sharable Content Object Reference Model (SCORM) is a framework and defines a Web-based learning Content Aggregation Model, a Run-Time Environment as well as Sequencing and Navigation for learning objects (Chew, 2008). SCORM is a collection of specifications adapted from multiple sources to provide a comprehensive suite of e-learning capabilities that enable interoperability, accessibility and reusability of Web-based learning content.

*Figure 1. CLIX framework (IMC AG) (CLIX Learning Management Architectures, 2008)*

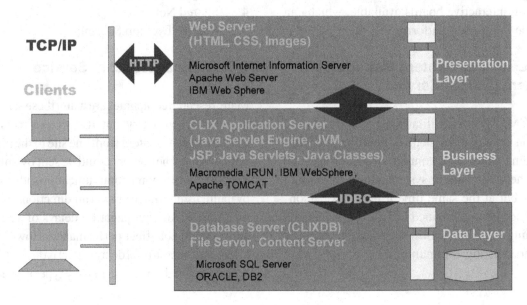

## 2.6. Isabel Application

The Isabel computer support cooperative work (CSCW) (Quemada et al., 2005) application is a group collaboration tool for the Internet (or other IP networks), which uses TCP-UDP/IP protocols (IPv4, IPv6 and dual stack). Isabel supports the realization of distributed meetings, classrooms, congresses, etc, by using a service concept which has a very effective management of multipoint configurations (ISABEL, 2007).

An Isabel terminal is a computer (PC) where the Isabel application is deployed (De Miguel et al., 2006) with all the additional hardware necessary to run Isabel (audio and video hardware, network hardware). Isabel application provides enhanced support to new distributed multimedia services (De Miguel et al., 2006).

The topology in Isabel sessions is tree-based; it has a root, interconnecting nodes and final nodes. There are several roles a terminal can fulfill in the session topology.

Isabel (see Figure 2) runs on top of its own overlay network. This overlay is composed of a media delivery layer and an interaction mode control layer. The content delivery overlay network can be configured to make use of the variety of network protocols and services existing today, such as unicast, multicast (ASM or SSM), IPv4 and IPv6 etc. Each Isabel element (master, interactive terminal, etc.) includes a flow server. The flow server is the core element used to construct the media delivery layer. The flow server can be run as an isolated platform element for performance reasons or to have several always-on entry points to the platform.

The flow server is a multipoint control unit (MCU) and gateway which fulfils the various functions in the Isabel platform that are needed to overcome the connectivity problems of the Internet, and they include (Quemada et al., 2005):

- Service proxy function which allows the access of a participant to the session through another terminal or flow server in places where no direct IP connectivity exists with the master of the session.
- MCU function which allows setting up multipoint configurations over IP unicast.
- Gateway function to connect IP multicast (ASM or SSM), IP unicast, IPv4 and IPv6, etc.
- Traffic shaping, limiting and merging functions. Each Isabel interactive terminal in-

*Figure 2. Typical Isabel platform (ISABEL, 2007)*

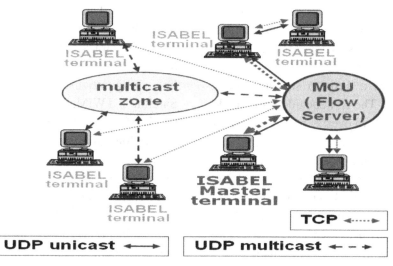

cludes a flow server inside and can be used for a service proxy, as an MCU or as a gateway for other participants of the session. However dedicated flow servers are recommended for performance reasons because they provide an always-on entry points to sessions.

An Isabel Terminal can be connected as a normal PC provided there is enough bandwidth to connect the session. The necessary bandwidth required to connect an Isabel Session is not a built-in parameter and can be decided by the session organizer. Link bandwidths can range from 128kbps to 10Mbps.

As Isabel uses TCP-UDP/IP protocols, the terminal must have an IP address. It is important to keep the Bidirectional UDP from 53009 to 53032 ports open in the routers. Most of configuration can be set up as required by the scenario such as audio and video codecs, transfer topology, error recovery features, and different interaction modes, etc. Isabel can handle the presence of NAT boxes with a flow server installed in the border of the network, and if the parent of a node is sited at an IP public address, a node behind a NAT box can join the session properly. In addition, it can handle heterogeneous network seamlessly for both multicast and unicast mode simultaneously. In addition, most of the traffic (except signalling) goes over UDP, which is the most suitable protocol to transport media flows over high-delay satellite links. That is why this system is an excellent choice for the testing scenarios.

Isabel includes a desktop sharing, and a whiteboard mode. The whiteboard allows mode runs on the Isabel own overlay network and it is transported via TCP.

The desktop sharing mode is based on VNC/RFB. It connects to any machine with a VNC server and distributes the desktop contents in real time to every other participant in the session. The Isabel machine can run its own VNC server, or an external server (i.e. a Windows machine).

The distribution of the Virtual Network Connection (VNC) desktop sharing mode in Isabel can be made in two ways: using the NEREDA mode or the Shared Display mode. The NEREDA mode distributes VNC data persistently using an overlay TCP distribution tree. The Shared Display mode encodes the desktop contents with the current video codec and distributes it through the UDP unpredictable Isabel distribution tree to deliver the participant's video streams. The whiteboard mode uses TCP as transport protocol which can be an issue of performance degradation and the contents on the whiteboard could take up to one second minimum delay if packets are lost.

## 3. TESTING ARCHITECTURES

The test bed of this study is the network developed in the BASE2 EU project, which has designed and deployed a hybrid, satellite- and wireless-based network infrastructure, and learning services to support distance learning for geographically isolated communities. BASE2 focuses on the empowerment (enabling learning) for members of the agrarian and maritime isolated communities. The BASE2 project involves the deployment of the service and network infrastructure and a number of trials. 10 agrarian community sites in Greece and 2 in Cyprus are now active with full network and service deployment. A number of different network testing scenarios have been carried out. These tests aim to study connectivity-related issues for the various architectural scenarios of BASE[2] link configurations. This includes Satellite only, Satellite and WiMax and finally Satellite, WiMax and WiFi as shown in Figure 3.

The four test machines are located close to the HUB station, while the DVB-RCS terminal and the intermediate WiMax/WiFi nodes are connected to the Inter/Intra-net via a separate interface so that no extra management traffic influences the satellite/WiMax/WiFi link measurements. In the actual implementation of network, all machines

*Figure 3. Test bed infrastructure*

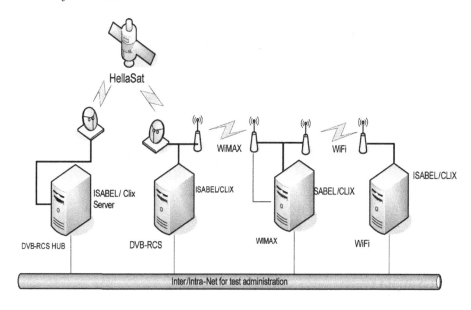

behind DVB-RCS machine are connected through an Isabel flow server. The Isabel flow server machines connect to Isabel server in NCSR through public internet. The Clix server is also at NCSR which connects through public internet to the DVB-RCS hub which in turns connects the user behind DVB-RCS terminals.

## 4. RESULTS ANALYSIS

To check the connectivity and delay initially a *'ping'* test was carried out between Wi-Fi –WiMAX, WiMAX-WiMAX and DVB-RCS Hub and Various Sites. In Figures 4 and 5 are the graphs which show the RTT results. The average RTT between Wi-Fi and WiMAX is 0.025 ms, and between DVB-RCS to WiMAX is 27 ms. The overall RTT is around 30ms.

The RTT to NAT IP is around 600ms as shown in Figure 6. Again in this, there are few peaks at the start of the ping response. These figures show that the jitter is very small.

## 4.1. TCP Measurements

Native TCP performs rather poorly over links with rather long RTTs (long fat pipe problem). Satellite links are a very good example. The performance limitations are caused by the TCP flow control mechanisms (i.e. slow start, window size limitations & congestion control).

The main limiting factor is the standard TCP window size limit of 64Kbytes. Assuming an RTT of about 600ms, the maximum sustained throughput is capped at about 110Kbyte/s. The current maximum windows size to be utilized is controlled by the TCP congestion avoidance algorithm. They, too, are often RTT driven. The classic 'Reno' is a good example.

Modern TCP stacks usually support Window Scaling, which allows the TCP window to grow exponentially to a maximum of 1 GByte. A number of less RTT-dependent (i.e. Vegas) or even satellite-optimized (i.e. Hybla) congestion avoidance algorithms have been proposed, but are not yet widely used.

Also since slow start is dependent on the RTT, it takes about 2-3 seconds for a TCP connection to reach its maximum throughput. Therefore, short

*Figure 4. WiMAX-Wi-Fi Ping statistics*

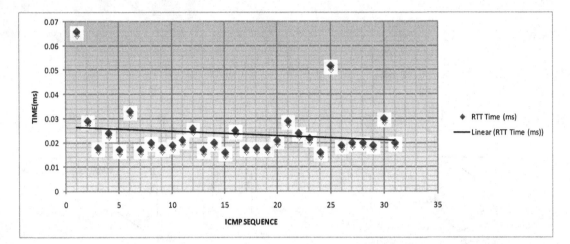

*Figure 5. DVB-RCS-WiMAX*

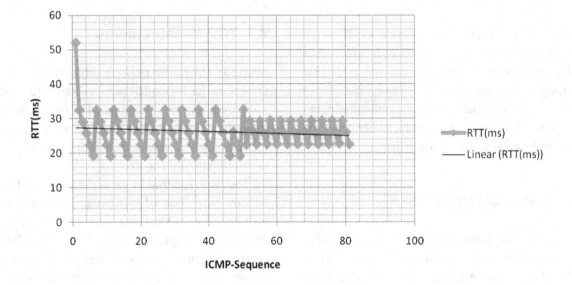

transfers, for example HTTP transactions, suffer from a significant drop in throughput. Similar limitations apply to recovery after packet loss or congestion.

Figure 7 shows the typical TCP throughput for DVB-RCS hub with the PEP enabled. The bandwidth limit of about 120kByte/s is configured at the hub station. The slow start effect is almost eliminated and the throughput is very constant.

## 4.2. UDP Measurements

To analyze the datagram forwarding behaviour, '*mgen*' was used to generate UDP traffic across the various links. The mgen scenarios used have been modelled after actual ISABEL traffic pattern. On the forward channel 950 kbps are used for the video stream while 96 kbps are used for the audio stream. On the return channel, only the 96 kbps audio stream is sent. In order to measure

*Figure 6. DVB-RCS-SITS*

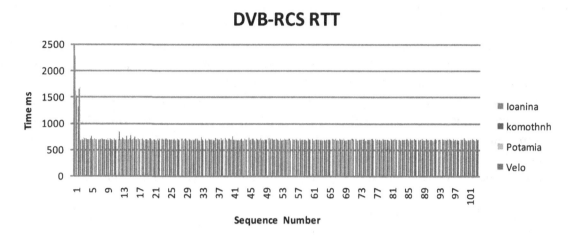

accurate latency times the clocks on the tow test machines where synchronized using the NTP protocol before the test. After the test, the clocks where synchronized again and a possible (linear) drift was corrected for (this functionality is part of the Net Analyzer package as developed by FOKUS, Germany).

The measurements show that the main impact in terms of packet trip time and jitter is caused by the satellite links and the WiMAX connection. The impact of Wi-Fi is within the tolerance band. We present here the graphical summary of the measurements using the DVB-RCS platform with CRA turned on in connection with WiMAX

*Figure 7. TCP throughput hub station (PEP enabled)*

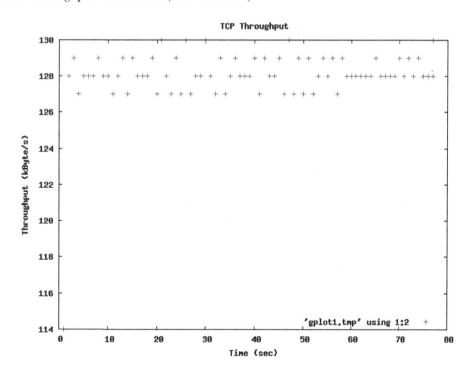

and Wi-Fi. There is no packet loss and jitter is very low for a shared satellite channel which is around 25ms.

The results show that on an idle link loss is minimal, the trip time is constant and therefore the inter-arrival jitter is very low. The forward and return channels of a DVB-RCS system have very different characteristics, especially concerning jitter. Proper hub station configuration can hide those quite well so that the system performs nicely. If the link is to be shared with other traffic (web access, etc.), QoS enforcement (i.e. DiffServ) should configured to prioritize the conferencing traffic over other traffic in order to guarantee an uninterrupted session.

## 4.3. ISABEL RTP Analysis

The following charts (see Figure 8) visualize the RTP stream statistics of an ISABEL conference between three sites. Further passively listening participating sites do not add to the traffic load, due to the multicast distribution of the content. The top row represents the bandwidth, jitter and loss figures of the audio streams, while the bottom row represents the video stream figures. The jitter statistics of the video streams have a limited significance since the video frames are not sent at fixed intervals. The inter-arrival jitter should be smaller than 100ms assuming a frame rate of 10 frames per second and at least one RTP packet per frame. Higher numbers indicate jitter incurred during transmission. Participant SITE1 and SITE2 were permanently active while participant SITE3 had its audio channel muted for most of the time and only communicated occasionally.

Adding up the bandwidth of the audio and video streams, it can be shown that the total amount does not exceed the 1Mbps limit. The Packet loss rate (averaged) is less than 0.2%, with a few occasional spikes. Those could be caused by transmission errors, a packet scheduler in any of the involved devices. The jitter of the audio signal is below 20ms, while the jitter of the video signal is below 50ms, which suggests that there no considerable jitter on the transmission links. Hence, the satellite link under real-world load performs within the expected parameters

*Figure 8. RTP stream statistics of an ISABEL conference*

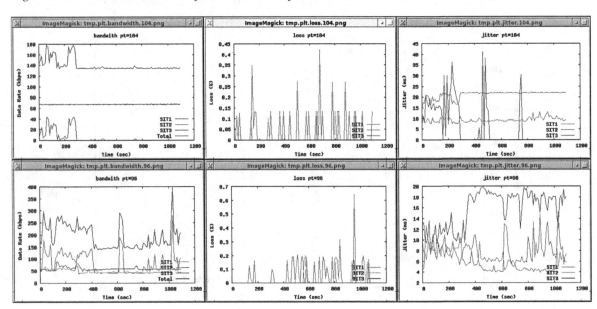

## 5. CONCLUSION

In this paper we have described various services and tested a Hybrid Satellite Terrestrial Network designed to meet the special tele-education needs of geographically isolated/remote communities, employing a number of networked services including the Isabel application platform. Terrestrial services, like WiMAX IEEE802.16 can transport and deliver IP data symmetrically in both directions. Round trip time is around 20 – 40 ms between sector controller and subscriber station. The maximum throughput is around 23 Mbps in both directions, i.e. channel size does not matter with regards to broadband channel requirements.

Satellite services, such as DVB-RCS, have a substantial round trip time of approximately 640 to 680 ms due to speed of light when communicating over the geostationary satellites (such as Hellas-Sat 2 on 39 degrees East, which was used in our testing scenarios). Since RCS is a highly asymmetric service (large Mbps-sized bandwidth on downlink and some tens or hundreds of Kbps throughput on the individual uplink) broadband requirements can be met when delivering through downlink towards the target area. Additionally, by introducing intelligent traffic prioritization and carrier management on the return channel, it was demonstrated that the jitter of the round trip time can be minimized and throughput numbers have been optimized at the same time. Therefore, it has been demonstrated that the proposed network architecture is suitable for tele-education and e-learning applications, and fully interoperable network can be designed, comprising all kinds of terrestrial and satellite components, capable of offering suitable tele-education services to a large number of sites.

E-learning in such remote and geographically isolated areas has now demonstrably got past the research phase. It has efficiently and successfully worked in the context of our study and a valuable experience related not only with the technical implementation but also with the process of organizing such e-learning delivery mechanisms was gained.

The bridging of the digital divide and the development of basic digital literacy is a direct benefit of these training sessions for all the participants of both selected remote communities (agrarian and maritime). Especially among the people of the agrarian community there is a very strong percentage of people who had never come in contact with these technologies. So this contact with these e-learning platforms provided them a familiarity with new technologies which is a great social benefit that emerged from the BASE2 project.

## ACKNOWLEDGMENT

This work was carried out as part of the Broadband access satellite enabled education (BASE2) project (Contract no.: 516159). BASE2 is supported by the Aeronautics and Space programme of European Commission. The overall objective of this project was the implementation of an end-to-end system for tele-education applications, integrating broadband terrestrial networks with satellite broadband technologies in order to empower remote communities with the capability of tele-education applications. The authors would like to thank all the members of the BASE2 project consortium for their excellent support and collaboration, and the European Commission for the generous financial support and guidance.

## REFERENCES

Abuelma'atti, O., Merabti, M., & Askwith, B. (2006). A wireless networked appliances interoperability architecture. In *Proceedings of the 1st International Symposium on Wireless Pervasive Computing* (p. 6).

Chew, L. K. (2008). Scorn 3rd edition specification and intelligent tutoring system – the difference and similarities. *Syenthesis Journal*, 79-86.

Chitre, D. M., & Henderson, T. (1995). Seamless integration of satellite and terrestrial networks. In *Proceedings of the Tenth International Conference on Digital Satellite Communications* (pp. 220-227).

De Miguel, T. P., Pavón, S., Salvachua, J., Quemada Vives, J., Chas Alonso, P. L., Fernandez-Amigo, J., et al. (2006). ISABEL experimental distributed cooperative work application over broadband networks. In R. Steinmetz (Ed.), *Proceedings of the Second International Workshop on Multimedia: Advanced Teleservices and High-Speed Communication Architectures* (LNCS 868, pp. 353-362).

Evans, B., Werner, M., Lutz, E., Bousquet, M., Corazza, G. E., Maral, G., & Rumeau, R. (2005). Integration of satellite and terrestrial systems in future multimedia communications. *IEEE Wireless Communications*, *12*(5), 72–80. doi:10.1109/MWC.2005.1522108

ISABEL. (2007). *ISABEL technical documentation*. Retrieved from http://www.agora-2000.com/products/ISABEL/documentation.html

Kraan, W. (2007). *No one standard will suit all*. Retrieved from http://metadata.cetis.ac.uk/content/20030513175232

Learning Management Architectures, C. L. I. X. (2008). *Micro-framework designed for creating micro-sites and small web applications*. Retrieved from http://code.google.com/p/clix-framework/

Quemada, J., de Miguel, T., Pavon, S., Huecas, G., Robles, T., Salvachua, J., et al. (2005). ISABEL: An application for real time collaboration with a flexible floor control. In *Proceedings of the International Conference on Collaborative Computing: Networking, Applications and Worksharing* (p. 9).

Shave, N. P. (2002). Roaming between satellite and terrestrial networks. In *Proceedings of the Third International Conference on 3G Mobile Communication Technologies* (pp. 58-63).

Stergioulas, L. K., Abbasi, M., Pitsilis, V., Constantine, M., et al. (2008). Satellite-enabled education for geographically isolated communities of farmers and maritime workers, The BASE[2] Project. In *Proceedings of the International Conference on Bridging the Digital Divide in Rural Communities: Practical Solutions and Policies*, Athens, Greece.

Sugarbroad, I. (1990). An OSI-based interoperability architecture for managing hybrid networks. *IEEE Communications Magazine*, *28*(3), 61–69. doi:10.1109/35.52893

## APPENDIX

## List of Acronyms

**3G:** 3rd Generation
**CLIX:** Corporate Learning and Access Platform
**DVB-S:** Digital Video Broadcasting –Satellite
**DVB-RCS:** Digital Video Broadcasting Return Channel through Satellite
**HTTP:** Hypertext Transfer Protocol
**ICMP:** Internet Control Message Protocol
**IP:** Internet Protocol
**Kbps:** Kilo bits per second
**LCMS:** Learning Content Management Services
**LTE:** Long Term Evolution
**MAC:** Medium Access Control
**Mbps:** Mega bits per second
**NAT:** Network Address Translation
**PEP:** Protocol Extension Protocol
**QoS:** Quality of Service
**RTP:** Real Time Protocol
**RTT:** Round Trip Time
**SIT:** Satellite Interactive Terminal
**TCP:** Transmission Control Protocol
**UDP:** User Datagram Protocol
**VSAT:** Very Small Aperture Terminal
**VNC:** Virtual Network Connection
**VoIP:** Voice over IP
**WAN:** Wide Area Network
**Wi-Fi:** Wireless Fidelity
**WiMAX:** Worldwide Interoperability for Microwave Access
**WLAN:** Wireless Local Area Network

*This work was previously published in the International Journal of Digital Literacy and Digital Competence, Volume 2, Issue 2, edited by Antonio Cartelli, pp. 40-52, copyright 2011 by IGI Publishing (an imprint of IGI Global).*

# Compilation of References

Abuelma'atti, O., Merabti, M., & Askwith, B. (2006). A wireless networked appliances interoperability architecture. In *Proceedings of the 1st International Symposium on Wireless Pervasive Computing* (p. 6).

Adams, T. L. (2010). Gender and feminization in health care professions. *Social Compass, 4*(7), 454–465. doi:10.1111/j.1751-9020.2010.00294.x

Adler, S. (1991). The reflective practitioner and the curriculum of teacher education. *Journal of Education for Teaching, 17*(2), 139–150. doi:10.1080/0260747910170203

Adomi, E. E. (2005). Internet development and connectivity in Nigeria. *Program, 39*(3), 257–268.

Adomi, E. E. (2008). Africa and the challenges of bridging the digital divide. In Garson, G. D., & Khosrow-Pour, M. (Eds.), *Handbook of research on public information technology* (Vol. 1, pp. 303–313). Hershey, PA: Information Science Reference. doi:10.4018/978-1-59904-857-4.ch029

Adomi, E. E., Okiy, R. B., & Ruteyan, J. O. (2003). A survey of cybercafes in Delta State, Nigeria. *The Electronic Library, 21*(5), 487–495. doi:10.1108/02640470310499876

Ahmed, A. M., & Yousif, E. (2007). *Problems and factors that influence use of internet by the Sudanese doctors.* Retrieved August 20, 2011, from http://www.sjph.net.sd/files/vol2i3p177-182.pdf

Ahn, J., Han, K., & Han, B. (2005). Web-based education: Characteristics, problems, and some solutions. *International Journal of Innovation and Learning, 2*(3), 274–282. doi:10.1504/IJIL.2005.006370

Ajayi, L. (2009). English as a second language learners: Exploration of multimordal texts in a junior high school. *Journal of Adolescent & Adult Literacy, 52*(7), 585–595. doi:10.1598/JAAL.52.7.4

Ajuwon, G. A. (2004). Use of computer and the Internet in a Nigerian teaching hospital. *Journal of Hospital Librarianship, 4*, 73–78. doi:10.1300/J186v04n04_06

Alkan, C. (2005). *Educational technology.* Ankara, Turkey: Ani Publishers.

Allen, I. E., Seaman, J., & Garrett, R. (2007). *Blending in: The extent and promise of blended education in the United States.* Needham, MA: Sloan-C. Retrieved from http://www.blendedteaching.org

Alrichter, H., & Posch, P. (1989). Does the 'grounded theory' approach offer a guiding paradigm for teacher research? *Cambridge Journal of Education, 19*(1), 21–31. doi:10.1080/0305764890190104

Altet, M. (1994). *La formation professionnelle des enseignants.* Paris, France: PUF.

Altet, M. (2001). L'analyse de pratiques. Une démarche de formation professionnalisante? *Recherche et Formation, 35*, 25–41.

Altet, M. (2002). Une démarche de recherche sur la pratique enseignante: l'analyse plurielle. *Revue Française de Pédagogie, 138*, 85–93. doi:10.3406/rfp.2002.2866

Ananiadou, K., & Claro, M. (2009). *21st Century skills and competencies for new millennium learners in OECD countries.* Retrieved from http://www.oecd.org/LongAbstract/0,3425,en_2649_35845581_44303186_119684_1_1_1,00.html

Anderson, L. W., & Krathwohl, D. (2001). *A taxonomy for learning, teaching and assessing: A revision of bloom's taxonomy of educational objectives*. New York, NY: Longman.

Anderson, R. E., & Dexter, S. (2005). Technology leadership: Its incidence and impact. *Educational Administration Quarterly, 41*(1), 49–82. doi:10.1177/0013161X04269517

Ang, P. H. (1997). *How countries are regulating Internet content*. Retrieved from http://cad.ntu-kpi.kiev.ua/events/inet97/B1/B1_3.HTM

Angelaina, S., & Jimoyiannis, A. (in press). Educational blogging: Developing and investigating a students' community of inquiry. In Jimoyiannis, A. (Ed.), *Research on e-learning and ICT in education*. New York, NY: Springer.

Ankeny, J. (2008). Five mobile social networking services you should get to know. *Fierce Mobile Content*. Retrieved July 20, 2011, from http://www.fiercemobilecontent.com/special-reports/five-mobile-social-networking-services-you-should-get-know

Anstey, M., & Bull, G. (2006). *Teaching and learning multiliteracies*. Newark, DE: International Reading Association.

Aouag, S. (2007). Designing learning activity to be individualized. In *Proceedings of the International Conference on Web Information Systems and Technologies*.

Apodaka, P. (2001). Calidad y evaluación de la educación superior: Situación actual y prospectiva. *Revista de Investigación Educativa, 19*(2), 367–382.

Ardizzone, P., & Rivoltella, P. C. (2008). *Media e tecnologie per la didattica*. Milano, Italy: Vita e pensiero.

Area de Tecnologias, P. L. D. Grupo G9 (2010). Qué es el Campus Virtual del Compartido del G9. Retrieved from http://www.uni-g9.net

Arnold, M. (1999). The virtual university. *Arena Journal, 13*, 85–100.

Arnold, N. (2007). Reducing foreign language communication apprehension with computer-mediated communication: A preliminary study. *System, 35*, 469–486. doi:10.1016/j.system.2007.07.002

Arua, E. A. (2009). *Reading comprehension skills for college and university students*. Ibadan, Nigeria: CELL.

Ashoori, M., Miao, C., & Cai, Y. (2007, November 2-5). Socializing pedagogical agents for personalization in virtual learning environments. In *Proceedings of the IEEE/WIC/ACM International Conferences on Web Intelligence and Intelligent Agent Technology*, Silicon Valley, CA.

Atkins, S., & Murphy, K. (1995). Reflective practice. *Nursing Standard, 9*(45), 31–35.

Atkinson, P., & Hammersley, M. (1994). Ethnography and participant observation. In Denzin, N. K., & Lincoln, Y. S. (Eds.), *Handbook of qualitative research*. Thousand Oaks, CA: Sage.

Awouters, V., Jans, R., & Jans, S. (2008, April). E-learning competencies for teachers in secondary and higher education. In *Proceedings of the International Conference on E-Learning*, Saragossa, Spain.

Bain, C. D., & Rice, L. (2007). The influence of gender on attitudes, perceptions, and uses of technology. *International Journal of Research on Technology in Education, 39*(2), 119–132.

Bandura, A. (1986). *The social foundations of thought and action: A social cognitive theory*. Englewood Cliffs, NJ: Prentice Hall.

Barber, M., & Moursched, M. (2007). *How the world's best-performing school systems come out on top*. London, UK: McKinsey & Co.

Barker, P., & Manji, K. (1991). Designing electronic books. *Educational and Learning Technology International, 28*(4).

Baron, G.-L., & Bruillard, É. (2000). Technologies de l'information et de la communication dans l'éducation: Quelles compétences pour les enseignants? *Educations & Formations, 56*, 69–76.

Bass, S. B. (2003). How will internet use affect the patient? A review of computer network and closed internet-based system studies and the implications in understanding how the use of the internet affects patient populations. *Journal of Health Psychology, 8*(1), 25–38. doi:10.1177/1359105303008001427

Bateson, G. (1991). A sacred unity. In Donaldson, R. (Ed.), *Further steps to an ecology of mind*. San Francisco, CA: HarperCollins.

Bath, P. A. (2008). Health informatics: Current issues and challenges. *Journal of Information Science, 34*(4), 501–518. doi:10.1177/0165551508092267

Baylor, A. L., & Ritchie, D. (2002). What factors facilitate teacher skill, teacher morale, and perceived student learning in technology-using classrooms? *Computers & Education, 39*(4), 395–414. doi:10.1016/S0360-1315(02)00075-1

Bazalgette, C. (2005). Incontro com Cary Bazalgette nel suo ufficio. *Boletim da Academia Nacional de Medicina, 3*.

Bazzoli, F. (2000). Gateways to the Internet. *Internet Health Care Magazine, 1*, 70–77.

Beauvois, M. H. (1998). Conversations in slow motion: computer-mediated communication in the foreign language classroom. *Canadian Modern Language Review, 54*(2), 198–217. doi:10.3138/cmlr.54.2.198

Beck, P., Kung, M., Park, Y., & Yang, S. (2004). E-learning architecture: Challenges and mapping of individuals in an internet-based pedagogical interface. *International Journal of Innovation and Learning, 1*(3), 279–292. doi:10.1504/IJIL.2004.004884

BECTA. (2003). *What the research says about barriers to the use of ICT in teaching.* Coventry, UK: British Educational Communications and Technology Agency.

BECTA. (2004). *Barriers to the uptake of ICT by teachers.* Coventry, UK: British Educational Communications and Technology Agency.

BECTA. (2010). *Digital literacy: Teaching critical thinking for our digital world.* Retrieved from http://schools.becta.org.uk/upload-dir/downloads/digital_literacy_publication.pdf

Beillerot, J. (1998). *Formes et formations du rapport au savoir.* Paris, France: L'Harmattan.

Bennett, S. (2011). Social media showdown: Top 10 social networking sites of 2011. *Infographic.* Retrieved August 2, 2011, from http://www.mediabistro.com/alltwitter/social-networking-2011_b12969

Beran, T., & Violato, C. (2005). Ratings of university teacher instruction: How much do student and course characteristics really matter? *Assessment & Evaluation in Higher Education, 30*(6), 593–601. doi:10.1080/02602930500260688

Berge, Z., & Huang, Y. (2004). A model for sustainable student retention: A holistic perspective on the student dropout problem with special attention to e-learning. *DEOSNEWS, 13*(5).

Bernard, R. M., Brauer, A., Abrami, S., & Surkes, M. (2004). The development of a questionnaire for predicting online learning achievement. *Distance Education, 25*(1), 31–47. doi:10.1080/0158791042000212440

Biggs, J. (1999). *Teaching for quality learning at university.* Philadelphia, PA: The Society for Research into Higher Education and Open University Press.

Biggs, J. (2007). Zannel: Twitter with pictures and video. *Aol Tech.* Retrieved August 2, 2011, from http://techcrunch.com/2007/10/01/zannel-twitter-with-pictures-and-video/

Binder, C. (1996). Behavioral fluency: Evolution of a new paradigm. *The Behavior Analyst, 19*, 163–197.

Blanchet, A., & Gotman, A. (2000). *L'indagine e i suoi metodi: l'intervista, trad. e cura di F. G. Merlina, A. Nuzzaci.* Roma, Italy: Kappa.

Bliuc, A., Goodyear, P., & Ellis, R. (2007). Research focus and methodological choices in studies into students' experiences of blended learning in higher education. *The Internet and Higher Education, 10*, 231–244. doi:10.1016/j.iheduc.2007.08.001

Bloom, B. S. (1956). *Taxonomy of educational objectives, Handbook I: The cognitive domain.* New York, NY: David McKay.

Bogdan, R., & Biklen, S. (1982). *Qualitative research for education: An introduction to theory and methods.* Boston, MA: Allyn and Bacon.

Bolasco, S. (1999). *Analisi multidimensionale dei dati.* Rome, Italy: Carocci.

Bonnici, J. P. M., & de vey Mestdagh, C. N. J. (2005). Right vision, wrong expectations: The European Union and self-regulation of harmful Internet content. *Information & Communications Technology Law, 14*(2), 133–149. doi:10.1080/13600830500042665

Boud, D., Keogh, R., & Walker, D. (Eds.). (1985). *Reflection: turning experience into learning.* London, UK: Kogan Page.

Bourdieu, P. (1972). *Esquisse d'une théorie de la pratique*. Genève, Switzerland: Droz.

Bourdieu, P. (1990). *The logic of practice*. Cambridge, UK: Policy Press.

Boyd, D. M., & Ellison, N. B. (2007). Social network sites: Definition, history, and scholarship. *Journal of Computer-Mediated Communication, 13*(1), 11. Retrieved August 11, 2011, from http://jcmc.indiana.edu/vol13/issue1/boyd.ellison.html

Boyd, E., & Fales, A. (1983). Reflective learning: the key to learning from experience. *Journal of Humanistic Psychology, 23*(2), 99–117. doi:10.1177/0022167883232011

Bradley, L., Lindstrom, Rystedt, H., & Vigmo, S. (2010). Language learning in a wiki: Student contributions in a web based learning environment. *Themes in Science and Technology Education, 3*(1-2), 63–80.

Brandhorst, A. R. (1976). Toward a taxonomy of educational objectives in the relational domain. In *Proceedings of the Annual Meeting of the National Council for Social Studies*. Washington, DC. Retrieved August 4, 2010, from http://www.eric.ed.gov/ERICWebPortal/search/detailmini.jsp?_nfpb=true&_&ERICExtSearch_SearchValue_0=ED134505&ERICExtSearch_SearchType_0=no&accno=ED134505

Brandl, K. (2002). Integrating Internet-based reading materials into the foreign language curriculum: from teacher-to-student-centered approaches. *Language Learning & Technology, 6*(3), 87–107.

Breivik, P. S. (2005). 21st century learning and information literacy. *Change, 37*(2), 20–27. doi:10.3200/CHNG.37.2.21-27

Bremer, J. (2005). The Internet and children: Advantages and disadvantages. *Child and Adolescent Psychiatric Clinics of North America, 14*(3). doi:10.1016/j.chc.2005.02.003

Broady, T., Chan, A., & Caputi, P. (2010). Comparison of older and younger adult' attitudes towards and abilities with computers: implications for training and learning. *British Journal of Educational Technology, 41*(3), 473–485. doi:10.1111/j.1467-8535.2008.00914.x

Brookfield, S. (1991). The development of critical reflection in adulthood. *New Education, 13*(1), 39–48.

Brookfield, S. (1995) *Adult learning: An overview*. Retrieved from http://nlu.nl.edu/ace/resources/documents/adultlearning.html

Brookfield, S. (1995). *Becoming a critically reflective teacher*. San Francisco, CA: Jossey-Bass.

Brown, J., Bryan, J., & Brown, T. (2005). *Past issues*. Retrieved from http://www.innovateonline.info/

Bucker, A. J., & Lamboy, C. (2002). Are professors ready for the technology age? In *Proceedings of the Selected Papers on the Research of Educational Communications and Technology Presented at the National Convention of the Association for Educational Communications and Technology Sponsored by the Research and Theory Division*, Dallas, TX.

Bucker, A. J., & Lamboy, C. L. (2003). An investigation of faculty technology skills in a Puerto Rican university. *Quarterly Review of Distance Education, 4*(2), 143–152.

Buckingham, D. (2003). *Media education: Literacy, learning and contemporary culture*. Cambridge, UK: Polity Press.

Buckingham, D. (2005). *Media education: Literacy, learning and contemporary culture*. Cambridge, UK: Polity Press.

Bugga, M. (2006). Facing the Facebook. *The Chronicle of Higher Education, 52*(21), C1–C4.

Burkhardt, G., Monsour, M., Valdez, G., Gunn, C., Dawson, M., & Lemke, C. (2003). *21st century skills: Literacy in the digital age* (pp. 42–83). Naperville, IL: North Central Regional Educational Laboratory.

Burnett, K., Bonnici, L., Miksa, S., & Kim, J. (2007). The development of a facet analysis system to identify and measure the dimensions of interaction in online learning. *Journal of the American Society for Information Science and Technology, 58*(11), 1569–1577. doi:10.1002/asi.20641

Byram, M., & Zarate, G. (1997). *The sociocultural and intercultural dimension of language learning and teaching*. Strasbourg, France: Council of Europe.

Byron, T. (2008). *Safer children in a digital world: The report of the Byron review*. Retrieved from http://webarchive.nationalarchives.gov.uk/tna/+/http://www.dcsf.gov.uk/byronreview/

Cabero, J. (2002). *Diseño y Evaluación de un Material Multimedia y Telemático Para La Formación y Perfeccionamiento del Profesorado Universitario para la utilización de las Nuevas Tecnologías Aplicadas a la Docencia.* Sevilla, Spain: Universidad de Sevilla. Retrieved from http://tecnologiaedu.us.es/nweb/htm/pdf/EA2002_0177

Calderhead, J. (1989). Reflective teaching and teacher education. *Teaching and Teacher Education, 5*(1), 43–51. doi:10.1016/0742-051X(89)90018-8

Calderhead, J., & Gates, P. (Eds.). (1993). *Conceptualizing reflection in teacher development.* London, UK: Falmer.

Calvani, A. (2011). *Principi dell'istruzione e strategie per insegnare.* Italy: Carocci.

Calvani, A., Cartelli, A., Fini, A., & Ranieri, M. (2008). Models and instruments for assessing digital competence at school. *Journal of E-learning and Knowledge Society, 4*(3), 183–193.

Calvani, A., Fini, A., & Ranieri, M. (2010). La competenza digitale nella scuola. Modelli, strumenti, ricerche. *Giornale Italiano della ricerca educativa, 3*, 5.

Calvin, J., & Freeburg, B. W. (2010). Exploring adult learners' perceptions of technology competence and retention in web-based courses. *Quarterly Review of Distance Education, 11*(2), 63–72.

Cambi, F. (2003). *Manuale di storia della pedagogia.* Roma-Bari, Italy: Editori Laterza.

Canady, R., & Rettig, M. (1995). The power of innovative scheduling. *Educational Leadership, 53*(3), 4–10.

Caravita, L. (2003). *Insegno/Imparo. PT software.* Milano, Italy: ORSEC.

Carreira, S. (2001). Where there's a model, there's a metaphor: Metaphorical thinking in students' understanding of a mathematical model. *Mathematical Thinking and Learning, 3*(4), 261–287. doi:10.1207/S15327833MTL0304_02

Cartelli, A. (2005). Towards an information system making transparent teaching processes and applying informing science to education. *Journal of Issues in Informing Science and Information Technology, 2*, 369–381.

Cartelli, A. (2010). Theory and practice in digital competence assessment. *International Journal of Digital Literacy and Digital Competence, 1*(3), 24–39. doi:10.4018/jdldc.2010101902

Cartelli, A., Dagiene, V., & Futschek, G. (2010). Bebras contest and digital competence assessment. *International Journal of Digital Literacy and Digital Competence, 1*(1), 24–39. doi:10.4018/jdldc.2010101902

Castells, M. (2000). Materials for an exploratory theory of the network society. *The British Journal of Sociology, 51*(1), 5–24. doi:10.1080/000713100358408

Cavallini, F. (2005). Finalmente fluenza tra i banchi! *Journal of Applied Radical Behavior Analysis, 1*, 49–69.

Cawelti, G. (1994). *High school restructuring: A national study.* Arlington, VA: Educational Research Service. (ERIC Document Reproduction Service No. ED366070).

Cedefop. (2008). *Terminology of European education and training policy: A selection of 100 key terms.* Luxembourg: Office for Official Publications of the European Communities.

Chaffee, J. (1998). *Critical thinking: The cornerstone of remedial education.* Paper presented at the Conference on Replacing Remediation in Higher Education, Stanford, CA.

Chambers, P., Clarke, B., Colombo, M., & Askland, L. (2003). Significant learning incidents and critical conversations in an international context: promoting reflexivity with in-service students. *Journal of In-service Education, 29*(1), 101–122. doi:10.1080/13674580300200239

Chaney, B. (2009). A primer on quality indicators of distance education. *Health Promotion Practice, 10*(2), 222–231. doi:10.1177/1524839906298498

Chang, W. (2005). The rewards and challenges of teaching innovation in university physics: 4 Years' Reflection. *International Journal of Science Education, 27*(4), 407–425. doi:10.1080/0950069042000323728

Chao, J. (2007). Student project collaboration using wikis. In *Proceedings of the 20th Conference on Software Engineering Education & Training* (pp. 255-261).

Chatti, M. A., Jarke, M., & Specht, M. (2010). The 3P learning model. *Journal of Educational Technology & Society, 13*(4), 74–85.

Chen, C., & Shaw, R. (2006). Online synchronous vs. asynchronous software training through the behavioral modeling approach: A longitudinal field experiment. *International Journal of Distance Education Technologies*, *4*(4), 88–102. doi:10.4018/jdet.2006100107

Chew, L. K. (2008). Scorn 3rd edition specification and intelligent tutoring system – the difference and similarities. *Syenthesis Journal*, 79-86.

Chickering, A. W., & Ehrmann, S. (1996). Implementing the seven principles: Technology as lever. *AAHE Bulletin*, *49*(2), 3–6.

Chikamatsu, N. (2003). The effects of computer use on L2 Japanese writing. *Foreign Language Annals*, *36*(1), 114–127. doi:10.1111/j.1944-9720.2003.tb01937.x

Childnet International. (2008). *Types of social networking service*. Retrieved August 5, 2011, from http://www.digizen.org/socialnetworking/downloads/Young_People_and_Social_Networking_Services_full_report.pdf

Chitie, D. M., & Henderson, T. (1995). Seamless integration of satellite and terrestrial networks. In *Proceedings of the Tenth International Conference on Digital Satellite Communications* (pp. 220-227).

Choy, S. (2002). *Nontraditional undergraduates (Tech. Rep. No. NCES 2002-012)*. Washington, DC: National Center for Education Statistics.

Christensen, S., & Kreiner, K. (1991). *Projektledelse i løst koblede systemer – ledelse og læring i en ufuldkommen verden*. Copenhagen, Denmark: Jurist- og Økonomforbundets Forlag.

Clark, C. M. (1995). *Thoughtful teaching*. New York, NY: Teachers College.

Clark, M. C. (2010). Controlling privacy on social networking services. *UX Matters*. Retrieved August 4, 2011, from http://www.uxmatters.com/mt/archives/2010/04/controlling-privacy-on-social-networking-services.php

Clark, R. C., & Mayer, R. E. (2007). *E-learning and the science of instruction* (2nd ed.). San Francisco, CA: Jossey-Bass.

Clarke, B. L., & Chambers, P. A. (1999). The promotion of reflective practice in European teacher education: conceptions, purposes and actions. *Pedagogy, Culture & Society*, *7*(2), 291–303.

Cole, D., & Moyle, V. (2010). Cam-capture literacy and its incorporation into multiliteracies. In Pullen, D. L., & Cole, D. (Eds.), *Multiliteracies and technology enhanced education: social practice and the global classroom* (pp. 116–129). Hershey, PA: IGI Global.

Collins, B. (2008). Privacy and security issues in social networking. *Fast Company*. Retrieved August 2, 2011, from http://www.fastcompany.com/articles/2008/10/social-networking-security.html

Collis, B. (1996). The internet as an educational innovation: lesson from experience with computer implementation. *Educational Technology*, *36*(6), 21–30.

Commission of the European Communities. (2008). *Improving competences for the 21st century: An agenda for European cooperation on schools*. Retrieved from http://ec.europa.eu/education/school21/sec2177_en.pdf

ComScore. (2011). *2010 digital year in review*. Retrieved July 15, 2011, from http://www.comscore.com/Press_Events/Presentations_Whitepapers/2011/2010_US_Digital_Year_in_Review

Conti-Ramsden, G., Durkin, K., & Walker, A. J. (2010). Computer anxiety: A comparison of adolescents with and without a history of specific language impairment (SLI). *Computers & Education*, *54*, 136–145. doi:10.1016/j.compedu.2009.07.015

Cooper, J. M. (1999). The teacher as a decision-maker. In Cooper, J. M. (Ed.), *Classroom teaching skills* (pp. 1–19). Boston, MA: Houghton-Mifflin.

Council of European Parliament. (2005). *Recommendation of the European Parliament and of the Council on key competences for lifelong learning*. Retrieved December 3, 2010, from http://ec.europa.eu/education/policies/2010/doc/keyrec_en.pdf

Cox, G., Carr, T., & Hall, M. (2004). Evaluating the use of synchronous communication in two blended learning courses. *International Journal of Computer Assisted Learning*, *20*, 183–193. doi:10.1111/j.1365-2729.2004.00084.x

Coyle, C. L., & Vaughn, H. (2008). Social networking: Communication revolution or evolution? *Bell Labs Technical Journal*, *13*(2), 13–18. doi:10.1002/bltj.20298

Cranton, P. (1996). *Professional development as transformative learning: New perspectives for teachers of adults*. San Francisco, CA: Jossey-Bass.

Cruickshank, D. (1985). Uses and benefits of reflective teaching. *Phi Delta Kappan, 66*(10), 704–706.

Csikszentmihalyi, M. (1982). *Beyond boredom and anxiety*. San Francisco, CA: Jossey-Bass.

Dagienė, V. (2008). Teaching information technology and elements of informatics in lower secondary schools: Curricula, didactic provision and implementation. In R. T. Mittermeir & M. M. Syslo (Eds.), *Proceedings of the International Conference on Informatics Education: Supporting Computational Thinking* (LNCS 5090, pp. 293-304).

Dagienė, V., Zajančkauskienė, L., & Žilinskienė, I. (2008). Distance learning course for training teachers' ICT competence. In R. T. Mittermeir & M. M. Syslo (Eds.), *Proceedings of the Third International Conference on Informatics Education – Supporting Computational Thinking* (LNCS 5090, pp. 282-292).

Dani, D. E., & Koenig, K. M. (2008). Technology and reform-based science education. *Theory into Practice, 47*(3), 204–211. doi:10.1080/00405840802153825

Daniel, E. L. (2000). A review of time shortened courses across disciplines. *College Student Journal*. Retrieved from http://findarticles.com/p/articles/mi_m0FCR/is_2_34/ai_63365186/

Daszko, M., & Sheinberg, S. (2005). *Survival is optional: Only leaders with new knowledge can lead the transformation*. Retrieved from http://www.mdaszko.com/theoryoftransformation_final_to_short_article_apr05.pdf

Daudelin, M. W. (1996). Learning from experience through reflection. *Organizational Dynamics, 24*(3), 36–48. doi:10.1016/S0090-2616(96)90004-2

Davenport, J. (1993). Is there any way out of the andragogy mess? In Thorpe, M., Edwards, R., & Hanson, A. (Eds.), *Culture and Processes of Adult Learning*. London, UK: Routledge.

Davis, C., & Kim, J. (2001). Repeating and remembering foreign language words: Implications for language teaching systems. *Artificial Intelligence Review, 16*, 37–47. doi:10.1023/A:1011086120667

De Kerckhove, D. (2000). *La pelle della cultura*. Genoa, Italy: Costa & Nolan.

De Miguel, T. P., Pavón, S., Salvachua, J., Quemada Vives, J., Chas Alonso, P. L., Fernandez-Amigo, J., et al. (2006). ISABEL experimental distributed cooperative work application over broadband networks. In R. Steinmetz (Ed.), *Proceedings of the Second International Workshop on Multimedia: Advanced Teleservices and High-Speed Communication Architectures* (LNCS 868, pp. 353-362).

Dede, C. (2004). If design-based research is the answer, what is the question? *Journal of the Learning Sciences, 13*(1), 105–114. doi:10.1207/s15327809jls1301_5

Dede, C. (2005). Planning for neo-millennial learning styles. *EDUCAUSE Quarterly, 1*, 7–12.

Del Moral, M. E. (1999, July 5-7). *Metáforas, recursos interactivos y ambientes hipermedia para el aprendizaje*. Paper presented at the 1st Educational Multimedia Conference, Barcelona, Spain.

Del Moral, M. E. (2004). Redes como soporte a la docencia: Tutoría online y aplicaciones telemáticas. In Rodríguez, R. (Ed.), *Docencia Universitaria- Orientaciones para la formación del profesorado* (pp. 193–212). Oviedo, Spain: Universidad de Oviedo.

Del Moral, M. E. (2004). Sistemas interactivos hipermedia educativos. In Del Moral, M. E. (Ed.), *Sociedad del conocimiento, ocio y cultura: Un enfoque interdisciplinar* (pp. 33–64). Oviedo, Spain: Ediciones KRK.

Del Moral, M. E., Cernea, D. A., & Villalustre, L. (2007, September 12-14). Contributions of the Web 2.0 to collaborative work around learning objects. In *Proceedings of the International Conference on Technology, Training and Communication*, Salamanca, Spain. Retrieved from http://ftp.informatik.rwth-aachen.de/Publications/CEUR-WS/Vol-361/paper13.pdf

Del Moral, M. E., & Villalustre, L. (2005, February, 7-27). *Indicadores de calidad para un interfaz gráfico centrado en el aprendiz*. Paper presented at the V Congreso Internacional Virtual de Educación (CIVE), Seville, Spain.

Del Moral, M. E., & Villalustre, L. (2008). Desarrollo de competencias y estilos de aprendizaje en contextos virtuales: Prácticas colaborativas y trabajo autónomo en Ruralnet. In Del Moral, M. E., & Rodríguez, R. (Eds.), *Docencia Universitaria- Experiencias docentes y TIC* (pp. 97–129). Barcelona, Spain: Editorial Octaedro.

Del Moral, M. E., & Villalustre, L. (2009). *Modalidades de aprendizaje telemático y resultados interuniversitarios extrapolables al nuevo EEES (Proyecto MATRIX)*. Barcelona, Spain: Editorial Octaedro.

Dervin, B. (1992). From the mind's eye of the user: The sense-making qualitative-quantitative methodology. In Glazier, J. D., & Powell, R. R. (Eds.), *Qualitative research in information management* (pp. 61–84). Englewood, CO: Libraries Unlimited.

Dervin, B., & Frenette, M. (2003). Sense-making methodology: Communicating communicatively with campaign audiences. In Dervin, B., Foreman-Wernet, L., & Lauterbach, E. (Eds.), *Sense-making methodology reader: Selected writings of Brenda Dervin* (pp. 233–250). Cresskill, NJ: Hampton Press.

Dewey, J. (1916). *Democracy and education. An introduction to the philosophy of education*. New York, NY: Free Press.

Dewey, J. (1933). *How we think: a restatement of the relation of reflective thinking to the educative process*. Boston, MA: Heath.

Di Nuovo, S. (2000). *Attenzione e concentrazione* [CD-ROM]. *7 test e 12 training di potenziamento*. Trento, Italy: Edizioni Erickson.

Dillenbourg, P., Baker, M., Blaye, A., & O'Malley, C. (1996). The evolution of research on collaborative learning. In Spada, E., & Reiman, P. (Eds.), *Learning in humans and machine: Towards an interdisciplinary learning science* (pp. 189–221). Oxford, UK: Elsevier.

Distance Education Report. (2000). *Global village: Focus on Europe*. Madison, WI: Magna Publications.

Dodge, B. (1995). *Some thoughts about WebQuest*. Retrieved from http://webquest.sdsu.edu/about_webquests.html

Dolan, P. L. (2010). *86% of physicians use Internet to access health information*. Retrieved August 20, 2011, from http://www.ama-assn.org/amednews/2010/01/04/bisc0104.htm

Donlevy, J. (2003). Teachers, technology and training. *International Journal of Instructional Media, 30*(2), 117–121.

Doyle, W. (1986). Paradigm in research of teachers' effectiveness. In Crahay, M., & Lafontaine, D. (Eds.), *L'art et la science de l'enseignement* (pp. 435–481). Bruxelles, Belgium: Labor.

Drenoyianni, H., Stergioulas, L. K., & Dagiene, V. (2008). The pedagogical challenge of digital literacy: Reconsidering the concept – envisioning the curriculum' – reconstructing the school. *International Journal on Social and Humanistic Computing, 1*(1), 53–66. doi:10.1504/IJSHC.2008.020480

Dreyfus, H. L., & Dreyfus, S. (1988). *Mind over machine: The power of human intuition and expertise in the era of the computer*. New York, NY: Simon and Schuster.

Drotner, K. (2001). *Medier for fremtiden: Børn, unge og det nye medielandskab*. Copenhagen, Denmark: Høst.

Durkin, K., Simkin, Z., Knox, E., & Contiramsden, G. (2009). Specific language impairment and school outcomes II: Educational context, student satisfaction, and post-compulsory progress. *International Journal of Language & Communication Disorders, 44*(1), 36–55. doi:10.1080/13682820801921510

Duval, R. (2002). The cognitive analysis of problems of comprehension in the learning of mathematics. *Mediterranean Journal for Research in Mathematics Education, 1*(2), 1–16.

Dzenowagis, J., Kuruvilla, S., & Aronson, B. (2002). Access to information for health and development: the health internetwork *Information Development, 18*(3), 177-180.

Eastman, M. J. (2011). A survey of social media issues before the NLRB. *U.S. Chamber of Commerce*. Retrieved August 18, 2011, from http://www.uschamber.com/sites/default/ files/reports/NLRB%20Social%20Media%20Survey.pdf

Ehrmann, S. C. (1997). *Asking the right question: What does research tell us about technology and higher learning?* Retrieved from http://www.tltgroup.org/resources/Flashlight/AskingRightQuestion.htm

Ehrmann, S. C. (1999). Asking the hard questions about technology use and education. *Change, 31*(2), 25–29. doi:10.1080/00091389909602676

Electronic Commerce and Transactions Act. (2006). *Federal Law 1 442 Muhurram 1427.* Retrieved from http://www.rafed.net/en/index.php?option=com_content&view=category&id=164&Itemid=853

Ellickson, R. C. (1991). *Order without law: How neighbors settle disputes.* Cambridge, MA: Harvard University Press.

Emejulu, O. (2006, January 23-24). *Literacy as a backbone of African development.* Paper presented at the Workshop on Literacy Training With Focus on Nomadic Fulani, Kaduna, Nigeria.

Emokykla. (2007). *Reikalavimai mokytojų kompiuterinio raštingumo programoms: Patvirtinta švietimo ir mokslo ministro 2007 m. kovo 29d. įsakymu ISAK-555.* Retrieved from http://www.emokykla.lt/

Emokykla. (2008). *Pedagogų rengimas IKT taikymo aspektu: Mokslinio tyrimo ataskaita.* Retrieved from http://www.emokykla.lt

Epper, R., & Bates, A. W. (2004). *Enseñar al profesorado cómo utilizar la tecnología. Buenas prácticas de instituciones líderes.* Barcelona, Spain: Editorial UOC.

Eraut, M. (1994). *Developing professional knowledge and competence.* London, UK: Falmer.

Eraut, M. (1995). Schön shock; a case for reframing reflection-in-action? *Teachers and Teaching, 1*(1), 9–22. doi:10.1080/1354060950010102

Eraut, M. (2004). The practice of reflection. *Learning in Health and Social Care, 3*(2), 47–52. doi:10.1111/j.1473-6861.2004.00066.x

Erstad, O. (2005). *Digital kompetanse i skolen – en innføring.* Oslo, Norway: Universitetsforlaget.

Ertmer, P. (2003). Transforming teacher education: visions and strategies. *Educational Technology Research and Development, 51*(1), 124–128. doi:10.1007/BF02504522

Ertmer, P. A. (1999). Addressing first- and second-order barriers to change: Strategies for technology integration. *Educational Technology Research and Development, 47*(4), 47–61. doi:10.1007/BF02299597

Eshet-Alkalai, Y. (2004). Digital literacy: A conceptual framework for survival skills in the digital era. *Journal of Educational Multimedia and Hypermedia, 13*(1), 93–106.

Eshleman, J. W. (1985). Improvement pictures with low celerations: An early foray into the use of SAFMEDS. *Journal of Precision Teaching, 6*, 54–63.

Espana, J. (2004). Teaching a Research-Oriented, Graduate Global marketing Course to Adult Learners in a One-Month Format. *Journal of American Academy of Business, 4*(1-2), 418.

ETS. (2002). *Digital transformation: A framework for ICT literacy.* Princeton, NJ: Educational Testing Service.

European Commission. (2005). *Common European principles for teacher competences and qualifications.* Retrieved from http://ec.europa.eu/education/policies/2010/doc/principles_en.pdf

European Commission. (2007). *Key competencies: A developing concept in general compulsory education.* Retrieved from http://www.eurydice.org

European Commission. (2010). *FP7 projects in technology-enhanced learning.* Retrieved from http://cordis.europa.eu/fp7/ict/telearn-digicult/telearn-projects-fp7_en.html

European Information Society. (2003). *eLearning: Better eLearning for Europe.* Brussels, Belgium: Directorate-General for Education and Culture, Office for Official Publications of the European Communities. Retrieved from http://ec.europa.eu/information_society/eeurope/2005/all_about/elearning/index_en.htm

European Schoolnet. (2005). *Assessment schemes for teachers' ICT competence.* Retrieved from http://www-old.eun.org/insight-pdf/special_reports/PIC_Report_Assessment%20schemes_insightn.pdf

European Union. (2008). Recommendation the European Parliament and the Council of 18 December 2006 on key competences for lifelong learning. *Official Journal of the European Union. L&C, L394*, 10–18.

Evans, B., Werner, M., Lutz, E., Bousquet, M., Corazza, G. E., Maral, G., & Rumeau, R. (2005). Integration of satellite and terrestrial systems in future multimedia communications. *IEEE Wireless Communications, 12*(5), 72–80. doi:10.1109/MWC.2005.1522108

Fabrizio, M. A., & Moors, A. L. (2003). Evaluating mastery: Measuring instructional outcomes for children with autism. *European Journal of Behavior Analysis, 4*, 23–36.

Facer, K. (2003). *Computer games and learning: Why do we think it's worth talking about computer games and learning in the same breath?* Retrieved from http://www.coulthard.com/library/Files/facer-futurelabs_2003_computergamesandlearning_discpaper.pdf

Fan, H., & Poole, M. S. (2006). What is personalisation? Perspectives on the design and implementation of personalisation in information systems. *Journal of Organizational Computing and Electronic Commerce, 16*(3-4), 179–202. doi:10.1080/10919392.2006.9681199

Fantin, M. (2006). *Mídia-educação: Conceitos, experiências e diálogos Brasil Itália*. Florianópolis, Brazil: Cidade Futura.

Fantin, M. (2008) Os cenários culturais e as multiliteracies na escola. *Revista Comunicação e Sociedade, 13.*

Fantin, M. (2010). Perspectives on media literacy, digital literacy and information literacy. *International Journal of Digital Literacy and Digital Competence, 1*(4), 10–15. doi:10.4018/jdldc.2010100102

Fantin, M., & Giradello, G. (2008). Digital literacy and cultural mediations to the digital divide. In Rivoltella, P. C. (Ed.), *Digital literacy: Tools and methodologies for information society* (pp. 310–340). Hershey, PA: IGI Global.

Farrah, H. (1988). The reflective thought process: John Dewey re-visited. *The Journal of Creative Behavior, 22*(1), 1–8.

Fechenda, E. J. (2011). Social vs. professional networking sites. *Healthcare IT News*. Retrieved August 2, 2011, from http://healthcareitnews.com/blog/social-vs-professional-networking-sites

Feiman-Nemser, S. (1990). Teacher preparation: structural and conceptual alternatives. In Houston, W. T. (Ed.), *Handbook of research on teacher education*. New York, NY: Macmillan.

Fisher, M. (2007). Computerphobia in adult learners. *Computers & Education*, 14–19.

Fitzgerald, M. (1994). Theories of reflection for learning. In Palmer, A., & Burns, S. (Eds.), *Reflective practice in nursing*. Oxford, UK: Blackwell Scientific.

Flanagan, J. C. (1954). The critical incident technique. *Psychological Bulletin, 5*(4), 327–358. doi:10.1037/h0061470

Forte, A., & Bruckman, A. (2007). Constructing text: Wiki as a toolkit for (collaborative?) learning. In *Proceedings of the International Symposium on Wikis*, Montréal, QC, Canada (pp. 31-41).

Francis, S. (1997). A time for reflection: learning about organizational learning. *The Learning Organization, 4*(4), 168–179. doi:10.1108/09696479710170860

Freire, P. (1972). *Pedagogy of the oppressed*. London, UK: Shedd and Ward.

Gagel, C. W. (1997). Literacy and technology: Reflections and insights for technological literacy. *Journal of Industrial Teacher Education, 34*(3), 6–34.

Galliani, L., Zaggia, C., & Serbati, A. (Eds.). (2011). *Adulti all'Università*. Lecce, Italy: Pensa Multimedia.

Gardner, H. (1993). *Multiple intelligences: The theory in practice*. New York, NY: Basic Books.

Garnham, C., & Kaleta, R. (2002). Introduction to hybrid courses. *Teaching with Technology Today, 8*(6). Retrieved from http://www.uwsa.edu/ttt/articles/garnham.htm

Gaubatz, N. (2003). Course scheduling formats and their impact on student learning. *National Teaching and Learning Forum, 12*(1).

Geeks Desk. (2011). *Top ten social networking sites*. Retrieved August 9, 2011, from http://www.geeksdesk.com/top-10-social-networking-websites/

Geertz, C. (1973). Thick description: Toward an interpretive theory of culture. In Geertz, C. (Ed.), *The interpretation of cultures: Selected essays* (pp. 3–30). New York, NY: Basic Books.

General Command of Abu Dhabi Police. (2008). *Internet and networks, and their effects on society and security*. Retrieved from http://www.alittihad.ae/print.php?id=52907&adate=2008

Geyer, R. W. (1997). Approaching ground zero with today's technology tools. *T.H.E. Journal, 25*(1), 56–59.

Ghaye, T., & Lillyman, S. (2000). *Reflection: principles and practice for healthcare professionals.* Wiltshire, UK: Mark Allen.

Gibbs, G. (1981). *Teaching students to learn: a student centred approach.* Oxford, UK: Oxford University Press.

Gibbs, G. (1988). *Learning by doing: a guide to teaching and learning method.* Oxford, UK: Further Education Unit, Oxford Polytechnic.

Gimbert, B., & Cristol, D. (2004). Teaching curriculum with technology: Enhancing young children's technological competence during early childhood. *Early Childhood Education Journal, 31*(3), 209–218.

Ginsburg, M. B. (1988). *Contradictions in teacher education and society: a critical analysis.* New York, NY: Falmer.

Giovannella, C. (2007). An organic process for the organic era of the interaction. In Silva, P. A., Dix, A., & Jorge, J. (Eds.), *HCI educators 2007: Creativity3: Experiencing to educate and design* (pp. 129–133). Rome, Italy: University of Rome Tor Vergata.

Giovannella, C. (2009). DULP: Complexity, organicity, liquidity. *IxD&A, 2009*(7-8), 11-15.

Giovannella, C. (2010). Beyond the media literacy. Complex scenarios and new literacies for the future education: The centrality of design. *International Journal of Digital Literacy and Digital Competence, 3*(1), 18–28. doi:10.4018/jdldc.2010070102

Giovannella, C. (in press). Is complexity tameble? Toward a design for the experience in a complex world. In. *Proceedings of the Conference on Human Factors in Computing.*

Giovannella, C., & Graf, S. (2010). Challenging technologies, rethinking pedagogy, being design-inspired. The grand challenge of this century. *eLearn Magazine, 2010*(2), 8.

Giovannella, C., Spadavecchia, C., & Camusi, A. (2010). Educational complexity: Centrality of design and monitoring of the experience. In G. Leitner, M. Hitz, & A. Holzinger (Eds.), *Proceedings of the 6th Symposium of the Workgroup Human-Computer Interaction and Usability on HCI in Work and Learning, Life and Leisure* (LNCS 6389, pp. 353-372).

Glassman, M., & Kang, M. J. (2011). The logic of wikis: The possibilities of the Web 2.0 classroom. *Computer-Supported Collaborative Learning, 6*, 93–112. doi:10.1007/s11412-011-9107-y

Global Security. (2011). *Nigeria space programs.* Retrieved from http:www.globalsecurity.org/space/world/nigeria/index.html

Goetz, J. P., & Lecompte, M. D. (1988). *Etnografía y diseño cualitativo en investigación educativa.* Madrid, Spain: Morata.

Gold, R. (1958). Roles in sociological field observations. *Social Forces, 36*, 217–223. doi:10.2307/2573808

Gore, J. (1987). Reflecting on reflective teaching. *Journal of Teacher Education, 55*(2), 33–39. doi:10.1177/002248718703800208

Gore, J., & Zeichner, K. (1991). Action research and reflective teaching in preservice teacher education: a case study from the United States. *Teaching and Teacher Education, 7*(2), 119–136. doi:10.1016/0742-051X(91)90022-H

Grabauskiene, V. (2005). *Formation of geometric images at primary school stage.* Unpublished doctoral dissertation, Vilnius Pedagogical University, Studentu, Lithuania.

Graham, C. R. (2006). Blended learning systems: Definition, current trends, and future directions. In Bonk, C. J., & Graham, C. R. (Eds.), *Handbook of blended learning: Global perspectives, local designs.* San Francisco, CA: Pfeiffer Publishing.

Grant, C., & Zeichner, K. (1984). On becoming a reflective teacher. In Grant, C. (Ed.), *Preparing for reflective teaching* (pp. 1–18). Boston, MA: Allyn & Bacon.

Gulikers, J. T. M., Bastiaens, T. J., & Kirschner, P. A. (2004). A five-dimensional framework for authentic assessment. *Educational Technology Research and Development, 52*, 67–86. doi:10.1007/BF02504676

Gynther, K. (2010). *Didaktik 2.0.* Aarhus, Denmark: Akademisk Forlag.

Habermas, J. (1990). *Conoscenza e umano interesse.* Bari, Italy: Laterza.

Habermas, J. (1990). *Moral consciousness and communicative action.* Cambridge, MA: MIT Press.

Hafner, W., & Ellis, T. J. (2004, January). Project-based, asynchronous collaborative learning. In *Proceedings of the IEEE Hawaii International Conference on Systems Science,* Waikoloa, HI.

Halkier, B. (2008). *Fokusgrupper* (2nd ed.). Copenhagen, Denmark: Samfundslitteratur.

Hamachek, D. (1999). Effective teachers: what they do, how they do it, and the importance of self-knowledge. In Lipka, R., & Brinthaupt, T. (Eds.), *The role of self in teacher development* (pp. 189–224). Albany, NY: State University of New York Press.

Hamilton, K. C. (2002). *Teaching adult learners: A supplemental manual for faculty teaching in the GBM program at FDU.* Madison, NJ: Fairleigh Dickinson University. Retrieved from http://www.fdu.edu/webresources/sitewidesearch.html

Hanluain, D. (2011). Money rushes into social networking. *Mobiledia Network.* Retrieved August 2, 2011 from, http://www.mobiledia.com/news/85010.html

Hannan, A., & Silver, H. (2000). *Innovating in higher education: Teaching, lerning and institucional cultures.* Buckingham, UK: Open University Press.

Harpe, L. D. (2009). Social networks and employment law. *Peopleclick Research Institute.* Retrieved August 1, 2011, from http://www.iowaabi.org/documents/filelibrary/ events/social_media/Social_Networks_Employment_Law_eBoo_C3A386C1048E1.pdf

Hartley, D. (2009). Personalisation: The nostalgic revival of child-centred education? *Journal of Education Policy, 24*(4), 423–434. doi:10.1080/02680930802669318

Hartnell-Young, E. (2006). Teachers' roles and professional learning in communities of practice supported by technology in schools. *Journal of Technology and Teacher Education, 14*(3), 461–480.

Haterick, R. (2000). Time is nature's way of making sure everything doesn't happen at once. In Haterick, R. (Ed.), *The learning market space: A publication of the leadership forum at the center for academic transformation.* Troy, NY: Rensselaer Polytechnic.

Hatton, N., & Smith, D. (1995). Reflection in teacher education: towards definition and implementation. *Teaching and Teacher Education, 11*(1), 33–49. doi:10.1016/0742-051X(94)00012-U

Hemmi, A., Bayne, S., & Land, R. (2009). The appropriation and repurposing of social technologies in higher education. *Journal of Computer Assisted Learning, 25,* 19–30. doi:10.1111/j.1365-2729.2008.00306.x

Herrington, J., & Kervin, L. (2007). Authentic learning supported by technology: Ten suggestions and cases of integration in classrooms. *Educational Media International, 44*(3), 219–236. doi:10.1080/09523980701491666

Hiltz, S. R. (1994). *The virtual classroom: Learning without limits.* Norwood, NJ: Ablex.

Hobbs, R. (2006). *Multiple vision of multimedia literacy: Emerging areas of synthesis.* Retrieved December, 17, 2007, from http://reneehobbs.org/renee's%20web%20site/publications/Hobbs%20final%20PDF%20Literacy%20and%20Technology%20Vol%202.pdf

Hof, R. (2009). Facebook to introduce new, simpler privacy settings. *Bloomberg Businessweek.* Retrieved August 6, 2011, from http://www.businessweek.com/the_thread/techbeat/archives/2009/07/facebook_introd.html

Hoffmann, R. (2008). A wiki for the life sciences where authorship matters. *Nature Genetics, 40*(9), 1047–1051. doi:10.1038/ng.f.217

Holborn, P., Wideen, M., & Andrews, I. (Eds.). (1992). *Devenir enseignant, à la conquête de l'identité professionnelle.* Montréal, QC, Canada: Èditions Logiques.

Hole, S., & McEntee, G. (1999). Reflection is at the heart of practice. *Educational Leadership, 56*(8), 34–37.

Horkheimer, M., & Adorno, T. W. (1976). *The culture industry: Enlightenment as mass deception.* London, UK: Continuum International Publishing.

Horn, L. (1996). *Nontraditional Undergraduates.* Washington, DC: U.S. Department of Education. (ERIC Document Reproduction Service No. ED402857).

Hostetler, K. (2005). What is "good" education research? *Educational Researcher, 34*(6), 16–21. doi:10.3102/0013189X034006016

Hottenstein, D., & Malatesta, C. (1993). Putting a school in gear with intensive scheduling. *The High School Magazine, 2,* 28–29.

Hsu, J. (2008). Innovative technologies for education and learning: Education and knowledge-oriented applications of blogs, wikis, podcasts, and more. *International Journal of Web-Based Learning and Teaching Technologies, 3*(3), 62–81. doi:10.4018/jwltt.2008070106

Hsu, J., & Hamilton, K. (2010). Facilitating adult learner persistence through innovative scheduling and teaching methods. *International Journal of Management in Education, 4*(4), 407–424. doi:10.1504/IJMIE.2010.035608

Huang, H. M. (2002). Toward constructivism for adult learners in online learning environments. *British Journal of Educational Technology, 33*(1), 27–37. doi:10.1111/1467-8535.00236

Hughes, J. E., & Narayan, R. (2009). Collaboration and learning with wikis in post-secondary classrooms. *Journal of Interactive Online Learning, 8*, 63–82.

Hughes, M. A. (1998). Active learning for software products. *Technical Communication, 45*(3), 343–352.

Hurt, A. (2007, February 28-March 4). *Exploring the process of adult computer software training using andragogy, situated cognition, and a minimalist approach.* Paper presented at the International Research Conference in the Americas of the Academy of Human Resource Development, Indianapolis, IN.

Ikpeze, H. C. (2009). Integrating technology in one literacy course: Lessons learned. *Journal of Literacy and Technology, 10*(1).

International Society for Technology in Education. (2000). *Educational technology standards and performance indicators for all teachers.* Retrieved from http://cnets.iste.org/

International Technology Education Association. (2000). *Standards for technological literacy: Content for the study of technology.* Reston, VA: Virginia.

Internet World Stats. (2011). *World Internet users and population stats.* Retrieved from http://www.internetworldstats.com/stats.htm

ISABEL. (2007). *ISABEL technical documentation.* Retrieved from http://www.agora-2000.com/products/ISABEL/documentation.html

Ivanova, M., & Chatti, M. A. (2011). Competences mapping for personal learning environment management. In *Proceedings of the PLE Conference*, Southampton, UK (pp. 1-13).

Iverson, P., Kuhl, P. K., Akahane-Yamada, R., Diesch, E., Tohkura, Y., Kettermann, A., & Siebert, C. (2003). A perceptual interference account of acquisition difficulties for non-native phonemes. *Cognition, 87*, B47–B57. doi:10.1016/S0010-0277(02)00198-1

James, S. (1984). *Reading for academic purposes.* New York, NY: Holt, Rinehart and Winston.

Jarvis, P. (1987). Malcolm Knowles. In Jarvis, P. (Ed.), *Twentieth century thinkers in adult education* (pp. 169–187). London, UK: Croom Helm.

Jarvis, P. E., & Jarvis, C. P. (1991). A tool to assist in the serial testing of attention as a means of monitoring the effectiveness of rehabilitation. *Cognitive Rehabilitation, 9*, 20–23.

Jewels, T., Ghanem, A., Mongeal, A., Nuaimi, E., Aljaaidi, A., Al-Kaf, A., & Nuaimi, A. (2009, August 6-9). E-Business use in the United Arab Emirates: Lessons for evolving markets. In *Proceedings of the 15th Americas Conference on Information Systems*, San Francisco, CA.

Jewitt, C., & Kress, G. (2003). *Multimodal literacy.* New York, NY: Peter Lang.

Jimoyiannis, A. (2010, April 8-9). Integrating Web 2.0 in education: Towards a framework for Pedagogy 2.0. In *Proceedings of the Web 2.0 Conference Abstracts*, London, UK (p. 5).

Jinoyiannis, A., & Gravani, M. (2010). Digital literacy in a lifelong learning programme for adults: Educators' experiences and perceptions on teaching practices. *International Journal of Digital Literacy and Digital Competence, 1*(1), 40–60. doi:10.4018/jdldc.2010101903

Johns, C. (1991). The Burford nursing development unit holistic model of nursing practice. *Journal of Advanced Nursing, 16*(9), 1090–1098. doi:10.1111/j.1365-2648.1991.tb03370.x

Johnson, M. (2009). *Adult Learners and Technology: How to deliver effective instruction and overcome barriers to learning.* San Jose, CA: San Jose State University. Retrieved from http://ic.sjsu.edu/mjportfolio/found/AdultLearnersAndTechnology

Jonassen, D. H., & Grabowski, B. L. (1993). *Handbook of individual differences, learning, and instruction.* Mahwah, NJ: Lawrence Erlbaum.

Jones-Kavalier, B. R., & Flannigan, S. L. (2006). Connecting the digital dots: Literacy of the 21st century. *EDUCAUSE Quarterly, 29*(2).

Judge, S., Puckett, K., & Cabuk, B. (2004). Digital equity. *International Journal of Research on Technology in Education, 36*(4), 383–397.

Juels, A. (2010). The primal cue. *Communications of the ACM, 53*(3), 120–119. doi:10.1145/1666420.1666448

Julfar, A. A. (2006). Empowering the Arab media through the Internet. In Emirates Center for Strategic Studies and Research (Ed.), *Arab media in the information age.* Abu Dhabi, United Arab Emirates: The Emirates Center for Strategic Studies and Research.

Junker, B. (1960). *Field work.* Chicago, IL: Chicago University Press.

Kalas, I. (2006). Discovering informatics fundamentals through interactive interfaces for learning. In R. T. Mittermeir (Ed.), *Proceedings of the International Conference on Informatics Education: The Bridge between Using and Understanding Computers* (LNCS 4226, pp. 13-24).

Kalas, I., & Winczer, M. (2008). Informatics as a contribution to the modern constructivist education. In R. T. Mittermeir & M. M. Syslo (Eds.), *Proceedings of the Third International Conference on Informatics Education: Supporting Computational Thinking* (LNCS 5090, pp. 229-240).

Kalyuga, S., Chandler, P., & Sweller, J. (2000). Incorporating learner experience into the design of multimedia instruction. *Journal of Educational Psychology, 92,* 126–136. doi:10.1037/0022-0663.92.1.126

Kasper, L. F. (2000). The role of information technology in the future of content-based ESL instruction. In Kasper, L. K. F., Babbitt, M., Mlynarczyk, R. W., Brinton, D. M., Rosenthal, J. W., & Master, P.,(Eds.), *Content-based college ESL instruction* (pp. 202–212). Mahwah, NJ: Lawrence Erlbaum.

Kasper, L. F. (2000). New technologies, new literacies: Focus discipline research and ESL learning communities. *Language Learning & Technology, 4*(2), 105–128.

Katz, I. R. (2007). *Beyond technical competence: Literacy in information and communication technology.* Retrieved from http://www.ets.org/Media/Tests/ICT_Literacy/pdf/ICT_Beyond_Technical_Competence.pdf

Kear, K., Woodthorpe, J., Robertson, S., & Hutchison, M. (2010). From forums to wikis: Perspectives on tools for collaboration. *The Internet and Higher Education, 13,* 218–225. doi:10.1016/j.iheduc.2010.05.004

Keller, L., Komm, D., Serafini, G., Sprock, A., & Steffen, B. (2010). Teaching public-key cryptography in school. In J. Hromkovic, R. Kralovic, & J. Vahrenhold (Eds.), *Proceedings of the 4th International Conference on Teaching Fundamentals Concepts of Informatics* (LNCS 5941, pp. 112-123).

Kember, D. (1989). A longitudinal process model of drop out from distance education. *The Journal of Higher Education, 60*(3), 278–301. doi:10.2307/1982251

Kester, L., Kirschner, P., & Corbalan, G. (2005). Learner control over information presentation in powerful electronic learning environments. In Verschaffel, L., De Corte, E., Kanselaar, G., & Valcke, M. (Eds.), *Powerful environments for promoting deep conceptual and strategic learning* (pp. 199–212). Leuven, Belgium: Leuven University Press.

Killen, L. (1989). Reflecting on reflective teaching. *Journal of Teacher Education, 40*(2), 49–52. doi:10.1177/002248718904000209

Kirkwood, A., & Price, L. (2005). Learners and learning in the 21st century: What do we know about students' attitudes and experiences of ICT that will help us design courses? *Studies in Higher Education, 30*(3), 257–274. doi:10.1080/03075070500095689

Kiser, A. I. T., Porter, T., & Vequist, D. (2010). Employee monitoring and ethics: Can they co-exist? *International Journal of Digital Literacy and Digital Competence, 1*(4), 30–45. doi:10.4018/jdldc.2010100104

Knežević-Florić, O. (2008). Lifelong leaning as a basis of the sustainable development concept. In Popov, J., Wolhuter, C., Leutwyler, B., Kysilka, M., & Ogunleye, J. (Eds.), *Comparative education, teacher training, education policy and social inclusion* (pp. 199–203). Sofia, Bulgaria: Bureau for Educational Services, Bulgarian Comparative Education Society.

Knight, J. (1997). Internationalisation of higher education: A conceptual framework. In Knight, J., & de Wit, H. (Eds.), *Internationalisation of higher education in Asia Pacific countries* (pp. 5–19). Amsterdam, The Netherlands: European Association for International Education.

Knowles, M. (1984). *Andragogy in action: Applying modern principles of adult education*. San Francisco, CA: Jossey-Bass.

Knowles, M., Holton, E., & Swanson, R. (1998). *The adult learner* (5th ed.). Houston, TX: Gulf Publishing.

Knowles, M. S. (1975). *Self-directed learning: A guide for learners and teachers*. Englewood Cliffs, NJ: Prentice Hall.

Knowles, M. S., Holten, E. F. III, & Swanson, R. A. (2005). *The adult learner* (6th ed.). Amsterdam, The Netherlands: Elsevier.

Koc, M. (2005). Individual learner differences in web-based learning environments: From cognitive, affective and social-cultural perspectives. *Turkish Online Journal of Distance Education, 6*(4), 12–22.

Koh, J. H. L., Herring, S. C., & Hew, K. F. (2010). Project-based learning and student knowledge construction during asynchronous online discussion. *The Internet and Higher Education, 13*, 284–291. doi:10.1016/j.iheduc.2010.09.003

Kolb, A. Y., & Kolb, D. A. (1984). Learning styles and learning spaces. Enhancing experiential learning in higher education. *Academy of Management Learning & Education, 4*(2), 193–212. doi:10.5465/AMLE.2005.17268566

Kolb, D. A. (1984). *Experiential learning: Experience as the source of learning and development*. Upper Saddle River, NJ: Prentice Hall.

Koller, M., Grütter, R., Peltenburg, M., Fischer, J. E., & Steurer, J. (2001). *Use of the Internet by medical doctors in Switzerland*. Retrieved August 20, 2011, from http://www.smw.ch/docs/pdf200x/2001/17/smw-09719.pdf

Koohang, A. (2009). Learner-centred model for blended learning design. *International Journal of Innovation and Learning, 6*(1), 76–91. doi:10.1504/IJIL.2009.021685

Kottamp, R. (1990). Means of facilitating reflection. *Education and Urban Society, 22*(2), 182–203. doi:10.1177/0013124590022002005

Kraan, W. (2007). *No one standard will suit all*. Retrieved from http://metadata.cetis.ac.uk/content/20030513175232

Krug, S. (2000). *Don't make me think: A common sense approach to web usability*. New York, NY: ACM Press.

Kurilovas, E. (2007). Digital library of educational resources and services: Evaluation of components. *Informacijos Mokslai, 42-43*, 69–77.

Kwan, P., & Ng, P. (1999). Quality indicators in higher education - comparing Hong Kong and China's students. *Managerial Auditing Journal, 14*(1-2), 20–27. doi:10.1108/02686909910245964

Labbo, L. D., & Reinking, D. (1999). Negotiating the multiple realities of technology in literacy research and instruction. *Reading Research Quarterly, 34*(4), 478–492. doi:10.1598/RRQ.34.4.5

LaBoskey, V. K. (1994). *Development of reflective practice: a study of preservice teachers*. New York, NY: Teachers College.

LaDuke, B. (2008). Knowledge creation in collective intelligence. In Tovey, M. (Ed.), *Collective intelligence: Creating a prosperous world at peace* (pp. 65–74). Oakton, VA: Earth Intelligence Network.

Landrum, T. J., & McDuffie, K. A. (2008). Learning styles in the age of differentiated instruction. *Exceptionality, 8*, 6–17.

Lankshear, C., & Knobel, M. (2003). *New literacies: Changing knowledge and classroom learning*. Buckingham, UK: Open University Press.

Larrosa, J. (2004). *Linguagem e educação depois de Babel*. Belo Horizonte, Brazil: Autêntica.

Larusson, J. A., & Alterman, R. (2009). Wikis to support the "collaborative" part of collaborative learning. *Computer-Supported Collaborative Learning, 4*, 371–402. doi:10.1007/s11412-009-9076-6

Lasley, T. (1990). Editorial. *Journal of Teacher Education, 40*(2), 2–8.

Latour, B. (1988). *The pasteurization of France*. Cambridge, MA: Harvard University Press.

Latour, B. (1992). Where are the missing masses? The sociology of a few mundane artifacts. In Bijker, W. E., & Law, J. (Eds.), *Shaping technology/building society: Studies in sociotechnical change* (pp. 225–258). Cambridge, MA: MIT Press.

Latour, B., & Wolgar, S. (1986). *Laboratory life – the Construction of Scientific Facts*. Princeton, NJ: Princeton University Press.

Lave, J. (2008). Everyday life and learning. In Murphy, P., & McCormick, R. (Eds.), *Knowledge and practice: Representations and identities* (pp. 3–14). London, UK: Sage.

Law, J. (1999). After ANT: Complexity, naming and topology. In Law, J., & Hassard, J. (Eds.), *Actor network theory and after* (pp. 1–14). Oxford, UK: Blackwell Publishers.

Law, N., Pelgrum, W. J., & Plomp, T. (2008). *Pedagogy and ICT use in schools around the world*. New York, NY: Springer. doi:10.1007/978-1-4020-8928-2

Lawson, K. G. (2005). Using eclectic digital resources to enhance instructional methods for adult learners. *OCLC Systems & Services*, *21*(1), 49–60. doi:10.1108/10650750510578154

Leach, D., Coyle, C. A., & Cole, P. G. (2003). Fluency in the classroom. In Waugh, R. F. (Ed.), *On the forefront of educational psychology*. New York, NY: Nova Science.

Learning Management Architectures, C. L. I. X. (2008). *Micro-framework designed for creating micro-sites and small web applications*. Retrieved from http://code.google.com/p/clix-framework/

Lechner, J. P. (2010). Employers: Be careful when checking employees' social networking sites. *Greenberg Traurig, LLP*. Retrieved August 3, 2011, from http://www.gtleblog.com/ 2010/04/articles/privacy/employers-be-careful-when-checking-employees-social-networking-sites/

Lee, L. (2002). Enhancing learners' communication skills through synchronous electronic interaction and task-based instruction. *Foreign Language Annals*, *35*(1), 16–24. doi:10.1111/j.1944-9720.2002.tb01829.x

Leu, D. J. (2002). The new literacies: Research on reading instruction with the Internet and other digital technologies. In Farstrup, A. E., & Samuels, S. J. (Eds.), *What research has to say about reading instruction* (3rd ed., pp. 310–337). Newark, DE: International Reading Association.

Levinsen, K. (2006). Watch out – the power users are coming. *International Electronic Journal of E-learning*, *5*(1), 79–86.

Levinsen, K. (2010). Effective use of ICT for inclusive learning of young children with reading and writing difficulties. In Mukerji, S., & Tripathi, P. (Eds.), *Cases on interactive technology environments and transnational collaboration* (pp. 56–73). Hershey, PA: IGI Global.

Levinsen, K., & Sørensen, B. H. (2008). *It, faglig læring og pædagogisk videnledelse*. Copenhagen, Denmark: The Danish University School of Education. Retrieved from http://junior-pc-koerekort.dk/Rapport_PIL_2008.pdf

Lewin, K. (1951). *Teoria e sperimentazione in psicologia sociale*. Bologna, Italy: Il Mulino.

Li, Q., & Edmonds, K. A. (2005). Mathematics and At-Risk Adult Learners. *International Journal of Research on Technology in Education*, *38*(2), 143–166.

Lieb, S. (1999). *Principles of adult learning*. Retrieved from http://www.hcc.hawaii.edu/intrnet/committees/facdevcom/guidebk/teachtip/adults-2.htm

Liebowitz, M. (2011). Facebook apps leak private info again. *Security News Daily*. Retrieved August 9, 2011, from http://www.securitynewsdaily.com/facebook-apps-leak-private-info-again-0780/

Lindsley, O. R. (1991). Precision teaching's unique legacy from B. F. Skinner. *Journal of Behavioral Education*, *1*, 253–266. doi:10.1007/BF00957007

Lin, H., & Kelsey, K. D. (2009). Building a networked environment in wikis: The evolving phases of a collaborative learning in a wikibook project. *Journal of Educational Computing Research*, *40*, 145–169. doi:10.2190/EC.40.2.a

Lin, Q. (2008). Student satisfactions in four mixed courses in elementary teacher education program. *The Internet and Higher Education*, *11*(1), 53–59. doi:10.1016/j.iheduc.2007.12.005

Lin, S., & Overbaugh, R. C. (2007). The effect of student choice of online discussion format on tiered achievement and student satisfaction. *Journal of Research on Technology in Education*, *39*(4), 399–415.

LinkedIn. (2011). *About us*. Retrieved August 2, 2011, from http://press.linkedin.com/about

Liston, D., & Zeichner, K. (1996). *Culture and teaching.* Mahwah, NJ: Lawrence Erlbaum.

Livingstone, D. (2001). *Adults' Informal Learning.* Toronto, ON, Canada: University of Toronto. Retrieved from http://www.oise.utoronto.ca/oise/Home/index.html

Livingstone, S., & Bowill, M. (2001). *Children and their changing media environment: A European comparative study.* Mahwah, NJ: Erlbaum.

Love, S., & Scoble, R. (2006). Developing a quality assurance metric: A panoptic view. *Active Learning in Higher Education, 7*(2), 129–141. doi:10.1177/1469787406064749

LowTax.net. (2008). *Dubai e-commerce special feature - offshore e-commerce: Ready for action?* Retrieved from http://lowtax.net/lowtax/html/dubai/jdbecom.html

Luehmann, A. L., & Tinelli, L. (2008). Teacher professional identity development with social networking technologies: Learning reform through blogging. *Educational Media International, 45*(4), 323–333. doi:10.1080/09523980802573263

MacGregor, R., & Vrazalic, L. (2007). *E-Commerce in regional small to medium enterprises.* Hershey, PA: IGI Global. doi:10.4018/978-1-59904-123-0

MacMillan, D. (2008). Cyberscams befriend social networks. *Bloomberg Businessweek.* Retrieved August 1, 2011, from http://www.businessweek.com/print/technology/Content/nov2008/tc20081119_974324.htm

Maconato, G. (2008). *Usi didattici delle tecnologie: quale stato dell'arte.* Trento, Italy: Erikson.

Maddux, C. D., Johnson, D. L., & Willis, J. W. (1997). *Educational computing, learning with tomorrow's technologies 2/E.* Needham Heights, MA: Allyn and Bacon.

Malyn-Smith, J. (2004). Power users of technology - Who are they? Where are they going? Why does it matter? *UN Chronicle Online Edition, 2,* 58. Retrieved from http://www.un.org/Pubs/chronicle/2004/issue2/0204p58.asp

Marcelo, C. (2008). Evaluación de la calidad para programas completos de formación docente a través de estrategias de aprendizaje abierto y a distancia. *Revista de Educación a Distancia, 8*(7), 2–6.

Marsh, G. E. (2003). Blended instruction: Adapting conventional instruction for large classes. *Online Journal of Distance Learning Administration, 6*(4). Retrieved from http://www.westga.edu/~distance/ojdla/.

Martin, A. (2006). A European framework for digital literacy. *Digital Kompetanse, 2,* 151–161.

Martinez, M. (2003). High attrition rates in e-learning: Challenges, predictors, and solutions. *The eLearning Developer's Journal.*

Martyn, M., & Bash, L. (2002, October 9-12). Creating new meanings in leading education. In *Proceedings of the Twenty-Second National Conference on Alternative and External Degree Programs for Adults*, Pittsburgh, PA.

Massachusetts Department of Elementary & Secondary Education. (2008). *School reform in the new millennium: Preparing all children for 21st century success: Recommendations of the 21st century skills task force.* Malden, MA: Massachusetts Department of Elementary & Secondary Education.

Mayer, R. E. (2001). *Multimedia learning.* Cambridge, UK: Cambridge University Press.

Mayer, R. E., & Moreno, R. (1998). A split-attention effect in multimedia learning: evidence for dual processing systems in working memory. *Journal of Educational Psychology, 90,* 312–320. doi:10.1037/0022-0663.90.2.312

McDowell, M., & Morda, D. (2011). Socializing securely: Using social networking services. *United States Computer Emergency Readiness Team.* Retrieved August 8, 2011, from http://www.us-cert.gov/reading_room/safe_social_networking.pdf

McKinney, V. R., Wilson, D. D., Brooks, N., O'Leary-Kelly, A., & Hargrave, B. (2008). Women and men in the IT profession. *Communications of the ACM, 51*(2), 81–84. doi:10.1145/1314215.1340919

McNamara, D. (1990). Research on teachers' thinking: its contribution to educating student teachers to think critically. *Journal of Education for Teaching, 16*(2), 147–160. doi:10.1080/0260747900160203

Media Council for Children and Young People. (2003). *SAFT.* Retrieved from http://www.medieraadet.dk/html/saft

Menon, M., Rama, K., Lakshmi, K., & Bhat, D. (2007). *Quality indicators for teacher education*. Vancouver, BC, Canada: Commonwealth of Learning. Retrieved from http://www.col.org/resources/publications/Pages/detail.aspx?PID=244#

Merriam, S., & Caffarella, R. (1999). *Learning in adulthood 2/E*. San Francisco, CA: Jossey-Bass.

Meskill, C., & Anthony, N. (2005). Foreign language learning with CMC: forms of on-line instructional discourse in a hybrid Russian class. *System, 33*(1), 89–105. doi:10.1016/j.system.2005.01.001

Mezirow, J. (1990). *Fostering critical reflection in adulthood*. San Francisco, CA: Jossey-Bass.

Mezirow, J. (1991). *Transformative dimensions of adult learning*. San Francisco, CA: Jossey-Bass.

Mezirow, J. (2003). *Apprendimento e trasformazione*. Milano, Italy: Cortina Editore.

Milheim, K. (2007). Influence of technology on informal learning. *Adult Basic Education and Literacy Journal, 1*(1).

Mittermeir, R. T., Bischof, E., & Hodnigg, K. (2010). Teaching kids to teach their teachers. In J. Hromkovic, R. Kralovic, & J. Vahrenhold (Eds.), *Proceedings of the Fourth International Conference on Teaching Fundamentals Concepts of Informatics* (LNCS 5941, pp. 143-154).

Molero, D., & Ruiz, J. (2005). La evaluación de la docencia universitaria: Dimensiones y variables más relevantes. *Revista de Investigación Educativa, 23*(1), 57-84.

Molyneaux, T., & Brumley, J. (2007). The use of wikis as a management tool to facilitate group project work. In *Proceedings of the AAEE Conference*, Melbourne, Australia.

Monroe, B. (2004). *Crossing the digital divide: Race, writing, and technology in the classroom*. New York, NY: Teachers College Press.

Moran, T. J., & Payne, M. (1998). Humanizing the integration of technology. *New Directions for Community Colleges, 101*, 43–47. doi:10.1002/cc.10105

Moreno, R., & Mayer, R. E. (2000). A coherence effect in multimedia learning: the case for minimizing irrelevant sounds in the design of multimedia messages. *Journal of Educational Psychology, 92*, 117–125. doi:10.1037/0022-0663.92.1.117

Morris, M. G., & Venkatesh, V. (2000). Age differences in technology adoption decisions. *Personnel Psychology, 53*(2), 375–403. doi:10.1111/j.1744-6570.2000.tb00206.x

Munby, H., & Russell, T. (1989). Educating the reflective teacher: an essay review of two books by Donald Schon. *Journal of Curriculum Studies, 21*(1), 71–80. doi:10.1080/0022027890210106

Murnane, R., & Levy, F. (2004). *The new division of labor: How computers are changing the way we work*. Princeton, NJ: Princeton University Press and Russell Sage Foundation.

Murphy, R. (2003). *English grammar in use*. Cambridge, UK: Cambridge University Press.

Nagata, N. (1996). Computer vs. workbook instruction in second language acquisition. *CALICO Journal, 14*(1), 53–75.

Nagata, N. (1997). An experimental comparison of deductive and inductive feedback generated by a simple parser. *System, 25*(4), 515–534. doi:10.1016/S0346-251X(97)00052-3

Naismith, L., Lee, B.-H., & Pilkington, R. M. (2010). Collaborative learning with a wiki: Differences in perceived usefulness in two contexts of use. *Journal of Computer Assisted Learning, 26*, 1–15.

Nash, G. (1970). Teach Your Children [Recorded by Crosby, Stills, Nash, & Young]. On *Déjà vu* [Record]. New York, NY: Atlantic Records.

National Center for Research in Vocational Education (1987). *Report on education*. Berkley, CA: National Center for Research in Vocational Education. Retrieved from http://vocserve.berkeley.edu/

Neumann, D. L., & Hood, M. (2009). The effects of using a wiki on student engagement and learning of report writing skills in a university statistics course. *Australasian Journal of Educational Technology, 25*, 382–398.

New London Group. (1996). A pedagogy of multiliteracies: Designing social futures. *Harvard Educational Review, 66*(1), 60–92.

Newmann, F., & Wehlage, G. (1993). Five standards of authentic instruction. *Educational Leadership, 55*(2), 72–75.

Nick. (2008). *Top 10 countries censoring the Web.* Retrieved from http://www.dailybits.com/top-10-countries-censoring-the-web/

Nilsen, J. (2000). *Designing web usability: The practice of simplicity.* Indianapolis, IN: New Riders Publishing.

Noffke, S., & Brennan, M. (1988, April). *The dimensions of reflection: a conceptual and contextual analysis.* Paper presented at the Annual Meeting of the AERA, New Orleans, LA.

Noordhoff, K., & Kleinfeld, J. (1988). Rethinking the rhetoric of 'reflective inquiry' in teacher education programs. In Waxman, H., Freiberg, H., Vaughan, J., & Weil, M. (Eds.), *Images of reflection in teacher education* (pp. 27–29). Reston, VA: Association of Teacher Educators.

Norlander-Case, K., Reagan, T., & Case, C. (1999). *The professional teacher: preparation and nurturance of the reflective practitioner.* San Francisco, CA: Jossey-Bass.

Norton, L., Richardson, J. T. E., Hartley, J., Newstead, S., & Mayes, J. (2005). Teachers' beliefs and practices concerning teaching in higher education. *Higher Education, 50*(4), 537–571. doi:10.1007/s10734-004-6363-z

Nuzzaci, A. (2004). *Profili di competenza e trasformazioni sociali. Insegnare ed apprendere,* Cosenza, Italy: Lionello Giordano.

Nuzzaci, A. (Ed.). (2004). *Profili di competenza e trasformazioni sociali. Insegnare e apprendere.* Cosenza, Italy: Lionello Giordano.

Nuzzaci, A. (2006). Per la costruzione di una banca dati italiana dei progetti di ricerca internazionali. In C. LANEVE, C. GEMMA (EDS.), *La ricerca pedagogica in Europa. Modelli e temi a confronto* (pp. 375-387). Atti del XXII Convegno Nazionale della Società Italiana di Pedagogia (SIPED), Cassino, 24-26 maggio 2006, Lecce. Italy: Pensa Multimedia.

Nuzzaci, A. (2007). For a community of the European educational research. *Revista Complutense de Educación, 18*(1), 217–232.

Nuzzaci, A. (2009, December 11-13). Il Progetto LEONARDO REFLECT. Competenze riflessive e processi valutativi: per un'analisi dell'azione dentro l'azione. In G. Domenici & R. Semeraro (Eds.), *Le nuove sfide della ricerca didattica tra saperi, comunità sociali e culture* (pp. 35-51). Atti del Convegno SIRD (Società Italiana di Ricerca Didattica), Roma, Italy. Roma, Italy: Monolite.

Nuzzaci, A. (2009). La riflessività nella progettazione educativa: verso una riconcettualizzazione delle routine. *Giornale Italiano della Ricerca Educativa, 1*(2-3), 59–76.

Nuzzaci, A. (2009). La riflessività nella pedagogia della progettazione: il ruolo delle routine. In Paparella, N. (Ed.), *Il progetto educativo* (Vol. 3, pp. 71–81). Roma, Italy: Armando.

Nuzzaci, A. (2011, December 2-3). La dimensione transculturale della didattica (e della ricerca). In L. Galliani (Ed.), *Il docente universitario: Una professione tra ricerca, didattica e governance degli Atenei: Atti dell'VIII Biennale Internazionale sulla Didattica Universitaria* (Vol. 2, pp. 263-286). Lecce, Italy: Pensa Multimedia.

Nuzzaci, A. (2011). Pratiche riflessive, riflessività e insegnamento. *Studium Educationis, 12*(3), 9–27.

O'Reilly, T. (2007). What is Web 2.0: Design patterns and business models for the next generation of software. *Communications & Strategies, 65*(1), 17–37.

Oblinger, D. (2003). Boomers, gen-exers and millennials: Understanding the new students. In *Proceedings of the EDUCAUSE Annual Conference, 38,* 36–43.

Oblinger, D., & Oblinger, J. (2005). Educating the net generation. In *Proceedings of the EDUCAUSE Annual Conference.* Retrieved from http://www.educause.edu/educatingthenetgen/

Oduwole, A. A., & Oyewumi, O. (2010). Accessibility and use of web-based electronic resources by physicians in a psychiatric institution in Nigeria. *Program, 44*(2), 109–121.

OECD. (1997). *Electronic commerce: Opportunities and challenges for government.* Paris, France: Organisation for Economic Co-operation and Development.

Ogoegbulem, S. (2010). *Nigeria's SAT-1 replacement next year.* Retrieved fromhttp://www.itnewsafrica.com/2010/11/nigeria%E2%80%99s-sat-1-replacement-next-year/

Okereke, G. E. (1993). Literacy as a redemptive factor in Nigerian politics in Chinua Achebe's "A Man of The People" and "Anthills of the Savannah". In Aboderin, A. O., (Eds.), *Literacy and reading in Nigeria (Vol. 6).* Calabar, Nigeria: Reading Association of Nigeria.

Oliver, M., & Trigwell, K. (2005). Can 'blended learning' be redeemed? *E-learning, 2*(1), 17–26.

Onukaogu, C. E. (2008). *Biliteracy and the attainment of sustainable development in multilingual Nigeria.* Ibadan, Nigeria: CELL.

Onwuegbuzie, A. J., Witcher, A. E., Collins, K. M. T., Filer, J. D., Wiedmaier, C. D., & Moore, C. W. (2007). Students' perceptions of characteristics of effective college teachers: A validity study of a teaching evaluation form using a mixed-methods analysis, *American Educational Research Journal, 44*(1), 113–160. doi:10.3102/0002831206298169

Ormrod, J. (2004). *Human learning* (4th ed., p. 456). Upper Saddle River, NJ: Prentice Hall.

Ornstein, A. C., & Hunkins, F. P. (1998). *Curriculum: Foundations, principles, and issues* (3rd ed.). Needham Heights, MA: Allyn and Bacon.

Osterman, K. F. (1990). Reflective practice: a new agenda for education. *Education and Urban Society, 22*(2), 133–152. doi:10.1177/0013124590022002002

Paas, F. G., Renkl, A., & Sweller, J. (2004). Cognitive load theory: instructional implications of the interaction between information structures and cognitive architecture. *Instructional Science, 32*, 1–8. doi:10.1023/B:TRUC.0000021806.17516.d0

Padilla, A. M. (2006). Second language learning: Issues in research and teaching. In Alexander, P. A., & Wine, P. H. (Eds.), *Handbook of educational psychology* (2nd ed.). Mahwah, NJ: Lawrence Erlbaum.

Papert, S. (1987). Microworlds: Transforming education. In R. W. Lawler & M. Yazdani (Eds.), *Artificial intelligence and education, vol. 1: Learning environments & tutoring systems* (pp. 79-95). Norwood, NJ: Ablex.

Papert, S. (1993). *Mindstorms: Children, computers and powerful ideas.* Boston, MA: Basic Books.

Paquay, L., Altet, M., Charlier, E., & Perrenoud, P. (Eds.). (1996). *Former des enseignants professionnels. Quelles stratégies? Quelles compétences?*Bruxelles, Belgium: De Boeck.

Parker, K. R., & Chao, J. T. (2007). Wiki as a teaching tool. *Interdisciplinary Journal of Knowledge and Learning Objects, 3*, 57–72.

Parker, S. (1999). *Reflective teaching in the postmodern world.* Buckingham, UK: Open University Press.

Pascual, I. (2007). Análisis de la Satisfacción del Alumno con la Docencia Recibida: Un Estudio con Modelos Jerárquicos Lineales. *RELIEVE, 13*(1), 127–138.

Pedersen, J. E., & Yerrick, R. K. (2000). Technology in science teacher education: A survey of current uses and desired knowledge among science educators. *Journal of Science Teacher Education, 11*(2), 131–153. doi:10.1023/A:1009468808876

Pence, H. E. (2009). Teaching in the 21st century. *Journal of Educational Technology Systems, 38*(2), 103–110. doi:10.2190/ET.38.2.c

Pennypacker, H. S., Gutierrez, A., & Lindsley, O. R. (2003). *Handbook of the standard celeration chart.* Cambridge, UK: Cambridge Center for Behavioral Studies.

Pennypacker, H. S., Heckler, J. B., & Pennypacker, S. F. (1977). The personalized learning center: A university wide system of personalized instruction. In Brigham, T. A., & Catania, A. C. (Eds.), *Handbook of applied behavioral research* (pp. 591–617). New York, NY: Irvington.

Perrenoud, P. (1994). *La formation des enseignants entre théorie et pratique.* Paris, France: L'Harmattan.

Perrenoud, P. (2001). *Développer la pratique réflexive dans le métier d'enseignant.* Paris, France: ESF.

Perry, W. G. (1970). *Forms of intellectual and ethical development in the college years: A scheme.* New York, NY: Holt, Rinehart, and Winston.

Pescheux, M. (2007). *Analyse des pratiques enseignantes en FLE/S. Mémento pour une ergonomie didactique du FLE.* Paris, France: L'Harmattan.

Pew Internet & American Life Project Surveys. (2010). *Typical daily Internet activities of adult Internet users* (U.S. Census Bureau Publication No. 1159). Retrieved August 3, 2011, from http://www.census.gov/compendia/statab/2011/tables/11s1159.pdf

Piaget, J. (1973). *To understand is to invent: The future of education*. New York, NY: Grossman.

Piaget, J. (1974). *La prise de conscience*. Paris, France: PUF.

Piaget, J. (1974). *Réussir et comprendre*. Paris, France: PUF.

Piaget, J. (1977). *Recherche sur l'abstraction réfléchissante*. Paris, France: PUF.

Pingdom. (2011). *Internet 2010 in numbers*. Retrieved August 2, 2011, from http://royal.pingdom.com/2011/01/12/internet-2010-in-numbers/

Pinto, M. (2005). A busca da comunicação na sociedade multi-ecrãs: Perspectiva ecológica. *Comunicar, 25*, 259–264.

Plass, J. L., Chun, D. M., Mayer, R. E., & Leutner, D. (1998). Supporting visual and verbal learning preferences in a second language multimedia learning environment. *Journal of Educational Psychology, 90*, 25–36. doi:10.1037/0022-0663.90.1.25

Polanyi, M. (1968). Logic and psychology. *Journal of the American Psychoanalytic Association, 23*, 27–43.

Pollard, A. (2002). *Reflective teaching: effective and evidence-informed professional practice*. London, UK: Continuum.

Posner, G. J. (1996). *Field experience: a guide to reflective teaching*. White Plains, NY: Longman.

Pozzali, A., & Ferri, P. (2010). The media diet of university students in Italy: An exploratory research. *International Journal of Digital Literacy and Digital Competence, 1*(2), 1–10. doi:10.4018/jdldc.2010040101

Prensky, M. (2001). *Digital natives, digital immigrants on the horizon*. Bradford, UK: MCB University Press.

Prensky, M. (2001). Digital natives, digital immigrants, part II: Do they really think differently? *Horizon, 9*(6). doi:10.1108/10748120110424843

Prensky, M. (2009). H. sapiens digital: From digital immigrants and digital natives to digital wisdom. *Innovate, 5*(3).

Prime, G. (1998). Tailoring assessment of technological literacy learning. *Journal of Technology Studies, 24*(1), 18–23.

Process, B. (1999). *European higher education area*. Retrieved from http://www.bolognaprocess.it

Quellmalz, E. S., & Kozma, R. (2003). Designing assessments of learning with technology. *Assessment in Education, 10*(3), 389–405. doi:10.1080/0969594032000148208

Quemada, J., de Miguel, T., Pavon, S., Huecas, G., Robles, T., Salvachua, J., et al. (2005). ISABEL: An application for real time collaboration with a flexible floor control. In *Proceedings of the International Conference on Collaborative Computing: Networking, Applications and Worksharing* (p. 9).

Rabardel, P. (2005). Instrument subjectif et développement di pouvoir d'agir. In Rabardel, P., & Patré, P. (Eds.), *Modéles du sujet pour la conception; dialectique activités développement* (pp. 11–29). Toulose, France: Octarés.

Ramsden, P. (1991). A performance indicator of teaching quality in higher education: The Course Experience Questionnaire. *Studies in Higher Education, 16*(2), 129–150. doi:10.1080/03075079112331382944

Rao, R. (2009). Digital divide: Issues facing adult learners. *Canadian Center of Science and Education Journal, 2*(1), 132–136.

Rashid, F. Y. (2011). *Network breaches, social media, smartphones worry administrators: Survey*. Retrieved August 4, 2011, from http://www.eweek.com/c/a/Security/Network-Breaches-Social-Media-Smartphones-Worry-Administrators-Survey-430279/

Reagan, T., Case, C., & Brubacher, J. (2000). *Becoming a reflective educator: how to build a culture of inquiry in the schools*. Thousand Oaks, CA: Corwin Press.

Reid, B. (1993). But we're doing it already! Exploring a response to the concept of reflective practice in order to improve its facilitation. *Nurse Education Today, 13*, 305–309. doi:10.1016/0260-6917(93)90058-A

Reinking, D. (1998). Synthesizing technological transformations of literacy in a post-typographic world. In Reinking, D., McKenna, M. C., Labbo, L. D., & Kieffer, R. D. (Eds.), *Handbook of literacy and technology: Transformations in a post-typographic world* (pp. xi–xxx). Mahwah, NJ: Lawrence Erlbaum.

Report, A. (2008). *Aho report on EU high-tech research: A wake-up call for innovation in Europe.* Brussels, Belgium: European Commission.

Ribble, M. S., & Bailey, G. (2005). Developing ethical direction. *Learning and Leading with Technology, 32*(7), 36–38.

Ribble, M. S., Bailey, G. D., & Ross, T. W. (2004). Digital citizenship: Addressing appropriate technology behavior. *Learning and Leading with Technology, 32*(1), 6–12.

Ritchie, J., & Wilson, D. (2000). *Teacher narrative as critical inquiry.* New York, NY: Teachers College.

Rivoltella, P. C. (2005). *Media education: Fondamenti didattici e prospettive di ricerca.* Brescia, Italy: La Scuola.

Rivoltella, P. C. (2008). From Media Education to Digital Literacy: A Paradigm Change? In Rivoltella, P. C. (Ed.), *Digital literacy: Tools and methodologies for information society* (pp. 217–229). Hershey, PA: IGI Global.

Roblyer, M. D., & Knezek, G. A. (2003). New millennium research for educational technology: A call for a national research agenda. *Journal of Research on Technology in Education, 36*(1), 60–71.

Rogoff, B. (2003). *The cultural nature of human development.* Oxford, UK: Oxford University Press.

Rosenberg, D. (2005). *Towards the digital library: Findings of and investigation to establish the current status of university libraries in Africa.* Retrieved June 6, 2005, from http://www.inasp.info/pubs/INASP/digilalhb.pdf

Rummler, G. A., & Brache, A. P. (1988). The systems view of human performance. *Training (New York, N.Y.), 25*(9), 45–53.

Ryberg, T. (2007). Patchworking as a metaphor for learning: Understanding youth, learning and technology. *E-Learning Lab Publication, 10.*

Rychen, D., & Salganik, L. (2003). *Key Competencies for a Successful Life and Well-Functioning Society.* Cambridge, MA: Hogrefe & Huber.

Saade, R. G., & Kira, D. (2007). Mediating the impact of technology use on perceived ease of use by anxiety. *Computers & Education, 49,* 1189–1204. doi:10.1016/j.compedu.2006.01.009

Saint-Arnaud, Y. (1992). *Connaître par l'action.* Montréal, QC, Canada: Presses de l'Université de Montréal.

Sangani, K. (2010). Who owns your personal data? *Engineering & Technology, 5*(11), 28–29. doi:10.1049/et.2010.1103

Sarramona, J. (2004). *Factores e indicadores de calidad en la educación.* Barcelona, Spain: Editorial Octaedro.

Scanlan, J. M., Care, W. D., & Udod, S. (2002). Unravelling the unknowns of reflection in classroom teaching. *Journal of Advanced Nursing, 38*(2), 136–143. doi:10.1046/j.1365-2648.2002.02157.x

Schaffert, S., Bischof, D., Bürger, T., Gruber, A., Hilzensauer, W., & Schaffert, S. (2006, June 11-14). Learning with semantic wikis. In *Proceedings of the First SemWiki Workshop - From Wiki to Semantics, co-located with the 3rd Annual European Semantic Web Conference,* Budva, Montenegro.

Schön, D. (1983). *The reflective practitioner: how professionals think in action.* New York, NY: Basic Books.

Schön, D. (1987). *Educating the reflective practitioner: toward a new design for teaching and learning in the professions.* San Francisco, CA: Jossey Bass.

Scott, P. A. (1993, November). A comparative study of students' learning experiences in intensive and semester-length courses. In *Proceedings of the North American Association of Summer Sessions,* Portland, OR.

Scott, P. A. (1995). Learning experiences in intensive and semester-length classes: Student voices and. experiences. *College Student Journal, 29,* 207–213.

Scott, P. A. (1996). Attributes of high-quality intensive course learning experiences: Student voices and experiences. *College Student Journal, 30*(1), 69–77.

Scott, P. A., & Conrad, C. F. (1991). *A critique of intensive courses and an agenda for research.* Madison, WI: University of Wisconsin. (ERIC Document Reproduction Service No. ED337087).

Scott, P. A., & Conrad, C. F. (1992). A critique of intensive courses and an agenda for research. In Smart, J. C. (Ed.), *Higher education: Handbook of theory and research.* New York, NY: Agathon Press.

Selfe, C. L., & Hilligoss, S. (1994). *Literacy and computers: The complications of teaching and learning with technology.* New York, NY: Modern Language Association.

Selwyn, N., Potter, J., & Cranmer, S. (2009). Primary pupils' use of information and communication technologies at school and home. *British Journal of Educational Technology, 40*(5), 919–932. doi:10.1111/j.1467-8535.2008.00876.x

Seng, J., & Lin, S. (2004). A mobility and knowledge-centric e-learning application design method. *International Journal of Innovation and Learning, 1*(3), 293–311. doi:10.1504/IJIL.2004.004885

Serdyukov, P., Subbotin, I., & Serdyukova, N. (2003). Short-term intensive college instruction: What are the benefits for adult learners? *Technology and Teacher Education Annual, 2*, 1550–1552.

Settlage, J., Odom, A. L., & Pedersen, J. E. (2004). Uses of technology by science education professors: Comparisons with teachers: Uses and the current versus desired technology knowledge gap. *Contemporary Issues in Technology & Teacher Education, 4*(3).

Shave, N. P. (2002). Roaming between satellite and terrestrial networks. In *Proceedings of the Third International Conference on 3G Mobile Communication Technologies* (pp. 58-63).

Sheehy, G. (2008). The wiki as knowledge repository: Using a wiki in a community of practice to strengthen K-12 education. *TechTrends, 52*(6), 55–60. doi:10.1007/s11528-008-0219-9

Siegle, D. (2004). The merging of literacy and technology in the 21st century: A bonus for gifted education. *Technology (Elmsford, N.Y.), 27*(2), 32–35.

Singh, P., & Martin, L. R. (2004). Accelerated degree programs: Assessing student attitudes and opinions. *Journal of Education for Business, 79*(5), 299. doi:10.3200/JOEB.79.5.299-305

Skiba, D. J. (2010). Digital wisdom: A necessary faculty competency? *Nursing Education Perspectives, 31*(4), 251–253.

Skinner, B. F. (1938). *The behavior of organisms.* Upper Saddle River, NJ: Prentice Hall.

Skinner, B. F. (1968). *The technology of teaching.* New York, NY: Appleton-Century-Crofts.

Sloffer, S. J., Dueber, B., & Duffy, T. M. (1999). Using asynchronous conferencing to promote critical thinking: two implementations in higher education. In *Proceedings of the 32nd Hawaiian International Conference on Systems Science,* Maui, HI.

Smith, C., & Kanalley, C. (2010). Fired over Facebook: 13 posts that got people CANNED. *Huffington Post.* Retrieved August 1, 2011, from http://www.huffingtonpost.com/2010/07/26/fired-over-facebook-posts_n_659170.html#s115707&title=Swiss_Woman_Caught

Smith, D., & Lovat, T. (1991). *Curriculum: action on reflection.* Wentworth Falls, Australia: Social Science Press.

Smyth, J. (1989). Developing and sustaining critical reflection in teacher education. *Journal of Teacher Education, 40*(2), 2–9. doi:10.1177/002248718904000202

So, H. J., & Brush, T. A. (2008). Student perceptions of collaborative learning, social presence and satisfaction in a blended learning environment: Relationships and critical factors. *Computers & Education, 51*(1), 318–336. doi:10.1016/j.compedu.2007.05.009

Soini, H. (2000, October 20-22). *Critical learning incident technique as a research method for studying student learning.* Paper presented at the Workshop on Qualitative Research in Psychology, Blaubeuren, Germany.

Sonwalkar, N. (2008). Adaptive individualisation: The next generation of online education. *Horizon, 16*(1), 44–47. doi:10.1108/10748120810853345

Sørensen, B. H. (1999). *Projektarbejde fra begyndertrinnet – medier og formidling.* Copenhagen, Denmark: Lærerhøjskole.

Sørensen, B. H., Audon, L., & Levinsen, K. (2010). *Skole 2.0.* Aarhus, Denmark: KLIM.

Sørensen, B. H., Hubert, B., Risgaard, J., & Kirkeby, G. (2004). *Virtuel Skole* (Tech. Rep. No. 153). Copenhagen, Denmark: Danmarks Pædagogiske Universitetsskole.

Sørensen, B. H., Jessen, C., & Olesen, B. R. (2002). *Børn på nettet- kommunikation og læring.* Copenhagen, Denmark: Gads Forlag.

Sørensen, B. H., Olesen, B. R., & Audon, L. (2001). *Det hele kører parallelt - de nye medier i børns hverdagsliv.* Copenhagen, Denmark: Gads Forlag.

Sparks-Langer, G., Simmons, J., Pasch, M., Colton, A., & Starko, A. (1990). Reflective pedagogical thinking: how can we promote it and measure it? *Journal of Teacher Education, 41*(4), 23–32. doi:10.1177/002248719004100504

Sponder, B. (2004). Technology and adult education: New tools for new experiences. In *Proceedings of the Adult Learning Colloquium: Current Issues in Adult Learning and Motivation,* Ljubljana, Slovenia (pp. 150-160).

Spradley, J. P. (1979). *The ethnographic interview.* New York, NY: Holt, Rinehart, and Winston.

Stald, G. (2009). *Globale medier – lokal unge. Institut for Medier, erkendelse, formidling.* Copenhagen, Denmark: Københavns Universitet. Retrieved from http://mef.ku.dk/

Steffensky, M., & Wilms, M. (2006). Chemisches Experimentieren im Sachunterricht – welche Impulse geben Schülerlabore und Lehrerfortbildungen? *Chemie konkret, 13*(1), 14-20.

Stein, D. S. (2009). How a novice online learner experiences transactional distance. *Quarterly Review of Distance Education, 10*(3), 305–311.

Stergioulas, L. K., Abbasi, M., Pitsilis, V., Constantine, M., et al. (2008). Satellite-enabled education for geographically isolated communities of farmers and maritime workers, The BASE² Project. In *Proceedings of the International Conference on Bridging the Digital Divide in Rural Communities: Practical Solutions and Policies,* Athens, Greece.

Stolle, E. (2008). Teachers, literacy & technology: Tensions, complexities. *National Reading Conference Yearbook, 57,* 56-69.

Stones, E. (1994). Reform in teacher education: the power and the pedagogy. *Journal of Teacher Education, 45*(4), 310–318. doi:10.1177/0022487194045004012

Strickland, J. (2011). Top ten social networking sites. *Discovery News.* Retrieved August 2, 2011 from http://news.discovery.com/tech/top-ten-social-networking-sites.html

Stroobants, H., Chambers, Ph., & Clarke, B. (Eds.). (2007). *Reflective journeys.* Leuven, Belgium: Belgium by Acco.

Study, S. A. (2011). *Medical practitioner.* Retrieved August 23, 2011, from http://www.sastudy.co.za/index.php?option=com_content&view=article&id=2109&Itemid=428

Sugarbroad, I. (1990). An OSI-based interoperability architecture for managing hybrid networks. *IEEE Communications Magazine, 28*(3), 61–69. doi:10.1109/35.52893

Sweller, J., & Chandler, P. (1994). Why some material is difficult to learn. *Cognition and Instruction, 12*(3), 185–233. doi:10.1207/s1532690xci1203_1

Tan, S. M., Ladyshewsky, R. K., & Gardner, P. (2010). Using blogging to promote clinical reasoning and metacognition in undergraduate physiotherapy fieldwork programs. *Australasian Journal of Educational Technology, 26*(3), 355–368.

Tapp, D. (n. d.). *Doctors and their continuing medical education: Interactions with the Internet.* Retrieved August 23, 2011, from http://www.mcnz.org.nz/portals/0/publications/summerstudentships/Dylan%20Tapp%20-%20Doctors%20and%20their%20Continuing%20Medical%20Education.pdf

Tardif, J. (1992). *Pour un enseignement stratégique: L'apport de la psychologie cognitive.* Montréal, QC, Canada: Éditions Logiques.

Taylor, M. C. (2006). Information adult learning and everyday literacy practices. *Journal of Adolescent & Adult Literacy, 49*(6), 500–509. doi:10.1598/JAAL.49.6.5

Tejedor, F. J. (2002). La Complejidad Universitaria del Rendimiento y la Satisfacción. In Villar, L. M. (Ed.), *La Universidad: Evaluación Educativa e Innovación Curricular* (pp. 3–40). Seville, Spain: Kronos.

Telecommunications Regulatory Authority. (2008). *eCommerce.* Retrieved from http://www.tra.gov.ae

Tennant, M. (1996). *Psychology and adult learning.* London, UK: Routledge.

Thomas, P., King, D., & Minocha, S. (2009). The effective use of a simple wiki to support collaborative learning activities. *Computer Science Education, 19,* 293–313. doi:10.1080/08993400903384943

Thompson, A. (2005). Scientifically based research: Establishing a research agenda for the technology in teacher education community. *Journal of Research on Technology in Education, 37*(4), 331–337.

Tibbs, E. R. (2010). *History of Shelfari.* Retrieved August 5, 2011, from https://wiki.itap.purdue.edu/display/INSITE/Shelfari#Shelfari-History

Tondeur, J., van Braak, J., & Valcke, M. (2007). Curricula and the use of ICT in education: Two worlds apart? *British Journal of Educational Technology, 38*(6), 962–976. doi:10.1111/j.1467-8535.2006.00680.x

Trageton, A. (2004). *At skrive sig til læsning.* Copenhagen, Denmark: Gyldendal.

Trentin, G. (2009). Using a wiki to evaluate individual contribution to a collaborative learning project. *Journal of Computer Assisted Learning, 25,* 43–55. doi:10.1111/j.1365-2729.2008.00276.x

Tripp, D. (1993). Critical incidents in teaching. In Fish, D., & Coles, C. (Eds.), *Developing professional judgement.* London, UK: Routledge.

Truzoli, R. (2004). Il Precision Teaching nei trattamenti comportamentali finalizzati all'acquisizione di comportamenti fluenti. *Psicoterapia Cognitiva e Comportamentale, 10,* 37–49.

Tse, S. K., Yuen, A. H. K., Loh, E. K. Y., Lam, J. W. I., & Ng, R. H. W. (2010). The impact of blogging on Hong Kong primary school students' bilingual reading literacy. *Australasian Journal of Educational Technology, 26*(2), 164–179.

Tsou, W., Wang, W., & Li, H. (2002). How computers facilitate English foreign language learners acquire English abstract words. *Computers & Education, 39,* 415–428. doi:10.1016/S0360-1315(02)00078-7

Turban, E., King, D., Liang, T., & Turban, D. (2010). *Electronic Commerce 2010* (6th ed.). Upper Saddle River, NJ: Prentice-Hall.

Turkle, S., & Papert, S. (1990). Epistemological pluralism: Styles and voices within the computer culture. *Signs, 16*(1), 128–157. doi:10.1086/494648

Tyler-Smith, K. (2006). Early attrition of first time e-learners. *MERLOT Journal of Technology and Learning, 2*(2), 73–85.

Tyner, K. (1998). *Literacy in a digital world.* Mahwah, NJ: Erlbaum.

U.S. Department of Education. (2002). *The Condition of Education (Tech. Rep. No. NCES 2002-025).* Washington, DC: NPO.

Underwood, J., & Szabo, A. (2003). Academic offences and e-learning: Individual propensities in cheating. *British Journal of Educational Technology, 34*(4), 467–478. doi:10.1111/1467-8535.00343

Underwood, J., & Szabo, A. (2004). Cybercheats: Is information and communication technology fuelling academic dishonesty? *Active Learning in Higher Education, 5*(2), 180–199. doi:10.1177/1469787404043815

UNESCO. (2008). *ICT competency standards for teachers: Implementation guidelines.* Retrieved from http://unesdoc.unesco.org/images/0015/001562/156209e.pdf

UNESCO. (2008). *ICT competency standards for teachers: Competency standard modules.* Retrieved from http://unesdoc.unesco.org/images/0015/001562/156207e.pdf

UNESCO. (2008). *ICT competency standards for teachers: Policy framework.* Retrieved from http://unesdoc.unesco.org/images/0015/001562/156210E.pdf

Usher, R., Bryant, I., & Johnston, R. (1997). *Adult education and the postmodern challenge.* London, UK: Routledge.

Usun, U. (2003). Advantages of computer based educational technologies for adult learners. *The Turkish Online Journal of Educational Technology, 2,* 4.

Valcke, M., Bonte, S., De Wever, B., & Rots, I. (2010). Internet parenting styles and the impact on Internet use of primary school children. *Computers & Education, 55,* 454–464. doi:10.1016/j.compedu.2010.02.009

Valdez, G., McNabb, M., Foertsch, M., Anderson, M., Hawkes, M., & Raack, L. (2000). *Computer-based technology and learning: Evolving uses and expectations.* Oak Brook, IL: North Central Regional Educational Laboratory.

Valli, L. (1992). *Reflective teacher education: cases and critiques.* Albany, NY: State University of New York Press.

Valverde, L. (1982). The self-evolving supervisor. In Sergiovanni, T. (Ed.), *Supervision of teaching* (pp. 81–89). Alexandria, VA: Association for Supervision and Curriculum Development.

Van Manen, M. (1977). Linking ways of knowing with ways of being practical. *Curriculum Inquiry, 6*(3), 205–228. doi:10.2307/1179579

Van Patten, J. R., Chao, C. I., & Reigeluth, C. M. (1986). A review of strategies for sequencing and synthesizing information. *Review of Educational Research, 56*(4), 437–472. doi:10.3102/00346543056004437

Van Soest, D., Canon, R., & Grant, D. (2000). Using an interactive website to educate about cultural diversity and societal oppression. *Journal of Social Work Education, 36*(3), 463–479.

Vergnaud, G. (1996). Au fond de l'action, la conceptualisation. In Barbier, J.-M. (Ed.), *Savoirs théoriques, savoirs d'action* (pp. 275–292). Paris, France: PUF.

Vermersch, P. (1994). *L'entretien d'explicitation.* Paris, France: ESF.

Villar, L. M., & Alegre, O. M. (2004). *Manual para la excelencia en la Enseñanza Superior.* Madrid, Spain: McGraw-Hill.

Vinatier, I. (2006, May 18-20). Des dispositifs de co-explicitation: un travail de conceptualisation de son activité par l'enseignant, le formateur. In *Proceedings of Faciliter les apprentissages autonomies 7ème Colloque européen sur l'autoformation,* ENFA Toulouse-Auzeville, France.

Vratulis, V., & Dobson, T. M. (2008). Social negotiations in a wiki environment: A case study with pre-service teachers. *Educational Media International, 45,* 285–294. doi:10.1080/09523980802571531

Vygotsky, L. S. (1978). *Mind in society.* Cambridge, MA: Harvard University Press.

Wakefield, J. F. (2003). The development of creative thinking and critical reflection: Lessons from everyday problem finding. In Runco, M. A. (Ed.), *Critical creative processes* (pp. 253–274). New York, NY: Hampton Press.

Walling, D. R. (2009). Idea networking and creative sharing. *TechTrends, 53*(6), 22–24. doi:10.1007/s11528-009-0339-x

Wang, L. (2005). The advantages of using technology in second language education. *T.H.E. Journal, 32*(10), 1–6.

Ward, D. (2000). Catching the wave of change in American higher education. *EDUCAUSE Review, 35*(1), 22–30.

Ware, P. D. (2004). Confidence and competition online: ESL student perspectives on web-based discussions in the classroom. *Computers and Composition, 21,* 451–468. doi:10.1016/S8755-4615(04)00041-6

Wasserman, S., & Faust, K. (1994). *Social network analysis: Methods and applications.* Cambridge, UK: Cambridge University Press.

Waxman, H., Freiberg, H., Vaughan, J., & Weil, M. (1988). *Images of reflection in teacher education.* Reston, VA: Association of Teacher Educators.

Wechtersbach, R. (2008). Lo sviluppo delle competenze digitali nella scuola slovena. *Tecnologie Didattiche, 43,* 17–22.

Weisbord, M. R. (1987). *Productive workplaces.* San Francisco, CA: Jossey-Bass.

Wenger, E. (1998). *Communities of practice: learning, meaning, and identity.* Cambridge, UK: Cambridge University Press.

West, R. P., & Young, K. R. (1992). Precision teaching. In West, R. P., & Hamerlynck, L. A. (Eds.), *Designs for excellence in education: The legacy of B. F. Skinner* (pp. 113–146). Longmont, CO: Sopris West.

West, R. P., Young, K. R., & Spooner, F. (1990). Precision teaching: An introduction. *Teaching Exceptional Children, 22*(3), 4–8.

Wheeler, S. (2009). Learning space mashups: Combining Web 2.0 tools to create collaborative and reflective learning spaces. *Future Internet, 1,* 5–13. doi:10.3390/fi1010003

Wheeler, S., Waite, S. J., & Bromfield, C. (2002). Promoting creative thinking through the use of ICT. *Journal of Computer Assisted Learning, 18,* 367–378. doi:10.1046/j.0266-4909.2002.00247.x

Wheeler, S., & Wheeler, D. (2009). Using wikis to promote quality learning in teacher training. *Learning, Media and Technology, 34*(1), 1–10. doi:10.1080/17439880902759851

Wheeler, S., Yeomans, P., & Wheeler, D. (2008). The good, the bad and the wiki: Evaluating student-generated content for collaborative learning. *British Journal of Educational Technology, 39*(6), 987–995. doi:10.1111/j.1467-8535.2007.00799.x

Whipp, J. L., & Chiarelli, S. (2004). Self-Regulation in a web-based course: A case study. *Educational Technology Research and Development, 52*(4), 5–22. doi:10.1007/BF02504714

Wildman, T., & Niles, J. (1987). Reflective teachers: tensions between abstractions and realities. *Journal of Teacher Education, 38*(1), 25–31. doi:10.1177/002248718703800405

Wlodkowski, R. J. (2003). Accelerated learning in colleges and universities. *New Directions for Adult and Continuing Education, 97*, 5–15. doi:10.1002/ace.84

Womack, B. (2010, August 2). Social networking and games leap in web use. *Bloomberg Businessweek*. Retrieved August 5, 2011, from http://www.businessweek.com/technology/content/aug2010/tc2010081_994774.htm?link_position=link6

Woo, M., Chu, S., Ho, A., & Li, X. (2011). Using a wiki to scaffold primary-school students' collaborative writing. *Journal of Educational Technology & Society, 14*(1), 43–54.

Wu, J. (2011). *How to make Skype work in UAE*. Retrieved from http://www.ehow.com/how_5006502_make-skype-work-uae.html

Xiao, Y., & Lucking, R. (2008). The impact of two types of peer assessment on students' performance and satisfaction within a Wiki environment. *The Internet and Higher Education, 11*, 186–193. doi:10.1016/j.iheduc.2008.06.005

Xiaoqiong, H., & Xianxing, J. (2008). Using film to teach EFL students English language skills. *Changing English, 15*(2), 235–240. doi:10.1080/13586840802052468

XING AG. (2011). *What is XING?* Retrieved August 2, 2011, from http://www.xing.com/help/help-and- faqs-2/my-xing-and-my-network-55/about-us-155/what-is-xing-159

Yang, F., Shu, Y., Lin, M., & Hsu, C. (2007). Study of basic computer competence among public health nurses in Taiwan. *The Journal of Nursing Research, 12*(1), 1–9.

Yang, S.-H. (2009). Using blogs to enhance critical reflection and community of practice. *Journal of Educational Technology & Society, 12*(2), 11–21.

Yier, R., & Luke, C. (2010). Multimodal, multiliteracies: Texts and literacies for the 21st century. In Pullen, D. L., & Cole, D. (Eds.), *Multiliteracies and technology enhanced education: Social practice and the global classroom* (pp. 18–34). Hershey, PA: IGI Global.

Yin, R. K. (1994). *Case study research: Design and methods* (2nd ed.). Thousand Oaks, CA: Sage.

Young, G. (2002). Hybrid teaching seeks to end the divide between traditional and online instruction. *The Chronicle of Higher Education*, 33–34.

Zeichner, K. M. (1994). Research on teacher thinking and different views of reflective practice in teaching and teacher education. In Carlgren, I., Handal, G., & Vaage, S. (Eds.), *Teachers' minds and actions - Research on teachers' thinking and practice* (pp. 9–27). London, UK: Falmer Press.

Zeichner, K. M., & Liston, D. (1990). *Traditions of reform and reflective teaching in US teacher education*. East Lansing, MI: National Centre for Research in Teacher Education, Michigan State University.

Zeichner, K. M., & Liston, D. (1996). *Reflective teaching: an introduction*. Mahwah, NJ: Lawrence Erlbaum.

Ziegler, S. (2007). The miseducation of Generation M. *Learning, Media and Technology, 32*(1), 69–81. doi:10.1080/17439880601141302

Zorko, V. (2009). Factors affecting the way students collaborate in a wiki for English language learning. *Australasian Journal of Educational Technology, 25*(5), 645–665.

# About the Contributors

**Antonio Cartelli** is Associated Professor for Experimental Pedagogy at the University of Cassino and Southern Latium in Italy. He manages the Laboratory for Technology of Education and Knowledge Management in the Department of Human, Social and Health Sciences. Among his interests can be included misconceptions, mental schemes, Information Systems for research and teaching, Web Technologies in teaching and research, and their everyday application for the improvement of teaching and learning. He authored many papers and books concerning the themes he is interested in and is currently Editor-in-Chief of the *International Journal of Digital Literacy and Digital Competence.*

\* \* \*

**Munir Abbasi** is currently working towards PhD in Hybrid Wireless Communication Technologies (Wi-Fi, WiMAX, SCPC, DVB-S/S2 and DVB-RCS) in the Department of Information Systems and Computing at Brunel University, UK. He did a degree in Electrical communication engineering and MBA in Management Information System. Mr. Abbasi has extensive experience in projects life cycle particularly RF, microwave and wireless system's design and development, system integration technical support, quality plan, business models, work packages, value added engineering, Failure Mode Effect Analysis (FMEA), Critical Path Analysis (CPA), and Key Performance Indicator (KPI). He has worked for both the public and private sector and has successfully completed many internationally collaborative projects.

**Esharenana E. Adomi** holds BEd, MEd. MLS and PhD degrees. He attended University of Ibadan, Ibadan and Delta State University, Abraka both in Nigeria.He is an Associate Professor at the Department of Library and Information Science, Delta State University, Abraka, Nigeria. He was secretary of Nigerian Library Association (NLA) 2000 – 2004 and currently the chairman, NLA, Delta State Chapter. He was Acting Head, Department of Library and Information Science, delta State University, Nigeria. January 2008 – February 2009. He received the 2004 Award for Excellence of the Most Outstanding Paper published in *The Electronic Library*, 2003 volume with an article entitled: "A survey of cybercafés in Delta State, Nigeria" co-authored with two other colleagues. He is a member of Editorial Advisory Board, *The Electronic Library*, formerly contributing editor, *Library Hi-Tech News* and currently the editor of Delta Library Journal. He has published over 45 articles in reputable national and international journals, chapters in books and four textbooks. He is the editor of *Security Software for Cybercafes* published, *Frameworks for ICT Policy: Government, Social and Legal Issues* and *Handbook of Research on Information Communication Technology: Trends, Issues and Advancements* published by IGI Global, Hershey, PA. His interests lie in ICT policies, community informatics, information/internet security, Internet/web technology and services, and application of ICTs in different settings.

**Rozz Albon**, educational psychologist, currently teaches final year Bachelor of Education students at the Higher Colleges of Technology's, Sharjah Woman's College in the United Arab Emirates. During her 22 year career in teaching at various universities she has been the recipient of many teaching awards. She was inspired through these appointments to further explore how culture impacts on learning. As Director of Teaching and Learning at Curtin University of Technology's Malaysian campus she started specifically investigating learning strategies of non-native English speaking students. At the UAE's Higher Colleges of Technology she is focused on researching pedagogical issues relating to digital literacy.

**Francesca Cuzzocrea** is assistant professor of Developmental Psychology at the Faculty of Education, University of Messina, Italy. Research efforts are directed towards data analysis and psychological assessment.

**Valentina Dagienė** published over 200 research and methodological papers and wrote more than 50 textbooks in the field of informatics and ICT for high schools. She has been working in various expert groups and work groups, interested in localization of software and educational programs, e-learning, and problem solving. She is a national representative and vice chair of the Technical Committee of IFIP for Education (TC3), a member of the Group for Informatics in Secondary Education (WG 3.1) and a member of the International Committee of Olympiads in Informatics. She is an Executive Editor of international journals "Informatics in Education" and "Olympiads in Informatics".

**Claudia Di Lorenzo** graduated in Media Science and Communication at the Tor Vergata University of Rome. She was LIFE's e-tutor for the course in Photographic languages. At present she works at Communication Service of the Italian Civil Protection Department.

**Angela Di Nuzzo** graduated in Educational Sciences in 2010 with best marks and honours. She worked on a thesis studying digital competences in university students and analyzed the answers of the students in her Faculty to a survey on this topic.

**Ericson Egbaivwie** is a librarian at Petroleum Training Institute Library PMB 20, Effurun, Delta State, Nigeria.

**Monica Fantin** is PhD in Education and Lecturer at Department of Teaching Methodology and in the Post-graduate Program in Education, in the Education and Communication line of research, at Federal University of Santa Catarina (UFSC), Brazil. She coordinates the Research Group "Childhood, Communication and Art" (NICA, UFSC/ CNPq). She has published many texts on subjects related to childhood, ludic culture, *media-education* and teaching education. She is also coordinating the Faculty of Pedagogy at UFSC.

**Carlo Giovannella** is currently the scientific and ICT coordinator and chair of the ISIM_garage (Interfaces and Multimodal Interactive Systems - http://www.scuolaiad.it/isimgarage - only Italian) at the IaD School (Distance Learning Center) of the University of Tor Vergata - http://www.scuolaiad.it. He is also teaching at the Faculty of Science, Physics Department. At present he deals with design for the experience (including interaction design), natural computer-mediated communication, augmented places and pervasive computing, collaborative learning and working (environments/tools/methods/strategies/ processes). He is designer and chair of the project LIFE, an innovative learning environment of new generation (http://www.scuolaiad.it/life). He is deeply involved in the research on the definition of a set of experience styles and on the ecological monitoring of experience style's indicators in education at, but not only, cognitive, emotional/affective and social levels. He is currently the vice-chair of IFIP WG 13.1. He has been co-chairing several international workshop and conferences, among the latest: HCIEd2008, CHItaly2009, DULP2010. Workshop co-chair of ICALT in 2011, he is, currently, the general co-chair of ICALT 2012. Editor in chief of the journal IxD&A (Interaction Design & architecture(s)), he has been also editor in chief of the Magazine F&D and deputy editor of the magazine Je-LKS (Journal of e-learning and Knowledge Society) of the SIeL (E-Learning Italian Society). Since more than 15 years is involved in the design and management of interdisciplinary curricula that integrate technologies, sciences and humanities: Master in "New Media and Communication", Honored Master in "Advanced Technologies for Interactive Communication", Bachelor in "Media Science and Technologies", Honored Master in "E-learning: methods, techniques and applications", Master in "Theory & Design of New Media", etc. He has published more than 50 papers in the domain of Technology Enhanced Learning and Design for the experience (2003 -), more than 90 papers in Physics (Solid State Physics and Complex Systems (1983 - 1999), more than 20 papers on Photography and communications (1995 - 2002).

**Vaiva Grabauskiene** is Postdoctoral Fellowship at Vilnius University Institute of Mathematics and Informatics. Also she works as associate professor of social sciences (educology) at Vilnius pedagogical university Department of Basic Education. Besides academic work, she collaborated in projects regarding information technology within the primary education. She interested in visual mathematical education, interrelations between mathematical and esthetical education, integrated training of geometry and hand-work at primary school, application of computer-based technologies in formation of geometric images at primary school. Her research outcomes have been published in methodological and computer science journals, conference proceedings, and books.

**Karin Hamilton** is the Director of Graduate Program Development at the Silberman College of Business at Fairleigh Dickinson University. She has extensive experience in both business and academic administration in the areas of strategic and tactical planning, project management and training and development. She has written numerous guides and manuals that have been used by business professionals, educational administrators, faculty and students. Her research interests are primarily in learning, pedagogy, and use of technology to improve learning outcomes. Karin was one of the originators of a program for teaching adult learners using a partial distance-learning format. She received her M.B.A. at Fairleigh Dickinson University and her B.A. at Valparaiso University.

**Jeffrey Hsu** is an Associate Professor of Information Systems at the Silberman College of Business, Fairleigh Dickinson University. He is the author of numerous papers, chapters, and books, and has previous business experience in the software, telecommunications, and financial industries. His research interests include human-computer interaction, e-commerce, IS education, and mobile/ubiquitous computing. He is Managing Editor of the International Journal of Data Analysis and Information Systems (IJDAIS), Associate Editor of the International Journal of Information and Communication Technology Education (IJICTE), and is on the editorial board of several other journals. Dr. Hsu received his Ph.D. in Information Systems from Rutgers University, a M.S. in Computer Science from the New Jersey Institute of Technology, and an M.B.A. from the Rutgers Graduate School of Management.

**Tony Jewels** is an experienced industry professional who joined academia in the late 90's. In 2007 as a senior lecturer with Queensland University of Technology he became a recipient of a national teaching award after winning a number of teaching awards at both faculty and university levels. He took up a position at Al Ain's United Arab Emirates' research intensive university, (UAEU) where he has been researching and teaching for 3 years within their Faculty of Business & Economics, in the areas of e-business, project management and enterprise information systems.

**Athanassios Jimoyiannis** is an Associate Professor of Science and ICT in Education at the Department of Social and Educational Policy, University of Peloponnese, in Greece. Prior to his current position he has been an assistant professor at the Department of Preschool Education, University of the Aegean. His current research interests include e-learning and ICT in education, teachers’ preparation about ICT in education, computer science education and science education. He is a co-editor of the international journal THEMES in Science and Technology Education. He is also a member of the Scientific Review Board in various international journals and conferences in the areas of e-learning and ICT in education.

**Angelina I. T. Kiser** is currently an Associate Professor and the Department Coordinator for Management and International Business in the HEB School of Business and Administration at the University of the Incarnate Word in San Antonio, TX, USA. She works closely with the Coordinator for Management Information Systems to ensure that she is utilizing up-do-date technology in her management courses. Dr. Kiser enhances her curriculum through technology and works to successfully prepare students for the workforce. She is specifically interested in research that considers the students' points of views with regards to technology in the classroom as well as technology that will benefit the students in their future careers. Dr. Kiser strives to harness the power of technology as students learn both fundamental and advanced aspects of management within a global society.

**Karin Tweddell Levinsen** is an associate professor in online education at university level at the Danish School of Education at Aarhus University. She is a member of the internationally acknowledged Research Programme on Digital Media and ICT in a Learning Perspective. Currently her research is focused on both university pedagogy and ICT and ICT and learning in the primary school. Of special interest is the study in digital literacy and competence building for the network society. She has published several papers on the subject and a book on school in the network society in collaboration with Birgitte Holm Sørensen and Lone Audon.

**Lourdes Villalustre Martínez** is a teacher of ICT for Education at the University of Oviedo. Visiting professor at other universities, including San Martin de Porres (Peru). Member of research group "Tech @". She is coauthor of several books ("*Education in rural areas: teaching guide*", among others) and numerous book chapters (*Competences development and learning styles in virtual environments: collaborative and independent work practices in Ruralnet*, 2008; *Evaluation of teaching competences and tutorials for teachers in virtual environments and their implications*, 2009, etc.) as well as numerous articles in journals of impact. She has participated in numerous research projects funded by the MEC, the University of Oviedo, etc.

**Anna Maria Murdaca** is associate professor of Special Education with teaching at the undergraduate degrees in Psychology, Physical education, Physiotherapy and Health professions, University of Messina, Italy. She presents regularly at national and international conferences and has published in the field.

**Antonella Nuzzaci** is associate professor of Experimental Pedagogy at the Faculty of Educational Sciences, University of L'Aquila, Italy. She is interested in the influence of cultural hertiage on education and in school evaluation and assessment; she also published several papers in journals and books on the above topics.

**Jonathan C. Ogugua** is a librarian at Federal University of Technology Library, Owerri, Imo State, Nigeria.

**Christopher Babatunde Ogunyemi** is a PhD research fellow at the Leiden University's Institute of Cultural Disciplines in The Netherlands. Born in Lagos he was educated at the University of Uyo, Akwa Ibom State in Nigeria. He holds a prestigious European Master Degree in Comparative Literature from Dalarna University in Sweden and he lectures English and Literature at Joseph Ayo Babalola University Ikeji Arakeji, Osun State in Nigeria. He is the author of Male Autobiographical Narratives and Gender Imperatives, Topical Issues in Literature and Globalization and Narratology and Contemporary Fiction which were all published by VDM-Publisher and Lap-Lambert Academic Publishing in Germany. He has leading papers in international journals of high repute.

**Patrizia Oliva** is adjunct professor at the Faculty of Education, University of Messina, Italy. Research efforts are directed towards the analysis of influences of family and educational systems on child development.

**M. Esther del Moral Pérez** is a Professor of Information Technologies and Communication in Education (ICTE) at the University of Oviedo. Research Group Coordinator "Tecn@": Technology and learning. Teacher of the virtual course *"Education in rural areas"* Shared Virtual Campus of the G9. His publications include: *Learning Methods and Results Telematics Interuniversity extrapolated to the new EEES: MATRIX Project* (2009), *Teaching experience and ICT* (2008), *Knowledge Society: Leisure and Culture* (2004), *Reflections on ICT and Education* (1998). Author of chapters of books in collaboration with others and numerous magazine articles and communications in national and international congresses. Researcher R & D Project funded by MEC.

**Corrado Amedeo Presti** is Anaesthesiologist and I Level Manager at Anaesthesia and Intensive Care UOC of the Hospital OMPA, Ragusa Provincial Health District-RG1 He holds Honored Master degrees in "Applied Remote Health Sciences and Technology in Medicine" (University of Catania), "Pain Management" and "E-learning: Methods, Techniques and Applications" (Iad School - Tor Vergata University of Rome. He is, at present, e-tutor of the Master in "E-learning: Methods, Techniques and Applications".

**Dimitrios Roussinos** holds a bachelor degree in Computer Science. He is a high school teacher, currently working at the Department of Social and Educational Policy, University of Peloponnese, in Greece. He has a great experience with teaching ICT and computer science at various levels; high school, vocational education and university, as well. His main research interests include e-learning and Web 2.0 tools in educational practice.

**Birgitte Holm Sørensen** is a professor in ICT and Learning. She is head of the Department of Curriculum Research, DPU, Aarhus University. She has been director of the research programme *Media and ICT in a learning perspective* during several years. Her research interests are children's use of ICT inside and outside school, ICT, formal and informal learning, game based learning and designs for learning. She has written and edited several books on ICT, children and learning. She is leader of the project *Serious Games on a Global Market Place (2007-2011)*, funded by The Danish Council for Strategic Research. In this project universities collaborate with companies. Her latest publication is 2.0 – Children In and Outside School in Carlsson, Ulla (2010): Children and Youth in the digital Media Culture. From a Nordic Horizon. Nordicom University of Gothenburg.

**L. K. Stergioulas** is currently a Reader in the Department of Information Systems and Computing at Brunel University, UK. He is a qualified Chartered Engineer and has studied Informatics and Physics in his first degree at the University of Athens, and received a M.Sc. and Ph.D. in Electrical Engineering from the University of Liverpool, UK, specialising in Information Engineering and Communications. He has published over 150 refereed papers in journals and international conferences and has supervised and examined numerous PhD dissertations in information systems and computer science. He has held many national and EU grants in information systems, technology-enhanced learning, human-centred communications and computing, medical and health informatics. He has been principal investigator in numerous EU projects, including UNIVERSAL (FP5), TIME2LEARN (FP5), PROLEARN (FP6), BASE2 (FP6), OpenScout and iCOPER European research projects. He is the coordinator of the TEL-Map project on Technology Enhanced Learning and the e-START EU Digital Literacy Network. He also chairs IFIP's Special Interest group in Digital Literacy (TC3 – SIG3.9). His research interests include technology-enhanced learning, educational and health information systems, human-centred computing, educational computing, and information systems for society.

**Zhongxian Wang** is a professor at Montclair State University, New Jersey, USA. Professor Wang teaches Decision Support & Expert Systems, Operations Analysis, Production/Operations Management, Business Statistics, Operations Research, and Management Sciences. He is a member of Information Resources Management Association (IRMA), Institute for Operations Research and the Management Sciences (INFORMS), The Decision Sciences Institute (DSI), The Production and Operations Management Society (POMS).

# Index